Praise for *God's Shadow*

T0268660

"Alan Mikhail's *God's Shadow* is a stunning work of global history. By examining the Catholic Atlantic's long, vexed engagement with the Islamic Mediterranean, Mikhail offers a bold and thoroughly convincing new way to think about the origins of the modern world. . . . A tour de force."
—Greg Grandin, author of *The Empire of Necessity:
Slavery, Freedom, and Deception in the New World*

"*God's Shadow* is full of fine details of this cross-cultural encounter, but its most arresting aspect is Mikhail's second claim: that 'the Ottoman Empire made our modern world.' He calls his book 'a revisionist account . . . demonstrating Islam's constituent role in forming some of the most fundamental aspects of the history of Europe, the Americas, and the United States.' . . . The highest praise for a history book is that it makes you think about things in a new way."
—Ian Morris, *New York Times Book Review*

"[A] refreshingly readable history book that offers a new world view. . . . A radical picture of the Ottoman Empire emerges 'as a unified juggernaut' conquering and controlling three continents, while Europe was a 'mosaic of squabbling polities.'"
—Diana Darke, *Times Literary Supplement*

"The Ottoman Empire lurks behind much of the modern world. Alan Mikhail's new book makes a great introduction to one of the key figures in Ottoman history, Sultan Selim I."
—Mary Beard, author of *SPQR: A History of Ancient Rome*

"[Alan Mikhail] makes it his mission to demonstrate how this utterly compelling leader helped define his age, bending the world to his will. And he succeeds with a flourish. . . . Mikhail offers a refreshingly Ottoman-centric picture of the 15th- and 16th-century Mediterranean." —Justin Marozzi, *Spectator*

"Alan Mikhail is a very original and inventive historian."
—Orhan Pamuk, winner of the Nobel Prize in Literature

"*God's Shadow* is a radical revision of the narrative of modern history, a revision that restores the Ottoman Empire to the central role it played in provoking Columbus's voyages, in haunting the fears and ambitions of European nation states, and in profoundly influencing the self-understanding of both Catholics and Protestants. . . . Along the way, Mikhail shows that the Muslim culture over which Selim reigned was in many respects far more progressive, tolerant, and cosmopolitan than anything known in the Christian West."
—Stephen Greenblatt, author of *Tyrant: Shakespeare on Politics* and *The Rise and Fall of Adam and Eve*

"Alan Mikhail's bold study of Sultan Selim, his conquests, and [his] reforms rightfully gives the Ottoman Empire and Islam a central place in early modern history. An important book and a lively read as well."
—Natalie Zemon Davis, author of *Trickster Travels: A Sixteenth-Century Muslim Between Worlds*

"In *God's Shadow*, Alan Mikhail challenges readers to recalibrate their sense of history. . . . Mikhail traces the global reverberations of this seismic development from China to Mexico, arguing that the Ottoman sultanate was the pivotal power in a world of ambitious polities." —Leslie Peirce, author of *Empress of the East: How a European Slave Girl Became Queen of the Ottoman Empire*

"In vivid prose, Alan Mikhail offers us a history written not from the cramped confines of Europe's kingdoms but from the heights of the Ottoman Empire, circa 1492. . . . *God's Shadow* will change how you think about both the past and the present."
—David Nirenberg, author of *Neighboring Faiths: Christianity, Islam, and Judaism in the Middle Ages and Today*

ALSO BY ALAN MIKHAIL

*Under Osman's Tree:*
*The Ottoman Empire, Egypt,*
*and Environmental History*

*The Animal in Ottoman Egypt*

*Nature and Empire in*
*Ottoman Egypt:*
*An Environmental History*

*Water on Sand:*
*Environmental Histories of the*
*Middle East and North Africa*
(editor)

# GOD'S SHADOW

...

*Sultan Selim,*

*His Ottoman Empire,*

AND THE

*Making of the Modern World*

...

# ALAN MIKHAIL

LIVERIGHT PUBLISHING CORPORATION

A DIVISION OF W. W. NORTON & COMPANY

INDEPENDENT PUBLISHERS SINCE 1923

FRONTISPIECE:

*Selim takes aim*

· · ·

Copyright © 2020 by Alan Mikhail

For information about permission to reproduce selections from this book, write to
Permissions, Liveright Publishing Corporation, a division of
W. W. Norton & Company, Inc., 500 Fifth Avenue, New York, NY 10110

For information about special discounts for bulk purchases, please contact
W. W. Norton Special Sales at specialsales@wwnorton.com or 800-233-4830

Manufacturing by LSC Communications
Book design by Barbara M. Bachman
Production manager: Anna Oler

Library of Congress Cataloging-in-Publication Data

Names: Mikhail, Alan, 1979– author.
Title: God's shadow : Sultan Selim, his Ottoman empire, and the
making of the modern world / Alan Mikhail.
Description: First edition. | New York : Liveright Publishing Corporation, [2020] |
Includes bibliographical references and index.
Identifiers: LCCN 2020010516 |
ISBN 9781631492396 (hardcover) | ISBN 9781631492402 (epub)
Subjects: LCSH: Selim I, Sultan of the Turks, 1470-1520. |
Turkey—History—Selim I, 1512-1520. | Ayşe Gülbahar Hatun, consort of
Bayezid II, Sultan of the Turks, –1505.
Classification: LCC DR504 .M55 2020 | DDC 956/.015092 [B]—dc23
LC record available at https://lccn.loc.gov/2020010516

ISBN 978-1-324-09102-8 pbk.

Liveright Publishing Corporation, 500 Fifth Avenue, New York, N.Y. 10110
www.wwnorton.com

W. W. Norton & Company Ltd., 15 Carlisle Street, London W1D 3BS

1 2 3 4 5 6 7 8 9 0

# CONTENTS

# MAPS

*All maps drawn by David Lindroth, Inc.*

# GOD'S SHADOW

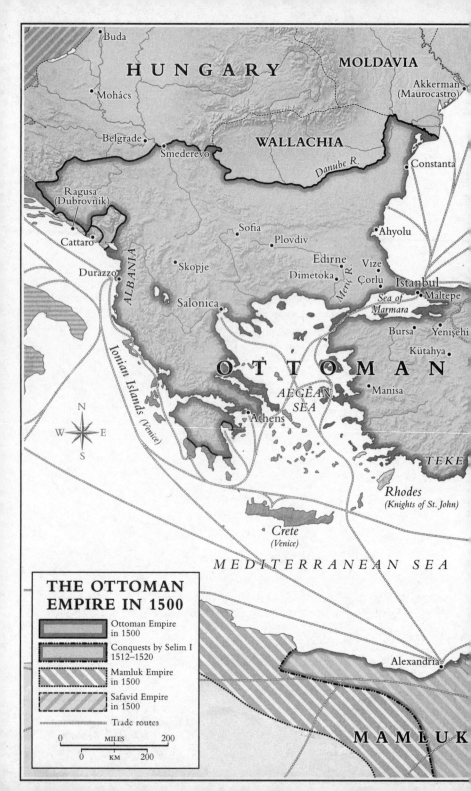

Buda

HUNGARY

Mohács

MOLDAVIA

Akkerman
(Maurocastro)

Belgrade

WALLACHIA

Smederevo

Danube R.

Constanta

Ragusa
(Dubrovnik)

Sofia

Ahyolu

Cattaro

Plovdiv

ALBANIA

Skopje

Edirne

Vize

Durazzo

Dimetoka

Çorlu

Istanbul

Maltepe

Salonica

OTTOMAN

Sea of
Marmara

Bursa

Yenişehi

Kütahya

Ionian Islands (Venice)

AEGEAN
SEA

Manisa

N
W        E
S

Athens

TEKE

Rhodes
(Knights of St. John)

Crete
(Venice)

MEDITERRANEAN SEA

## THE OTTOMAN
## EMPIRE IN 1500

Ottoman Empire
in 1500

Conquests by Selim I
1512–1520

Mamluk Empire
in 1500

Safavid Empire
in 1500

Trade routes

0        MILES        200

0        KM        200

Alexandria

MAMLUK

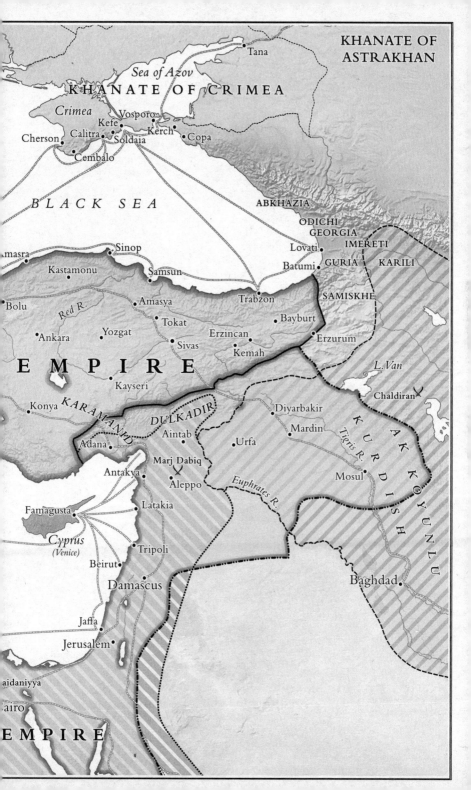

KHANATE OF
ASTRAKHAN

*Sea of Azov*

•Tana

KHANATE OF CRIMEA

*Crimea*

Cherson•    •Calitra  Vosporo•  •Kerch
         •Kefe  •Soldaia    •Copa
            •Cembalo

B L A C K   S E A

ABKHAZIA

ODICHI
GEORGIA

•masra        •Sinop              Lovati•    IMERETI
     Kastamonu•                  Batumi•  GURIA    KARILI
•Bolu           Samsun•        Trabzon•
      *Red R.*    •Amasya              SAMISKHE
•Ankara   •Yozgat  •Tokat    •Erzincan  •Bayburt
              Sivas•   Kemah•        •Erzurum

E M P I R E            *L. Van*

        •Kayseri                    •Chaldiran ✗

•Konya  KARAMANID          Diyarbakir•       A
                DULKADIR      •Mardin    K
   Adana•    •Aintab   •Urfa      *Tigris R.*   K
                                         O
Antakya•  Marj Dabiq ✗              •Mosul  Y
          Aleppo•                          U
Famagusta•  •Latakia   *Euphrates R.*        N   K
                                            L   U
*Cyprus*                                       R
(Venice)  •Tripoli                             D
     Beirut•                                   I
  Damascus•                    Baghdad•        S
                                              H
•Jaffa
Jerusalem•

•aidaniyya
•airo

E M P I R E

# INTRODUCTION

. . .

*Selim*

On the border between Texas and Mexico, precisely where the Rio Grande flows into the Gulf of Mexico, lies a sleepy town with the unlikely name of Matamoros. "Mata" comes from the Spanish verb *matar*, to kill, while *moros*—the Spanish equivalent of the English word "Moors"—is the derogatory name Spanish Christians reserved for Muslims. To be a Matamoros, then, is to be a Moor-slayer, a title with seemingly no connection to the American past or present. Why would a sunny border town in northeastern Mexico be named "Moor-slayer"? Were Muslims ever an existential enemy to kill in Mexico or Texas?

The word "Matamoros" was coined by Catholic Spaniards. For them, it was the duty of every Christian soldier to be a Moor-slayer. Much of Spain had been under Muslim rule from 711 until 1492—a fateful year in geopolitical history, for in 1492 not only did Spain's Christian armies take (or retake, as they preferred to say) the last Muslim stronghold on the Iberian peninsula, but one particular Matamoros by the familiar name of Christopher Columbus opened up a new front in Spain's war against Islam. Having been a common soldier in Isabella and Ferdinand's conquest of Granada, Columbus showed himself to be a religious man. Throughout his life, in battle after battle against Muslims and, specifically, against the Ottoman Empire, Spain's major rival throughout the Mediterranean, he had refined his palate for the taste of Muslim blood, and he felt the burden of holy war deep in his soul. Thus, as he bobbed westward on the high seas, his mind was occupied by neither a secular passion for discovery nor a calculating commercial vision. More than anything else, he sailed to the Americas imbued with a zeal for waging Christianity's war against its foremost enemy—Islam.

Despite their great victory on the Iberian peninsula, Christians were losing captives, commercial influence, and territory to the Ottomans almost everywhere else. The ideological wind propelling the white sails of Columbus's three ships was the fifteenth-century world's most exigent political struggle—the one between Catholic Europe and the Muslim Ottoman Empire. The Ottoman Empire, contrary to nearly all conventional accounts of world history, was the very reason Europeans went to America.

For half a century before 1492, and for centuries afterward, the Ottoman Empire stood as the most powerful state on earth: the largest empire in the Mediterranean since ancient Rome, and the most enduring in the history of Islam. In the decades around 1500, the Ottomans controlled more territory and ruled over more people than any other world power. It was the Ottoman monopoly of trade routes with the East, combined with their military prowess on land and on sea, that pushed Spain and Portugal out of the Mediterranean, forcing merchants and sailors from these fifteenth-century kingdoms to become global explorers as they risked treacherous voyages across oceans and around continents—all to avoid the Ottomans.

From China to Mexico, the Ottoman Empire shaped the known world at the turn of the sixteenth century. Given its hegemony, it became locked in military, ideological, and economic competition with the Spanish and Italian states, Russia, India, and China, as well as other Muslim powers. The Ottomans influenced in one way or another nearly every major event of those years, with reverberations down to our own time. Dozens of familiar figures, such as Columbus, Vasco da Gama, Montezuma, the reformer Luther, the warlord Tamerlane, and generations of popes—as well as millions of other greater and lesser historical personages—calibrated their actions and defined their very existence in reaction to the reach and grasp of Ottoman power.

The challenge of the Ottoman brand of Islam, as the empire pushed westward into Europe, was a major impetus behind Martin Luther's Protestant Reformation. On the empire's eastern border, its wars with Safavid Iran intensified the divide between Sunni and Shiite that roils the Muslim world even today. Ottoman military conquests and economic acumen created one of the world's first truly global commodities, coffee, and spurred capitalist consumerism through their invention of the coffeehouse.

Europe's forced departure—more like ejection—from the Mediterranean contributed to an apocalyptic mind-set in Christian Europe. Christianity and Islam seemed to be battling for the body and soul of creation. Once in the New World, self-styled soldiers of Christ continued their old war, waging it now against the indigenous peoples of a distant land. These Moor-slayers used their experiences of Islam in the Old World to understand the Americas and their peoples, and even—with the spiritual and legal backing of the pope—invoked their perceived duty to counter Islam to justify their importation of West African slaves to the Americas. By ignoring Islam, we have thus failed to understand Columbus and his age fully and, indeed, correctly.

In tracing the global influence of Ottoman power, *God's Shadow* offers an innovative, even revolutionary, account of the role of Islam and the Ottoman Empire in defining the shape of the Old and New Worlds. Over the past five centuries, the bulk of this story has been dismissed or ignored by professional historians and lay readers alike. Yet, Muslims were integral to what is inevitably a shared history. The ineluctable fact is that the Ottoman Empire made our modern world—which is, admittedly, a bitter pill for many in the West.

Why is this so? A primary reason is that in the twenty-first-century West—as, indeed, in fifteenth- and sixteenth-century Europe—

Muslims are often seen reflexively as enemies and terrorists, diametrically opposed to the religion that defined our culture and to the political systems we hold sacred. From popular culture to global politics, among conservatives and liberals alike, Islam—in the United States especially—is seen as "the great other," a problem that somehow needs to be "fixed." Muslims are targets of both popular and official vilification and often outright physical violence.

Other facts, too, have blotted out our recognition of the Ottoman influence on our own history. Foremost, we tend to read the history of the last half-millennium as "the rise of the West." (This anachronism rings as true in Turkey and the rest of the Middle East as it does in Europe and America.) In fact, in 1500, and even in 1600, there was no such thing as the now much-vaunted notion of "the West." Throughout the early modern centuries, the European continent consisted of a fragile collection of disparate kingdoms and small, weak principalities locked in constant warfare. The large land-based empires of Eurasia were the dominant powers of the Old World, and, apart from a few European outposts in and around the Caribbean, the Americas remained the vast domain of its indigenous peoples. The Ottoman Empire held more territory in Europe than did most European-based states. In 1600, if asked to pick a single power that would take over the world, a betting man would have put his money on the Ottoman Empire, or perhaps China, but certainly not on any European entity.

Since the Industrial Revolution and the so-called European glories of the nineteenth century, this history has been rewritten to portray European ascendancy as somehow stretching back to Columbus. This is a historical absurdity. Not only does it paper over the deep fissures in early modern Europe, it also masks the fact that the Ottoman Empire struck fear into the world for centuries before it earned its derogatory nineteenth-century sobriquet, "the sick man of Europe." Some historians claim that the Ottoman Empire began to decline from its peak of imperial might around 1600, just as the English began their settlement of the Americas. While it is true that the empire lost wars and ceded territory more often after that date, it remained the most hegemonic force in the Middle East and one of the most formidable states in Europe, Asia, and Africa for another three hundred years—until World War I. Indeed, the combined longevity of the empire and its centrality to world affairs is one of the most striking features of its history. The Ottoman Empire, as all empires invariably do, did end, but only after more than six hundred years of rule. Reading sixteenth-century Ottoman history through the lens of the nineteenth century, or even through the lens of Edward Gibbon's once canonical eighteenth-century account of the decline and fall of Rome, takes us down a historically indefensible dead-end path.

While not diminishing the intense conflicts between Europe and the Ottoman Empire, an examination of how the Ottomans constructed our modern world shows that the histories of Islam and Europe (and later America) were not exclusively or necessarily oppositional or divergent. These conjoined histories involve far more than just violence; the much-ballyhooed "clash of civilizations" represents a minuscule portion of a richly interwoven tapestry. Such an examination also explains how the town of Anahuac, so named by its native inhabitants, became Matamoros, a remnant symbol of Christian Spain's brutal wars against Islam.

THE EPIC STORY OF the Ottoman Empire begins far from the Middle East. The people who would eventually become the Ottomans started marching westward from China as early as the sixth century, making their way across Central Asia to the Mediterranean. For nearly a millennium, they continued their steady trek. Along the way, they fought wars and converted to various religions. In doing so, they also converted others to those religions, built cities and towns, exchanged goods and foodstuffs, learned and spread languages, invented new breeds of horses, created artistic masterpieces, and wrote spectacular poetry. Most of the descendants of those who started the journey settled down along the way, on or near the historic Silk Road, marrying into local families, adopting and altering the cultures of their new homes.

An intrepid few trekked all the way to Anatolia—also called Asia Minor—the land bridge between the Black and Mediterranean seas where Asia reaches out to touch Europe. Most of those who made it that far west were a Turkic-speaking nomadic tribe. Their long migration explains why today's Turks share bonds of language, culture, and ethnicity with peoples throughout Central Asia, even as far as China and beyond. (Korean and Turkish are both in the Altaic language group, for example.) Once in Anatolia, these new arrivals sought out for themselves and their animals the undulating plains of the Mediterranean and Aegean coasts, where they entered a fractured Byzantine entity. In thirteenth-century Anatolia, they became one of dozens of small family principalities—Muslim and Christian, Turkish and Greek— existing within and sometimes fighting against a waning Byzantine Empire. Their loosely-bound tribal group was led by a man named Osman, who died in the mid-1320s. He would later come to be seen as the first Ottoman (the word being an anglicized derivation of Osman). Every sultan down to the twentieth century was his blood descendant.

While Osman succeeded in chipping away some territory from the Byzantine Empire, it was his son who scored the first real victory for those early Ottomans. In 1326, Orhan took Bursa, a cosmopolitan city set in a lush valley not far from the Sea of Marmara. As a center of the international silk trade, its seizure provided a major boost to the Otto-

*Osman*

mans' rising ambitions. From this first Ottoman capital, the bearers of the mantle of Osman notched up victory after victory, taking control of an impressive range of territory in western Anatolia and the Balkans. There, the mostly Christian communities accepted the mostly Muslim Ottomans in large measure because these new arrivals from the Asian steppes excelled in cutting favorable deals with strong families and other local power brokers. The Ottomans' conquering armies promised military protection, along with more favorable tax and trading terms than the Byzantines offered, in exchange for allegiance to the family of Osman and the contribution of some troops every now and then.

After roughly a century of squeezing the Byzantines, the Ottomans dealt them a lethal blow in 1453, when the empire's seventh sultan, Mehmet II, stormed through the walls of the Byzantine capital, Constantinople. This earth-rattling victory, a conquest both actual and symbolic, won the Ottomans Christendom's eastern capital and one of the world's largest and most strategic cities, situated as it was at the fulcrum between Europe and Asia, commanding one of the principal routes from West to East. Mehmet took the title of Caesar, proclaiming the Ottomans a new Roman Empire. For most of Europe's Christians, the young Columbus included, the capture of one of "the two Romes" by a Muslim power was a sign that the end of days was nigh. The Ottomans had, as a contemporary European described it, plucked out one of the eyes of Christianity.

For close to four centuries, from 1453 until well into the exceedingly fractured 1800s, the Ottomans remained at the center of global politics, economics, and war. As European states rose and fell, the Ottomans stood strong. They battled Europe's medieval and early modern empires, and in the twentieth century continued to fight in Europe, albeit against vastly different enemies. Everyone from Machiavelli to Jefferson to Hitler—quite an unlikely trio—was forced to confront the challenge of the Ottomans' colossal power and influence. Counting from their first military victory, at Bursa, they ruled for nearly six centuries in territories that today comprise some thirty-three countries. Their armies would control massive swaths of Europe, Africa, and Asia; some of the world's most crucial trade corridors; and cities along the shores of the Mediterranean, Red, Black, and Caspian seas, the Indian Ocean, and the Persian Gulf. They held Istanbul and Cairo, two of the largest cities on earth, as well as the holy cities of Mecca, Medina,

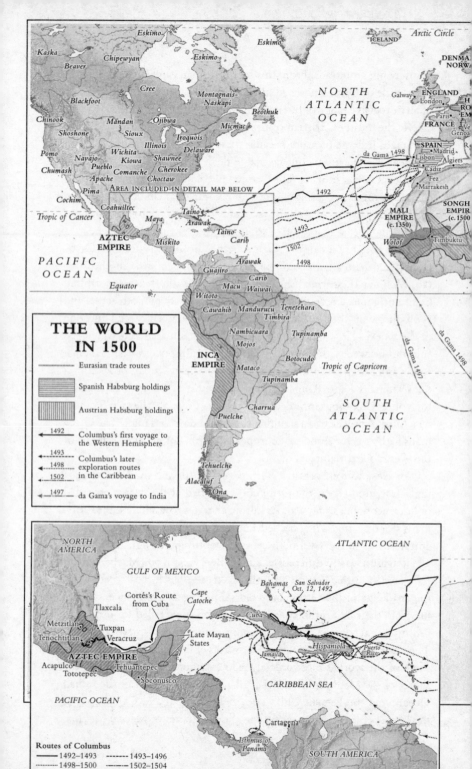

# THE WORLD IN 1500

Eurasian trade routes

Spanish Habsburg holdings

Austrian Habsburg holdings

1492 — Columbus's first voyage to the Western Hemisphere

1493 / 1498 — Columbus's later exploration routes in the Caribbean / 1502

1497 — da Gama's voyage to India

**Routes of Columbus**

1492–1493 — — — 1493–1496 ······· 1498–1500 — — 1502–1504

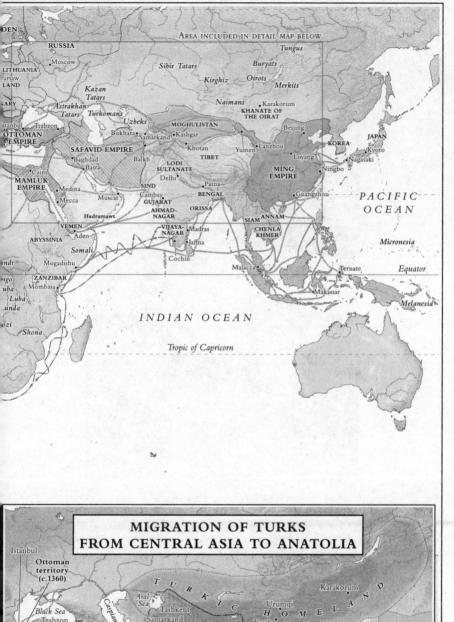

RUSSIA
Moscow

LITHUANIA
arsaw
LAND

ARY

Sibir Tatars

Tungus

Buryats

Kirghiz

Oirots

Merkits

Naimans

Karakorum

KHANATE OF
THE OIRAT

Kazan
Tatars

Astrakhan
Tatars

Turkomans

Uzbeks

Bukhara

Samarkand

MOGHULISTAN

Kashgar

Beijing

JAPAN

Kyoto

stanbul
OTTOMAN
EMPIRE

Trabzon

SAFAVID EMPIRE

Baghdad

Basra

Balkh

Khotan

TIBET

Yumen

Lanzhou

KOREA

Nagasaki

Loyang

Ningbo

MAMLUK
EMPIRE

Cairo

Medina

Mecca

Muscat

LODI
SULTANATE

Delhi

SIND

Patna

BENGAL

MING
EMPIRE

Guangzhou

PACIFIC
OCEAN

Hadramawt

Cambay

GUJARAT

AHMAD-
NAGAR

ORISSA

YEMEN

ABYSSINIA

Aden

Somali

VIJAYA-
NAGAR

Madras

Jaffna

SIAM

ANNAM

CHENLA
KHMER

Micronesia

Equator

Cochin

ndi

ngo
uba

Luba
unda

ozi

Shona

ZANZIBAR

Mombasa

Mogadishu

Malacca

Ternate

Makassar

Melanesia

INDIAN OCEAN

Tropic of Capricorn

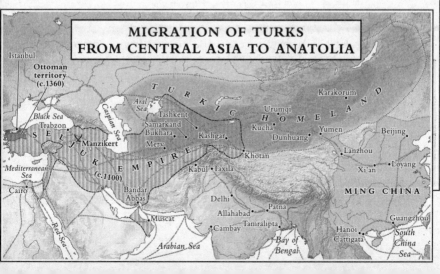

# MIGRATION OF TURKS
# FROM CENTRAL ASIA TO ANATOLIA

Istanbul

Ottoman
territory
(c.1360)

Black Sea

Trabzon

T U R K I C

Aral
Sea

Caspian Sea

Tashkent

Samarkand

Bukhara

Merv

HOMELAND

Karakorum

Urumqi

Kucha

Dunhuang

Yumen

Beijing

SELJUK

Manzikert

Kashgar

Lanzhou

Mediterranean
Sea

E M P I R E

Khotan

Xi'an

Loyang

Cairo

(c.1100)

Kabul

Taxila

MING CHINA

Bandar
Abbas

Delhi

Muscat

Allahabad

Patna

Tamralipta

Cambay

Red Sea

Arabian Sea

Bay of
Bengal

Hanoi

Cattigata

South
China
Sea

Guangzhou

*Mehmet II in the Hippodrome*

and Jerusalem, and what was the world's largest Jewish city for over
four hundred years, Salonica (Thessaloniki in today's Greece). From
their lowly beginnings as sheep-herders on the long, hard road across
Central Asia, the Ottomans ultimately succeeded in proving themselves
the closest thing to the Roman Empire since the Roman Empire itself.

ONE MAN, MORE THAN any other, made the Ottoman Empire the trans-
formative global power that it was. Selim was his name, and although
born of a sultan, he was never supposed to amount to much. The fourth

of his father's ten sons, he was born in 1470 in a small Anatolian town, the son of an enslaved concubine. Given his pedigree, a life of leisurely wealth and princely comfort was to be his lot—but it would likely be a short life, given the fratricidal maneuverings that often accompanied the death of a sultan and the accession of the next. Implacable and unflappable, callous and visionary, Selim had other plans. The story of his life—the power plays that brought him to the throne, his military ventures and techniques of governing, his personal charisma, his religious piety—presents a sovereign narrative of how the Ottoman Empire made the modern world.

Selim was the grandson of Mehmet II, the sultan who in 1453 captured Constantinople and renamed it Istanbul. His father, Bayezit, continued the empire's gains, extending its borders in all directions by invading Italy, Iran, Russia, and Hungary. Surpassing all of his predecessors, Selim achieved a conquest far more significant than even Constantinople—the near tripling of the empire's territories through wars in the Middle East, North Africa, and the Caucasus. When he died in 1520, the empire was stronger than it had ever been, a behemoth, far more powerful than any other state on Earth, bestriding the three continents of the Old World and aiming for more. Selim was the first sultan to rule over an Ottoman Empire with a majority Muslim population and the first Ottoman to hold the titles of both sultan and caliph.

Selim was also one of the first non-firstborn sons to become sultan, the first to have but one son himself, and the first to depose a sitting sultan. Monomaniacally obsessed with accruing power, Selim systematically and ruthlessly eliminated his domestic and foreign rivals, slaughtering two of his half-brothers in order to gain the throne. A nineteenth-century historian described him in the voluptuously sinister prose of that century as a "sanguinary tyrant, whose fierce blazing eyes and choleric complexion well accorded with his violent nature." Sending a message to the living as well as the dead, he often kicked the decapitated heads of those he executed. Not for nothing did he come to be known as Selim the Grim (*Yavuz*, in Turkish). "His eyes betray a cruel streak," the Venetian doge Andrea Gritti wrote. "Ferocious and cunning," he was, quite simply, "a warmonger."

Selim's life and reign spanned perhaps the most consequential half-century in world history. He proved the most influential of the line of Osman's thirty-six sultans—more so than even his son, perhaps the

Ottoman Empire's most famous sultan, Suleyman the Magnificent—his legacy shaping the empire until its end in the twentieth century, along with the geopolitical realities of our own day. As with Christ—though Christians would find the comparison invidious, to say the least—there was the empire and world before Selim, and the empire and world after Selim. We all live in Selim's shadow, a fitting reflection of another of his sobriquets, "God's Shadow on Earth."

Because of his prominence in Ottoman history and world politics, Selim's life has been chronicled many times. Ottoman histories written both before and after his death provide many details. The foremost corpus of sources is known collectively as the *Selimname*, the "Book of Selim," and it grew out of an effort after Selim's death to paint the sultan in as flattering a light as possible. During the sixteenth and seventeenth centuries, Ottoman historians copied and adapted earlier texts, creating a set of distinct yet tightly interlinked versions. In using the *Selimname*—which is indispensable for any understanding of Selim— we must weigh its often laudatory, nearly hagiographic accounts of Selim's life against other evidence that is often fleeting or incomplete. Combining a critical reading of the *Selimname* and other Ottoman sources with contemporary materials from Spain, the Mamluk Empire, Venice, the world of the Indian Ocean, and the Americas provides a balanced view of Selim and his empire and underscores the extent of his global influence.

GOD'S SHADOW THUS SERVES as a revisionist account, providing a new and more holistic picture of the last five centuries, and demonstrating Islam's constituent role in forming some of the most fundamental aspects of the history of Europe, the Americas, and the United States. If we do not place Islam at the center of our grasp of world history, we will never understand why Moor-slayers are memorialized on the Texas–Mexico border or, more generally, why we have blindly, and repeatedly, narrated histories that miss major features of our shared past. As we chronicle Selim and his age, a bold new world history emerges, one that overturns shibboleths that have held sway for a millennium. Whether politicians, pundits, and traditional historians like it or not, the world we inhabit is very much an Ottoman one. This is a story only Selim can tell.

# PART ONE

# PRINCE

## (1470–87)

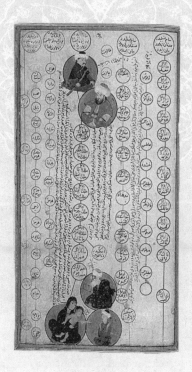

IMAGE ON PREVIOUS PAGE:
*Ottoman lineage*

# PERFUME OF THE WORLD

*Amasya*

ON A BED OF PURPLE VELVET SHEETS AND GREEN-EMBROIDERED pillows in Amasya's imperial palace, Gülbahar Hatun gave birth on October 10, 1470. Scribes noted that the royal birth occurred on a Wednesday in the early evening. Simultaneously, just outside the walls of the imperial residence in this landlocked city seventy miles from the Black Sea, a roving Sufi mystic with unkempt hair and a bushy beard held court for a small group of devotees and a growing number of curious listeners. He knew nothing of the goings-on of imperial politics, nor was he a trusted adviser or even an acquaintance of Bayezit, the city's governor, yet he shared his vision of what was occurring within the palace walls. "Today, at this court which is the abode of prosperity, a fortunate child, a chosen son who is destined to attain happiness, will be born," the mystic prophesied. "The light of the lamp of his dominion will illumine the horizons; the fragrant scents of his prosperity will perfume the nostrils of the inhabitants of the world. He will become sovereign in the place of his father, a protector of dominions in the dynasty of the line of Osmān." Such bold prognostications were hardly unique in the Ottoman world. A vast collection of soothsayers and learned men of every ilk roamed the empire, claiming to know an unknowable present as well as the future. Predicting the birth of the next sultan was not uncommon for those trading in prophecy, and every so often these merchants—like all fortune-tellers with well-timed intuition—got something right, enough to keep their customers returning for more.

The Amasya Sufi's predictions, however, soon veered off in a peculiar direction. "On his body," he continued, "the mark of which is happiness and the home of which is good fortune, he will have seven moles of royal omen. In accordance with the number of those moles, he will overcome seven rulers from among the evil-natured enemies, and be made triumphant and victorious."

The mention of seven moles was no accident—seven is an auspicious number in Islam. Heaven consists of seven levels; seven verses make up the first chapter of the Qur'an; and pilgrims circumambulate the Kaaba, Islam's holiest place, seven times. Most significantly, the number seven pointed to the seven climes. The whole world was divided into seven regions, or climes—an early notion that the earth has seven continents. Seven moles on a newborn's body would thus mark him as the future sovereign of the known world.

As Gülbahar gave a final heave—the child's father, as was customary, was absent from the scene—her weariness turned to joy and her screams surrendered to cries of elation. The newborn was a boy. His name would be Selim. And, indeed, he had seven moles.

GÜLBAHAR HAD BEEN BORN a Christian in Albania. The story of how she became Prince Bayezit's fourth consort underscores the increasingly dominant position of the Ottoman Empire in the fifteenth-century world—the last century before the emergence of the transoceanic empires of Spain, Portugal, Britain, and the Netherlands. The major empires of the fifteenth century ruled over large swaths of territory and controlled the seas, but they rarely sent navies across oceans. Eurasia was home to the Chinese, Byzantine, Mamluk, Venetian, and Spanish empires; in the Americas were the Incas and the Aztecs; in Africa, the Songhai and Mutapa empires. Before their conquest of the Byzantine capital in 1453, the Ottomans entered the region we know as the Middle East overland, as upstarts from the east, surging into territories controlled by the Byzantine, Mamluk, and Venetian empires—some of the world's largest states at the time, but still orders of magnitude less powerful than the Chinese or the Aztecs. Albania, one of those hinge territories on the border between empires, was batted back and forth between different imperial overlords.

The Venetian Empire, nestled on the north and east coasts of the Adriatic Sea, increasingly found itself fending off Ottoman raids on its territories in Albania. After their gains in Anatolia, a few decades before they took Constantinople, the Ottomans had crossed the Dardanelles into Europe to open a new phase in their expansion, marching their armies across the Balkans—then held, tenuously, by the Byzantine Empire—and deep into the forbidding mountains and valleys of coastal Albania. Possession of this stretch of coast allowed naval and pirate ships to monitor traffic, and trade, between the Adriatic and the wider Mediterranean; it was a key choke point in the theater of war between Venice and the Byzantines as they vied for control of the Greek peninsula and the eastern Mediterranean. As was their regular practice, the Ottomans cut deals with local notables, promising to respect their autonomy and offering protection. Many preferred Ottoman sovereignty to Venetian rule and agreed to pay the Ottomans taxes in kind or in cash.

By winning these European territories, the Ottomans not only advanced closer to the ultimate prize of Byzantine Constantinople but also were able to launch further attacks on the Catholic Venetians. Although many of these military skirmishes took place at sea, Albania was one of the prime terrestrial battlegrounds.

As the Ottomans accumulated territory in Europe, they integrated people from these captured regions into their imperial system

**EUROPE IN 1500**

- Spanish Habsburg holdings
- Austrian Habsburg holdings
- Church lands
- Trade routes

0    MILES    200
0    KM    200

SWEDEN
Göteborg

TEUTONIC ORDER

COURLAND

BALTIC SEA

alborg

DENMARK

penhagen

Lübeck
MECKLEN-
BURG
mburg.

POMERANIA

TEUTONIC ORDER

Danzig    PRUSSIA

Vilna

LITHUANIA

Minsk

BRANDENBURG

Warsaw

POLAND

SAXONY

BOHEMIA

Nuremberg

Prague

Krakow

Lvov

EMPIRE

Vienna
AUSTRIA

Buda

HUNGARY

MOLDAVIA

VENICE

Zagreb

Mohács

Venice

Belgrade
Smederevo    WALLACHIA

Florence

Pisa

Spoleto

Ragusa
(Dubrovnik)

Cattaro

Constanta

PAPAL STATES

Rome

Sofia

Ahyolu

Skopje

Plovdiv    Edirne

Durazzo

Dimetoka

Naples

Salonica

Istanbul

KINGDOM OF NAPLES

Otranto

Bursa

Palermo

Sicily

OTTOMAN EMPIRE

Manisa

inis

Athens

Mahdia

MEDITERRANEAN SEA

Crete
(Venice)

and developed an institution known as the *devşirme*. Teenage Christian boys were seized and taken to Ottoman centers of power. With all family ties severed, these boys converted to Islam, received every material advantage, and were taught the military arts, becoming a devoted, privileged cadre of Ottoman soldiers. In this way, the Ottomans created a loyal military elite. Some older Balkan Christian men also sought upward mobility by attempting to ingratiate themselves into the empire's military ranks.

As best we know, Gülbahar's father was one such man who converted to Islam in order to enter Ottoman military service. He gained further potential social advantage by giving his daughter to the sultan as a concubine. This would pay untold dividends, if she gave birth to a son. Indeed, Gülbahar's father could entertain the prospect of becoming the Ottoman sultan's grandfather—a stunning turn of events for a man who started adult life as a lowly Albanian regular. For Gülbahar herself, the benefits were likewise considerable. Not only would she live a more comfortable life in the palace than she would in her native village (where, instead of being owned by a sultan's son, she would simply have been owned by her husband), but she also had the chance of becoming the mother of a sultan and therefore the most important woman in the empire—truly one of the most powerful women in the world. Because, in this period, Ottoman sultans and princes produced sons not from their wives but from their concubines, all Ottoman sultans were the sons of foreign, usually Christian-born, slaves like Gülbahar.

Probably shy and apprehensive at first, Gülbahar would have had support from at least some of her fellow concubines in making the jarring transition to a prince's harem. Others, however, asserting their dominance in the harem hierarchy, would have delighted in making this young woman's new life excruciating. Gülbahar—as we can surmise from her later life—was able to navigate her new situation deftly and maximize her opportunities.

ALIENATION PERVADED THE LIFE of the Ottoman royal family. As a seventeen-year-old concubine, Gülbahar had barely spotted Bayezit in the harem courtyard before their sexual congress, her reputed coquettish charms and alluring beauty having been enough to pique his interest. In the coital union of master and concubine—uncouth and functionalist—love rarely played a part. Sultans and princes focused on producing as many male heirs as possible, to ensure the continuation of the dynasty and therefore the empire in a world in which death—during childbirth, in battle, from disease—was commonplace. Since Bayezit already had three sons, Gülbahar must have feared that her own son, if she bore one, might not be favored by his father. Such was the life of a younger Ottoman prince—celebrated at birth, then, at best, luxuriously ignored.

For the sultan, or a sultan-in-waiting like Bayezit, having many sons was a double-edged sword. Leaving behind a son was every sultan's ultimate duty, since the empire would fall if the line of Osman died out. Yet each new male descendant of Osman, in the most Darwinian of terms, represented an existential threat to his father, as a potential successor who might eye the throne a little too prematurely. More directly, he was a threat to his half-brothers. A refrain heard throughout the Ottoman Empire went, "There are no ties of kinship between princes." From the moment of their birth, half-brothers were set against one another to jockey for the throne, with their mothers acting as their strongest advocates. The mother–son relationship within the imperial family proved more important, both personally and politically, than any other. Fathers remained aloof, and the system ensured that sons viewed their father and half-brothers as enemies more than kin. Sophocles could not have scripted it better.

Succession was never straightforward in the Ottoman Empire. While the eldest son usually inherited the throne, technically any male descendant of Osman was entitled to it, and so most sultanic successions involved bloodshed. A sultan might favor one son over the others, but that guaranteed nothing. This was as true for Bayezit and his half-brothers as it was for Bayezit's sons. Bayezit thus bequeathed to his ten sons not only his almond-shaped eyes but also murderous fraternal rivalry, which their mothers fostered. The triumphant son and mother took the palace; the losing sons were killed. Their mothers lost not only their children but also the prestige and fortune that accrued from being the mother of a prince—or, clearly better, the mother of the sultan. The best these women could hope for was exile to the palace of the former Ottoman capital, Bursa—a kind of imperial retirement home for the forgotten mothers of murdered princes. Obviously, no son and no mother would aspire to such a fate.

As a laboratory for the mercilessly fierce politics of that era, the harem perfectly incubated future sultans. The leader of the Ottoman Empire had to be conniving and ruthless, and he had to be a brilliant strategist—all this in order to outwit and outsmart his rivals, whether Venetians, Safavids, Hungarians, or his own siblings and sons. The prince who emerged from the harem stronger than his half-brothers, the thinking went, would become the sultan most suited to ensuring that the Ottomans remained the strongest geopolitical power in the world.

Once a concubine bore a son, sexual relations ceased. It was a single equation: one woman, one son. Within the harem in Amasya, each mother and son occupied separate quarters, but encountered the others daily in the harem's passages and salons. Women like Gülbahar were the mothers of potential future sultans—a status that brought responsibilities and advantages, opportunities and risks. Above all, royal mothers had to keep their sons alive; secondly, they had to ensure that their sons received a princely education. In those early years in Amasya, the precocious Selim learned Ottoman Turkish (the language of the imperial administration), Arabic (the language of the Qur'an and the key to the religious sciences), and Persian (the language of literature and poetry). A prince's education also included lessons in archery, medicine, writing a royal edict, and hunting. Meanwhile, Gülbahar and her attendants taught him how to pray, dress, and carry himself as a future sultan. Thus, the harem—often an object of fantasy and myth, more opulent and well appointed than anything a commoner could have imagined—functioned in reality more as a schoolhouse than a seraglio.

WHEN SELIM WAS BORN, Bayezit had been the governor of Amasya for sixteen years. Every Ottoman prince was sent off during his youth to be a provincial governor, a key role in which to prove his mettle. As the eldest son of Mehmet II, the conqueror of Constantinople, Bayezit was set a daunting standard. A year after that conquest, he was posted to Amasya with his mother and—not surprisingly, given that he was just seven—a whole coterie of advisers and attendants. He remained there for the next twenty-seven years until, in 1481, he became sultan and moved his extensive household—which included the eleven-year-old Selim—to Istanbul.

Amasya was a sleepy agricultural town in northern Anatolia with a

*Bayezit on the throne*

temperate climate, renowned for its apples, tucked into a narrow valley cut by the Green River and bounded on nearly all sides by rugged
mountains. Sheer cliffs protected the town and guaranteed Amasya a
remarkably consistent shape over the centuries, as structures could be
built only along the slender banks of the river. As with many towns and
cities in Anatolia, Amasya had been continuously inhabited for close to
seven thousand years by the time Bayezit arrived there.

Neither a hub of trade nor a locale of great strategic importance,
Amasya distinguished itself over the centuries as both an intellectual
center—Strabo, the ancient Greek geographer, was born there—and
the adolescent home of generations of future sultans. Almost all princes,
not just those dispatched there to be governor, journeyed to Amasya to
imbibe all a sultan would need to know. With its gaze fixed outward on

the wider world, Amasya functioned as a sort of Ottoman West Point. There, future sultans studied statecraft, warfare, equitation, economics, history, and administration, and learned how to balance the interests and passions of competing bureaucrats and family members. Like other Anatolian towns and cities, Amasya had established communities of Armenians, Greeks, Bosnians, Jews, Turks, and others. Thus, as a microcosm of the diversity of the Ottoman Empire, Amasya was an ideal venue for preparing potential sultans for rule.

In the exceedingly cosmopolitan empire, the harem ensured that a non-Turkish, non-Muslim, non-elite diversity was infused into the very bloodline of the imperial family. As the son of a mother with roots in a far-off land, a distant culture, and a religion other than Islam, Selim viscerally experienced the ethnically and religiously amalgamated nature of the Ottoman Empire, and grew up in provincial Amasya with an expansive outlook on the fifteenth-century world. Although his elevation to the throne was far from certain, Selim entered his teenage years conscious of the map Gülbahar laid down to prepare him to navigate the world beyond the harem walls.

EVEN AS YOUNGSTERS, all Ottoman princes, ever so gingerly, were exposed to the delicate and perilous world of early modern diplomacy. One of the primary vehicles for showcasing a new male in the line of Osman to foreign leaders was the imperial circumcision festival. Somewhat like bar mitzvahs, these lavish ceremonies—which tended to occur nearly every year, given the structure (and collective fertility) of the royal family—celebrated the entry of a boy into manhood. They also served a diplomatic function: they were a pretext for inviting foreign envoys, heads of state, and other international dignitaries to the imperial palace in Istanbul, a new structure in the recently conquered city that would eventually be named Topkapı Palace. Along with the gift-giving, congratulatory messages, and an endless parade of sumptuous dishes, Ottoman officials and their counterparts could deepen their ties in a social setting and conduct business on the side. Selim's circumcision festival occurred in the summer of 1479, when he was almost nine. He and his parents traveled the four hundred miles to Istanbul so that the many foreign guests, as well as emissaries resident in the city, could easily attend the ceremony.

As a prince's introduction to the world beyond the palace and a means to prove the effectiveness of a mother-and-son pair, the circumcision ceremony had to proceed flawlessly. The prince's mother took charge of the arrangements but, as was then customary, she did not attend the public festivities. The circumcision ceremony thus embodied the dual role of the imperial mother: nurturing parent, and manager of her son's eventual takeover of the empire. Not only did she soothe her young son after his painful surgical entry into manhood, but she helped to organize the first major international event of his life.

Selim's circumcision festival came at a nadir in Ottoman–Venetian relations. Before the conquest of Constantinople in 1453, Ottoman and Venetian forces had come close to full-scale war on several occasions, but economic interests in maintaining the flow of east–west trade nearly always prevailed. After 1453, however, war became inevitable, as Ottoman advances in the Balkans further encroached on Venetian territories with the capture of Serbia in 1459.

A few years later, in 1462, an Ottoman military commander of Albanian origins—he had been captured in one of the raids that regularly brought Balkan boys into the empire—defected to a Venetian fortress near Athens. The Ottomans, understandably, demanded his return. When the Venetians refused, war ensued. In truth, the Ottomans used the fugitive as a pretext to justify their invasion of Athens and their continuing expansion in the Peloponnese and on into the Balkans, as far west as Bosnia, which they conquered the following year, and further into Albania soon after that.

This period of conflict finally ended in 1479 with the Ottoman siege of the Venetian-held city of Shkodra (in the north of modern-day Albania), a victory that allowed the Ottomans to project their power further north along the Adriatic coast. The Treaty of Constantinople, signed on January 25, 1479, brought peace to both sides. After decades of war, Ottoman ascendancy in the eastern Mediterranean—indeed, on the very doorstep of Venice—became official, as did the Italian state's vastly diminished regional status. Thus, it was understandable that, just a few months after this ignominious defeat, the Venetian senate was in no mood to send a favored representative to Selim's circumcision ceremony. They did not send anybody, in fact, snubbing Selim—and, more to the point, his grandfather, Sultan Mehmet II.

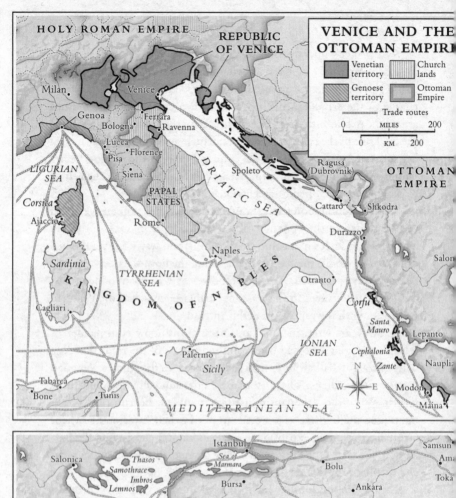

⁂

BAYEZIT'S HAREM, WHILE LAVISH, was crowded with his twenty-seven children, several wives, and a retinue of concubines. Of his ten boys, sons two through four emerged as viable contenders for the throne: Ahmed, Korkud, and Selim. His firstborn son, Abdullah, died in 1483 at the age of eighteen, and the other six never amounted to much beyond their sinecure posts as governors of various Anatolian towns. Like Selim, Ahmed and Korkud were born to concubines in Amasya—in 1466 and 1467, respectively. All enjoyed similar harem educations in languages, philosophy, religion, and the military arts. Early on, Bayezit seems to have tapped Ahmed as his eventual successor (he would certainly favor him later)—perhaps because he was the eldest surviving son, or perhaps because Bayezit deemed him the ablest. Whatever the reason, his father folded Ahmed into imperial governance long before his brothers. As a boy, he attended meetings, assembled a team of advisers, and developed relationships with important military figures. Despite these advantages, or perhaps because of this privilege, Ahmed grew indolent. As a result, his body became corpulent, his mind sluggish. According to a Greek account from the seventeenth century, Ahmed "only cared for eating, drinking, and sleeping." He enjoyed the pleasures of life in the palace and saw the throne more as a birthright than as something he had to win from his younger brothers.

Korkud was the most bookish of the three half-brothers. Like many cerebral children with a domineering older sibling, he preferred quiet contemplation to meetings and military exercises. "Korkud," the same Greek source offered, "had applied himself to literature and displayed no other concerns." He enjoyed poetry and penned several treatises on theological esoterica. As he grew up, Korkud became far more pious than his brothers, philosophically accepting the vagaries of fate. If Allah wanted him to be sultan, it would happen. During his youth, Korkud did not push for what he considered ephemeral, and generally avoided affairs of state.

Shrewd even in his earliest days, Selim observed these fraternal crevices. He saw an opportunity to set himself apart from his older brothers by holding the middle ground between the two—crafty and political like Ahmed, deep-thinking and munificent like Korkud. Unlike Ahmed, though, Selim was not lazy, and, unlike Korkud, he did not retreat into books. As a boy, he was—again, as the Venetian doge Andrea Gritti described him—"more ferocious and cunning than his brothers . . . extremely generous, and at the same time a warmonger": winning attributes for anyone who hoped to rule a world empire. Even with their struggle for the throne many years away, Bayezit's sons developed a deep hatred for one another. As rambunctious youngsters, they chased one another through the harem courtyards for sport; as grown men, they would chase one another around Anatolia with armies.

Before one of them could take over the empire, though, their father first had to become sultan. If Bayezit failed to seize the throne, they would likely be killed.

WHEN SELIM WAS TEN, his grandfather, Mehmet the Conqueror—a man he deeply respected and loved (far more than his father, according to some observers), a leader whose style he would seek to emulate—suffered severe abdominal pains while on a military campaign just east of Istanbul, the capital he had won a few decades earlier. Having spent most of his adult life at war, he was soothed by the sound of horses galloping outside his tent, but even so a deep panic gripped him. Religious men and doctors came to succor him, and his closest advisers hovered at his bedside. Around four o'clock on the afternoon of May 3, 1481, at the age of forty-nine, Mehmet—the greatest sultan the empire had yet known—drew his last breath. Tearfully, the grand vizier closed the eyes of his now soulless sultan and began to organize the transfer of the body to Istanbul's Fatih Mosque, which Mehmet had built to be his eternal home.

Suspicious circumstances surrounded the sultan's death. All evidence pointed to poison, a ubiquitous fear in the halls of the palace. Disgruntled advisers and military commanders, foreign agents, and above all Mehmet's own sons all had their reasons to dispatch the sultan. Because poison was difficult to trace back to a specific source, and could kill from afar slowly over time, it was an ideal weapon; an assassin could administer a concoction that would lead to death months later. Without exaggeration, however, the Ottoman sovereign's body was perhaps the most protected corporeal form on Earth—palisaded by an elaborate system of food sampling, physician surveillance, and water management—so dosing him with poison approached the impossible. Palace administrators, for example, forced the imperial chefs to serve their own children from the sultan's plate before it was delivered to him. During the recent years of war between Venice and the Ottomans, Venice had made at least a dozen attempts on Mehmet's life, and some believed that Venice had bribed one of the sultan's personal physicians, a Persian, to kill him. Others believed that one of his sons was the culprit. But despite the many rumors, at the time and since, the exact reason for the sultan's death remains a mystery.

Mehmet died, fittingly, just a few kilometers from the grave of Hannibal of Carthage, the renowned military commander and strategist of antiquity. Hannibal had battled the Roman Empire in the third century BCE; eighteen hundred years later, Mehmet crushed the last remnants of the Romans in the east—the Byzantine Empire. Mehmet's empire would assume the mantle of the Romans—something Hannibal was never able to accomplish. After decades of neglect and depopulation, Constantinople—now Mehmet's Istanbul—experienced a rebirth, instilling fear in every European leader from Henry VI of England to Pope Nicholas V, who saw this as a sign of impending eschatological violence, with Mehmet as the Antichrist and the Ottomans as the devil's foot soldiers. From the second Rome, the Ottoman sultan might mobilize a strike on the first, a cataclysm that seemed all too real to Europeans in 1480, when Mehmet seized the tiny port city of Otranto on the Italian peninsula. With his demise, however, and the subsequent Ottoman retreat from Otranto, the outlook brightened, encouraging Europeans to believe that God might be on their side after all.

It took a few weeks for news of the sultan's death to spread throughout Europe, and the elation was literally explosive. Fireworks pierced the night skies and church bells tolled in every European capital. On the day of Mehmet's death, the earth itself had jolted the island of Rhodes with tremors—another cosmic omen. "This second Lucifer, this second Mohammed, this second Antichrist," this seizer of the second Rome, had departed. "It was fortunate for Christendom and for Italy," wrote the procurator of St. Mark's Basilica in Venice, "that death checked the fierce and indomitable barbarian." With Mehmet's death, Europe received a much needed, albeit momentary, respite from the periodic Crusades it felt obligated to wage against its Muslim enemies, for example, after 1453—though then, as on many occasions, feelings of Christian duty fell short of actual war, since European powers often could not organize a proper fighting force. More practically, with Armageddon averted, numerous European princes' financial obligations to the Ottoman Empire—which were considerable—now appeared potentially renegotiable.

In contrast to Europe's elation, a mood of impending chaos and mounting crisis pervaded the Ottoman Empire. The succession struggle that inevitably followed a sultan's death was only beginning. As a perceptive, crafty ten-year-old, Selim would watch this dramatic spectacle unfold and learn a great deal about politics and violence, and also about his own family.

CHAPTER

2

# EMPIRE BOYS

*Bayezit and Cem battle*

WHEN NEWS OF MEHMET'S DEATH REACHED AMASYA, BAYEZIT set out immediately for Istanbul, taking only his most trusted advisers and military men. He could be sure that his younger half-brother Cem (pronounced "Jem") was on the road as well—and whoever arrived first at the palace usually kept the throne. Distance from the seat of power invariably proved a major factor in Ottoman succession struggles, and the location of Cem's governorship gave him a slight head-start.

Selim had heard about Cem, but had never met him. As, from his child's perspective, he absorbed the uncertainty and panic that pervaded the palace and the empire, he began to understand the brutal realities of his own future. This crisis foreshadowed the crisis that would come when Bayezit himself died; Selim would then find himself in the perilous position his father found himself in now. That is, if Bayezit succeeded in seizing the throne. If he did not, Selim's future would be short indeed.

Gülbahar's role as Selim's mentor and adviser proved key in this moment. She alone could explain to him the complicated and potentially deadly world of imperial succession, and teach him how to navigate it. They would eventually leave Amasya, the only home Selim had known, and follow Bayezit to the palace. Each mother-and-son pair could have also considered a strategic alliance with Cem. Although sons were generally pitted against fathers and brother against brother in the Ottoman dynastic system, succession jumbled these interests, creating one of the few instances in which sons—usually—supported their fathers unconditionally. Only after a father had secured the sultanate could his sons become his primary challengers for power.

The questions facing those *outside* the Ottoman Empire were similarly weighty. With the leader of the largest and, thanks to Mehmet, strongest polity in the Mediterranean now gone, power shifted decisively toward Europe. Ottoman succession battles always inspired the empire's enemies to hope that they could claw back some lost territory. As the conqueror not only of Constantinople but also of parts of Italy and Albania, Mehmet had proven more consequential than any sultan before him, so his demise proved equally significant as a moment of possibility. Would Europe unite long enough to wage an effective war against the Ottomans, and perhaps mount the Crusade for Jerusalem that had been dreamed of for centuries? And would Europeans regain some control of the precious trade with the East? The world waited on geopolitical tenterhooks as the Ottoman dynasty worked out its family quarrels. Soon the struggle would spill beyond the borders of the empire.

❈

BAYEZIT AND CEM WERE nearly polar opposites. Bayezit was a serious, even dour man. A devout Muslim, he enjoyed studying Islamic philosophy and supported the empire's religious establishment by building mosques, hospitals, and colleges. The Venetian ambassador to Istanbul described him as "very melancholic, superstitious, and stubborn," a comment perhaps inspired by Bayezit's removal of the paintings by Italian artists his father had commissioned for the palace. Cem, on the other hand, was a bon vivant. Handsome and charismatic, he enjoyed hunting and sport, poetry and wine. His womanizing was legendary, with much-embroidered tales of maidens throwing themselves at his feet. On the inside of his favorite wine chalice, he had had seven lines engraved, to represent the seven climes. Each draft of wine thus exposed a new line, drawing him closer to possessing the entire world. In his drunkenness, he would be able to see the earth laid open in front of him while he imagined his power over all of creation. Ultimately, his shrewd political acumen and desire for the throne surpassed his love of wine and women.

A couple decades after Bayezit became the governor of Amasya in the mid-1450s, Cem assumed the governorship of Konya, another ancient Anatolian town. Konya had seen the apostle Paul arrive to spread the gospel; during the Renaissance, it would become a renowned center of carpet production. It is most famous today as the home and burial site of the Persian poet Rumi, whose death in 1273 inspired his followers to found the Mevlevi Sufi order, based on his teachings of universal love and the unification of God and man. The order's use of music, mystical poetry, whirling hypnotic dance, and even wine to unite man with God made it one of the most distinct religious orders in all of Islam. No doubt the Sufis' combined message of love and worldly pleasure appealed to Cem during his governorship of the city, though there is no evidence that he actually joined the ranks of their brotherhood.

Mehmet's grand vizier, Karamani Mehmed Pasha, who had closed the sultan's eyes for the last time, supported Cem for the succession, whom he and other imperial functionaries viewed as the more pliable of the two sons, easier to influence and control. Conspiring to keep news of Mehmet's death secret for as long as possible, he furtively implored

Cem to rush to Istanbul and seize the throne before Bayezit was any the wiser. But the grand vizier was no match for the Janissaries—the empire's elite and powerful military corps. They had long supported Bayezit, as they considered he would be more likely to support their agenda for a militarily aggressive, expansionist empire. Because Mehmet died while on campaign, the news of his death was no secret to the Janissaries. Immediately they sent word to Bayezit and bolted into action, thundering into Istanbul with armaments and horses to secure the palace until Bayezit could arrive. Although the grand vizier and his allies tried to prevent this, the soldiers easily overwhelmed the civilian administrators, slaughtering many of them in the streets and taking over much of the city. They soon captured the grand vizier himself and killed him, too. Without a sultan, without a clear successor, and now without a grand vizier, the empire fell into a fragile and parlous state of turmoil.

One of the most powerful constituencies in the empire, the Janissaries were a unique fighting force in the early modern world. The Ottomans' professional military, always at the ready for battle, far outshone any force in Europe, where states had to round up an army of mercenaries and irregulars every time they went to war. Not only was this cumbersome and slow, but the recruits were woefully unreliable and undertrained, often fighting for personal gain rather than for the interest of the state. It was no wonder, observed Niccolò Machiavelli, that the Ottomans were in the ascendancy in the Mediterranean. Machiavelli was correct in his assessment of how the Ottoman army stacked up against European armies, but he missed a salient point. The very same advantages of strength that the standing army afforded the empire could also be turned against it. While theoretically the Janissaries were subservient to the sultan, the reality was much more complicated. They took sides, as in the succession battle between Bayezit and Cem; they used the threat of violence against organs of the state and sometimes the populace at large to exact money, resources, and power; and they almost always pushed for war, hungry for their portion of the spoils seized in battle and the opportunities for pillage. Thus, to keep the Janissaries happy, sultans had to cut deals with them, grant them favors, and keep their ranks flush with newly captured recruits. In contrast to Cem's foppish lifestyle, Bayezit's serious, stoic nature earned him the Janissaries' support.

For nearly three weeks, the throne remained vacant, as Bayezit and Cem sprinted from Anatolia to Istanbul. Bayezit arrived first, reaching the outskirts of Istanbul on May 21, 1481. After killing the grand vizier, the Janissaries had imposed strict controls on the city—enforcing a curfew, patrolling the streets, chasing down rabble-rousers, and securing neighborhood squares. The normal chaos of a city of half a million people—the steady hum of vegetable and fruit peddlers, merchants hawking their wares, and crowds of men socializing on street corners—had hushed to an eerie calm. He rendezvoused with a detachment of Janissaries at a prearranged city gate, and they formed a phalanx around him to rush him through the city to the palace.

Once safely within the palace walls, Bayezit received obeisance from the Janissary commanders and the imperial governing elite. The grand mufti, the empire's chief religious figure, proclaimed him sultan

*Bayezit converses with his advisers, including Korkud*

of the entirety of creation, ruler of the first clime to the seventh, of time immemorial to the end of days. After this simple ceremony in the palace garden, Bayezit proceeded with full military accompaniment to the Mosque of Eyüp, a structure his father had ordered built after his conquest of Constantinople; it encircled the tomb of Eyüp, a companion of the Prophet Muhammad. There the empire's elite bestowed upon Bayezit the sword of the first Ottoman sultan, Osman, his thirteenth-century ancestor. After these two simple ceremonies—conferring on him the recognition of the dynasty, of God, and of his family (except for Cem, of course)—Bayezit became the empire's eighth sultan on May 22, 1481, one day after his arrival in the capital.

Meanwhile, Cem found himself bogged down in Anatolia. He had made it only as far as İnegöl, a town in a bowl-shaped mountain valley near the first Ottoman capital of Bursa, when word reached him that his half-brother had taken the palace. He exploded in a fit of rage.

Bayezit knew that to secure his rule, he had to eliminate Cem. Thus, in the first military venture of his sultanate, just a week into his rule, Bayezit ordered an army contingent to İnegöl. Arriving in the mountain town on May 28, the new sultan's forces encountered an inspired and fierce group of soldiers. Channeling their leader's fury, Cem's men routed Bayezit's. With this victory, Cem took control of Bursa, the first seat of the empire and a center of the international silk trade. Ensconcing his forces in the palace, Cem proclaimed himself Sultan of Anatolia, a clear declaration of his intention to continue his war against his half-brother. He struck coins in his own image, and the mosques in Bursa intoned Friday prayers in his name. Now the empire had two palaces, two capitals, and two sultans. A civil war loomed, jeopardizing the empire's very existence.

Cem understood the perilous nature of his position and tried to negotiate, suggesting that he rule Anatolia while Bayezit took everything west of the Bosphorus Strait, a roughly equal division of imperial territory. Bayezit refused. As far as he was concerned, he was the empire's rightful sultan and Cem was a rebel enemy of the state. Bayezit responded to Cem's "offer" by dispatching another army. Again, the forces met outside Bursa, but this time Bayezit's men scored a decisive victory, driving Cem not only out of Bursa but all the way to Syria, out of the Ottoman Empire altogether. To Bayezit's dismay, they failed to kill or capture him.

Secure on the throne and with his half-brother now on the run, Bayezit summoned his wives, children, and concubines from Amasya. Apart from his circumcision ceremony nearly two years earlier, Selim, now eleven, had never left Amasya. From a provincial, landlocked town, he arrived in the very heart of the empire, where his father was the sultan and his new home the nucleus of power.

The palace harem was as grand as anything imaginable: a sprawling complex of innumerable apartments with high vaulted ceilings linked by a warren of passageways, and dozens of buildings to explore. Perched on one of Istanbul's fabled seven hills overlooking the Bosphorus, the palace, with its gardens and balconies, offered a panorama of spectacular views. After his daily lessons in language, history, and religion, Selim would gambol from one vantage point to another to gaze out at Europe and Asia and enjoy the sea breezes. He loved watching

*Defending Bayezit against an assassination attempt*

the boats glide between continents and listening to the calls of eagles and buzzards migrating south from the Black Sea. As a prince, he was kept at some remove from the city beyond the walls, but its loud noises and pungent smells inevitably found their way into the palace.

Even while he enjoyed nonstop attention as the son of the new sultan, Selim sensed the tension. His father, especially in the early years of his rule, remained on the defensive, ever wary of Cem. Selim learned early that the imperial ground beneath him would be eternally unstable.

EUROPEAN POWERS, ALWAYS COGNIZANT of affairs on their eastern flank, were scheming to take advantage of this perceived moment of Ottoman weakness. On June 4, 1481, a mere two weeks after Bayezit took the throne, Pope Sixtus IV wrote to Christian leaders across Europe, hoping to organize a new Crusade against the Ottomans and other Muslims. A month later, the pope's naval forces joined a fleet from Naples to attack Otranto, the Ottomans' single territorial possession on the boot of Italy. Fighting began in July 1481 and lasted until September, when Ottoman forces surrendered, bringing to a close their thirteen-month sojourn. Buoyed by this victory, the Christian alliance set its sights on repelling the Ottomans from the Mediterranean. With a reinforcement of twenty-five ships from Portugal, the pope planned to cross the Adriatic from Otranto to Valona (today's Vlorë) on the Albanian coast. A victory there would secure both sides of the strategic mouth of the Adriatic and create a foothold for reconquering the parts of Albania and Greece that Mehmet had captured during the previous decades. But an outbreak of plague in Albania and a group of disgruntled ship's captains stalled these plans. Through no action of his own, the new sultan had, at least for now, managed to retain the eastern coast of the Adriatic.

To the east, the Mamluk Empire, the Ottomans' major adversary in the Muslim world, took advantage of the power vacuum to strengthen their military and economic influence in the Middle East and throughout the eastern Mediterranean. The longer the House of Osman remained divided, the better, as far as the Mamluks were concerned. Thus, they welcomed Cem to Cairo, the Mamluk capital, as their guest, which transformed the Ottomans' internecine enmity into a matter of international intrigue, one that ricocheted through much of global politics.

Cem could not have asked for a more powerful set of arrows for his quiver—an empire to help to win an empire. He felt at ease in the wealthy Mamluk court, where respect, comfort, and luxury were lavished on him. Outside the palace walls, though, Cairo was an entirely different matter. When Cem first reached the city on September 30, 1481, he gaped in awe at its imposing strangeness and grand scale. Of the two largest cities in the Mediterranean, Istanbul was bigger than Cairo, but Cairo had been spared the depopulation that had occurred in Istanbul immediately before and after 1453. Having never lived in Istanbul as an adult, Cem was overwhelmed by Cairo's size, noisome streets, and the maddening intimacy of its tightly packed neighborhoods. The imperial court conducted its business in Arabic, rather than Turkish or Persian; Cem had some facility with Arabic, thanks to his harem education, but still it challenged him. Overall, Cairo was far more Arab and Muslim than any place in the Ottoman Empire, whose population still retained a Christian majority. The call to prayer reverberated throughout the alleyways of the Mamluk capital more forcefully than Cem had ever experienced.

Ramadan began a few weeks after Cem arrived in Cairo. As an honored guest of the Mamluk sultan Qaitbay, Cem dined as part of the sovereign's entourage every night during the holy month. The sunset feasts that broke the fast of the day were sumptuous affairs, with poets and musicians offering entertainment. Over bulgur and lamb and desserts of saffron milk and dried apricots, Cem broached the topic of Mamluk support for his bid to overthrow his half-brother. Qaitbay, who had a long beard and spiky eyebrows, listened patiently but kept delaying promises of support, saying he would have to consult his advisers first, or would have to wait until the end of Ramadan, or offering some other excuse. In fact, Qaitbay wanted the fraternal rivalry to last as long as possible, as Ottoman disarray advantaged the Mamluks in the control of the East–West trade.

Intensely frustrated by Qaitbay's stalling, Cem decided to leave Cairo and make the *Hajj*—the Islamic pilgrimage to the holy cities of Mecca and Medina—in December 1481. The Prophet Muhammad, born in Mecca in the year 570, had died in Medina in 632. In Mecca, he received the revelations that eventually became the Qur'an; no matter where they are in the world, all Muslims face Mecca to pray five times a day. The *Hajj* is one of the Five Pillars of Islam and is considered a duty that every able Muslim should undertake. Yet Cem was the only Ottoman sultan or prince in over six hundred years of Ottoman history to observe this important tenet of the faith. And even in his case, his motivation seems to have been more political than religious. The annual pilgrimage—the largest gathering anywhere in the Muslim world—showcased the cosmopolitanism of Islam, bringing together people from Morocco in the west to China in the east, who spoke languages ranging from Russian to Bengali. Cem saw it as an opportunity to project an image of himself as the Caliph of all Muslims and Protector of the Holy Cities; the *Hajj* would be evidence of his fitness to rule.

Cem's arrival in Mecca with the caravan from Cairo sparked intense excitement. Just as he had hoped, his pilgrimage became what we would call today a publicity tour. Everywhere he went—from the Kaaba, Islam's holiest site, to the Tomb of the Prophet in Medina—crowds followed him, seeking his prayers and words of wisdom. He inspired Medina's despondent residents to elevate their spirits and rebuild their Great Mosque (*al-Masjid al-Nabawi*), which had been engulfed by fire after lightning struck its minaret a few months before he arrived in the city. For centuries thereafter, the reconstruction of the mosque was credited to Cem's influential visit.

Inspired and emboldened by his pilgrimage, Cem returned to the Mamluk capital with the Cairo caravan on March 11, 1482, and duly wrote the following challenge in verse to his half-brother:

> *While you lie on a bed of roses in sheer happiness,*
> *Why should I be covered by ashes in sorrow's furnace?*
> *If one observes piety, shouldn't justice favour him?*
> *Is that not a legitimate right claimed by the pilgrim?*

Upon receiving this dispatch, Bayezit scoffed and responded with a verse of his own, mocking Cem's feigned piety and lack of respect for the empire:

> *Since time immemorial we were given this state,*
> *Why then are you unwilling to accept preordained fate?*
> *"I went on the pilgrimage," you say to advance your claim;*
> *Why then are these worldly gains and sovereignty your chief aim?*

In Cairo that spring, Cem plotted his comeback. With reluctant Mamluk support—just enough to keep the brothers fighting—propelling him forward, Cem knew he would need help from within the Ottoman Empire. Through his network of emissaries and contacts, he started making overtures throughout Anatolia. There was no shortage of power brokers and local potentates ready to welcome an alliance with an Ottoman prince. Anatolia was still a tessellated landscape of minor regional powers, remnants of Byzantine military factions, and large household polities. The goal of early modern states like the Ottoman Empire was not necessarily to eliminate these mostly autonomous domestic elements but rather to co-opt, subdue, or otherwise manage them. Cem understood this politics of negotiation and cooperation; he therefore felt confident that he could secure the forces he needed to mount an effective challenge to Bayezit.

CEM'S FIRST MOVE WAS to enter into an alliance with the leader of the Kasıms, one of the largest tribal principalities in Anatolia. They were among the many very old families of pastoral nomads who had interests and influence around major Anatolian towns and had managed to cut deals with ruling powers over the centuries—from the Romans to the Byzantines and now the Ottomans. The Kasıms' strongholds centered on areas near Konya, where Cem had been governor. Although the town now was, at least ostensibly, under his half-brother's control, Cem shared a long history with the leaders of the clan and knew they could find common purpose. The arrangement could not have been more propitious for each side. By allying with Cem, the Kasıms transformed themselves from one of many local power brokers into an existential threat to the dynasty. The previous year, in hopes of capturing more territory from the empire, the Kasıms had sought a coalition with the Knights Hospitaller of St. John, rulers of the tiny island of Rhodes, but they were rebuffed as the Knights thought it best to honor the peace treaty with the Ottomans they had been forced to sign three years previously. The Kasıms clearly wanted a global power alliance; they found it in Cem. For his part, Cem gained a military force he could use against his half-brother.

With this collaboration in place, Cem secretly returned to

Anatolia—against the protestations of Sultan Qaitbay—to finalize with the Kasıms his plans for an attack on Konya. He left behind his mother, concubines, and some of his four children (one of Cem's daughters married Qaitbay's son in this period). Having traveled overland through Syria to Cairo, then to the holy cities, and now back to Anatolia, Cem traced a path through the Mamluk Empire that presaged the conquests his nephew Selim would undertake thirty-four years later.

Upon reaching the rocky hills on the outskirts of Konya, Cem made his way to the Kasım encampments. Like Alexander the Great, the Seljuks, the Crusaders, and so many others, Cem and the Kasıms prepared for their invasion of Konya by amassing troops, weapons, and other resources on the plains beyond the city. This would, Cem hoped, be the first in a cascade of battles that would win him the throne. Instead, when fighting commenced in late May 1482, his forces were beaten back in mere hours by the city's new governor, Abdullah—Bayezit's eldest son, Selim's half-brother, Cem's nephew.

Denied Konya, Cem and the Kasıms decided to move on Ankara. As they headed north, word reached them that Bayezit himself, having heard that Cem was in Anatolia, had set off from Istanbul with a huge army, eager to welcome his half-brother back to the empire with a freshly dug grave. Rightly fearful for his life, Cem halted his march toward Ankara and retreated southward. Bayezit then dispatched one of his soldiers to catch up with Cem and the Kasıms and deliver a letter outlining terms of surrender. In exchange for relinquishing his interest in the throne and recognizing Bayezit as the one and only legitimate sultan, Cem would receive a yearly sum of gold and a protected retirement in Jerusalem, far away from Istanbul. Cem rejected the offer out of hand. Aside from requiring him to surrender any chance of becoming sultan, which was instantly unacceptable, Bayezit's deal might also have been a ruse to assassinate him.

Cem's quest for the throne had already taken him to Cairo and the Arabian peninsula. Before the succession was finally resolved, he would take the struggle through the royal courts of France, Italy, and Rhodes, grafting the politics of Ottoman succession into the politics of early modern Europe and then the globe.

# AN OTTOMAN ABROAD

*Pope Pius II blesses a Crusading fleet at Ancona,
with Cem in attendance*

ADJUSTING TO HIS NEW LIFE IN THE PALACE WHILE ABSORBING
the lessons of the sanguinary imperial politics around him, eleven-year-
old Selim remained safely within the confines of the harem as his fam-

ily's succession drama unfolded. With a child's fretfulness, he watched his uncle jockeying to gain the support of foreign powers against his father.

After his failure to establish a foothold in Anatolia, Cem knew his half-brother's forces would soon drive him out of the empire altogether. The Mamluks had already made clear that they would support Cem only so far. Persia was an option, but it was too internally fractured to be interested in waging a major campaign against the far more powerful Ottoman Empire. By contrast, European powers, all weaker than the Ottomans in this period, were eager for any geopolitical advantage they could muster. Cem, while still encamped with the Kasıms outside Konya, began reaching out across the Mediterranean. In the early 1480s, the head of the family helped Cem to write and dispatch letters to disparate sovereigns, understanding that a war between Bayezit and a European state would open up space in Anatolia for the Kasıms to advance their forces. This was a slow process in the early modern world, where communication moved only as fast as a human on horseback or on a ship.

Cem's first letter was to Venice, in January 1482; his request for asylum and alliance was refused. The Venetians had recently signed a peace treaty with the Ottomans and had no interest in upsetting the delicate balance of relations. Cem turned next to the rulers of Rhodes, the Knights Hospitaller of St. John, whom the Kasıms had approached a few years earlier, but his first messenger was captured and killed by Bayezit's forces. Realizing that Bayezit was aware of his schemes, Cem entrusted his next emissary with a verbal message, which ensured that the envoy, if captured, would not—unless tortured, perhaps— divulge any important information. The man chosen for the task was one Firenk Suleyman Bey, a Christian convert to Islam who spoke fluent French ("Firenk" is a corruption of Frank, a common title carried by Christian converts to Islam). Little is known about his origins. He may have been a captive who agreed to convert and serve the Ottoman state in exchange for his freedom. Alternatively, he could have voluntarily "turned Turk," as the phrase went, as many Crusading soldiers did when they reached the Middle East, for various reasons: genuine faith, the love of a Muslim woman, awe at the superior power and majesty they discovered in the East, or the opportunities available to them in the Muslim world.

Rhodes, just off the southwestern Anatolian coast, is a parched and craggy island, strategically located where the Aegean meets the Mediterranean. In the summer of 1482, Firenk Suleyman Bey reached the island without incident and relayed Cem's message to Pierre d'Aubusson, Grand Master of the Knights, who knew Cem personally from the truce negotiations in 1479, when Cem had been entrusted with that task by Mehmet II, his father. D'Aubusson, well aware of the tactical potential that Cem represented, leaped at the chance to serve as his protector. Buffeted on all sides by much larger and stronger enemies, the Knights viewed an internal challenger to the Ottoman throne as a potentially enormous weapon. Not only could Cem rattle the entire carapace of the Ottoman Empire, but should he gain the throne through their support, he would be forever in the Knights' debt. For his part, Cem did all he could to encourage the Catholics' expectations by promising to deliver something he could not: peace between Islam and Christendom. Desperate and perhaps naïve, the Knights saw Cem's overture as an opportunity to forge a Christian–Muslim alliance against a shared Muslim enemy. Politics did not always trump religion in the early modern Mediterranean, but in this instance it clearly did. In the middle of July 1482, Cem boarded a ship at Korikos (modern-day Kızkalesi) on the southeastern Anatolian shore. Although he was unaware of it then, this was his last moment in the Ottoman Empire.

IT TOOK OVER A week for the small merchant ship to cover the three hundred miles between Korikos and the city of Rhodes on the northeastern tip of the island; the trip was uneventful, given the sea's placid summer currents. Yet Cem's mind was tortured. He talked to no one and hardly slept. He knew well that the longer Bayezit held the throne—and it had already been more than a year—the harder it would be to uproot him. Leaving the territory of the empire once again was, clearly, a gamble for Cem, yet, given his debacle with the Kasıms at Konya, he had little choice. Looking overboard into the limpid blue of the northern Mediterranean, Cem saw the darkness of his circumstances—forced once more to put his fate in the hands of another power. But should he stay in Anatolia, he would surely be hunted down.

While he clearly had his trepidations, Cem could not have known the depth of the political morass into which he was stepping when he reached Rhodes. There, he would become one of the early modern world's most valuable bargaining chips, a hostage who did not know he was a hostage—at least, not yet. Any entity that gave Cem refuge, however small or unimportant, immediately became a sponsor of Bayezit's potential demise and could therefore make demands of the empire. Rhodes would be the first of many European powers to vie for Cem.

In the grand game of imperial politics, each party needed the other, even as each tried to outwit the other. Cem bargained for as much support as he could get from the Knights—money, ships, troops, diplomatic protection—to sustain his bid for the Ottoman throne. For their part, the Knights viewed Cem as a stepping-stone toward their larger ambition—a new Crusade to capture Jerusalem from the Muslims. The Knights had started as a Crusading order, and they remained a Crusading order. Cem was useful to them not as a spark to ignite an infernal war with the Ottomans—a war they wanted to avoid at all costs, because they knew they would lose disastrously—but because he bought them time. They wagered that Cem was enough of a threat to Bayezit that they could leverage him for peace, and perhaps money too. A temporary *Pax Mediterranea* would enable them to rebuild their military strength and financial resources for the planned Crusade.

When he arrived on the island on July 29, 1482, representatives of the Knights met him at the docks with a royal welcome. Carpets embroidered with gold and silver softened his first steps ashore, and he was given a "most beautiful horse" to ride from the coast into the city. Crowds cheered him along the route, which was strewn with flowers. The Knights—as well as Italian, Greek, French, and Flemish merchants on Rhodes—hailed Cem as a prince as well as a kind of celebrity who might tip the Mediterranean's balance of power against the Ottoman sultan. Cem, the Knights, and the Mediterranean's Christian merchant communities shared the same political program, but their interests would converge for only so long. After thanking those who had accompanied him from the harbor and handing over the horse's reins, Cem made the short, steep climb up to the imposing stone walls of the palace of the Grand Master of the Knights of Rhodes.

Since as early as the sixteenth century BCE, Rhodes had been continuously inhabited. Its location made it a coveted speck on the sea

*The Knights Hospitaller receive Cem in Rhodes*

as long as maritime routes were the principal means of long-distance travel. Along with Crete, Rhodes served as the key border crossing from the Aegean—and beyond it, Istanbul and the Black Sea—into the eastern Mediterranean, and then on to Egypt, Cyprus, Syria, the rest of the Middle East, North Africa, and points west. Rhodes also controlled one of Anatolia's richest supply zones of rare coastal timber, which was coveted for shipbuilding and other uses. The ramparts of the city, first built by the Greeks in the fourth century BCE, had been restored by the Knights of St. John in the early fourteenth century. Not long before Cem approached the walls in the early afternoon of July 30, they had had to do so again.

Almost exactly two years earlier, Mehmet II had attacked Rhodes with what one of the Knights described as "an Armada of one hundred and nine vessels" with "a great many cannons, bombards and wooden towers with other engines of war" manned by nearly seventy thousand soldiers. This huge force besieged the city of Rhodes for more than two months, with Ottoman infantry advancing to the top of the palace's ramparts before d'Aubusson was able to mount a counterattack with the help of reinforcements from the king of Naples. In the end, the Ottomans were rebuffed, but not before close to half of the Knights' three thousand men and more than nine thousand Ottoman soldiers were slaughtered and the palace left in shambles. In the early modern Mediterranean, alliances changed as quickly as the sea's currents; now the son of the destroyer of the Knights' palace was an honored guest.

Most of what we know of Cem's sojourn on Rhodes comes from the account of a vice-chancellor and secretary of the Knights named Guillaume Caoursin. Caoursin sought to paint the rule of the Knights in the rosiest hues possible, but, read judiciously, his writings provide invaluable details of Cem's time on the island. While Cem was always comfortable on Rhodes—with a well-appointed apartment, sumptuous meals every night in the Grand Master's palace, and frequent hunting trips around the island—he remained worried about his precarious position as a captive diplomatic asset. Caoursin wrote that Cem "observes those around him and always seems a little sad and pensive. . . . He is so fidgety that he can't stay long in one place." Still, "even as an exile and a fugitive, he does not lose his aristocratic dignity," which apparently enabled him "to swim every day in the sea, naked, without prudishness in sight of everybody." Cem was melancholy on Rhodes, perhaps resigned to his fate, even as he remained committed to achieving the outcome he feared was slipping away. Each day, he drowned his sorrows in luxurious food and wine and distracted himself with Alméida, a slave woman he purchased on the island.

After thirty-four days, the Knights decided to send Cem, against his will, to one of their castles in France—for his own safety, they said, but in reality for their own. Fearing that Bayezit might invade Rhodes to try to capture him, they thought it best to move him as far away as possible. This plan allowed the Knights to maintain control over their royal hostage while removing the imminent threat of an Ottoman invasion. The same day Cem set sail for France, on September 1, 1482, d'Aubusson sent a delegation to Istanbul, offering to hold Cem in France in exchange for an Ottoman guarantee of peace. To their delight, Bayezit immediately agreed to their terms. From the sultan's perspective, this superb deal allowed him essentially to hire the Knights as prison guards to keep his half-brother far from Istanbul. In return, Bayezit agreed to pay the Knights 45,000 Venetian gold ducats annually to cover the costs of Cem's imprisonment. Furthermore, Bayezit promised not to invade Rhodes or Otranto, as his father had done two years earlier. The only Ottoman royal ever to go on the *Hajj*, Cem also earned the distinction of sailing farther west than any member of the House of Osman had gone before. The fraternal struggle for the Ottoman throne now spanned the Mediterranean.

Cem learned of this bargain when he landed in Nice six weeks later, on October 17, 1482. Bewildered, angry, and depressed that the Knights had ransomed him, the twenty-three-year-old prince found himself in an even stranger new land. As on Rhodes, the Knights kept Cem comfortable but under close watch. A prisoner but still a prince, he was placed under a kind of lax house arrest in the well-appointed acropolis of Nice, which was owned by an associate of the Knights, a wealthy Genoese merchant named Gaspare Grimaldi. On Cem's first night there, Grimaldi's oldest daughter took a bed-warmer to their new guest, and, if we are to believe the French accounts, offered herself to the prince. Later, her sisters and cousins took their turns spending the night with Cem, suggesting that Grimaldi hoped to marry one of his daughters or nieces into the Ottoman royal family. When allowed to venture beyond the walls, Cem moved on to the city's female prostitutes and "charming well-made boys / each the son of a noble." Cem reveled in this sexual diversion. "What a wonderful place is this city of Nice," he wrote, apparently unconcerned about venereal disease, "a man can stay there and do as he please!" Alienating at first, the city eventually reminded him of Konya, where he had been governor, with its narrow winding streets and small neighborhood squares. He loved the azure coastline and picturesque red-roofed buildings. His debauches, however, were an unsatisfactory salve for the lost sultanate so far away.

Cem's exile was only just beginning. He would spend the next seven years being shuffled around southeastern France from castle to castle as local rulers maneuvered to earn the princely purse Bayezit was paying his half-brother's captors. Cem's captivity was thus, rather peculiarly, an enormous boon to the region's economy, as 45,000 gold ducats represented a formidable sum in the mid-1480s.

At the same time, at the far end of the Mediterranean, the Ottomans and the Mamluks tussled in a series of indecisive wars—skirmishes that

Cem's nephew Selim would continue and ultimately win a few decades later. Like the Knights, the minor potentates of southeastern France, and other Mediterranean powers, the Mamluks also coveted Cem as a weapon against the Ottomans, enabling them to terrify Bayezit with the threat that his half-brother might storm the palace. In addition, someone else was lobbying for Cem's return to Cairo—his mother. She had stayed behind in the Mamluk capital after her son left for his ill-fated attempt to capture Konya and yearned to have him back in Cairo, both out of maternal longing and in order to continue the fight against Bayezit. Thus, the Mamluk sultan wrote to the Knights of St. John, imploring them to return Cem to Egypt in return for the full support of the Mamluk army in any future confrontation with the Ottomans as well as 100,000 gold ducats. Despite these generous terms—more than Bayezit was offering—the Knights refused to relinquish their Ottoman prince. He was proving too valuable, and, besides, other plans were afoot.

Soon after the Mamluk approach, Pope Innocent VIII—famous for his papal decrees on witchcraft and his lifelong efforts to further the Inquisition—convinced the Knights to transfer Cem from France to Rome for, he said, "the general good of Christendom." The "good," as he saw it, was that moving Cem closer to the Ottoman Empire increased the threat to Bayezit should Cem be released, and this would serve to check Ottoman advances against Christians in the Balkans. Fearing—though perhaps also seeking—a kind of Mediterranean world war, the pope thus hoped to orchestrate a three-way alliance among Rome, Hungary (at the time, one of the Ottomans' primary rivals in the Balkans), and Cem against Bayezit. This, of course, was part of the larger goal: the preparation of a new Crusade to "win back" Jerusalem and deliver the death blow to Islam.

When Cem arrived in Rome on March 4, 1489, nearly eight years after his father's death, he became in essence a reified weapon in Renaissance Europe's bloodlust against Islam—a more compelling obsession than the classics of antiquity, art, or personal salvation. In the words of one of the foremost historians of the Renaissance, James Hankins, "The humanists wrote far more often and at far greater length about the Turkish menace and the need for crusade than they did about such better-known humanist themes as true nobility, liberal education, the dignity of man, or the immortality of the soul." In effect, much of the "civilization" of the Renaissance developed from Christianity's atavistic hatred of Islam.

Reacting against the culture of fire-breathing religious loathing that surrounded him, Cem became ever more pious during his years in Europe. A pleasure-seeking orgiast in his youth and in Nice, Cem paradoxically became a devout Muslim for the first time in his life in the very heart of Christian Europe, the Vatican. Before his European sojourn, his relationship to Islam had been shaped more by politics than by faith. While he was in the Ottoman Empire, then in Mamluk Cairo, and even on his *Hajj*, Cem's commitment to Islam had always seemed half-hearted; when he undertook the pilgrimage—the most quintessentially Islamic of Islamic acts—he did so to drum up support for his bid for the throne. In Europe, though, his Muslim faith was both a statement of defiance against his captors and a wellspring of strength against hardship and loneliness. As for so many who turn to religion in times of adversity, Islam represented for Cem a source of both political and spiritual freedom in the absence of physical freedom.

In Cem's mind, there was no contradiction between emphatically marking one's political identity as a Muslim in Europe while acting un-Islamically. He loved wine and regularly had sex with both Christian women and boys. According to some accounts of his years in Europe, he may even have married a Christian woman—a possibility that in Europe (but not in the Ottoman Empire) would have required at least a nominal conversion. If he did indeed convert to Christianity, he likely did so through a practice known to Muslims as *taqiyya*. Usually translated as "dissimulation," *taqiyya* allows one to affect a temporary outward conversion to a religion other than Islam, usually for reasons of survival, while inwardly preserving one's true Islamic identity. Apart from the rumors of this marriage, all other indications point to Cem having remained a Muslim throughout his years in Europe.

Ten days after arriving in Rome, and fuming about his mistreatment at the hands of the Knights, Cem met privately with Pope Innocent. When the tall, rotund pope tempted him with the worldly power that would come from leading a new Crusade—leadership Cem could only undertake as a Christian—he reportedly vowed never to help Rome or indeed any Christian power against a Muslim empire, his own or any other, "even for the rule of the whole world." In this, of

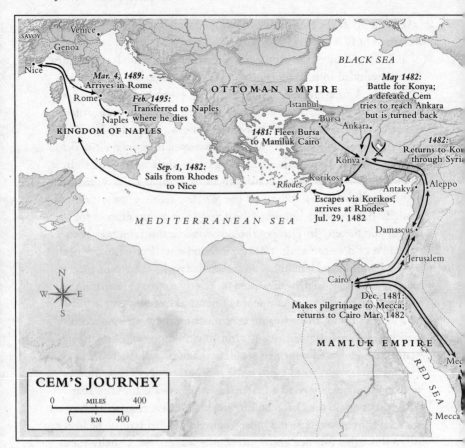

CEM'S JOURNEY

SAVOY
Venice
Genoa
Nice
*Mar. 4, 1489:*
Arrives in Rome
Rome
*Feb. 1495:*
Transferred to Naples
Naples where he dies
KINGDOM OF NAPLES

OTTOMAN EMPIRE
Istanbul
Bursa
*1481:* Flees Bursa
to Mamluk Cairo

BLACK SEA

*May 1482:*
Battle for Konya;
a defeated Cem
tries to reach Ankara
but is turned back
Ankara

Konya

*1482:*
Returns to Kor
through Syri

*Sep. 1, 1482:*
Sails from Rhodes
to Nice

Korikos
*Rhodes*

Escapes via Korikos;
arrives at Rhodes
Jul. 29, 1482

Antakya
Aleppo

Damascus

MEDITERRANEAN SEA

Jerusalem

Cairo

*Dec. 1481:*
Makes pilgrimage to Mecca;
returns to Cairo Mar. 1482

MAMLUK EMPIRE

RED SEA

Mec

Mecca

0 MILES 400
0 KM 400

course, he was demonstrating his anti-European politics as much as his steadfast belief in Islam. Furthermore, he demanded that Innocent release him immediately so that he could travel to Cairo and live the rest of his life in a Muslim land. Unaffected by these protestations, the pope promptly ordered Cem returned to his prison cell.

Cem was twenty-nine, and had been on the run for close to a decade. "Stocky and robust," as described by the cleric Matteo Bosso, he had been well taken care of while he was shuttled from exile to exile, prison to prison. No longer an unmoored libertine, he finally admitted defeat. In a series of letters to his half-brother, he expressed remorse for challenging Bayezit's claim to the throne and pledged allegiance to him. Cem even wrote that he forgave Bayezit for killing his three-year old son while he was in France. Humbling himself at his half-brother's feet, a broken Cem apparently would have done whatever was asked of him in order to live out the rest of his days in freedom in the Ottoman Empire—or, failing that, in a Muslim land such as India, Iran, or the Arab world. While there is no way to confirm whether or not Cem's intentions were sincere, Bayezit took no chances. Interpreting Cem's pleas as a potential ruse, he rejected them.

Despite Cem's strident unwillingness to support a new Crusade, Pope Innocent remained hopeful. The shockwaves from the 1453 fall of Constantinople still reverberated in Europe's ears, roaring again in 1480 with the Ottomans' capture of territory on the Italian peninsula. The medieval Crusades, despite what Western students have imbibed for centuries, were far more than discrete military adventures—they amounted to a nearly unbroken strategy across centuries, an ongoing European military stance against the Muslim world that peaked and waned as needs dictated. Plans for Christian Crusades against Islam continued well into the seventeenth century, and it could be argued that they have not yet disappeared. From a European Christian perspective, the ascendancy of the Ottomans at the expense of Europe fueled notions that Armageddon was near, so it was more than ironic that Pope Innocent now looked to the Muslim East for help. Clarifying that his interest was in a Crusade specifically against the Ottomans, rather than all of Islam, Innocent dispatched envoys to Cairo seeking Mamluk support for a new war against their coreligionists.

In a kind of early modern *entente cordiale*, Christian Europe and the Mamluks knew they needed each other against the superior military power of the Ottomans. Each side had previously made overtures to the other, but achieving common cause continued to prove elusive—for reasons not of religion or culture, but of politics. In 1489, the fly in the ointment was Cem. The Mamluks made Cem's return a condition of any alliance with the pope. The pope refused, thus scuttling any hope of a joint papal–Mamluk fighting force. Innocent then turned to the European powers, who once again swiftly declined his invitation to join a fresh Crusade. Political conditions in the Mediterranean skewed so heavily in favor of the Ottomans that most European leaders judged a Crusade at this time to be a suicide mission.

Unable to rally the interest and manpower he needed, Innocent, like the Knights of St. John before him, settled for something less than total war and entered into negotiations with the Ottoman Empire. Having Cem in Rome, of course, increased the pope's leverage. He threatened to release the Ottoman prince, intimating that Cem would ally with the Hungarians against the Ottomans in the Balkans even while knowing full well that he would not, and pushed for guarantees that the Ottomans would never invade the Italian peninsula again, would allow Christians freedom of worship in the Ottoman Empire, and would afford safe passage to Jerusalem for Christian pilgrims. If Bayezit acceded to these demands, the pope pledged to continue to hold Cem hostage—albeit still insisting on a fee. From Bayezit's perspective, this was a splendid deal, for his overriding goal in the years around 1490 remained keeping Cem at bay in Christian Europe. Besides, he had no intention of invading Italy, and he had already upheld Ottoman Christians' freedom of worship and offered protection to European Christian pilgrims visiting Jerusalem. Not only did he agree to Innocent's terms, he offered several other small concessions. He handed over to Rome the head of the lance that allegedly pierced Christ's side during the Crucifixion, one hundred Moorish slaves, and an advance payment of 120,000 gold ducats to support three years of Cem's captivity. This sum was a pittance for the Ottomans, yet it was the equivalent of an entire year's income for the papacy.

HAVING GROWN UP IN the 1470s and 1480s, Selim witnessed firsthand the power of religion in international affairs and in his own family. After all, he, together with Cem, his father, and all Ottoman sultans and princes in the empire's first three centuries, were the sons of Christian converts, female slaves who had often, but not always, been captured in war. Rumors of his uncle's conversion to Christianity and his potential participation in a Crusade against Islam further underscored for Selim both the political stakes of religion and the religious stakes of politics.

As participant, observer, beneficiary, and victim, both of the religious politics of the age and his own family's dynastic structure, Cem could compare what he witnessed in Europe to what he knew of his own empire. By any measure, religious violence in the Mediterranean peaked in the 1490s. Not only did Europe renew its persistent calls for a Crusade against Islam, but the Ottoman Empire furthered its holdings in the Christian Balkans, and Spain's long-running Inquisition reached its bloody climax. With their conquest of Granada in 1492, the Catholic monarchs defeated the last of Spain's Muslim kingdoms. As we will see, they expelled nearly all of the peninsula's Jews and Muslims, then moved to extend their war against non-Christians in Africa, Asia, and the Americas.

Although all religious minorities throughout the Mediterranean were subjected to much hardship, the Ottomans, despite what Innocent thought, never persecuted non-Muslims in the way that the Inquisition persecuted Muslims and Jews—and, despite the centuries of calls for Christian Crusades, Muslims *never* attempted a war against the whole of Christianity. While considered legally inferior to Muslims, Christians and Jews in the Ottoman Empire (as elsewhere in the lands of Islam) had more rights than other religious minorities around the world. They had their own law courts, freedom to worship in the empire's numerous synagogues and churches, and communal autonomy. While Christian Europe was killing its religious minorities, the Ottomans protected theirs and welcomed those expelled from Europe. Although the sultans of the empire were Muslims, the majority of the population was not. Indeed, the Ottoman Empire was effectively the Mediterranean's most populous Christian state: the Ottoman sultan ruled over more Christian subjects than the Catholic pope.

Of course, Christian leaders did not only target Muslims with their Crusades. As European armies marched out against Islam, they slaughtered many Jews on their way eastward. Some of the survivors, and the majority of Spain's expelled Jews, eventually made their way to the relative safety of the Ottoman Empire. Thus, to a young Selim, the religious clashes of the early modern world seemed not a matter of Christianity versus Islam but rather of Ottoman Islam's ecumenical view of the world versus European Christianity's violent efforts to achieve religious homogeneity.

POPE INNOCENT VIII, one of the leading proponents of his religion's savagery, fell ill and died on July 25, 1492, just a week before his Italian compatriot Christopher Columbus set off on his first voyage across the Atlantic. With Innocent's death, Cem became the property of his successor, Pope Alexander VI. Although he was handsome and gregarious—or perhaps precisely because he was handsome and gregarious—Alexander proved an ineffective political and religious leader. A member of the ruthless Borgia clan, he had many mistresses and sired at least nine illegitimate children. His papacy was dogged by accusations of sexual philandering and financial misdealings to support his children—ammunition for his political rivals' persistent fiery critiques.

One of the pope's adversaries was King Charles VIII of France, who coveted the Italian peninsula and especially the strategically import-ant kingdom of Naples. At the end of 1494, taking advantage of the political weakness created by the chaos of Alexander's personal life, Charles the Affable, as he was known, thundered an army of twenty-five thousand soldiers, about a third of whom were Swiss mercenaries,

*Cem is handed over to Charles*

into Rome, quickly forcing Alexander to accede to his demands, foremost among them being safe passage for his armies south to Naples. Charles then made another demand: he wanted Cem, who was still a desirable prize after all these years. Alexander reluctantly surrendered the peripatetic prisoner to Charles. The twenty-four-year-old king and his forces, with Cem in tow, reached Naples in February 1495.

Bayezit, as always, was keeping a close eye on Cem's whereabouts and gauging how his European captors might use him against the Ottomans. From France to Rome to Naples, Cem was steadily edging closer to Istanbul, with progressively more powerful captors pushing him in that direction. Charles posed a more direct threat to the Ottomans than either the pope or the Knights of St. John. Through marriages and other alliances, he boasted many relatives among the noble families of the Balkans. Tracing the roots of their power back to Byzantium and the Kingdoms of Serbia, these predominantly Christian families still reveled in their bygone glory during an era of Christian rule before the Ottoman conquests. Though they retained their landholdings, wealth, and prestige, they harbored an inherent distrust of their Muslim overlords. Bayezit feared that Charles would exploit his familial connections and the insecurity of the Balkans to move, with Cem, into the western provinces of the Ottoman Empire.

This was a risk Bayezit refused to tolerate, so in 1495 he began mobilizing his forces in and around Istanbul. They strengthened the city walls, reviewed tactical plans for operations in the Balkans, and tested artillery. Military reinforcements were deployed to the empire's western borders and a battle fleet headed for the Adriatic, tucking into the fjords of the Dalmatian coast to be ready at a moment's notice. Even in early 1495, nearly fourteen years after Bayezit had become sultan, Cem's threat to the empire remained so exigent that the mere whiff of his encroachment triggered a massive military mobilization.

Very soon, however, Cem would no longer pose a threat to Bayezit. When Charles's army reached Naples, a wilting weariness forced Cem to bed down in one of the city's castles, now in the possession of the French king, who tasked one of his personal physicians to monitor the captive and afford him all necessary comforts. The doctor kept watch as Cem's symptoms grew more serious. First his face, eyelids, and throat reddened and swelled. Then he was overcome by a fever, accompanied by shortness of breath. Cem seems to have had an infection, possibly pneumonia. Charles's physician finally succeeded in stabilizing the patient, cooling him down with cold compresses and bleeding him from time to time, but his condition worsened again and his pulse grew weak and irregular. Charles visited his bedside to offer encouragement. "Be in good spirits, my lord," he said to Cem. "As soon as you get well you'll find freedom and salvation, so don't be upset any longer about being a prisoner." After Charles left Cem's room, the Ottoman prince said, "Thank God the words freedom and salvation enter my ears. I have always prayed thus: 'Oh God, if the infidels want to take me on the pretext of marching on Muslims, then don't let me see those days, and take my soul first.'" Cem promptly lapsed into a coma. He returned to consciousness two or three times over the next few days, long enough on one occasion to have an attendant read out a letter from his mother, who was still in Cairo. Having lived as a prisoner in Europe for thirteen years, Cem finally achieved his freedom, and perhaps his salvation, dying in Naples on February 25, 1495, at the age of thirty-five, a few months before a coalition of Italian city-states forced Charles back to France.

CEM'S DEATH WAS A major blow to European designs on the Ottoman Empire. His father's conquest of Constantinople in 1453 had been a cataclysmic event for European Christians, and the capture of Otranto in 1480 was similarly jolting. In 1481, when Mehmet died, the Ottomans held more territory in Europe than any other polity. Searching for some advantage against its Muslim foe, Christian Europe seized on Cem. Some esurient European leaders thought that if they helped Cem overthrow his half-brother, they could win the powerful Ottoman Empire to their side as a stalwart military partner, thereby putting it in the position of European kingmaker. Cem's unexpected death fundamentally transformed this geopolitical landscape. While Cem had needed allies in Europe, Bayezit most certainly did not. Undisputed succession had now been achieved in the Ottoman Empire. At this point in the mid-1490s, Europe was weakened, whereas most of Mehmet the Conqueror's gains were solidified. Bayezit's Ottomans stood fully in the ascendancy. European delusions of Crusade, reconquest, and the "return" of Constantinople and Jerusalem receded into the distance.

For Bayezit, Cem's death represented a new chapter in his reign. The threat that had been hanging over his throne for fourteen years was gone. For the first time, Bayezit could focus single-mindedly on the task of ruling the most powerful state in the Mediterranean.

Bayezit's unfettered rule would not last long. Soon his own sons would rise to challenge him. Selim, now twenty-four, understood that, although birth order in large measure determined one's fate, it was not everything. Bayezit had triumphed not because he was the eldest, but because he was the more serious and warlike, the more shrewd and ruthless. As the third surviving son, Selim knew he was not likely to become sultan—up to this point, the eldest had almost always been his father's succeessor—but, having seen Cem die demoralized and diplomatically prostituted in exile in Naples, he was determined not to let his uncle's fate become his own. Possessed of an adamantine force of character, Selim set his sights on winning the throne, an act he knew would require killing his older half-brothers. He had learned from the example of Cem's life that an Ottoman prince could trust no one—especially his own blood.

# GOVERNOR

## (1487–1500)

CHAPTER

4

# LEARNING THE
# FAMILY BUSINESS

*In the Trabzon market*

TO WIN THE OTTOMAN THRONE, SELIM AND HIS HALF-BROTHERS had first to prove their mettle by governing a city in the east of the empire. As Bayezit's sons scattered across Anatolia, Selim was particularly disadvantaged, being appointed governor of the city of Trabzon, almost as far from Istanbul as one could go and still be in the empire.

Trabzon (formerly Trebizond), sits at the southeastern corner of the
Black Sea, at the junction of trade routes to the East. Selim arrived
there aged seventeen, in 1487—about eighteen months before Cem was
transferred from France to Rome—accompanied, as was the custom,
by his mother. He was tasked with integrating this recently conquered
city into the imperial administration, but more important, from his
point of view, was the job of building the foundation of independent
support he would need if he were to compete for the sultan's throne.
As he was an official representative of the empire, this would necessarily have to be a surreptitious undertaking. As well as his mother,
his concubines and servants made the long journey with him, along
with a cadre of imperial attendants and advisers. Over the twenty-
plus years he would spend on the eastern fringes of the empire, Selim's
small household would serve as his scaffolding of care, comfort, and
protection.

As he sailed along the Black Sea to Trabzon—perhaps occasionally
spotting the famous Black Sea dolphin, remarked on since antiquity—
Selim absorbed the verdant green of the soaring Pontic Mountains,
which push so close to the coast that the settlements of the northern
Anatolian shore appear like a ribbon of humanity between water and
stone. Like most of the region's towns, Trabzon grew the only way that
geography allowed, up into the hills, but still the port city's drab sand-
colored streets and buildings held close to the deep indigo sea, its source
of sustenance and commerce, its primary connection to the world. Like
Istanbul, Amasya, and most other cities in the empire, those along this
coastline boasted ancient roots. First settled in the eighth century BCE,
Trabzon became a Christian stronghold in the third century CE. Its
remote location, combined with the natural defense provided by the
Pontics, forged it into a stalwart outpost that fended off outsiders for
most of its history. Over the centuries, its Christian rulers rebuffed
streams of conquering armies, sometimes governing it as a sovereign
city-state, sometimes aligning with one or more of the larger polities
around it. When the Ottomans made their first attempts to seize the
city, they faced the same fate as most previous attackers: Trabzon's
well-armed populace successfully frustrated the newcomers' numerous
incursions. In fact, the city distinguished itself as the last of Byzantium's
client states to fall to the Ottomans, surviving independently for eight
years after the capture of Constantinople in 1453. Mehmet II needed no

fewer than two hundred galleys in Trabzon's harbor, plus eighty thousand infantry and sixty thousand cavalry coursing down through the mountain passes, to finally subdue Trabzon in August 1461.

By the time Selim arrived there twenty-six years later, the city was still only beginning its slow transition from a millennium of Christian rule. It was, so to speak, a frontier zone, a region of such tenuous ties to Ottoman hegemony that Selim would have to work hard to bring the area squarely within the fold. The religious makeup of the city did not help; more than 85 percent of the population adhered to some form of Christianity, mostly Orthodoxy, making Islam a small minority faith. Turkish culture barely registered. In Trabzon as elsewhere, the Ottomans' conquests resulted in minority rule over peoples very different from themselves, both religiously (in the case of Christians) and culturally (in the case of Greeks, Arabs, Serbs, and others). Like other imperial powers, the Ottomans cut deals with local strongmen and promised massive protections for the majority population.

At the turn of the sixteenth century, most of the era's expanding empires faced this same challenge: minority rule. Whether in the Americas or in Asia, small bands of military elites conquered vast new territories, thereby gaining the right to rule over huge populations. The ascendant Muslim Mughals, for example, moved south from Central Asia to India, where they governed an enormous restive population of Hindus and other non-Muslims. The Aztecs, in their conquest of the Yucatán peninsula, ruled over peoples who shared neither their culture nor their worldview. And European global expansion in this period brought the continent's armies face to face with peoples they had never before encountered, in places they did not fully understand. These early modern empires changed the ethnic, linguistic, economic, and religious landscape of the world, creating new cultural synergies and new political possibilities even as they foreclosed others.

SELIM FOUND HIS NEW home to be a dizzying entrepôt teeming with goods and people from all over the world. Given its strategic location on the southeastern corner of the Black Sea, Trabzon had long been an important way-station on the Silk Road, with trade goods coming overland from the East through the mountain passes, then making their way to the West by ship. The entire line of port cities on the southern coast of the Black Sea—from Istanbul eastward to Amasra and Sinop, and then finally Trabzon—served as a critical trading zone for Europeans seeking goods from India, China, and Central Asia. Merchandise, travelers, armies, even vermin, as well as ideas and technologies, were funneled through Trabzon. Like other nodes of global commerce, Trabzon became a highly cosmopolitan city, with many long-ingrained traditions of urban governance and social relations. Selim's first task was to stamp an Ottoman imprint on a city that predated the empire by millennia.

The Venetian itinerant Marco Polo arrived in Trabzon in the late thirteenth century, following established trade routes from Italy eastward. Like many travelers before him, he was foul-smelling and exhausted as he transferred from ship to caravan, sporting his signature red hat. More than twenty years later, in 1294 or 1295, he returned to the city as his final point of departure from Asia back home to Venice. Robbed, during this second sojourn in Trabzon, of much of the fortune he and his men had accrued during their decades in the East, Marco Polo and his entourage departed the city weary and embittered.

In the covered market, Sri Lankan cinnamon met Murano glass. Tall bags of brown wool rested on the gray cobblestones, with flaming Indian red pepper and iridescent yellow turmeric glowing like lava and fire. The spice district—riddled with the stray scents of peppers and ginger, then cassia, and, inevitably, the piercingly aromatic odor of cardamom— transitioned gradually into a warren of vendors hawking porcelain and gemstones from China, a more tranquil part of the market where purchases were made annually rather than weekly. Intricately woven Persian silks and wools carpeted whole sections of the cobbled ground, while rhubarb, cattle hides, and cottons from Russia and the Caucasus were piled high. Beyond the market's arched gate, its central thoroughfare spilled out to a plaza with sweeping views of the sea, before the road disappeared downward into the residential part of the city. Here men congregated, caught up with the gossip, and exchanged news.

Like other Silk Road cities, Trabzon, despite its distance—or perhaps because of its distance—from Byzantine Constantinople and later Ottoman Istanbul, boomed as a place of enormous wealth, attracting to its western shoreline and its dusty eastern gates Indians, Italians, Russians, Greeks, Iranians, Armenians, Arabs, Georgians, and many others. With long hair and even longer cloaks, Venetian and Genoese merchants were among the most frequent traders in Trabzon, eager to quench the increasingly Asian appetites of their customers back home. Acting as middlemen, these merchants offered primarily gold and finished textiles in exchange for the desired Eastern products. Europe produced little that the East wanted or needed; the major commodity Europeans had to trade was cash.

After 1461, when the Ottomans began to facilitate and benefit from Trabzon's central role in Eurasian trade, they quickly grasped that they would have to insinuate themselves into the city's age-old rhythms and customs. Trabzon had long been run by a handful of powerful families who resisted outside interference in their city's affairs, which, over the centuries, had become nearly inseparable from their own commercial interests. Rather than seeking to destroy or subdue Trabzon's prominent households, the Ottomans cut deals with them. They paid cash for loyalty, guaranteed market share, and learned how to achieve the delicate balance between stepping back and flexing their muscle. Before, during, and after Selim's tenure as governor, the overarching aim of the Ottomans in Trabzon, and in their other Black Sea port cities, was to divert into their coffers revenues from tariffs and other taxes. Indeed, the chronological course of the Ottomans' battles across northern Anatolia in the second half of the fifteenth century traces an inland line parallel to the Black Sea coast, along the overland routes of the silk-and-spices trade—thus forming a commercial highway of sorts from Istanbul to Bursa, Ankara, Tokat, Amasya, and eventually Trabzon. As with China's expansion westward and Aztec moves eastward, the Ottomans' military conquests were essentially a search for capital in the form of land and greater access to markets. War and commerce served as the two legs of the Ottomans' sprint eastward through Anatolia.

After subduing these cities and towns, the Ottomans used their system of Islamic law courts to encourage and regulate trade. In a port city like Trabzon, most small-scale business transactions occurred on the docks. As soon as merchants stepped off their boats, trade representatives would accost them with swatches of purple silk or a sniff of cardamom, trying to entice the new arrivals to their showrooms and offices up the hill. Still on the pier, they haggled over prices, the quality of merchandise, and rates of interest. Larger deals, though, always went through the courts. The logic was twofold. The court system protected the parties involved in financial transactions, while allowing the Ottomans to skim a bit off the top—small recompense for the empire's function as the ultimate commercial guarantor. No matter their language, birthplace, or religion, all merchants—locals and foreigners—conducting business in the empire relied on its courts for protection. When a Catholic Florentine merchant named Piero, for example, died in October 1478 in Bursa, his estate, with all its unresolved debts and credits, was adjudicated and settled in the city's Islamic law court. Records indicate that he owed a Damascene spice merchant named Abdurrahman 86,000 *akçe* (Ottoman silver coins) and had further outstanding debts on raw silk he had purchased from Iranian merchants in Trabzon and elsewhere; fortunately for Piero's creditors, he was also owed 67,200 *akçe* by an Italian resident of Istanbul. The judge assigned one of Bursa's Genoese merchants to be the executor of Piero's estate, to ensure that all creditors were paid. Such oversight of commerce assured foreign investors that their money and merchants would be safe in the Ottoman Empire. This kept cash and goods flowing between East and West.

At any given moment and for any reason, the Ottomans, as the middlemen of Eurasian trade, could turn off the spigot of silk and spices heading to Europe or dry up the stream of cash and finished products moving east. They used this privileged position to squeeze the Italian city-states in times of war, or to gain more favorable trading terms for the empire's merchants. When Iran's Safavid Empire proved particularly menacing, the Ottomans closed the major silk-trading routes west to the Black Sea, robbing their enemies of the cash that fueled their military campaigns.

⌘

MOST SEVENTEEN-YEAR-OLDS would be unprepared to rule a hub of global commerce like Trabzon, so how did Selim manage to govern a place so complex and potentially troublesome? The short answer was his mother, Gülbahar. As we have seen, the Ottoman policy of "one mother, one son" bound them together, with the expectation that a mother would be her son's guide even as far as the sultanic throne. Thus, the immature boys sent off to rule in the hinterlands were in reality only the junior half of a partnership; it was the partnership, rather than the boy himself, that was on trial. The dynasty's slave mothers were, in effect, largely in charge in the provinces, while their still mostly unformed sons—sultans-in-training—were, at least to begin with, hardly more than figureheads.

Removed from the capital and the rest of the imperial family, the empire's princes learned from their mothers how to govern, tamp down dissent, manage personalities, project their authority, and balance state budgets. In Trabzon, Gülbahar and Selim worked together diligently to integrate the city more fully into the empire. The most important theoretical underpinning of their efforts, and of Ottoman rule generally, was a philosophy of government known as the Circle of Justice. Adapted from a long tradition of political ideas originated by the Sumerians, the governing principles of the Circle of Justice describe a compact between a sovereign and the populace he rules. In summary form, the Circle of Justice is often expressed in the following way (sometimes elegantly written in a circle):

> *No power without troops,*
> *No troops without money,*

*No money without prosperity,*
*No prosperity without justice and good administration.*

The ultimate success of a ruler thus derives from his ability to recognize the mutually constitutive relationships between political power, military force, prosperity, and justice for his people. With no beginning and no end, the Circle of Justice suggests that power resides in the totality of the whole, not in any one place or person. Every point of the circle is equal and essential. God, of course, stands above all, casting his shadow on earth through the person of the sultan. Such a theory of governance, though perhaps never explicitly invoked by Selim or his mother, served as the foundation of their rule in Trabzon.

In the end, however, it was the messy day-to-day struggles, pressures, and forced compromises involved in the running of a bewilderingly multidimensional frontier town—not the idealized statutes of the Circle of Justice—that informed their decisions. In addition to successfully expanding the volume of commerce passing through Trabzon, the team of mother and son demonstrated their competence by solving mundane problems—not unlike the actions of municipal governments in the twenty-first century. When a fountain in one of the city's central squares ran dry, Gülbahar and Selim appointed someone to make it flow again. When roads became rutted, they allocated funds to recobble them. When a resident had a dispute with a neighbor or a dishonest merchant, he complained not to lower-level officials but directly to the governor and his mother. Together, the two hobbled thieving bureaucrats, oversaw the city's police, and ensured fair market prices. Above all, as imperial officials did throughout the realm, they levied taxes, the essential revenues that fortified the empire's coffers.

Although international trade propelled Trabzon to global prominence, its success would have been impossible without the foodstuffs grown in and around the city. Indeed, the prosperous people who were an essential part of the Circle of Justice were not merchants but rural farmers. As the overwhelming majority of the population, peasants produced most of the empire's cash in the form of tax revenues from assessments on what they grew. In Trabzon, in addition to cultivating copious amounts of wheat, barley, and other staples, farmers grew specialized delicacies in mass quantities for trade, the most important being cherries and hazelnuts. The region around Trabzon was then, and remains today, the world's most prolific producer of these crops. Forming a checkerboard pattern, the farms of red cherries and brown hazelnuts dominated the landscape around Trabzon, much as they do even now.

Some of these lucrative small farms were distributed as recompense for military service; in exchange for paying a specific amount of tax to the state and maintaining a modicum of order among the peasant farmers living on the land, soldiers could farm and manage—but not own—these plots. Others were sold at auction to the highest bidder, in an exchange of leasehold land for cash instead of military service. This form of imperial incorporation allowed the empire to outsource the quotidian complexities of land management, as well as the inherent risks, while ensuring a steady income stream and ultimate control over the land. Furthermore, the reliance of leaseholders on the recognition and permissions of the empire tied them ever more loyally and closely to the Ottoman system.

This delegation of authority over land to individuals proved a great boon to the imperial administration, sparing governors much of the minutiae of land and people management. Still, Selim and Gülbahar could not escape all of the intricacies of property contestations, taxation, and anxieties over crop yields. This was fifteenth-century life, after all. Livestock wandered onto fields, damaging crops. Droughts and floods regularly destroyed cultivated plots. Given the profit incentive, landholders often tried to extract too much from those working their fields, sparking small-scale peasant rebellions or the wholesale abandonment of land. As governor, one could only delegate so much; Selim served as the final arbitrator. If Selim wanted the Ottoman throne, he would first have to prove himself capable of dealing with such trivial matters as tracking down a runaway horse.

ONCE SELIM AND HIS mother had established their administrative control, they dedicated themselves to a thoroughgoing program of Ottomanization, aimed at replacing Trabzon's Christian and Greek character with a more distinct Muslim and Turkish ethos. They made their first moves in this direction by bringing in Ottoman Muslim bureaucrats from elsewhere in the empire. This reflected a longstanding Ottoman tactic for maintaining a monopoly of authority: the regular rotation of officials among vastly different parts of the empire, so that no one administrator could develop too much power in any one locale. Selim effectively cleared out the city's bureaucracy and brought in an entirely new slate of administrators loyal only to him and his vision of total Ottomanization. Selim and Gülbahar also curtailed the reach of the city's large trading families, who had historically helped themselves to much of the municipal tariff revenues, using a deft balance of force and persuasion to direct record amounts of money from Trabzon's international commerce into the imperial coffers.

In addition to appointing their own officials and taking control of more cash, mother and son sought to redesign the urban landscape. As Ottoman Muslims replaced Greek Christians in the city's administration, minarets now jostled with bell towers in the city's skyline (it would be another few decades before the Ottomans converted some of the city's churches to mosques). The city walls received a facelift of plaster and stone, which caught the sun reflecting off the sea. Relying on the advice of urban planners imported from the empire's older cities, Gülbahar and Selim refurbished streets, planted trees, and increased the number of water faucets throughout the city. Carved in the stone over these spigots were verses from the Qur'an and the seal of Sultan Bayezit, a reminder of the authorities that sponsored these sources of free, precious water. Some streets were redirected and others closed off to create a series of open plazas where carefully placed features projected Ottoman governance—charitable soup kitchens, fountains, hospitals, military offices, and schools. Over the years, Trabzon's physical landscape slowly morphed into something more similar to older Ottoman cities like Bursa or Amasya.

Perhaps most significant in the process of making Trabzon Ottoman was the newly endowed pious foundation that, under the direction of the Christian-to-Muslim convert Gülbahar, forever changed the city. The Islamic institution of the pious foundation, *vakıf* in Turkish, allowed one to endow a set of structures, plots of land, or businesses that could be held in perpetuity, with the revenue supporting a specific charity or other public good. Because these foundations were meant to endure forever, sponsoring one became a visible way to mold an urban landscape, both during and after one's lifetime. Gülbahar established the most opulent, imposing, and socially important pious foundation in Trabzon's history. At its center was the city's most exquisite mosque of that era, the Gülbahar Hatun Mosque—a sumptuous square stone structure with an ornate dome. Selim completed the mosque after his mother's death, but its planning and construction began during her lifetime. Its pencil-thin minaret soared higher than the many other minarets built in the period. "Gülbahar's needle" became a favorite of Trabzon's countless ravens and crows, constant competition for the imam who climbed to this highest point in the city five times a day to call the pious to prayer. Within the complex's walls was a school where children absorbed lessons about God and the world and recited the Qur'an. A soup kitchen provided the poor with a warm meal of lentils, bread, and rice on Trabzon's many chilly evenings. The foundation also held what would become the city's most renowned library, offering meditative respite from the clamorous world outside. The institution's financial holdings included residential and commercial properties elsewhere in the city and beyond, notably Trabzon's lucrative but fetid dye houses on the outskirts, as well as some farmland and water mills. The revenues earned from the rents on these properties and from the sale of agricultural products supported the work of the foundation's public mission and funded the upkeep of its physical structures. Some of this money also paid for the salaries of the teachers, cooks, scribes, and imams needed to run its various institutions.

*Gülbahar Hatun mosque complex*

The most popular and profitable of the foundation's holdings were its two bathhouses, one for women and one for men. Bathhouses were not just spaces of cleanliness and heat, but also of single-gender conviviality, conversation, and escape. Temporarily leaving behind life's worries, one entered the bathhouse once or twice a week to enjoy a scrub and a massage, as well as to learn about city affairs, to see friends, and to complain about one's job or family. Bathhouses provided both a necessary hygienic function and a recreational one, and became ubiquitous across the Ottoman Empire.

Gülbahar did not leave any writings, letters, or a diary. In the absence of such first-person accounts, we are fortunate to have her foundation as documentation of her life and worldview, as her achievements, which have not been fully recognized by past scholars, deserve our attention. The buildings Gülbahar endowed in perpetuity reveal her personality and interests. First, she clearly cared for Trabzon's disadvantaged. Her soup kitchen kept the hungry fed; her school educated children for free; and the library she built offered knowledge to all who cared to enter. Second, her foundation suggests to us the level of her devotion to her adopted faith, and to the Ottoman Empire. Using quintessentially Islamic legal precepts that make these pious foundations distinct from similar institutions in other religious traditions, Gülbahar built an infrastructure to support Islam in Trabzon, where it was still a minority religion. Her mosque and Qur'anic school played a key role in the city's transformation—which mirrored her own—from Greek Orthodoxy to Ottoman Islam.

Above all, Gülbahar's foundation evidenced her intense commitment to the city of Trabzon. Probably more than anywhere else in her life, Gülbahar felt at home in Trabzon, and thus was profoundly interested in stamping her mark on the city. While for Selim this posting was merely a stepping-stone to his ultimate goal, Gülbahar reveled in the power she was able to exercise there. From her lowly status as a slave, Gülbahar had risen to the top of the imperial structure with her successful governance of Trabzon. In her late thirties and early forties during her years there, she was a powerful figure of provincial rule. She held audiences almost weekly, where all bowed to her. With her high-arching eyebrows like angular hats over her dark, deep-set eyes, she shot daggers at those who prostrated in deference to her. Yet she knew that her administrative authority would soon wane, since the older Selim grew, the less important she would become. If he became sultan, her role as adviser would be diminished by the retinue of imperial functionaries. If he did not, either he would be killed or he would be given some other position in the bureaucracy, a position in which his mother would likely have little or no influence. So, in many ways, she ran Trabzon as *her* capital city.

In perhaps the strongest statement of her devotion, she made her bond to the city eternal by demanding to be buried in a tomb she helped design. Gülbahar died in 1505, and in 1514 Selim made good on his vow to build the tomb. An octagonal structure, it rises beside the mosque of her pious foundation, like a giant stone mushroom next to a gargantuan tree, smaller no doubt but no less beautiful. The complex, now known simply as the Lady's Foundation, endures as a prominent, still active institution in the city today.

GÜLBAHAR AND SELIM REMAIN forever connected to Trabzon for other reasons too. Most significantly, his children—her grandchildren—were born there. Since producing potential successors was a prerequisite for becoming sultan, Selim knew well that he had to achieve this during his governorship. Uncovering the full genealogical picture of Selim's progeny proves vexing, but even without clear answers, one essential thing is certain: at the age of twenty-four, Selim became, on November 6, 1494, the father of a son who would come to be known as Suleyman the Magnificent. Suleyman would rule longer than any other sultan in Ottoman history and expand the empire's territory even beyond his father's gains.

Suleyman's mother, Hafsa, was fifteen at the time of Suleyman's birth. Hailing from Crimea, Hafsa—plumpish, with long auburn hair and a prominent forehead—was one of Selim's two concubines. When her son assumed the throne after Selim's death, Hafsa became in her own right the most powerful woman in the empire, the first of the so-called Sultanate of Women, the name given to a century in which the mothers of sultans (and less often their wives) wielded enormous influence in imperial affairs—yet more evidence of the central role of women, and slave women no less, in Ottoman history. Hafsa and Selim's other consort, Ayşe, each bore him three daughters. As best we know, Selim had only the one son, which would have been highly unusual, given the reproductive politics of the empire. Indeed, when he took the throne, Selim became the first sultan to have only one son—yet another unique fact about him.

Given that Selim had six daughters survive into adulthood, it seems reasonable to assume that his two concubines produced a total of more than just one son. It is possible that all but Suleyman died young, but no mention of such births (or deaths) exists in any of the period's sources. One possibility is that Selim took what would have been at the time the extreme and unprecedented measure of killing his other sons to spare Suleyman a bloody succession battle of the sort he knew he was about to undertake against his own half-brothers. Both Ottoman custom and the Guardians of the Holy Law sanctioned fratricide, but father–son murder—in either direction—was considered a heinous crime against both God and state. If Selim did in fact kill his other sons, it is not clear why Suleyman would have been the chosen survivor. And again, no sources mention filicide. Even if he did favor Suleyman to such a degree that he wanted him to have no competitors, surely Selim knew that Suleyman might die long before he came close to the throne. No other sons then would mean no successor, the death of the Ottoman dynastic line. In everyday terms, had Suleyman slipped on a rainy cobblestone, choked on a fish bone, or fallen off his horse during a hunt, Selim might have gone down in history as the agent of the empire's demise, though the logic undergirding the empire's system of concubinage—the ability to produce many potential successors quickly—made this scenario exceedingly unlikely. In the back of his mind, Selim knew he could always produce another son should Suleyman die.

In the end, Suleyman survived to inherit his father's throne. But at the time of Suleyman's birth, it was not at all clear that Selim would have a throne to pass on.

# POWER AT THE EDGE

*The helmet of Uzun Hasan, leader of the Ak Koyunlu*

BETWEEN HIS ASSIGNMENT TO TRABZON IN 1487 AND THE BIRTH of Suleyman seven years later, Selim and his mother solidified their power base on the eastern edge of the empire. Gülbahar's pious foundation demonstrated that life for Trabzon's majority Greek Christian population was better under the rule of the Muslim House of Osman than it had been under the Orthodox Byzantine Empire. In fact, nearly everywhere the Ottomans came to rule, the local population recognized the advantages provided by the Ottoman system: freedom of worship, lower taxes, military protection, social stability, and the free flow of commerce.

Throughout the turbulent decade of the 1490s, empires across the globe pursued armed campaigns to fortify and expand their territory. In China, Ming authorities reinforced the Great Wall to fend off Mongol incursions and to serve as a base of operations for attacks farther west. Spain and Portugal dispatched their navies to the East and West Indies to defend their sovereignty and capture more territory. In Mexico, Aztec forces conquered the central city of Mitla, near Oaxaca, and continued to the south. None of these early modern empires had the capacity to unilaterally impose itself militarily or politically; rather, they had to earn recognition and acquiescence from the peoples they ruled. Given the cultural, religious, and linguistic diversity of the Middle East and eastern Mediterranean, the Ottomans proved to be masters of such rule, gaining control of territory while ceding enough political and cultural autonomy to win acceptance from populations with competing interests. Selim's rule in Trabzon was only one example of the larger triumph of the Ottomans' lightning expansion.

As Selim moved into adulthood, he assumed more of the daily administration of the city from his mother and their coterie of advisers. He interspersed walks in his palace garden holding young Suleyman's hand with adjudication of complex tax disputes and evaluation of the city's need for another pier. By the end of the fifteenth century, Gülbahar and Selim had, in roughly a dozen years, transformed Trabzon into one of the empire's eastern bulwarks. The later, laudatory *Selimname* described the order and prosperity of Selim's governorship this way: "He was a sun, which stayed in the constellation of honour. Through his coming, the dominion found happiness, and the seed of justice was scattered over the world. There was no trace of oppression in his time, and the temperament of the dominion was preserved from suffering." Elaborating on themes derived from the Circle of Justice, the chronicle continued: "The *re'āyā* [people] were comfortable under his protection; in the capital that he invested, everyone found profit."

The provincial governorships of Ottoman princes served, by design, both as tests of their leadership abilities and as staging grounds for their later attempts to take over the empire. Some posts, of course, were more lucrative, more prestigious, and more advantageous than others; proximity to the capital was often the greatest advantage a son could have. Of Bayezit's three eldest surviving sons, Ahmed in Amasya held the governorship nearest to Istanbul. Korkud, as governor first of Saruhan and then Teke in western Anatolia, was not much farther from Istanbul than Ahmed, but both of these postings lacked the prestige of Amasya. In this, and in sending Selim to the most distant city in the empire, Bayezit made clear whom he most favored to succeed him.

Selim would turn this disadvantage into an asset. If he hoped to pose a real challenge to his half-brothers, he would need a military force that operated beyond the purview of the Janissary Corps. Tucked away in distant Trabzon, he assembled a ragtag coalition that included upstarts, exiles from other states, disaffected soldiers, those passed over for imperial military service, leaders of various ethnic groups throughout Anatolia, and family members of those in his household.

Princely households—comprised of wives, concubines, children, advisers, tutors, and elite soldiers—created for the prince ties that spanned the empire. Each connection was a spoke in a complex network of semi-independent satrapies, as the various princes sought advantage over their rivals by doling out favors and striking deals. Selim, now in his mid-twenties, with his soon-to-be-hallmark mustache an impressive fixture on his upper lip, created, as other princes did too, what one might call an empire-in-training: a miniature Topkapı Palace, complete with advisers, servants, military officials, and a harem, all in provincial Trabzon. Given the geographic weakness of his posting in remote eastern Anatolia, Selim, more than his rivals, needed an exceptionally strong household, one with an independent spirit, ties across the empire, and unbreakable bonds of loyalty. Because Selim was governor of Trabzon for close to twenty-five years, living there longer than any other place in his life, he was able to forge durable and lasting connections. The regular rotation of governors was meant to prevent this very phenomenon, but his father never rotated Selim out of Trabzon because, he probably wagered, one could do no worse. Bayezit clearly had no fear of Selim—a gross error in judgment that would come to haunt him.

ONE PILLAR OF SELIM'S support was his partnership with some of the empire's often vilified ethnic minorities. In the borderlands of Trabzon, Selim recognized the crucial need to cooperate with the area's powerful

minority groups—not just for the success of the overall imperial enterprise in the east but for his own ends. This success rested on a formula
of what in the nineteenth century became known as *Realpolitik*. The
empire needed the support of its diverse ethnic groups to thrive, and
these same groups required the support of the empire. The dominant
ethnic groups in eastern Anatolia were the Kurds and the Karamanids.

Well before Selim's day and even down to the present, Kurds have
constituted the majority of the population in the rugged highlands and
unforgiving landscape of eastern Anatolia and northern Iraq and Iran.
Although mostly Muslim, they trace their lineage back to pre-Islamic
times—practicing, for example, tattooing, a custom formally forbidden
in Sunni Islam. Renowned as horsemen, poets, and weavers, the Kurds
have, over the centuries and still today, maintained their own distinct
culture, Indo-European language, cuisine, and identity. Although the
Ottomans were compelled to work with the Kurds, as they could tip
the balance of power in favor of any polity that wanted to rule in the
upper Tigris and Euphrates valleys, they generally denigrated them,
referring to them pejoratively as "mountain Turks" or "failed Turks"—
uncouth, uncultured, uncivilized, and unworthy of recognition as an
autonomous community with its own distinct identity.

In his decades in Trabzon, close to the Kurds' historic power base,
Selim achieved a rapprochement with the Kurds. To maintain authority
and relative calm in the region, he cut deals with Kurdish chieftains,
offering them advantages where other Ottoman officials had preferred
the sword. In return, they pledged their loyalty to him. Co-optation
nearly always proved more successful than force, so—as with all of the
Ottomans' negotiated deals—Selim and the various Kurdish factions
reached an arrangement of maximal mutual benefit. Tribal leaders won
open lines of communication with the empire, financial rewards, and
local spheres of autonomy. Most important for Selim and his ultimate
goal, the Kurds offered him armed manpower resources outside the
channels of the imperial military establishment.

Like the Kurds, the Karamanids had also felt the wrath of Ottoman
power, but here again the empire eventually settled on a strategy of
co-optation rather than outright elimination. Pushed westward from
Central Asia as they fled the Mongol invasions of the thirteenth century, the Karamanids were among the many large tribal confederations in Anatolia that resisted the imposition of Ottoman rule. Proud of

their Central Asian heritage and famed for their swift horses and ornate carpets, the Karamanids, with their distinctive helmets and flowing beards, were fearsome figures as they surged over the horizon. Their stronghold was the ancient south-central Anatolian city of Laranda, which they renamed Karaman. (A local breed of sheep is the source of a yogurt that has made the city regionally famous.) Karaman stood at the foot of the Taurus Mountains, near an extinct volcano. Its most prominent structure was its fortress, first constructed in the Bronze Age (approximately 3000–1000 BCE) and continuously rebuilt from then through the Roman period, until its last renovation by the Byzantines in the twelfth century. Stretching for more than five hundred miles between Karaman and Trabzon was some of the harshest territory in Anatolia: steep cliffs, narrow mountain passes, punishing wind, little edible vegetation. Despite the daunting obstacles of terrain and distance, Selim was able to establish an alliance with the Karamanids by manipulating his family's complicated dynastic politics.

Bayezit's fifth son, four years younger than Selim, was named Şehinşah. He seemingly had no desire for the throne and spent most of his life—nearly thirty years—in the comfortable governorship of the province of Karaman, which also included the important cities of Konya and Kayseri. Much as Selim had co-opted the Kurds, Şehinşah built alliances with the Karamanid tribal confederation. In fact, he devoted much of his time and energies to ensuring the Karamanids' well-being, security, and hence loyalty, offering them the choicest grazing lands and several key administrative positions, as he needed their military might to defend the territory he governed from other pastoral powers in the region. Yet of all the strident challenges Şehinşah faced over the course of his governorship, the strongest came from his half-brother Ahmed, then the governor of Amasya. Selfish and self-assured in his birthright as the eldest surviving son, confident that their father would guarantee him the throne, Ahmed coveted the province of Karaman, especially the city of Konya, with its wealth and religious significance as the home of several Sufi orders. He would later capture Karaman during his succession battle with Selim, but the various raids he led in the 1490s to seize the city from Şehinşah failed, largely because of Şehinşah's alliance with the Karamanids. As a kind of private fighting force, they thus functioned as armed arbitrators of intra-Ottoman clashes. Constant external threats made clear to both Şehinşah and the

Karamanid leaders that they shared a vested interest. Operating largely autonomously under Şehinşah's patronage, the Karamanids grasped that neither Ahmed nor any other leader might be as obliging.

Ahmed's insistent belligerency—coupled with Şehinşah's own lack of interest in becoming sultan himself—led Şehinşah and his mother, Hüsünşah, to support Selim over Ahmed and Korkud in the contest to become the next sultan. Ever since their days in the Amasya harem, this mother-and-son dyad had been closer to Selim and Gülbahar than to any of the other mother-and-son pairs. In the 1490s, the bond materialized militarily in the form of Şehinşah's offer to lend Selim his Karamanid forces as a kind of mercenary army. As the governor of a rich frontier city, Selim confronted exigent threats from the Caucasus and Iran to his east and was frequently in need of soldiers. Looking beyond his post in Trabzon, he understood as well that such a fighting force would aid him in a run for the throne. Selim promised to pay the Karamanid warriors whatever amount his half-brother paid them, and guaranteed their leaders that they could keep their lands near Karaman in perpetuity. To ensure their loyalty, he enticed them with some land near Trabzon as well. As a result, the Karamanids increasingly came to Selim's aid, willingly (and self-interestedly) offering their support to a leader who might soon become sultan. For his part, Şehinşah would never see Selim take the throne, dying in Konya in 1511 at the age of thirty-seven. In his last days, he was despondent, having lost his beloved youngest son the previous year, but he would have been pleased to know that the Karamanid force he had nurtured found a new patron in Selim. One of Selim's payroll registers from the early sixteenth century indeed reveals that he replaced his half-brother as the primary employer of the military components of the Karamanid confederation.

In addition to his strategic alliances with the Kurds and Karamanids, Selim employed a veritable army of soldiers for hire. More than any other force, warfare forged the politics, culture, and economy of the Ottoman Empire, with the Janissary Corps at the pinnacle of the empire's military hierarchy. With their tall hats and long swords, the imposing soldiers of this professional, salaried army were afforded every resource and luxury and trained as the Ottomans' elite fighters, the ultimate protectors of sultan and state, the envy of Machiavelli and countless other observers. The Ottoman state and its imperial military, however, did not possess a monopoly on armed violence. Countless other warriors—militiamen, ruffians, seasonal soldiers, even some disaffected former Janissaries—stood ready to fight. Mercenaries, brigands, and private soldiers proliferated throughout the countryside. Rural folk often possessed arms and employed violence, or sometimes the mere threat of violence, to gain money, influence, and power. On occasion, even soldiers from other states took their weapons to the Ottoman Empire, offering their services to whomever would pay. Awash in cash as the governor of a rich commercial city, Selim stood more than ready to pay these mercenaries to enable him to seize the throne.

The same payroll register provides a detailed snapshot of Selim's armed forces, which numbered 1,770 salaried soldiers. To put this number in perspective, Bayezit, as sultan, employed 7,000 salaried soldiers. As supreme commander of the Ottoman army, Bayezit of course had nearly infinite military and financial resources, as well as enormous responsibilities for the defense of his realm, so this comparison of the militaries of father and son shows how truly impressive Selim's collection of warriors was. In Trabzon, an outpost of empire, he assembled a fighting force equivalent to more than a quarter of what the world's most powerful sovereign had at the ready.

Although Selim's personal aim was to capture the Ottoman throne, the building of this powerful military coalition aided the empire's larger goal of expansion and consolidation. Selim's negotiations made the Kurds, Karamanids, and disparate groups of marauding fighters stakeholders in the Ottoman imperial project. Even as he planned to use them against his father the sultan, he was bringing them into the imperial system. Unlike his half-brothers, who presided over more stable and secure internal provinces, Selim had to deal with the constant pressures of border security. Looking beyond the weakness of his current posting, Selim cultivated the crucial tactical relationships that he would later utilize against them.

IN THE 1490S, ferocious wars raged in Burma, resulting in the rise of the First Toungoo Empire; Jewish and Muslim refugees from Spain streamed east and south across the Mediterranean; and the native peoples of the Americas fended off strangers from across the ocean. The rocky lands east of Selim's outpost in Anatolia buckled into chaos in that decade too, as, between the fall of one state and the rise of another, no single power controlled the Caucasus and northern Iran. The nearly continuous fighting among numerous small principalities and tribal groups fractured the region between the Black and Caspian seas. Much of this warfare spilled over into eastern parts of the Ottoman Empire, either as raiders pillaged towns for resources and slaves, or as various factions attempted to create alliances with power brokers within the empire.

From the fourteenth century—when the Byzantine Empire still controlled most of Anatolia—through to the 1490s, the Ak Koyunlu Confederacy ruled the Caucasus and northern Iran. This loose coalition of nomadic tribes collaborated to raid and trade and eventually to establish and control farms and raise revenue. Primarily Turkmen peoples, they shared with the Ottomans lineages stretching across Central Asia; the Ottomans and the Ak Koyunlu (literally, "White Sheep") were then, in essence, cousins. Determining when, why, and how the coalition adopted (or received) the name "White Sheep" proves difficult. Some historians ascribe it to a breed of sheep the group excelled in raising, while others think it derived from a ritual totem. The Ak Koyunlu reached their peak in the 1460s and 1470s, when they united under a single figure—first a chieftain named Uzun Hasan, and then his son Ya'kub, who seized power after killing his older brother. These two leaders formed marriage alliances with the Byzantine Empire and even pursued diplomatic relations with Venice and the pope, thereby becoming another potential Muslim ally for Europe against the common Ottoman enemy. This projected Venetian–Ak Koyunlu alliance—Christian and Muslim, lagoon and nomad—which would have squeezed the Ottomans, never materialized.

The death of Ya'kub in 1490 splintered the Ak Koyunlu Confederacy, as fighting broke out between his sons and nephews over who would succeed him. In the ensuing decade, the Ak Koyunlu fell into a vortex of civil war. As the internal struggle debilitated them, neighboring sovereigns became more empowered. To the west, Selim took advantage of his enemies' vulnerability and, deploying some of his recently attained military resources, enacted retribution on those who raided the countryside around Trabzon. He often sent his fighters to chase the Ak Koyunlu far to the east of Trabzon, sometimes all the way to northern Iran and the Caspian Sea, thus extending his influence throughout the region. At the same time, south of Ak Koyunlu territory, various tribal groups grew in size and power, constantly battling and continually reforging their coalitions.

A later historian of Selim's reign, who sought to depict the sovereign as superlatively as possible, wrote of the mayhem caused by the Ak Koyunlu's infighting and fragmentation, "The kingship having been left vacant, every unsound and foolish man was made possessor of a throne. The means of order and regularity became damaged, and the condition of the affairs of state was left neglected and disordered." The writer continued, "The most despicable men ascended the throne of glory; the vile acquired equal status with the good. The man who did not know became on a level with him who did; mean, petty fellows took precedence. There was no regard left for the old order; everyone would look to an unsound, false person." In a statement meant to be interpreted as the inverse image of everything Selim represented, we learn the result of the lack of central leadership that prevailed among the Ak Koyunlu:

> The carpets of justice and protection were hidden, not spread out, on the face of the earth, and the minds of rulers and sultans were intoxicated by the aromas of inclination and desire. . . . The established usages and laws of the realm had fallen into complete disorder, and evils and corruption had been spread in the traditional order of religion and kingdom.

Although a dramatically slanted view of Selim and his age, this account accurately depicts the Ottoman view of the Ak Koyunlu. Reflected in the mirror of Selim's perfection and prowess, their failures were manifest. Again invoking themes from the Circle of Justice, this passage employs the imagery of the unfurling of justice and honest rule "on the face of the earth" as a sign of the proper reconciliation of divine and worldly law, "of religion and kingdom."

Destabilizing succession battles, their inability to coalesce disparate interests into a united whole, and the increasing strength of the powers around them led eventually to the Ak Koyunlu's disintegration. The final blow came from the most successful of the region's many independent tribal groups. In 1501, one of the area's young upstarts, a teenager named Ismail, assumed power over his community, becoming the founder and first shah of the Safavid Empire, which would rule the former Ak Koyunlu territory for the next two hundred years and emerge as one of Selim's chief adversaries.

FOR THE OTTOMANS AT the end of the fifteenth century, the west proved easier to control than the east. After their conquest of Constantinople in 1453, they reached as far as Italy in the 1480s and, in pushing westward in the Balkans toward Venice, sent shudders through every court in Europe. The Ottoman navy formed a robust line of defense across much of the eastern Mediterranean and Black Sea. In Trabzon, Selim did his part to consolidate and bolster the empire's forces in the east, even while building his own personal base of power.

The Ottomans had not yet claimed Jerusalem or North Africa, but their mutually beneficial alliance with their fellow Muslims in Cairo essentially determined the course of European trade in the Middle East and North Africa. Muslims—specifically the Ottomans and the Mamluks—controlled all access to the East from the Mediterranean. Selim in Trabzon was just one of the many Ottoman toll-masters on the routes between West and East, between Europe and Asia. Indeed, when we view the period through the lens of Selim, we understand—in contrast to the traditional, culturally blinded story of European ascendancy during the Renaissance and the so-called "Age of Exploration"— the outsized role of the Ottomans in the shaping of world history. If Europeans wanted to trade with China and India, they would have to either agree to the Ottomans' terms or circumvent them. The effort by Venetian diplomats in the 1480s to strike a deal with the Ak Koyunlu was just one attempt at circumvention, and a rather feeble one at that. Another Italian would soon try a very different tack.

# THE
# OTTOMAN

*(1492)*

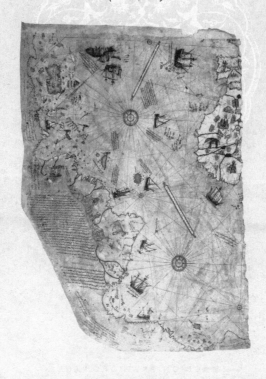

# COLUMBUS AND ISLAM

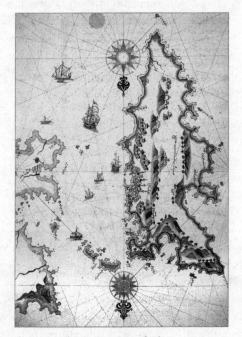

*Ottoman map of Chios*

CHRISTOPHER COLUMBUS WAS TWO YEARS OLD WHEN SELIM'S grandfather, Mehmet II, conquered Constantinople. Although we think we know the story of Columbus, it is in fact far more complicated than has been acknowledged. Throughout his life—from his first journeys around the Mediterranean, then down the western coast of Africa, and eventually across the Atlantic—Columbus bumped up against Europe's borders with the superior Muslim polities of his day. In myriad ways, all of his voyages were a response to the power of the Ottomans and other Muslims in the Old World—the political force that shaped Columbus and his generation more than any other.

As both civilizational kin and territorial rival to Christianity, Islam was Christianity's most imposing and lethal enemy. In the decades around 1500, it was not the Venetians nor the Spanish nor the Portuguese who set the standard for power and innovation; it was Islam. Islam shaped the ways in which European armies fought wars; it influenced European cuisine and clothing; it drove the direction of the continent's territorial expansion; and it spurred advances in European astronomy, architecture, and trade. Islam made much of European civilization, both directly and by reaction. To think beyond the familiar narratives handed down to us by generations of historians is to see that Columbus's life simply cannot be understood without taking Islam into account. Connecting Islam and Columbus, furthermore, revises our understanding of one of the most iconic years in world history: 1492. The Ottomans' influence on Columbus was a measure of the empire's global reach.

SO DOMINANT WAS THE culture of Christianity's Crusades that, even in the small Genoa neighborhood where Columbus spent most of his first two decades with his parents and four siblings, war with Islam was always an acknowledged peril, a part of their everyday world. For centuries before his birth, and indeed long before the rise of Islam and Christianity, forces in the region around Genoa had battled North Africans for control of the Tyrrhenian Sea. In Columbus's youth, Genoa proved a magnet for Crusaders because of the strong presence of the Knights Hospitaller of St. John, who offered free housing and medical care. Columbus and his family likely knew some of these religious warriors, and no doubt he grew up hearing their heroic tales of distant lands and infidel enemies. At the age of nine, between his lessons in Latin and mathematics, navigation and accounting, Columbus would rush down to the docks to bid farewell to fleets of inspired yet frightened men departing for Jerusalem on Crusade.

The city's San Lorenzo Cathedral, where Columbus would have

*Genoa*

attended Mass, held important treasures captured during earlier Crusades—an emerald-green bowl said to have been used by Jesus for washing his hands before the Last Supper, and a gold-plated silver reliquary purportedly containing the ashes of John the Baptist. Under the church's elegant striped arches of white marble and black slate, he would have learned that brave Christian soldiers had risked their lives to "recapture" these items from the hands of the wretched Muslim infidels. Such precious objects from the East were sprinkled all over Europe, from the smallest chapels to the largest cathedrals, and served as reminders that Muslims had held Jerusalem since 638 and that Christians had a God-given imperative to regain the city. Both the substance and idea of the Crusades were infused into the worship services of nearly every European neighborhood church and thus into most Europeans' lives.

Columbus also learned about other Europeans who traveled to the Muslim East. Genoa was primarily a mercantile port, not a military one. Blessed with a deep and protected harbor, Genoa was pushed to the sea by the Apennine Mountains, forced—like Selim's Trabzon—to spread along a narrow strip of coast. It was "one of the maritime wonders of Europe," in one historian's words, a key way-station on the "coastal highway" linking Italy and France. Over the centuries, the merchant families who ran the city developed connections far beyond this stretch of coast. Colonies of Genoese merchants prospered in Beirut, Alexandria, Tunis, Oran, Algiers, Naples, Paris, London, Bristol, Málaga, Jaffa, on various Aegean islands, and around the Black Sea, sometimes even exercising direct political control in these locales. In the fourteenth and fifteenth centuries, many of the ports and towns where

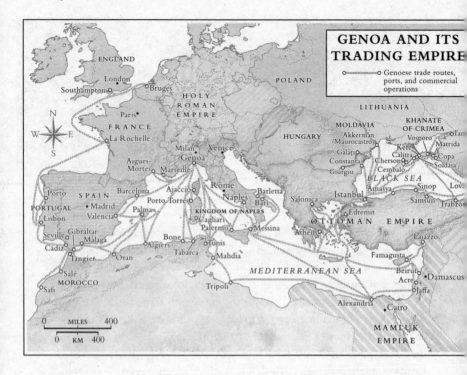

GENOA AND ITS TRADING EMPIRE

Genoese trade routes, ports, and commercial operations

Genoese held vested interests would be incorporated into the Ottoman Empire. Long before Selim became governor of Trabzon, for example, Genoese merchant families had built warehouses and offices in the city, from which they managed their active trade in goods from the East.

As a boy in this vibrant commercial city, Columbus likely spent hours at Genoa's docks, where, in addition to watching Crusaders sail off to the east and workers haul cargo and repair vessels, he would have seen ships, sailors, and wares arriving from Ottoman ports. It is likely that he saw Ottoman merchants, wearing unusual garb and speaking a language he could not understand. Undoubtedly he would have known about the Ottoman Empire and about Genoese trading interests in Black Sea cities such as Sinop and Trabzon, and he must have sensed the anxiety of Genoa's merchant community about Ottoman advances in the Black Sea and the Mediterranean. He was ten in 1461, when Selim's grandfather captured Trabzon, jolting Genoa and once again underscoring the immediacy of Ottoman dominance.

Columbus also learned important lessons about the East from

the still unpublished work of Marco Polo, which was circulating in Genoa in manuscript. Although Polo was Venetian by birth, he had an important connection to Columbus's hometown: he had been captured by the Genoese in the Battle of Curzola in 1298, and it was while he was imprisoned in Genoa that he regaled a cellmate, a man named Rusticello, with the tales of his travels in the East. As an escape from their dreary predicament, Polo transported Rusticello from Venice to China and back, and it was Rusticello, not Polo, who would eventually record—and embellish—these now legendary stories. When Polo traveled through Trabzon, in the late thirteenth century, the city's Genoese community was thriving—a fact that made the recent loss of the city to the Ottomans all the more personal.

A major figure in Polo's tales was the Grand Khan (most likely a fictionalized version of the Mongol emperor Kublai Khan), whose opulent court and persona especially fascinated Columbus. Polo supposedly reached this court far off in Asia—beyond Constantinople, Jerusalem, Baghdad, and Afghanistan—where he discovered a jewel-encrusted paradise of luxury, learning, and power. But what most intrigued Columbus about the Grand Khan was that, according to Polo, though he was not a Christian he wanted to become one. Thus, even though he had reached the pinnacle of wealth and power without the benefit of Christianity, the Grand Khan seemed to grasp the "truth" of the religion and might become a convert, thereby gaining for Christianity the souls of all his subjects, too. This fable of a Grand Khan who had seen the light of Jesus stoked the European imagination like nothing else. For Christians, he offered the mirror of everything Islam should have been—a civilization formed outside the realm of Christianity, yet one that recognized its own bankruptcy in the face of the glories of the supreme true religion.

The illusion of a Grand Khan of the East with Christian proclivities was not entirely fiction. The germ of this idea lay in the historical reality of the Eastern Nestorian Church, a branch of Syriac Christianity that spread from the Middle East throughout Central Asia and to parts of China. Although Christianity reached China in the first half of the seventh century, it was only in 1275 that the Yuan Mongol emperors of Beijing appointed that city's first Nestorian archbishop, and it was this Christian denomination that Polo encountered in China. At the end of the 1280s, the Mongols dispatched a Nestorian envoy to Pope Nicholas IV in Rome with the following message:

Today many Mongols are Christian. There are queens and children of kings who have been baptised and confess Christ. The Khans have churches in their camps. And as the King is united in friendship with the Catholics and proposes to take possession of Syria and Palestine, he asks your aid for the conquest of Jerusalem.

Given the Crusading fervor of the times, such statements kindled a belief in Europe that a global Christian alliance to conquer Jerusalem was possible. According to the fantasy, once the Grand Khan converted, the Muslims holding Jerusalem would be surrounded by Christians who, in one final, apocalyptic pincer movement, would destroy them forever, smashing the glistening Dome of the Rock that dominated Jerusalem's skyline and thus "retaking" the holy city. Although none of this ever came to pass, Catholic–Nestorian lines of communication remained open, even after the Ming took China from the Yuan in 1368. Well into the fifteenth century, descendants of the Yuan Mongol Grand Khans sent representatives of the Nestorian faith from China to Italy. Several of these envoys arrived in Italy during Columbus's youth—in 1460 and 1474, for example. Even though they were far from being the ecclesiastical allies many Europeans had imagined, the Nestorians of China were enough of a reality to keep Christian hopes alive in the fifteenth century.

It was the imagination—not reality—that mattered, for only imagination could propel Europeans to reach these Christians in the Far East. To Columbus and other pious Catholics, even if the khans were not Christians—or not yet Christians, or the wrong kind of Christians—they were still better than Muslims or Jews. And while Jews and Muslims could be forgiven for being born into their invidious religions, their unforgivable sin was refusing conversion once the light of Christianity had been revealed to them. This "problem" was nowhere more evident than in Spain, where western Europe's largest Muslim population and one of its primary Jewish populations resided. Although some Spanish Muslims and Jews did in fact convert—even as many Christians doubted their sincerity—most Iberian Jews and Muslims rejected conversion out of hand. This was their supreme blasphemy: willful rejection of the truth.

Thanks mostly to Polo, European Christians believed the Grand

Khan to be more open to conversion than the recalcitrant Muslims and Jews. The historical record, however, says otherwise. Most evidence points to the fact that, although a few members of the khans' families accepted Nestorian Christianity—and those mostly for exigent political reasons—the Mongol khans themselves never did. Nonetheless, after centuries of failed Crusades, and with the spectacular growth of Ottoman power blocking European access to the Asian trade, a desperate Europe's only hope against Islam seemed to be a mythical potentate thousands of miles away. *The Travels of Marco Polo*, which encouraged this hope, remained one of Europe's most widely printed texts for over half a millennium.

YET ANOTHER FANTASY ABOUT the religious conflict between Christianity and Islam captured Columbus's imagination during his youth: the legendary Seven Cities of Cibola. When Muslims first seized Christian Spain in 711, the story goes, seven bishops were able to escape with their faithful followers. As Muslim soldiers streamed inland, each bishop stole one of the ships left at Gibraltar by the invaders. This armada eventually reached an island in the "sea of darkness," where all disembarked. To combat any temptation to return to Spain—which they rightly assumed was now lost to the infidel Muslims—the bishops burned the ships. They then built seven cities, each governed by one of the bishops and populated by the flock in his care. Supposedly these cities were fashioned entirely of gold—rescued from Spain by the Christians to keep it out of the invaders' hands. Embellished over the years, this saga further stirred European imaginations. For would-be Crusaders, the Seven Cities of Cibola represented a vast repository of gold that could fund the holy army needed to retake Jerusalem from the infidels, and enrich them personally too.

Where, though, to find this island? Over the centuries, explorers, ambassadors, and mapmakers posited its existence somewhere in the Atlantic. The 1325 map of Dalorto, for example, depicted the island of Cibola as located west of Ireland. But, given their proximity to continental Europe, the more southerly islands of the eastern Atlantic offered the first tantalizing possibilities. These islands were only vaguely known to exist, and they were little visited—perfect fodder for the imagination. But over the course of Columbus's lifetime, as the

Azores, the Canaries, and the Cape Verdes were explored, no golden cities were unearthed from the islands' volcanic soil.

Such failures, rather than vanquishing the fantasy, only served to fuel hopes even more. As Europeans extended their ventures farther across the Atlantic, and eventually deep into the Americas at the end of the fifteenth century and throughout the sixteenth, the chimerical golden isle, though perpetually elusive, continued to sparkle. Its projected location was pushed ever farther west; it functioned as a kind of talisman of the unknown, calling Europeans siren-like forward. In the Americas, the most famous seeker of the Seven Cities in the mid-sixteenth century was Francisco Vázquez de Coronado. When he returned empty-handed from what is today the southwestern United States, Cibola was shunted out into the Pacific. Decades before Coronado's journey, however, Columbus believed firmly that the Seven Cities existed somewhere in the Atlantic, and that they would provide the gold needed to wrest Jerusalem from Muslim hands.

FILLED WITH SUCH FANTASIES and raised on legendary accounts of the Crusades, Columbus increased his interactions with Islam when he became an apprentice sailor in the Mediterranean at the age of thirteen or fourteen. As a merchant's assistant, he would have stowed trade goods on board, recorded weights and costs, secured lodgings in port for his captain and crew, and generally been available to help with navigational and business matters. Building a reputation as a reliable and efficient sailor for hire, Columbus enjoyed near-constant employment on merchant and military expeditions in the service of Europe's numerous small maritime principalities and larger polities. Some of these voyages took him to the edges of the Ottoman Empire and other Muslim states around the Mediterranean.

In 1472, when he was twenty-one, Columbus directly experienced the Muslim world for the first time. He had taken a job as a ship's captain for King René of Anjou during his war on Naples. One of the king's large three-masted galleasses, named *Fernandina*, had been commandeered by corsairs (officially sanctioned pirates in the employ of a state), and the king dispatched Columbus to Tunis, on the northern coast of Africa, to recapture it. At the time, Tunis was the stronghold of the Hafsid Empire, which ruled much of the North African shore, making money from piracy and the overland caravan trade. Like other mercantile city-states around the Mediterranean, Tunis had become a center of great wealth, art, and culture.

Columbus sailed with his crew from Naples west to Sardinia to resupply before turning south. There, they received intelligence that three Hafsid ships were guarding King René's vessel in the port of Tunis. The crew pleaded with Columbus to seek reinforcements before continuing on what they now feared would be a perilous mission. He preferred to forge ahead but, failing to convince his near-mutinous crew, he decided to lie to them. Setting sail from Sardinia by night, Columbus told his men they were heading to Marseille to secure naval support and take on more men and weapons. When day broke, however, the crew could see the ancient ruins of Carthage on the North African coast. Unfortunately, the outcome of this venture has never been established, though of course we know that Columbus survived. Most of our information about the Tunis expedition comes from a letter he wrote from Hispaniola over twenty years later, in 1495. The duplicity he displayed on his way to North Africa anticipated some of the connivances he would make later. Throughout his maritime career, Columbus was routinely mendacious, privileging his instincts and self-interest above all else: honesty, his crew, and even reason itself.

Whatever the uncertainties of the historical record, Columbus's sea crossing to Tunis brought him face to face with the awesome power of the enemy civilization that he had heard about only in church and in Crusader stories. While his first direct experience of the Muslim world proved foreboding and menacing, its true character remained mostly unknown to him.

He would gain more intimate firsthand experience of the Muslim world a few years later, in 1474 or 1475, when a branch of Genoa's eminent merchant house of Spinola sent him to Chios, a scrubby, hilly island in the Aegean Sea just off the Anatolian shore. In 1475, after Genoa lost Kefe in Crimea, its last possession on the Black Sea, Chios became the Italian city-state's easternmost territory. It was therefore of vital importance to Genoa's commercial interests in the Ottoman Empire and beyond. Chios had a further strategic advantage: it is the only place on earth where mastic is naturally produced. The crystallized sap of the island's trees—which have gnarled trunks and bushy tops that make them look like enormous bonsai trees—was a coveted

*Mastic*

luxury item used for cooking and in medicines, perfumes, and varnishes. Thus, whoever held Chios could earn enormous profits. In the 1470s, the Spinola firm protected its investment in Chios's mastic trade by sending only its most trusted representatives, men like Columbus, to ensure the resin's safe shipment to Genoa and to markets farther afield.

In traveling to Chios, Columbus had his first direct encounter with the imposing power of the Ottoman Empire. Though a Genoese colony, Chios lay very much in the Ottomans' orbit, as the empire controlled the seas around the island and all the harbors on the coast across the strait. The Ottomans had captured Enos, Imbros, Limnos, Samothrace, Lesbos, and other major Aegean islands over the previous two decades. Like the inhabitants of those islands, the majority of Chiots were Greek, but there was a growing Turkish population. While enjoying the pleasant sunshine of Chios, Columbus listened attentively and, one presumes, with dread to lurid tales of the Ottoman conquest of Kefe only a few months before and of the siege of Constantinople over two decades earlier. Memories of the loss of Constantinople, in particular, were still fresh on the island, since Genoese reinforcements from Chios had been sent to aid in its defense. The contingent suffered heavy losses that still reverberated in nearly every family on Chios.

Stories Columbus had heard in his youth about Christianity's existential wars with Islam were reified on Chios with baleful tales of lost loved ones. On the eastern frontier of Christendom, he witnessed the overwhelming dominion of the Ottoman Empire: its vicelike control over a tiny, if still nominally independent, island like Chios, its seizures of Italian-controlled ports around the Black Sea, and the portents that it might soon continue its march westward across Europe. Looking into the weary eyes of Chios's war veterans convinced Columbus that Christianity had to be boldly offensive against Islam or face cataclysmic disaster. In tracing a line of Muslim power from Tunis to Chios, Columbus came to realize that no polity on the European continent could match Muslims, especially the Ottomans, economically or militarily.

⬧

THE OTTOMANS' STRANGLEHOLD ON trade with the East forced Columbus, like countless other European merchants, to seek out distant lands and distant waters for markets far from the lucrative eastern Mediterranean, mostly in the eastern Atlantic. In 1476, twenty-five-year-old Columbus ventured beyond the Mediterranean for the first time. He carried a mastic shipment from Chios to the second-rate ports of England, a journey that would—quite unexpectedly—teach him something about the New World.

As Columbus and his five ships headed through the Strait of Gibraltar and turned northward along the southwestern Iberian coast, they noticed a convoy of four French cutters gaining on them in the unfamiliar waters. With their quicker and more nimble ships, the French privateers attacked the Italian vessels, first tossing explosives onto the decks and then boarding with brandished swords—excited for booty, hopeful for captives. Suddenly, just as the buccaneers took possession of the Spinolas' mastic and other merchandise, fire broke out on Columbus's vessel. Everyone abandoned ship, taking their chances on a swim to the shore seven or eight miles away. Columbus—clinging to an oar, weakened by the sun, and shaken by the horror of the raid—managed to fling himself onto the beach at the Portuguese port of Lagos. Spitting out saltwater, he gratefully buried his face in the wet sand. This is Columbus's own rendition of the episode, as later relayed to his son Ferdinand. All we know about how Columbus arrived in Lagos comes from this single account, described by one historian as a "garbled story." However he landed in Portugal, with his ships and cargo lost, Columbus spent the next several months in Lagos, recovering from the harrowing experience while making arrangements with the Spinolas about what to do next. They instructed him to wait in Lagos and join their next fleet sailing to England. He did so, improving his Portuguese in the meantime, and reached London's docks in the second half of 1476.

London in these years stood on the cusp of a major political and social transition, from a typical medieval European city to the Elizabethan metropolis that nurtured Marlowe and Shakespeare. The crucial turning point came in 1485, the year Henry VII ended the Wars of the Roses by seizing the throne, inaugurating the era of Tudor rule. Up to this point, fifteenth-century London had preserved its ancient core, shaped as much by the Romans as by any other power. When Columbus arrived, the streets retained some of the grid pattern the Romans had put down, and the Roman city wall, while decaying, still stood. The city, which sprawled along the north bank of the Thames, with ramparts and gates, tiled roofs and the occasional church spire, was still recovering from the ravages of plague. London had eighty thousand souls when the Black Death arrived in 1348 and would not reach that number again until 1500, when its population began to boom.

More than anything else, trade and religion forged the physical landscape of London in the fifteenth century. Merchants came from the Low Countries, Scandinavia, and Germany, as well as from the Mediterranean. Columbus himself had landed in the city representing an Italian merchant family. Commerce literally mapped the city—Wood Street, Milk Street, Ironmonger Lane, Cheapside, and so on. Churches, monasteries, and abbeys also framed the city, with thoroughfares bearing names like White Friars Street and Carmelite Street. Europe's Crusading spirit thrived in London, too; the Knights Hospitaller of St. John had built a monastery in the city in 1100, and other Crusading orders had bases there as well. The presence of the Knights in London—at a large geographical remove from the Ottoman Empire—no doubt helped to affirm in Columbus's mind just how exigent the anti-Muslim mission of the Crusades was for Christendom.

Still in England in the summer of 1477, the year Marco Polo's travelogue was printed and published for the first time—it was a German translation—Columbus joined a group of ships sailing the well-established trade route between Bristol and Iceland—a foray that would prove crucial to his later ventures. On his return trip at the end of the summer, Columbus docked in Galway, on the west coast of Ireland, where he penned the following enigmatic passage:

> Men of Cathay have come from the west. [Of this] we have seen many signs. And especially in Galway in Ireland, a man and a woman, of extraordinary appearance, have come to land on two tree trunks.

The individuals Columbus saw in Galway were most likely Native Americans, perhaps Inuit or Yupik in wooden kayaks or umiaks. Long before Columbus crossed the ocean, numerous Native Americans rode Atlantic currents eastward to Europe and Africa. Every July, the Davis Strait between Canada and Greenland flushes out a great rush of water, icebergs, logs, and anything else that happens to be caught in those waters into the North Atlantic, where strong currents carry everything to the east. Columbus was in Galway in August, so the timing would seem to explain why the two bodies were presumably still in good enough shape to be "recognized" as "Men of Cathay"—Cathay being the term of art at the time for China, or, more generally, some part of Asia.

This moment of encounter in Ireland between an Italian bringing mastic from a Greek island in the orbit of the Ottoman Empire and two Native American bodies floating east on wooden crafts—misinterpreted as coming from China—is as historically significant as it is peculiar. The presence of these "Men of Cathay" in Galway convinced Columbus that the distance across the Atlantic between Europe and Asia was not as great as some had presumed. If two corpses could make it across the ocean, conceivably he could too.

⸻ ※ ⸻

THIS SIGHTING OF NATIVE Americans in Galway in 1477 was the germ of Columbus's belief that an Atlantic route to Asia was possible. Seemingly, he had found an answer to suppositions with which he had long grappled. He concluded that in order to capture Jerusalem for Christendom as part of the global destruction of Islam, one needed to head west, not east—bypassing the Ottomans altogether. By crossing the Atlantic, one would find the gold of the Seven Cities of Cibola en route to the Christian-sympathizing Grand Khan in China, and thus take Jerusalem from the east, by the back door.

To us in the twenty-first century, this sounds beyond chimerical, but to Columbus, it made perfect sense: Christian Europe and the converted khan together would eliminate the Ottomans and all other Muslims in an epic battle for the soul of the world. As Columbus progressed westward—from his unpleasant first encounter with Muslim military power in Tunis to his startling glimpse in Galway—he devised a plan that, like a pole star, would steer the rest of his life and would lead to one of the most consequential, yet still largely misunderstood, ocean crossings in the history of the world.

# COLUMBUS'S CRUSADE

*Portuguese map of West Africa*

THE STORY OF COLUMBUS AND HIS GENERATION OF EXPLORERS
is indubitably one of Crusade. These sailors explicitly defined most
of their expeditions in religious terms, as crucial contributions to the

global civilizational war between Christendom and Islam. Like all Europeans of his era, Columbus grew up with this Crusading yeast baked into his daily bread. Without understanding the role of anti-Muslim Crusading in all of Columbus's voyages—even before his transatlantic crossing—we cannot fully explain their lasting and con-sequential outcomes. His earliest ventures in international commerce in the Mediterranean proved useful not only as coming-of-age experi-ences and for navigational training, but also as lessons about the global power and reach of Islam. He first journeyed north out of the Mediter-ranean to avoid the Ottomans. Following his adventures in the North Atlantic, Columbus, in his late twenties and back in Portugal, resolved to dedicate his skills toward a greater purpose—the destruction of Islam. Before crossing the Atlantic, he would sail south from Lisbon in one of his first attempts to extinguish Muslim power from the earth, eventually taking his Crusade to the New World, where, astonishingly, he understood Islam to exist.

During these early days of his seafaring career, Columbus devel-oped connections with some of Europe's most accomplished mariners. Once he resolved to focus on exploring an Atlantic route to Asia, he tried to enlist the best of these sailors to join him. Lisbon, as a center of European navigation, proved the perfect locale for him to pitch his ideas. In 1479, at the age of twenty-eight, Columbus married a Por-tuguese woman named Filipa Moniz, whose social background was radically different from his. She came from a long line of aristocracy on both sides, whereas Columbus, the son of a weaver, had quite lit-erally washed up as human flotsam on Portugal's shores a few years earlier. They most likely met in church, one of the few places where people from different social strata could interact. For Columbus, the professional advantages of this marriage were enormous. Filipa's fam-ily had deep roots in the world of Portuguese maritime exploration as well as in the Catholic wars against Islam. They were devout members of the Order of Santiago, named after St. James, the patron saint of Moor-slayers.

In 1415, Filipa's maternal grandfather had participated in the Por-tuguese conquest of Ceuta, on the North African coast. On a skinny peninsula at the tip of the continent, this prominent walled fortress, formerly ruled by the kingdom of Fez, would prove to be of the utmost strategic importance to Portugal's imperial expansion in Africa. He also served as governor in Algarve, Portugal's southernmost region, immediately after its capture from the Muslims, who had ruled it for centuries. Filipa's father had played an integral role in the Portuguese conquest of the island of Porto Santo near Madeira, and in 1516 one of her relatives would join Portugal's first mission to China. To symbolize Columbus's marital ties to the family's illustrious naval lineage and its Moor-slaying credentials—two vital markers of his ascension in the ranks of Europe's seafaring elite—Filipa's mother gave her new son-in-law navigational instruments and maps that family members had used decades earlier during voyages to Ceuta and Porto Santo with Prince Henry the Navigator, one of the mid-fifteenth century's most celebrated explorers.

Prince Henry was the third son of Portugal's King João I. Born in 1394, he had a stern face, an underbite, and a neat mustache. Never a real contender for the throne, he used his father's resources to fund various dalliances and hobbies. The love of his life proved to be naval exploration, and with money and time at his disposal, he quickly gained fame as one of the first Europeans to lead expeditions to the south and west of Portugal. Experimenting with new types of sail and new navigational technologies, Henry and his men ventured first to the islands off the coasts of Portugal and West Africa—the Azores, the Canaries, Madeira, and the Cape Verdes. Columbus took advantage of his new connections to ingratiate himself into the circle of mariners the prince had gathered, Henry himself having died in 1460.

According to one of his contemporaries, Gomez Eanes de Azurara, writing in the fateful year 1453, Henry "was actuated by the zeal for God, by the desire for alliance with the Eastern Christians [an allusion to the Grand Khan], by an eagerness to know how far the power of the 'infidel' existed, by the wish to convert people to Christianity, and by the desire to fight the Moors." This Crusading ethos provided Henry and his men with ideological justification and, crucially, financial backing from the king of Portugal, the pope, and other European rulers. They zealously believed in the truth of holy war and, like Columbus, longed to find the Grand Khan, who surely would help them destroy Islam. Thus, the voyages of Prince Henry and his successors were not, as they are usually described, driven by secular curiosity, motivated by the search for knowledge or technological innovation. They belong to the history of Christianity's Crusades.

Henry's most famous plan for outflanking the Muslim world rested on his belief in the possibility of a southern route around Africa. The primary problem with this idea, initially, was that it meant crossing the equator. Ancient wisdom held that anyone who tried to cross the Torrid Zone, as the equatorial latitudes were then known, would be, as if in some Dante-esque torture, scorched to death by this hottest of rings around the earth. Henry and his crew, however, pressed their luck, willing to test the Torrid Zone for themselves. They headed southward along the African coast, eventually making it around Cape Bojadar, and then, probably inadvertently, crossing the equator. Once they realized they were on the other side, near what is today Gabon, not only did they discover that they were still alive, but they happened upon a stunning coastline of lush greenery, rivers, thriving societies, and—perhaps most surprisingly—many Muslims. The ancients, it seemed, had been wrong on several counts.

Unbeknownst to Henry (as well as to Columbus), Islam had been introduced to West Africa in the eighth century by Muslim merchants from the East trading across the Sahel. By the time the Portuguese arrived there—as they found, to their utter dismay—Islam had grown from a minority faith of a few adherents to the state religion of several West African empires, most prominent among them the Mali Empire, which adopted Islam as its official religion in 1324. By then, West African Islam had incorporated and adapted longstanding local cultural practices, aesthetics, and even other religious ideas, becoming a unique version of the faith that today is a major force in the region. The "discovery" of Muslims in West Africa in the fifteenth century further deepened the belief among European Crusaders that their Christian faith had become sclerotic, was surrounded by the powerful forces of Islam, and could only be saved through drastic action.

As Prince Henry continued his explorations, revealing Muslims in places he had never known existed and proving the need to intensify Christianity's war against a flourishing Islam, he pushed for an enlarged legal purview to extend Catholicism's political and military reach beyond Europe. He received this from Pope Nicholas V, who, incidentally, established the Vatican Library using many of the Greek manuscripts that scholars fleeing Constantinople had taken with them. In 1452—the year before Constantinople fell—Nicholas issued a papal bull entitled *Dum Diversas*, which bestowed upon Portugal "official

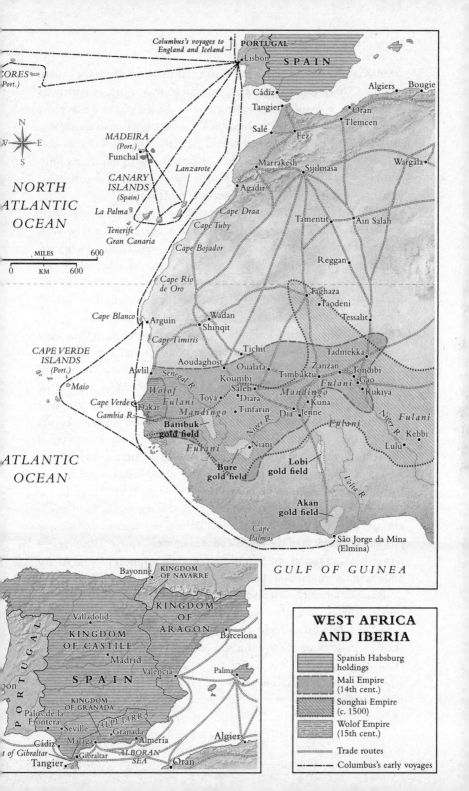

Columbus's voyages to
England and Iceland

PORTUGAL
Lisbon

SPAIN

Cádiz

Tangier

Salé

Fez

Algiers

Bougie

Oran

Tlemcen

Marrakesh

Sijilmasa

Wargala

AZORES
(Port.)

NORTH
ATLANTIC
OCEAN

MADEIRA
(Port.)
Funchal

Lanzarote

CANARY
ISLANDS
(Spain)

La Palma

Tenerife
Gran Canaria

Agadir

Cape Draa

Cape Tuby

Cape Bojador

Tamentit

Ain Salah

Reggan

Cape Río
de Oro

Taghaza

Taodeni

Tessalit

W
N
E
S

MILES
0        600
KM       600

Cape Blanco

Arguin

Cape Timiris

CAPE VERDE
ISLANDS
(Port.)

Maio

Cape Verde

Dakar

Gambia R.

Awlil

Wadan

Shinqit

Tichit

Aoudaghost

Koumbi
Saleh

Oualata

Diara

Toya

Tinfarin

Mandingo

Dia

Jenne

Kuna

Timbuktu

Tadmekka

Zanzan

Fulani

Tondibi

Gao

Kukiya

Niger R.

Fulani

Kebbi

Lulu

Wolof

Fulani

Bambuk
gold field

Senegal R.

ATLANTIC
OCEAN

Niani

Bure
gold field

Fulani

Lobi
gold field

Akan
gold field

Volta R.

Cape
Palmas

São Jorge da Mina
(Elmina)

GULF OF GUINEA

Bayonne

KINGDOM
OF NAVARRE

Valladolid

KINGDOM
OF
ARAGON

Barcelona

KINGDOM
OF CASTILE

Madrid

Palma

SPAIN

Valencia

PORTUGAL

KINGDOM
OF GRANADA

ALPUJARRA

Palos de la
Frontera

Seville

Málaga

Granada

Almería

Algiers

Cádiz

Gibraltar

Strait of Gibraltar

Tangier

ALBORAN
SEA

Oran

### WEST AFRICA
### AND IBERIA

Spanish Habsburg
holdings

Mali Empire
(14th cent.)

Songhai Empire
(c. 1500)

Wolof Empire
(15th cent.)

Trade routes

Columbus's early voyages

dominion" over the west coast of Africa and all the islands of the eastern Atlantic. This legalized Henry's territorial gains as a part of Portugal's empire. The bull specified that Portugal had the right to enslave any "Saracens" (another term for Muslims) and pagans living in the region. Still decades before Europeans would cross the Atlantic and centuries before the transatlantic slave trade would peak, the significance of this stunning papal document cannot be overstated. It provided the first legal basis for the European enslavement of Africans.

In a world of Christians Crusading against Islam, Europeans warring against the Ottomans, this bull equated the legal status of West African Muslims with that of pagans—both considered unbelievers, of course, and both now subject to enslavement by Christian Europeans. Given the history of encounters between Christendom and Islam, Muslims were the closest, most familiar, and ultimate "other" for Europeans—the political, military, and ideological enemy against whom all other enemies were measured and through whom they were understood. Because West Africa's non-Muslims were also non-Christians, they were interpreted through the primary category of non-Christian "otherness" available to Europeans—Islam. For Christians, then, *pagan* equaled *Muslim*, making it possible for the Portuguese in West Africa to understand both non-Muslims and Muslims as part of the same conceptual category of "Muslim"—a category of person which a Christian was allowed to treat with great force and violence.

The papal conjoining of Muslim and non-Muslim is what ultimately allowed both to be taken "legally" from West Africa to the New World as slaves. The repurposing of the category of "Muslim" to encompass non-Christians outside of Europe was hence a constituent element of the birth of the much-vaunted European age of discovery—an age built, of course, on Europe's territorial conquests in West Africa and the enslavement of its people.

Pushed out of the Mediterranean by Ottoman military and economic power, Columbus would export this conceptual innovation across the Atlantic, which would soon allow Europeans to expand their understanding of "Muslim" otherness to encompass not just West African non-Muslims but Native Americans as well. In the Americas, where of course no Muslims existed in 1492, European Christians again filtered the unknown peoples they encountered through their notions of Islam and anti-Muslim Christian Crusade.

THE FARTHEST POINT SOUTH on the African coast reached by the team of explorers Henry had organized was São Jorge da Mina, on the Gulf of Guinea—today, Elmina in Ghana. That town would soon prove the linchpin of Portugal's empire in West Africa, a key conduit for the funneling of African gold to Lisbon. In 1481, Portugal's new king, João II, recognized the need for a stronghold there, so he dispatched a heavily armed fleet to build a fortified trading post—the first European-built structure in sub-Saharan Africa. Aboard ten caravels and two transport ships, João sent foundation stones, roof tiles, nails, and provisions. Columbus, now thirty and leaving a young son in Lisbon, sailed south on one of these ships.

João's fort immediately proved its worth. Between 1487 and 1489, 8,000 ounces of gold went from São Jorge da Mina to Lisbon; 22,500 ounces were shipped between 1494 and 1496; and by 1500, shipments totaled 26,000 ounces. Owing in large measure to the infamous papal bull that Henry had negotiated, the commerce of São Jorge da Mina soon came to include slaves as well, with ten to twelve thousand West Africans transported to Lisbon between 1500 and 1535 alone. In subsequent centuries, the fort that Columbus helped construct became one of the main export hubs of the transatlantic slave trade.

While he was in São Jorge da Mina, Columbus collected three pieces of information that solidified his resolve to head westward across the Atlantic, where—more sure than ever—he was convinced he would find Asia. First, in this region of Africa that would later be known as the Gold Coast, he saw seemingly endless supplies of the precious metal in the soils and rocks near the coast. Contemporary interpretations of geography had taught him that regions of the globe at similar latitudes enjoyed comparable climates and natural features. In his understanding, then, he would find lands rich in gold if he headed due west from São Jorge da Mina—perhaps even the Seven Cities of Cibola that had fired his imagination for so many years. The second piece—hearing from sailors in the African port that they often saw logs washed up on shore that seemed to have been carved by human hands—confirmed his experience in Galway with the two Native American corpses: Asia, apparently, was close. Thirdly, in São Jorge da Mina Columbus gleaned an understanding of the Atlantic's predominant patterns of wind and

*São Jorge da Mina*

current. On the West African coast, the prevailing winds blow out to sea, and the ocean's dominant current is to the west as well. This is the exact opposite of the pattern in Portugal, where the ocean's eastward currents make it difficult to sail westward for most of the year. To head west, Columbus correctly understood, it would be best to sail south along the African coast in order to pick up the westerly current.

Columbus now had, he believed, nearly all the information necessary to execute his plan to bypass the Ottomans and find the Grand Khan. The only thing missing was a benevolent patron.

COLUMBUS'S YEARS OF BACK-AND-FORTH negotiations with different European sovereigns—Spanish, French, English, Portuguese, Venetian, and Genoese—is a well-known tale. Less well known is the role that Muslims and the Ottoman Empire played in this. Columbus's major push for money occurred in the 1480s—the decade during which Isabella and Ferdinand, the eventual financiers of his voyages, declared war on Islam. It is hardly a coincidence that Europe's war on Islam and Columbus's voyages transpired at the exact same time. In the minds of Columbus and the Spanish sovereigns, the two were pieces of the same global war: Christianity against Islam. Ferdinand—"fit and athletic" and "swarthy in a rakish way"—and Isabella—"her eyes between gray and blue" and "her face very beautiful and gay"—were resolute Moor-slayers, as well as second cousins. As part of their global strategy against Islam, they dispatched their navies eastward in the Mediterranean to fight the Ottomans, endeavored to clear the Iberian peninsula of Muslims, and sent Columbus and his fleet off to the west to Asia in an attempt to surprise and surround the Muslims of the Middle East.

Ottoman advances in the second half of the fifteenth century directly affected Spanish holdings in the Mediterranean. After his capture of Otranto in 1480, Mehmet the Conqueror sent ships to Sicily, the Mediterranean's largest island, to assess the prospects for a possible invasion. Once a Muslim possession, Sicily in the fifteenth century was nominally under the sovereignty of Ferdinand and Isabella, so this move by the much more powerful Ottoman sultan instantly captured their attention. "Every day," Isabella's court chronicler wrote, "news came to the King and Queen that the Turks had a great armada on the sea, and that they were sending it to conquer the kingdom of Sicily." At the center of the sea, Sicily functioned as a gateway between the eastern and western Mediterranean. Whoever controlled Sicily controlled the Mediterranean. The loss of Sicily to the Ottomans would mean, for example, that Chios, where Columbus had picked up the Spinolas' mastic, would almost certainly be lost as well. It would also give the Ottomans an important launching pad for further invasions—farther north on the Italian peninsula, toward the holy city of Rome, and farther west against Spanish and other Christian territories. The Spanish sovereigns therefore leaped into action after Mehmet's fleet was spotted off Sicily's rocky coast, dispatching their own fleet to Italy's western coast to join forces with the king of Naples, a cousin of Ferdinand's, to move on the Ottomans in Otranto. Luckily for this combined Spanish–Neapolitan force, Mehmet died while it sailed toward Otranto, and the subsequent succession crisis that brought Bayezit to the throne forced the empire to give up on Sicily and indeed to withdraw from Italy altogether. In the end, the Ottomans held Otranto and its tiny crystal-blue harbor for only a year.

*Isabella and Ferdinand with their daughter Joanna*

Despite this retreat, the Ottomans continued to push westward in the Mediterranean over the course of the 1480s, testing the resolve of Spain as well as other European powers. In 1488, Bayezit attacked, but failed to seize, another of the central Mediterranean's most strategic islands, Malta, prompting Spain to send reinforcements to its garrisons in Sicily. Between 1487 and the middle of the 1490s, Ottoman ships continued west, reaching Corsica, Pisa, the Balearic Islands, and even breaching the Iberian mainland itself at Almería and Málaga. Although these were not full-scale invasions resulting in permanent Ottoman settlements, the sight of a fleet of Ottoman ships pulling into port panicked already frightened European states, especially Spain, because of its large Muslim population. The propulsive power of the Ottomans was everywhere in the Mediterranean, even in Iberia itself.

These gains in the western Mediterranean made the already precarious situation of Spain's Muslims much more dire. Muslims on the peninsula were equated with Spain's external Muslim enemies—the Ottomans and the many independent Muslim principalities in North Africa that Spain had long sought to conquer. Especially in the fifteenth century, as Spain extended its empire in North Africa and after the Ottoman conquest of Constantinople, Spain's besieged Muslims sent desperate appeals for help to the most powerful Muslim states—the Ottomans and the Mamluks. Their pleas sparked the Spanish monarchs' deepest fears—the potential alliance of their Muslim "fifth column" population with the Mediterranean's Muslim powers in the impending, and to the royals' mind inevitable, global religious war. In the 1480s, the Mamluk navy proved far too weak to threaten Spain, because it was already stretched thin from doing battle with the Portuguese in the Indian Ocean. Indeed, the Mamluks too, like Spain's Muslims, eventually turned to the Ottomans for help in those years.

In 1487 or 1488, as Selim and Gülbahar settled into their new home in Trabzon, Bayezit, sensing opportunity, sent a privateer named Kemal Reis into the western Mediterranean on a reconnaissance mission, charging him to return with a realistic picture of the situation in Spain and the position of Muslims in Iberia and North Africa. Arriving first in the ports of Almería and Málaga, Kemal met clandestinely with members of Spain's Muslim community. He sent messages to Bayezit describing how weak and frightened they had become after repeated waves of Catholic repression, and advising that the only way to properly support them would be a full-scale Ottoman invasion of Iberia.

Such an offensive was a financial and logistical impossibility at that point, so Bayezit instructed Kemal to assess the possibilities of an alliance with the North African Muslim principalities in Spain's orbit— those directly under its rule as well as those that had managed to remain independent. From Spain, Kemal sailed south and followed the North African coast east from Ceuta to Tripoli, stopping in every port to see where alliances could be forged and where ramparts seemed weak, and also where inroads would be impossible. Typically, a single family or household controlled each of these walled cities. These families had submitted to Spain, successfully fought it off, or reached some sort of rapprochement with the far more powerful empire. Encouraged by the interest of the Ottomans, these North African potentates saw opportunities to alter the balance of power with Spain and extend their influence beyond their city walls.

For example, in the port of Bougie (now Béjaïa), east of Algiers and due south from Menorca, Kemal found a willing ally in the city's ruler, Sayyid Muhammad Tuwalli, who claimed to possess magical powers that had allowed him to fend off the Spanish. Sayyid Muhammad allowed Kemal and his men to stay in the city for a few weeks. From there, Kemal made further alliances with leaders in Bone, east of Bougie, and even as far east as the island of Djerba, off the southeastern Tunisian coast. While these agreements gave the Ottomans some degree of influence in North African affairs, their foothold remained tenuous, since the local leaders could renege on their promises or be ousted at any time. Even so, the alliances allowed Bayezit to maintain geostrategic pressure on Spain in the western Mediterranean. From 1490, when Kemal Reis first arrived in North Africa, until 1495, when Bayezit summoned him back to Istanbul, Kemal and his men, along with some of their new allies, undertook several successful raids against Spanish positions in Morocco and even on the Iberian peninsula.

Like Columbus, Henry, and Pope Nicholas V, Isabella and Ferdinand regarded their war against Islam as a civilizational struggle. The Ottomans' increasing influence on the threshold of their territory in the western Mediterranean, especially among their own reviled Muslim subjects, seemed to accelerate the arrival of the portended final apocalyptic conflict between Christendom and Islam. Spain in the 1480s was an amalgam of some half dozen independent states. Isabella ruled Castile, Ferdinand Aragon, and various independent Muslim emirs held territories in the south of the peninsula. At the end of the fifteenth century, Catholicism and antipathy toward Islam were the only shared tenets among Spain's non-Muslim states. Isabella especially took it as her duty, as sovereign of one of the largest and most influential of Spain's Christian states, to lead the global war against all Muslims— whether in Castile, across Iberia, in North Africa, in the Ottoman Empire, or anywhere else. (Ironically, there were more Christians in the Ottoman Empire at the time than in the *whole* of Spain.) For both

Ferdinand and Isabella, any Muslim anywhere was a potential threat, but they regarded those living under their own rule as the most dangerous. Iberia's independent Muslim south was also a potential territorial foothold for the Ottomans. As the Catholic sovereigns saw it, the only way to counter both these threats, the one internal and the other to their south, was to completely eliminate Muslims from the Iberian peninsula, a community with nearly eight hundred years of history.

The process of attempting to make Spain wholly Christian was known as the *Reconquista* (or "Reconquest"), a perceived (and expected) "return" to the status quo ante of the early eighth century, before Muslims arrived in Spain. The *Reconquista* sprang from the same ethos as the Inquisition: the belief that non-Christians threatened and weakened Christian Spain and therefore had to be eliminated either through conversion or expulsion. Thus, the *Reconquista* also targeted Spain's other major non-Christian community, the Jews. But unlike Jews, Muslims controlled territorial entities in Iberia and beyond and were thus perceived as a more dangerous military and political threat. Jews never had a formal state in Spain, nor an external state that was alleged to be supporting the Judeo-Spanish community. Spain's Jews, unlike Muslims, were not locked in a battle with Christendom for global territorial and religious domination. Spain hence justified violence towards its Jews, as we will see in more detail later, on the basis not of international politics but of anti-Jewish theology.

After the Ottomans' forays into the western Mediterranean in the 1480s and early 1490s, the *Reconquista* became something more than merely a campaign for political and religious consolidation on the Iberian peninsula. It became a crucial battle in the greater existential war to roll back Islam and its foremost representatives, the Ottomans, from the Mediterranean and eventually from the face of the earth altogether. It was, in short, a Crusade.

※

STEEPED AS COLUMBUS WAS throughout his life in the rhetoric and reality of the Crusades, he used the notion of a global civilizational war between Christendom and Islam—the idea that he and the Spanish sovereigns were all "Matamoros"—to push his case for the Atlantic voyage. He was confident that if he could demonstrate that heading west across the ocean would help to defeat Islam, Ferdinand and Isabella would finance his journey. But how to gain an audience with either of them? Given her consternation about the Ottomans, and locked as she was in battle with the Muslim kingdom of Granada and some of the smaller Muslim principalities in the south, Isabella had little time to heed what she must have assumed was a far-fetched—never mind expensive—proposal from a dreamy-eyed Genoese buccaneer. Although there is a stark lack of female leaders in the historical record, here we see how Columbus, like Selim, relied on powerful women. For several years, he tried to get a chance to pitch his ideas to the queen, following her from place to place, using his connections to try to set up a meeting. Columbus's exploring exemplar, Prince Henry the Navigator, was her great-uncle, but he had died decades earlier. Isabella captiously strung Columbus along until May 1486, when she finally offered him a few minutes of her time in Córdoba.

The so-called "Ornament of the World," Córdoba was a handsome city in southern Spain in which churches became mosques and mosques became churches; where Muslim, Jewish, and Christian scholars had worked and lived together for centuries along the ancient Guadalquivir River; where the three religions overlapped, conversed, and intertwined their beliefs. Around the year 1000, Córdoba was one of the world's largest and richest cities, with more than half a million residents. It was known as a place of ecumenical learning and, at times, religious cosmopolitanism—a medieval testament to the peaceful *convivencia* (coexistence) of Judaism, Christianity, and Islam. Córdoba, however, had been under Catholic rule since the thirteenth century, and thus by Isabella's day the city's culture of *convivencia* had been eroding for more than a century. In large measure, this was a consequence of the rise of the Ottoman Empire. With the balance of power in the Mediterranean tipping to the east, Christian leaders in Spain had adopted a more confrontational stance, lashing out at their mostly defenseless Muslim subjects as an impotent response to what they perceived as the looming threat of Islam.

When Isabella finally agreed to meet Columbus for what would be the first of many encounters, she discovered that they were in some ways kindred spirits, both interested in geography, exotic plants and animals, and fantastical stories of the wealth of far-off lands. They were also the same age—both were born in 1451, she a few months earlier, the same year that Selim's grandfather Mehmet II acceded to the Ottoman throne. They shared pale skin and red hair. One of the longest accounts of the adult Columbus's appearance and personality comes from roughly this period (his portrait was never painted during his lifetime). He was "taller than most, and with strong limbs." His face was described as "oblong," his nose aquiline, and his light eyes "lively." Columbus's "hair was very red and his face ruddy and freckled." Owing to his Genoese schooling, "he was a good Latinist and a very learned cosmographer, gracious when he wished, but hot tempered if he was crossed." By all accounts, he and Isabella got along splendidly, with their first conversation described by a courtier as "chatting," rather than a formal meeting. It helped that Columbus, in the words of another historian, "was clearly a charismatic figure, and women, including the queen, seemed to be attracted to him."

He laid out his case to the queen of Castile, drawing confidence from the fact that Isabella was, in his words, "devoted to the Holy Christian Faith and dedicated to its expansion and to combating the religion of Mahomet." He would sail westward to the court of the Grand Khan of the East, convince him to join forces with Christian Europe against the Ottomans, and together they would retake Jerusalem in an epic battle that would destroy Islam forever. He set out his belief that such an apocalyptic war was the only way to ensure the triumph of Christianity over Islam. He vouched that he had both the experience and the knowledge to guarantee this outcome. He buttressed his credentials by explaining that he had studied Marco Polo, Pliny's *Natural History*, and Ptolemy's *Geography*, and had pored over every map he could find. He regaled Isabella with tales of all he had learned during his days with Henry the Navigator's sailors—the narrowness of the Atlantic, its currents, the West African coast, and the latitude at which gold could be found in Asia. He told her about the two "Men of Cathay" he had seen in Ireland and the hand-carved wood that had washed up on the beach at São Jorge da Mina. He promised that, should she fund his venture, she would forever be known as the queen of the oceans and the ultimate executioner of Islam.

Her interest piqued, Isabella ordered her advisers to study Columbus's plan. At that point, in 1486, given the demanding war effort in the Iberian south, she was unable to devote the resources needed to do anything more than entertain Columbus's fancies. She did, however, offer to hire him as a soldier. Strapped for cash and without other viable patronage options, he agreed, joining the Spanish fight against the Moors. As a soldier in Isabella's army, Columbus wagered, he would have opportunities to remind her of his plan. In the late 1480s, the *Reconquista* was on the front foot, winning town after town near Granada, the ultimate prize, whose defeat would eliminate Muslim rule from the Iberian peninsula. In 1488, Spanish forces won important strategic victories by capturing the towns of Vera, Vélez-Blanco, and Vélez-Rubio, east of Granada, in the semi-arid hills toward the coast. Controlling the coast was critical, as rumors swirled that the Ottomans were sending reinforcements—a hundred thousand soldiers and 505 galleys—to support the Iberian Muslims. Whether or not such a long-feared alliance was indeed in the offing, the dreaded Ottoman forces never materialized. Two further Spanish victories tightened the vise around Granada; in 1489, Isabella's armies captured Jaén, north of the city, and Baza to its east. In both battles, Columbus reportedly played a decisive role.

After the conquest of Baza, two Franciscan friars arrived in Spain from Jerusalem's Church of the Holy Sepulchre—one of the holiest places in Christendom—carrying a message from the Mamluk rulers of Jerusalem. If Isabella and Ferdinand did not abandon their siege of Muslim territories in Spain, the message read, the Mamluks would destroy the sacred church and kill every Christian living in their empire. Isabella dismissed this as a toothless attempt at intimidation; she would not be deterred from pushing on to Granada. The queen sent away the envoys, dressed in their traditional brown habits, with one thousand gold ducats and a veil for the shrine in Jerusalem that she herself had embroidered. Rather than deterring Isabella and her generals, the Mamluk threat only added fuel to the Catholic zeal for a Crusade to take Jerusalem. Hearing about this and, like Isabella, burning wth anger, Columbus seized the moment to remind her of his own plan to "reclaim" the holy city.

The Franciscans' visit to Baza demonstrated that Muslim powers also viewed Spain as the crucible of a global war between Islam and Christianity. Both the Mamluks and the more dominant Ottomans saw southern Iberia as a Muslim borderland that had to be defended against Christian armies. Yet even as the Mediterranean's two major powers, Spain and the Ottoman Empire, jockeyed for territorial and civilizational influence and supremacy, they shared similar aspirations for universal rule, parallel dynastic structures, and comparably heteroge-

neous subject populations. In the 1490s, they also shared the perception
that multitudes of internal and external enemies posed never-ending
threats to their respective realms. For the Spanish, the primary danger
came from Muslims. For the Ottomans, the peril came not from their
empire's Christians—still the majority of the population—but rather
from Shiite Muslims, both in Anatolia and off to their east: the raiders
against whom Selim was ranging his formidable army.

IN JULY 1491, in her elaborate regal encampment at Santa Fe, just outside Granada, Isabella prepared for what she hoped would be the final
offensive. Her forces had successfully surrounded the city. Close to a
decade of war had stretched its resources: food shortages were rampant,
military morale was low and manpower was depleted, and many of the
advisers of the king of Granada, Abu ʿAbd Allah Muhammad XII—or
Boabdil, as he is more commonly known—were resigned to defeat.

Granada had once been a wealthy city of about thirty thousand,
exporting silk, leather, ceramics, nuts, and olives throughout the Mediterranean. Nestled in the foothills of the Sierra Nevada mountains at
the confluence of four rivers, the region around Granada produced
enormous quantities of pomegranates and also copious amounts of
millet which was ground in the city's 130 water mills. Atop a hill in
the city's eastern sector, seemingly floating on air, stood the majestic
Alhambra complex, with reflecting pools, towers, gardens, filigreed
porticoes, and façades of splendid Islamic calligraphy. The Arabic word
*Alhambra* means "the red woman," a reference to the red clay of the
region which was used to build this elegant fortress and its palace.

Columbus, camped with the forces of Ferdinand and Isabella outside
Granada's walls, bided his time with the other soldiers. After failing to
get support for his expedition from numerous monarchs across Europe,
he was frustrated, desperate, and poor, reduced to the lot of a mercenary soldier. It had been six years since he first approached the ambitious but cautious Isabella. That promising meeting was now hardly
more than a fleeting memory, but he chased her down once again in
Santa Fe to remind her of his plan. She shooed him away, but, annoyed
as she was, promised him an answer once the siege was over.

After years of fighting and months of negotiations, Boabdil,
ensconced with his family and advisers under the *muqarnas*—stalactite

vaulting—of the Alhambra's ceilings, formally surrendered on January 2, 1492, ending more than seven centuries of Muslim rule on the Iberian peninsula. The long, punishing strangulation of Granada had succeeded. On January 6, the feast of Epiphany, the Spanish, with Columbus among them, triumphantly entered the city of pomegranates. In one of his first acts in the conquered emirate, Ferdinand marched up the hill to the Alhambra complex with a large silver cross Pope Sixtus IV had given him to gird him in battle—clear evidence of the Vatican's keen interest in this war between Spanish Catholicism and Islam. This most important of Moorish structures in all of Spain—the palace and fortress of centuries of Muslim rulers, the city's citadel and most distinctive feature—was now in Catholic hands. On the day when Christians believe the Magi of the East brought gifts to the newborn Christ, Ferdinand, "darker-complexioned than Isabella," presented his queen, "white and fair," with the gift of the red Alhambra that they had yearned for so long to seize. All of Spain was now united under the flag of Catholicism.

With tears in his large, hazel-colored eyes and anguish on his bearded, saturnine face, Boabdil left the palace for the final time via a bridge that came to be known as the Bridge of Sighs. He fled to North Africa, where he reportedly died several years later in Fez. The Muslims who remained in Spain were given three years to leave, as were its Jews. In the millennial minds of Isabella and Ferdinand, their victory was preordained by God, a sure sign that their plans for a global Crusade would ultimately succeed. Just as in Spain, they resolved, Islam would be eradicated from the world.

Only days after the Spanish victory, one of Ferdinand and Isabella's court historians wrote that Granada was "the extinction of Spain's calamities." The euphoria of conquest made hyperbole the language of the day. Another historian asked the sovereigns rhetorically, "Will there ever be an age so thankless as will not hold you in eternal gratitude?" The Catholic victory at Granada "redeemed Spain, indeed all of Europe." Church bells rang out across European cities and the pope ordered days of festivities. Celebratory bullfights were organized across Spain, as were reenactments of the siege of Granada. Coming almost four decades after the 1453 loss of Constantinople to the Ottomans, Granada was for many Europeans an act of retribution, a Christian

*Boabdil hands over the keys to Granada to the Spanish*

rebuttal to the most powerful Muslim empire on earth. Not surprisingly, this feeling of revenge was most palpable in Spain, where, as we have seen, the threat of Ottoman support for the peninsula's Muslims was pungent. In the words of a Spanish court historian, the conquest of Granada "was famed and celebrated through all the realms of Christendom, and it extended to the farthest and most remote lands of the Turk and Sultan." While no doubt a true watershed of the last millennium, the fall of Granada, in fact, did little to stop Ottoman advances, in the Balkans and Central Europe or North Africa and the Middle East; and, moreover, there would be Muslims in the Iberian peninsula for more than another century, until their final expulsion in 1614.

The destruction of the kingdom of Granada spelled the end of Muslim rule in Europe, apart from Ottoman holdings in the Balkans. Not until the twentieth-century formation of Albania and Bosnia would another Muslim state arise on the continent. Granada represented the first major Christian victory over Islam since it had emerged in Arabia in the seventh century. With this defeat, Europe buried centuries of its centrally formative Muslim history, which had commenced in 711. The active suppression of over seven hundred years of Europe's domestic Muslim history began in January 1492, and it continues in various guises to the present day—making our story of Selim, the Ottomans, and Islam vital as a corrective to current understandings of the past.

꙰

AS ISABELLA AND FERDINAND'S troops streamed over the hills of Granada and along its picturesque stone lanes, elated and exuberant, Columbus could think only of his "project of discovering a world." Although he shared in the joy of the conquest, he could not help but feel "melancholy and dejected in the midst of the general rejoicing, [as] he beheld with indifference, and almost with contempt, the conclusion of a conquest which swelled all bosoms with jubilee, and seemed to have reached the utmost bounds of desire." What Columbus most wanted from the fall of Granada was a response from the parsimonious Spanish queen. Isabella finally made good on her promise. Against the judgment of her advisers and her husband and trusting her own intuition, she agreed to fund Columbus's expedition across the Atlantic.

As a solution to the problem of Muslim power in the Mediterranean, Columbus's proposed adventure was a desperate act in desperate circumstances. In the larger picture, the triumph at Granada was dwarfed by Ottoman incursions ever farther west in the Mediterranean, Europe, and North Africa. And the Ottoman (and Mamluk) hegemony over trade with the East—manipulated in places such as Trabzon by Ottoman officials such as Selim—enabled them to control contact with Eastern merchants and levy exorbitant tariffs on European traders, and even blockade the trade routes at will. With few viable options against the Ottomans, and buoyed by her victory, Isabella was willing to gamble on a perilous trip across an unfathomable ocean. And if Columbus's plan—risky and far-fetched though it seemed—could contribute in even a minor way to the destruction of the Ottoman Empire and Islam, then it would prove to be a more than worthy investment of her resources. Christ the forgiving savior would finally march upon the entire world as a belligerent, and Jerusalem would be won.

CHAPTER

CHAPTER
8

# NEW WORLD ISLAM

*Aztec dance*

I N COLUMBUS'S MIND, SPAIN'S GLORIOUS *RECONQUISTA* OVER ISLAM
surely would lead to Christianity's global *Conquista* over the vile religion. Hoping to do his part to advance Europe's Crusade, he set sail
from the Andalusian port of Palos de la Frontera on the evening of
August 3, 1492, a summer when Sultan Bayezit marched his armies to
Sofia, the capital of Bulgaria, and raided Transylvania.

The year 1492 is seen as a historical caesura, a rupture between all that was old and all that is new. For some, it is the year the modern world began; for others, it is the year the independent sovereignty of the Americas ended. To understand 1492 properly and fully, however, we must understand the continuities that made and shaped it. We must eschew the mythology about a secular Western march of progress. On their three square-sailed ships, Columbus and his eighty-seven crewmen carried across the Atlantic their long history of warring with Islam and their sense of inadequacy in the face of the Ottoman colossus. He and his royal patrons were launching a new phase in an epic war that already had lasted more than half a millennium. Having failed to capture the Jerusalem of the Old World, after 1492 Europe looked to a New Jerusalem across the ocean as a promised land free of Islam. Columbus sailed west on Crusade.

The opening lines of Columbus's logbook relate this explicitly: "On 2 January in the year 1492, when your Highnesses had concluded their war with the Moors who reigned in Europe, I saw your Highnesses' banners victoriously raised on the towers of the Alhambra, the citadel of that city, and the Moorish king come out of the city gates and kiss the hands of your Highnesses." In the very next sentence, Columbus pivoted to his overarching goal of finding and converting the Grand Khan, whom Marco Polo had vowed would help Christendom surround and defeat Islam:

> In that same month, on the grounds of information I had given your royal Highnesses concerning the lands of India and a prince who is called the Great Khan—which means in Spanish "King of Kings"—and of his and his ancestors' frequent and vain applications to Rome for men learned in the holy faith who should instruct them in it, your Highnesses decided to send me, Christopher Columbus, to see these parts of India and the princes and peoples of those lands and consider the best means for their conversion.

Yet even the three ships—*La Niña*, *La Pinta*, and the flagship *Santa María*, names that every American schoolchild must memorize—which Columbus believed would enable him to defeat Islam owed a debt to the enemy. Spanish and Portuguese shipbuilders took a navigational leap forward at the end of the fifteenth century by borrowing a technology from their Muslim rivals: the lateen sail, a triangular sail joined at 45 degrees to a ship's mast. Combining lateen sails with traditional European square rigs offered advantages of speed and maneuverability without sacrificing the stability of the square sail. The result was large ships that performed like smaller vessels. The "combined rig made possible a change in the nature of exploring voyages," quickly becoming the preferred means for crossing the Atlantic. In maritime historian J. H. Parry's words, "the Arabs were their teachers."

On these ships—on all four of his New World journeys, in fact—Columbus took with him speakers of several Middle Eastern languages, planning to use these men, some of whom were themselves converts to Christianity, to communicate with the Eastern Nestorians—the Christians described by Marco Polo and others, who supposedly were interested in aligning with European Catholicism—as well as with the silk and spice merchants he expected to find. Between them, they spoke Arabic, Hebrew, Chaldean, and of course Spanish. Ironically, even as the Spanish Crown was expelling its Jews and Muslims and attempting to destroy the Muslim empires of the Mediterranean, the languages of those very civilizations were crucial to the Catholic plans of conquest.

As Columbus had learned from his experience on the West African coast, it was necessary first to sail south in order to sail west, so he plotted a course for the Canary Islands. When the three ships arrived in the islands about a week later, trouble arose—the *Pinta*'s rudder broke loose. Frustrated by this early stroke of bad luck, Columbus had no choice but to wait on Grand Canary while the ship was repaired, and load more provisions. He set sail again on September 8. Once the islands had faded from view some of the crew wept, fearful they would never again touch solid ground.

For the next thirty-four days, Columbus followed a remarkably true course westward. With calm seas, steady winds, and sunny skies—fortunate conditions, given that this was hurricane season—Columbus beamed with confidence. His men, though, grew more skeptical as the days passed. They seized on every speck of ocean debris as a sign of nearby land, then fell into deepening despair when no shoreline came into view. At one point in mid-Atlantic, mutiny nearly broke out, with the crew threatening to toss Columbus overboard if he did not turn the ships around. As if in some Stygian perpetuity, they seemed to be moving only toward more open sea. As late summer yielded to autumn, the men's emotions proved choppier than the ocean's waves. Finally, near dusk on October 11, reeds, birds, and what looked like hand-carved wood floated by the ships. When darkness fell, some of the men reported seeing a light blinking out in the blackness. No one slept that night. As day broke, Columbus and his men laid their eyes on land. They had, it seemed, finally arrived, but no one knew quite where.

From that day until his death in 1506, Columbus remained convinced that he had found a western route to Asia. His first thought was that the flat, tree-covered island he and his crew had reached was a speck of land off the coast of India—hence the importation of that term to describe the inhabitants of the New World. In Columbus's day, "India" denoted a vague, all-encompassing concept of the whole of Asia. Of course, they were not in India or anywhere near it, but in the Bahamas. Columbus named the island where he anchored his ships San Salvador; the people who lived there called it Guanahani.

As he and his men gratefully hopped ashore, it took several minutes for their sea legs to adjust to solid ground. Then, with the banners of Ferdinand and Isabella fluttering in the warm fall breezes of the sea that Columbus understood to be the western Pacific, "many people of the island came to them." San Salvador and other Caribbean islands belonged to the Taino people, and Columbus's first descriptions of them illustrate how he intepretated the New World through his experiences of the Old to make the Indies intelligible to his patrons. The Taino, he writes, were a friendly people, "the colour of Canary Islanders (neither black nor white)." As "naked as their mothers bore them," they carried no arms, painted themselves, and were of "fine limbs and good proportions." They generously offered the Europeans food, water, balls of cotton thread, and parrots. In exchange, Columbus's men gave them beads, baubles, and bits of colored glass—and, unwittingly, yet monstrously so, also passed on their pathogens. The Taino, Columbus thought, "would easily be made Christians," and the fact that some wore gold pieces in their noses suggested riches to come.

Wasting no time, Columbus boarded his ship after just two days on San Salvador to sail for the Asian mainland, which he understood to be close. He took along six evidently willing Tainos to serve as guides and interpreters. Following the chain of the Bahamas southward, he claimed the Crooked Islands for Spain. On shrubby Southern Crooked Island, which he christened La Isabella, Columbus was told about a great king "who wears much gold."

Were it not for the impending annihilation of millions of native people, the follies of this first encounter in the Americas would seem comical. Given the difficulties of communication between Columbus and the Taino, he did not understand, for example, whether the king was on this island, the putative mainland, or elsewhere—but as the islanders knew about him, Columbus figured, he could not be far away. When a search party failed to find him on La Isabella, Columbus leapt to the conclusion that he must therefore be on the mainland—the Asian mainland—and was surely the Grand Khan, the very object of his voyage. His excitement swelled as he imagined his first glimpse of the khan's majestic court. As he wrote in his logbook on October 21, 1492, for Isabella and Ferdinand to read later, his crew's next stop would be "another very large island that I believe must be Cipango [Japan] according to the indications that these Indians that I have give me, and which they call Colba [Cuba]. In it they say there are many and very large ships and many traders. And from this island . . . I have already decided to go to the mainland and to the city of Quinsay [Hangzhou, China] and to give Your Highnesses' letters to the Grand Khan."

On October 28, having traveled south, Columbus's ships landed on the northern coast of Cuba. Maybe, he now thought, this was not Japan; Cuba appeared far too vast to be an island. Most of the other islands he had visited—the Canaries, Madeira, Chios, the Bahamas—were rather small. Ireland and Iceland are islands, too, of course, but fantasy was quickly overtaking reality. Columbus decided he must be in China itself, perhaps only steps away from the grandeur of the Grand Khan's court. From the coast of Cuba, he sent two of his interpreters into the interior to find the route to the Grand Khan.

Rodrigo de Jerez and Luis de Torres (a Spanish Jewish convert to Christianity), together with two of the Tainos Columbus had brought from San Salvador, were gone for two days. They returned to the shore with reports of a village whose inhabitants were very friendly and had shared sweet potatoes, maize, and beans—all novel crops for the two Europeans. The villagers had also offered them tobacco, making Rodrigo and Luis the first nonindigenous people to smoke it. Having no interest in either maize or tobacco, Columbus bemoaned the fact that the men had failed to find the Grand Khan or even a trace of Nestorian Christianity. And the promise of a bounty of gold that had glistened so tantalizingly in the noses of the Taino on San Salvador remained elusive. Columbus decided to continue probing the coast, this time following it eastward toward a harbor that looked promising. Having reached the eastern tip of Cuba, he sailed over to a mountainous island in the distance. Reminded of the splendors of Castile, Columbus dubbed the island La Isla Española, "the Spanish Island"—or, in Latin, Hispaniola.

In early December, Columbus, his crew, and their Taino guides spent a few more weeks sailing eastward along the northern coast of Hispaniola, landing and going ashore whenever they could. But winter threatened, and Columbus decided to sail back to Spain before supplies ran too low. On Christmas Day of 1492, the *Santa María*, the largest ship in the fleet, came up short, her rudder stuck fast in a coral reef. Columbus tried to float the ship by cutting away her heavy mast and offloading as much cargo as possible, but it was useless. The current pushed her farther onto the reef, and her seams opened. Water rushed through the *Santa María*'s hull. She was gone.

The men moved quickly to transfer the ship's cargo to the other two vessels. As Columbus reported to his patrons, "Not even a shoe string was lost." Ever the believer, ever the conqueror, Columbus wrote, "Our Lord had caused the ship to run aground there so that he would found a settlement there." He and his men built a small camp from the *Santa María*'s salvageable timbers, overlooking the wreck. He named it La Navidad, to commemorate the day of the ship's disaster. Since the remaining two vessels could not accommodate all the sailors, Columbus was forced to leave thirty-nine men behind. He left them enough food and supplies for a year, but when he returned eleven months later, he found the camp burned and all the men dead.

On January 16, 1493, in the depth of winter, Columbus and his two rickety, leaky ships departed La Navidad, pushing off from Cape Cabrón in eastern Hispaniola to head home. Columbus and his men had found only a few specks of gold, certainly no Christians, and not a hint of a Grand Khan. Yet thoughts of India, Japan, and China still danced in his head. The Europeans' few months in the Caribbean had been an almost otherworldly experience of incomprehensibility, imbued with surreal visions for all involved—indigenous as well as European.

Information on those first days of contact—dissected endlessly and infused in subsequent centuries with racialized and colonial overtones of conquest and destiny—is mostly lost to us. Columbus's few logbook pages are all we have. While we cannot know the Taino perspective on those last few months of 1492, one can imagine the overwhelming, almost spectral strangeness of their first sighting of people so pale, dressed so peculiarly, sailing vessels and carrying standards they had never seen before. To say this was one of the oddest moments—never mind one of the most dangerous—in these people's lives clearly understates their experience; indeed, this first encounter defies description. What we can safely surmise is that both the Taino and the Spanish refracted their first meeting through their past experiences.

When Columbus, Cortés, and eventually thousands of other Europeans crossed the Atlantic, they did not forget the long centuries of civilizational conflict that had formed them as soldiers, Christians, and conquerors. Although this fact is ignored in most historical accounts, many of those who fought against indigenous peoples in the New World had battled Muslims in the Old World. With these experiences of war in the Mediterranean having embedded Islam in their minds as an ever-present threat, *enemy* to them nearly always equaled *Muslim*. Thus, as they increasingly came to regard the indigenous peoples of the Americas as enemies, they viewed them through their unique definition of *enemy*: Muslim. This was in some ways all they could do, given the conceptual pathways that had been forged in Europe's collective consciousness for nearly a thousand years.

The transatlantic passage was the easy part for Europeans. Infinitely more complex was the mental journey required to assimilate the New World into their understanding of the globe. Columbus was never able to do this. He died, in 1506, too soon to understand his mistake—or, alternatively, perhaps he was simply unwilling to admit that the land he had found was not Asia. It would take several more decades for the mental gulf between the Old and New Worlds—a chasm far wider than the Atlantic—to be traversed. To understand the full range of this, and especially of the central role of Old World conflicts as the primary means of assimilating the New World into the Old, we must leap in time somewhat beyond 1492 and examine subsequent Spanish explorations of other parts of the New World.

THE FIRST EUROPEAN ACCOUNT of Mexico demonstrates how the Spanish imported to the New World their knowledge and fear of Islam in order to understand the culture and politics of the indigenous peoples of the Americas. In February 1517, the conquistador Francisco Hernández de Córdoba lobbied Diego Velázquez de Cuéllar, the savage first Spanish governor of Cuba, to allow him to sail from the island in search of new territories and exploitable resources for the Spanish Crown. After some haggling over the terms of the expedition, Hernández de Córdoba received permission and set off from Havana on February 8 with three ships and a hundred men.

Hernández de Córdoba navigated his fleet westward along the relative safety of the northern coast of Cuba to the island's tip at Cabo de San Antonio before setting off into open sea. Aboard one of these vessels, Bernal Díaz del Castillo recorded what happened next, revealing the perilousness of the journey and the cluelessness of Hernández de Córdoba and his crew.

> [O]nce in the open sea, we steered at a venture towards the west, without knowledge of the depths or currents, or of the winds that prevail in those latitudes. So we were in great hazard of our lives when a storm struck us which lasted two days and two nights and had such force that we were nearly wrecked. When the weather moderated we resumed our course, and twenty-one days after leaving port to our great joy we sighted land, for which we gave thanks to God. This land was as yet undiscovered, and we had received no report of it. From the ships we could see a large town, which appeared to lie six miles back from the coast, and as we had never seen one as large in Cuba or Hispaniola we named it the Great Cairo [*El Gran Cairo*].

Just as Columbus had initially assimilated Cuba as Japan and San Salvador as India, here the Maya city that would later be known as Cape Catoche, on the Yucatán peninsula, became Cairo. Egypt's most famous city was a touchstone, conjuring up in the Spanish imagination the image of a gargantuan metropolis of grandeur, threatening mystery, and bloodthirsty fantasy. Far more populous than any city in Europe, Cairo was the second largest city in the Mediterranean after Istanbul, and it had been the symbol of Muslim power for centuries before the conquest of Constantinople. Cairo had sent out ships to torment Spanish settlements in North Africa and on the Iberian peninsula. It had captured and imprisoned Christians and dispatched threatening missives to European capitals. Cairo controlled holy Jerusalem, and prevented Europeans from trading with India and China. Across the Atlantic, this center of enemy Muslim power in the Old World scripted the Spanish understanding of a vast Maya city. By 1517, Indians in the New World had become a new enemy for Spanish Catholics—effectively, the Muslims of the Caribbean.

Cairo, fatefully, mattered in another way in 1517. A few weeks after the Spanish christened Cape Catoche *El Gran Cairo*, Selim, as we will see, marched his Ottoman troops to conquer Mamluk Cairo.

In numerous other ways, the vocabulary of war with Islam became the language of Spanish conquest in the Americas. Columbus identified Taino weapons as *alfanjes*, a Spanish word derived from Arabic for a curved metal scimitar inscribed with Qur'anic verses. Despite the fact that Columbus himself observed that the Taino "have no iron," and of course knew nothing of the Qur'an, he likened them to Muslim soldiers by putting *alfanjes* in their hands. Later, when Columbus first saw the scarves of a group of indigenous women, he compared them to *almaizares*, Moorish sashes, citing them as evidence of some sort of contact between this part of "Asia" and Spain. A few decades later, Hernán Cortés wrote that the Aztecs wore "Moorish robes" and that Aztec women resembled "Moorish women." On Bonacca Island near the Honduran coast, the Spanish noticed that, "like the Moors, the women covered their faces."

Cortés was, like Columbus, a veteran of Spain's *Reconquista*. His encounter with the Aztecs proved especially fertile for comparisons with the Islamic civilizations the Spanish had fought in the Old World. In the Aztecs, Cortés and his men met a formidably complex empire with cities larger than any in Spain, a highly sophisticated political culture, and imposing armies. More than, for example, the Taino, the

Spanish recognized the Aztecs as a rival civilization akin to the Muslim empires of the Old World—"a familiar barbarian empire," in one historian's words. Cortés wrote in his diary that he saw more than four hundred mosques (*mezquitas*) in what is today Mexico. He called Montezuma a sultan, and described the ruler's palaces in terms that strikingly evoke Granada's Muslim palaces, even claiming to see styles of floor and roof tiles that only existed in Granada at the time. In the words of J. H. Elliott, one of the foremost scholars of Cortés, "Since the only political model for his conquest Cortés knew was the Reconquest, Moctezoma had to be treated in his narrative as a Muslim ruler would have been. Anahuac [meaning here the valley of Mexico at the core of the Aztec Empire] is thus described, as far as Cortés is able, in images more appropriate to Assyria or Persia or, closer to home, the Nasrid Kingdom of Granada, than to any possible Amerindian society."

Such cultural filtering of the New World through the Old would continue long after Columbus and Cortés. Over the course of the sixteenth century and beyond, this prism refracted what Europe encountered in the Americas. Thus, when the Spanish tried to subdue and Christianize Mexico's nomadic Chichimecs, they habitually referred to them as *alarabs*, "the Arabs." In Brazil, the children of Portuguese men and Indian women were called *mamelucos*, Mamluks. Plains Indians captured and transported by the Spanish to New Mexico as slaves came to be known as *genízaros*, a corruption of the Turkish word for janissary (*yeniçeri*). The famed adobe bricks of Spanish Mexico used a technology first developed by the Muslims of Spain, and the word *adobe* is itself an adaptation of the Arabic word for brick, *al-tub*. As these examples show, even as the Spaniards fled the Mediterranean to escape Islam, they had been so forged by the struggle with their Old World enemy that they could not get away from it in the New World. In fact, they unwittingly, and against their own interests, carried Islam with them to the Americas.

Particularly worrisome for the Spanish was, perhaps oddly, native dancing, which they identified as a key piece of cultural evidence for the link between Islam and the indigenous peoples of the Americas. Spanish observers of Aztec dancing wrote that it was derived from "the zambra of the Moors." In Spain, the *zambra* was associated with the Moriscos, Muslim converts to Christianity often suspected of harboring secret Muslim beliefs and plotting against Catholics—the most bloodthirsty of wolves in sheep's clothing. Having been baptized, Moriscos possessed all the rights of Christians; they could marry Christians, receive Communion, and participate in church life. But if they were Muslims masquerading as Christians, their actions threatened not only the Christian soul but also the Spanish body politic. The Spanish monarchs feared the Moriscos as a fifth column for the Ottomans, and the Inquisition tried hundreds of them, attempting to prove that they remained Muslim in their souls. As part of the attempt to snuff out any notion of a unique Morisco identity, as well as to assert that their practices remained tainted by Islam, the *zambra* was banned on the grounds that it was heretical. Thus, using the word to describe Aztec dancing linked indigenous Americans to Moriscos as elements of the global Islamic peril.

This imagined Muslim–Aztec link was expressed in other ways as well. In the summer of 1573, for example, an indigenous merchant in Mexico named Pero Ximénez reported spotting off the Pacific coast "ships that were said to be of Turks or Moors." A few weeks later, another indigenous Mexican reported seeing in the plaza of the town of Purificación "seven vassals of the Great Turk, all men of the sea, the spies of the princes." These reports were extremely worrisome for the Spanish administration, especially since these Muslim "spies" were seen off the western coast of Mexico, in what we now know to be the Pacific Ocean. Were the Ottomans about to invade New Spain from the far side? The Spanish had sailed west to escape the Ottomans and Islam in the Mediterranean. If the Ottomans were now about to land on the western coast of the Americas, clearly all was lost. Spanish officials immediately set out to investigate. "García [the Crown's agent] noted that the ships had been reported only by indigenous peoples living in the coastal towns whom Spanish authorities considered to be less reliable witnesses than Spaniards." Alarmingly, he added that these "less reliable" indigenous people were preparing to enter into an alliance with the "Turks or Moors" against the Spanish.

Were Indians and Ottomans now in cahoots against Spain in Mexico? Had Spain's historic nemesis outflanked them, to navigate up and down the Pacific coast? How had Islam reached so far? Were the Spanish perhaps close to Asia after all—but an Asia which the Ottomans had already conquered? In their paranoid imagination, Old World animosities and Old World threats had reached the New World and, in fact, surrounded it. Spain's *Reconquista* would thus have to continue its march in the Americas.

⁂

"THE CONQUEST OF THE Indians began," wrote one of the earliest sixteenth-century Spanish historians of the Americas, "after that of the Moors was completed, so that Spaniards would ever fight the infidels." From Old World to New, Ottoman to Taino, Muslim to Indian, *Reconquista* to *Conquista*, Spain conceived of itself as engaged in a perpetual Crusade against non-Christians. In the Spanish apocalyptic mindset, Islam had somehow penetrated every realm of human habitation. Europeans' ventures in the Americas "began as a kind of proxy war," in one scholar's rendition, "against the Islamic ghosts that still haunted their imaginations" after Granada. Thus, while the name *El Gran Cairo* did not stick as a place name in Mexico, Matamoros did.

Santiago Matamoros, St. James the Moor-slayer, was said to have descended from heaven on a white horse in the year 822 to save the armies of the king of Aragon from a far larger and more powerful force of Muslim invaders. St. James was often invoked in subsequent battles between Spanish Catholics and Muslims, and depicted on his white horse, brandishing a sword, in paintings commemorating these battles. He thus became the patron saint of Spain's wars with Islam, the patron saint of Moor-slaying. When the Catholic war against Islam crossed the ocean, it was only natural that Santiago would go with it.

In 1535, during the Spanish invasion of what is today the city of Cuzco in Peru, Santiago was said to have appeared when a Spanish garrison was surrounded by Andean Indians attempting to push the Spanish out of their territory. With their patron saint's help, the soldiers turned what surely would have been a bloodbath into a slaughter of the Indians. Santiago then became the patron saint of Cuzco, where large paintings of him were hung in the town's cathedral. In a telling reimagination, though, his sobriquet was changed from *Matamoros* to the more appropriate *Mataindios* (Indian-slayer). Santiago Matamoros was thus imported from Europe to Peru and recast to fight against Spain's new enemies. Interestingly, during a nineteenth-

*Santiago Matamoros, the patron saint of Moor-slaying*

century revolt against Spanish colonial rule, recently Christianized Indians in Peru reimagined Santiago as their patron, too, invoking his help as *Mataespañois*—the Spaniard-slayer. Such rhetorical inversions serve as telling markers of the durable influence of anti-Muslim Crusade in the Americas.

CHAPTER

9

# CHRISTIAN JIHAD

*Catholic torture of Native Americans*

SPECTACULAR OCEAN CROSSINGS AND SHIPWRECKS, SIGHTINGS OF massive New World cities, and dreams of grand transcontinental alliances soon yielded to a more mundane, but far more crucial aspect of early modern imperial expansion. Whether in Asia or the Caribbean, Trabzon or Hispaniola, all successful imperial conquests necessitated the administrative integration of the newly acquired territories. This was as true for the Spanish as it was for the Ottomans. Thus, Selim in eastern Anatolia and Columbus and Cortés in the Caribbean participated in a common venture in the years around 1500—attempting to bring new territories more securely under their empire's rule, co-opting conquered populations, and generating revenue.

An empire was, above all, the land it held. Columbus therefore devoted himself to the administration of land for the Spanish Crown—claiming it, registering it, surveying it, cultivating it, all ultimately to gain profit from it. He wrote to Isabella and Ferdinand, "No prince of Castile is to be found . . . who has ever gained more land outside of Spain, and Your Highnesses have these vast lands, which are an Other World where Christianity will have so much enjoyment and our faith so great an increase." To make such "vast lands" productive, the Spanish exported to the Americas a system of land tenure they had first developed in territories conquered from Muslim empires in the south of Iberia, known as the *encomienda*. As in the Ottoman system, plots were granted to soldiers and other settlers to cultivate; they did not actually own the land, but held the right to profit from its produce. Since the Spanish lacked the manpower to properly cultivate these *encomiendas*, they forced America's natives to provide labor, which was considered their "tax payment" to the Spanish Crown, and were under legal order to ensure that these subjugated laborers lived "like Christians." In certain gold-rich areas, such as Haina in Cuba, Columbus also demanded that the local people pay him tribute in gold. Soon, colonists were sending back to Spain gold, foodstuffs, timber, spices, cotton, and slaves. As the Ottomans did, the Spanish quickly converted territorial conquest to great profit.

Given the obvious vast potential of land in the Americas and the lack of previous Crown administration there, colonists, bureaucrats, and soldiers, along with all sorts of parvenus and treasure seekers, took advantage of the relative chaos of the first few decades of Spanish rule. The transition from being a maritime adventurer in pursuit of wealth and glory to being an agricultural colonial charged with crop rotation and roof thatching was a daunting one for many of the men who joined Columbus on his four voyages. In an unfamiliar locale, often in stifling heat, with insufficient food and rampant disease, many settlers succumbed. Only the lucky few, like Columbus, managed to sail back to Spain.

Once word reached Spain of the perils of life in the New World, fewer and fewer settlers crossed the Atlantic. Even though most Indians rejected amicable relations with the Spanish, a smaller number did cooperate, and soon learned how to use their labor as a weapon. In the end, the Spanish, quite clearly, needed the Indians more than the Indians needed the Spanish. Almost all of the settlers were men, and when their camps disbanded, which they often did because of disagreements or power struggles, some of them moved into Indian communities. To gain acceptance, these men quickly had to forgo the violence and greed, rape and destruction that dominated European life in the Caribbean in these early years. Relationships with indigenous communities throughout the Caribbean and Mexico were thus the key to Spanish survival and success. From these cominglings of people from entirely different worlds, a new, uniquely American culture would emerge.

AS AN ADMINISTRATOR, Columbus was largely a failure. He cared little for bureaucracy or turning a profit for the Crown. Desperate to rid himself of mundane responsibilities in order to concentrate on reaching the court of the Grand Khan and finding the gold that would fund the conquest of Jerusalem, he lobbied Ferdinand and Isabella to send judges to administer the new colonies and priests to convert the natives. So focused was he on his greater mission that he even forced all of the men who sailed with him on his four voyages to sign statements that they believed Cuba to be mainland Asia, and continued to bring interpreters whom he hoped would help him communicate with the Grand Khan and the Nestorians. He would spend his final years compiling a book of prophecies about a Spanish messianic figure who would lead the conversion of the world to Christianity. A far cry from land tenure and agricultural labor—or even the search for new trade routes to reach the riches of the East—imperial conquest and Armageddon are what consumed Columbus.

Columbus's administrative incompetence cost him whatever loyalty and respect he may once have enjoyed among the Spanish settlers. In part, this was because he had no royal rank or office that demanded deference. Complaints about his ineptitude made their way back to Spain, forcing him to spend valuable time defending himself. As he wrote to Isabella and Ferdinand about one accusation:

[It] was brought out of malice on the basis of charges made by
civilians who had revolted and wished to take possession of the
land. . . . In this endeavor I have lost my youth, my proper share
in things, and my honor. . . . I was judged as a governor who had
been sent to take charge of a well-regulated city or town under
the dominion of well-established laws, where there was no danger of everything turning to disorder and ruin; but I ought to
be judged as a captain sent to the Indies to conquer a numerous
and warlike people of manners and religion very different from
ours, living not in regular towns but in forests and mountains.

Columbus saw himself as a sailor, conquistador, and explorer, not as a
fastidiously tax-collecting, people-managing bureaucrat. He excelled
in the imagination of conquest, but he failed at the realities of its consequences. He was, essentially, nothing more than a driven, rogue
explorer.

Crippled by arthritis and denied the grants and privileges he had
previously enjoyed, Columbus died on May 20, 1506, in Valladolid,
Spain, surrounded by his family and shipmates. In his last years, he
lobbied the Spanish Crown for the profits from land in the Caribbean
he thought were his due as stipulated in various agreements, but given
his failings in the minutiae of governance, and the by now clear sense
of just how lucrative these Indies (whether they were East or West)
could be, the Spanish sovereigns refused to give him anything. This
did not make him destitute, in the end, but it did make him angry.
His will instructed that all his documents—including his unfinished
book prophesying the apocalypse—be sent to his family in Genoa, and
that his son Diego ensure that Mass was said for the souls of his father,
mother, and wife. Filipa had preceded her husband in death by at least
two decades; his testament is one of only two mentions Columbus ever
made of her.

AFTER COLUMBUS'S DEATH, THE Spanish realized that their possessions
in the Americas needed a legal basis beyond the personality of any single administrator. In 1513, the Crown promulgated a document known
as the Requirement (*Requerimiento*), which became the central assertion

of Spain's legal dominion over the peoples of the New World. As a writ
of conquest, the Requirement was nothing less than a doctrinal man-
ifesto announcing a Spanish Catholic *jihad* on American Indians. The
inherently Islamic features of Columbus's anti-Islamic mission were
unacknowledged, even suppressed, by nearly all his contemporaries;
subsequent historians have largely maintained this silence. The imposition of the Requirement in the New World, however, unquestionably
proves that Islam continued to shape Catholic Spain, even after its supposed defeat in Iberia, and, still more important for our purposes, that
it also shaped Catholic Spain's forays across the Atlantic.

The conquistadors, typically unaware of the motive, were legally
obliged to recite the Requirement's precepts aloud at the outset of each
new conquest. For the native peoples of the Americas, witnessing such
a puzzling performance paled in comparison to the violence it portended. The Requirement became a ritualized part of Spanish warfare,
an unsheathing of the sword before it was plunged into flesh. Its words
remain central to our understanding of the age.

It opened by proclaiming Christianity as God's one true faith. "God
our Lord one and eternal created heaven and earth . . . God our Lord
gave charge [of all peoples] to one man named Saint Peter, so that he
was lord and superior of all the men of the world . . . and gave him
all the world for his lordship and jurisdiction (*señorio y jurisdicción*)."
It then acknowledged all those who had already chosen, rightly, to
accept God's message. "Almost all who have been notified [of this] have
received His Majesty and obeyed and served him, and serve him as subjects . . . and turned Christian without reward or stipulation . . . and
His Majesty received them . . . as . . . subjects and vassals."

From here, the Requirement pivots to its central threatening
summons:

> Therefore I beg and require you as best I can . . . [that] you rec-
> ognize the church as lord and superior of the universal world,
> and the most elevated Pope . . . in its name, and His Majesty in
> his place as superior and lord and king . . . and consent that these
> religious fathers declare and preach . . . and His Majesty and I in
> his name will receive you . . . and will leave your women and
> children free, without servitude so that with them and with

yourselves you can freely do what you wish . . . and we will not compel you to turn Christians.

It then states directly that the choice before the peoples of the Americas was either Christianity or suffering:

> But if you do not do it . . . with the help of God, I will enter forcefully against you, and I will make war everywhere and however I can, and I will subject you to the yoke and obedience of the Church and His Majesty, and I will take your wives and children, and I will make them slaves . . . and I will take your goods, and I will do to you all the evil and damages that a lord may do to vassals who do not obey or receive him.

In a final affront, the Requirement blamed native peoples for any hardship that might befall them. "And I solemnly declare that the deaths and damages received from such will be your fault and not that of His Majesty, nor mine, nor of the gentlemen who came with me."

The tableau is ghastly to envision: bearded sailors about to make landfall screaming these Spanish imprecations from their ships to people who had no idea who these white men were or what they were shouting about. These indigenous Americans were *required* to acknowledge that the Catholic Church was the universal power of the world and that, by extension, their own belief system and culture were inferior if not infinitely wrong. They were granted the "freedom" to choose not to convert, at horrendous cost, though even this choice was eventually taken from them as the years wore on. What the conquistadors ultimately sought was an acknowledgment of the superiority of their religion. As long as this was recognized, native peoples could maintain their traditional beliefs and practices. Failure to acknowledge Christianity's perfection and authority, however, ensured death and slavery. For the indigenous people of the Americas, the equation was simple: whether they converted or not, they had to accept the superiority of Christianity or seal their own death warrant.

Warfare is always an arena of both belligerency and exchange. The Requirement's "unique ritual demand for submission," as opposed to conversion, derived directly from Spain's historical experience with the Muslim practice of *jihad*. Despite modern-day distortions, *jihad* does not always, or even usually, have a military connotation. Its most general meaning is to struggle, to accept the summons to follow the path designated by God. Most commonly, this meant to endeavor to become a better person, a better servant of God—to strive toward the advancement of one's personal faith, moral character, and religious practice. On occasion, when *jihad* did refer to taking up arms against an enemy, strict rules defined the combat. The first step of any *jihad* was to invite a non-Muslim enemy to convert to Islam, an act that, if performed, would eliminate the need for war. This invitation, which always occurred on the cusp of a potential war, was not only a way to avoid costly bloodshed but also a means of winning acknowledgment of Islam's superiority.

The summons in the Requirement was nearly identical in intent; Catholicism took the idea from Islam. In both the Catholic Requirement and Islamic *jihad*, "refusal to acknowledge religious superiority was the moment of truth, for in both cases rejection justified war." Again tracking Islamic beliefs, Catholicism's *jihad* against native peoples assigned the responsibility for the unbeliever's death solely to that individual. The Requirement was effectively *jihad* in Christian garb.

"No other European state," in the words of historian Patricia Seed, "created a fully ritualized protocol for declaring war against indigenous peoples." Other European powers found the Spanish Requirement odd, if not barbaric; British, French, and Dutch officials criticized and mocked it as a recognition of and concession to Islam, their collective enemy. It was, as we have seen, a direct descendant of a culture that had dominated Spain for centuries, and it was thoroughly alien to the rest of Europe, where Islam had never ruled.

There were Spaniards, too, who disapproved of the Requirement. The most famous dissenter was Bartolomé de Las Casas, a Dominican friar who served as the first Bishop of Chiapas and is often memorialized as the "Protector of the Indians." Las Casas eventually came to recognize that the atrocities Europeans were committing against indigenous Americans were indefensible. Unfortunately, his solution for overcoming this barbarity was no less barbaric—to ship African slaves to the New World instead of enslaving the natives. He wrote scathingly of the Requirement, considering the document vile. What would happen, he asked, if "Moors or Turks came to make the same requirement?" With this rhetorical question, he obviously meant to poke fun at the Requirement's manifest Islamic origins. "Did the Spaniards show superior proof by witnesses and truer evidence of what they declared in their requirement . . . than the Moors showed of their Muhammed?" Criticizing the Requirement and the entire project of Spanish conquest in the Americas it supported, he wrote that it was inspired by "the Mohammedan procedures that our Spanish people have had since [Muslims] entered these lands." He added, "Those who war on [indigenous American] infidels mimic Muhammad." He also noted that the Requirement mentioned neither the Trinity—for Muslims, evidence of Christianity's polytheism—nor Christ himself, both clear indications that the document was not born of the one true faith. For Las Casas to point to the Islamic origins of Spain's statement of its political and legal authority in the New World was to challenge that authority's legitimacy. As Spain's most vocal advocate for the Indies and its peoples, Las Casas aimed to strike at the very heart of Spain's violent overseas colonial project with his critique of the Requirement, while also cursing "Turks and Moors" as "the veritable barbarian outcasts of the nations." Because all Spanish Catholics agreed that Islam was an abomination, Las Casas believed that if the Requirement's connection to Islam was clarified, his fellow Spaniards would abandon it, along perhaps with the whole project of colonial empire. He was wrong.

JUST AS ISLAM INFLUENCED Spanish warfare in the Americas, it also affected the administrative structures of Spain's New World empire. In the fifteenth and sixteenth centuries, the Spanish faced a more extreme version of an earlier challenge: how, as Christian rulers, to govern a vast population of non-Christians—this time, on the far side of an ocean.

The sacking in 1085 of the picturesque city of Toledo, just south of Madrid, was the first major victory of the *Reconquista*. When the triumphant King Alfonso VI, a shrewd prince who had come to power through an Ottoman-like outmaneuvering of his older brother, began to grapple with the problem of ruling this majority-Muslim city, he sought the advice of Siznado David, a Portuguese Muslim convert to Christianity. David suggested that he follow the lead of the city's previous Muslim sovereigns, who, when they took control in 1035, imposed on the then majority-Christian population a head tax, known as the *jizya*, in return for protection. Recognizing the value of this advice, Alfonso adopted this and many other Muslim practices. Certainly no crypto-Muslim—in truth, he reviled Islam—Alfonso nevertheless saw that his religious enemy's governing strategies had proven their effectiveness. Moreover, maintaining them would ensure the least disruptive transition of power. Indeed, following the numerous waves of the *Reconquista*, Christian rulers often maintained the practices—from taxation schemes to market regulations to administrative assignments to modes of warfare—of the Muslim regimes they had just unseated.

Nearly all Muslim polities had assigned Jews, Christians, and other non-Muslims to the category of *dhimmi*. *Dhimmi*s were offered specific rights in exchange for certain obligations, the major one being the payment of the *jizya*. This was a personal tax, not a tax on property or commerce—a tax for simply being a non-Muslim in a Muslim state. Unquestionably, it represented a humiliating subjugation. Still, it enshrined a pact between the non-Muslim taxpayer and the Muslim sovereign: in exchange for payment of the *jizya*, the sovereign was obliged to protect *dhimmi* rights to freedom of worship and the open exercise of each community's religious laws. In stark contrast to Spain's bloody Inquisition, Muslim policies allowed non-Muslims to practice their religion without fear of death.

As occurred after the conquest of Toledo, Spain's Christian rulers sometimes instituted a variation of the *jizya* over the non-Christians they conquered, termed the *tributo* (tribute). The *tributo* was put into effect almost exclusively in cities and towns where the majority of the population was non-Christian and hence needed to be convinced to accept Spanish Christian rule. In locales with Christian majorities, the conquerors imposed the harsher policies of the Inquisition.

The Requirement took the *jizya*-inspired *tributo* to the New World. Like the Islamic tax, the Spanish version was a mark of vassalage. America's native peoples had to pay simply for existing as non-Christians in a Christian state. In assessing the Spanish colonial transfer of this Muslim practice to the New World, Seed writes that the "indigenous peoples of the Americas became New World dhimmīs." As with those subjected to the *jizya* and *tributo* in Spain itself, American Indians, in exchange for payment of this tax, were allowed to maintain the autonomy of their communities, to practice their beliefs, and to govern themselves according to their own rites and laws—that is, once they had acknowledged the superiority of the Christian faith. Given the haphazard nature of Spanish administration in the first few decades of colonization, however, the guarantee of these rights was often an unmet ideal.

AS THEY HAD DONE since 1453, Spain and the Ottoman Empire continued after 1492 to battle over the legacy of the Roman Empire, long understood as the Old World's paradigmatic political entity. An empire was not simply a succession of systems of rule on the ground but also an ideal, a set of universal governing principles put into practice. The Romans had, it was thought, perfected this seamless melding of real-world action and political theory, and so both the Ottomans and the Spanish (as well as others) sought to claim the Roman legacy for themselves. Asserting their descent from this universalistic tradition, both empires hoped to don the Romans' mantle—territorially, ideologically, administratively. Continuity with the Roman past bolstered the legitimacy and authority needed to govern in the early modern present.

Thus, the Ottomans would regularly refer to themselves as *Rum*, Turkish for "the Romans," and, by the end of Selim's reign, their empire would come the closest in world history to holding all the territory the Romans had once controlled. Not for nothing have the Ottomans been described as "the Romans of the Muslim world." The Spanish, too, often compared themselves to the Romans, especially during the reign of Charles V. In 1519, Charles joined the Spanish Empire to what remained of the Holy Roman Empire, politically unifying Europe as had not been done since Charlemagne, but still falling far short of the territorial breadth of the Roman Empire. Nevertheless, even as far away as Mexico, a resurgent Spain asserted its Roman heritage. Aiming to capture the maize-rich ancient city of Tlaxcala in the 1519 Battle of Otumba, Cortés inspired his troops by saying, "As for your observation, gentlemen, that the most famous Roman captains never performed deeds equal to ours, you are quite right. If God helps us, far more will be said in future history books about our exploits than has ever been said about those of the past." The complicated intertwining of the Romans, the Ottomans, and the Spanish grew ever more complex in the New World.

By adding some Christian elements to an embellished Aztec legend, Cortés claimed that the Aztec emperor Montezuma—described by the expedition's chronicler Bernal Díaz del Castillo as "of good height, well proportioned, spare and slight, and not very dark"—"donated" his empire to Charles V because the Aztecs believed Cortés to be the prophesied "Great Lord" who would one day come from the east. This invented "donation" deliberately echoed another fictitious Old World tale the Spanish used to justify their politics, both past and present: the Donation of Constantine. As the story goes, Constantine the Great, the first Roman emperor to convert to Christianity, in 330 transferred his capital to a new city, which he named Constantinople, thereby purposefully leaving—"donating"—Italy and the rest of western Europe to the pope and his successors. Charles V stood then as the rightful heir of both Constantine and Montezuma, a descendant of the Roman legacy and the custodian of New World imperial power. By logical extension, anyone in the Ottoman and Aztec empires who resisted Spanish rule prevented Charles V from fully possessing what was rightfully given to him as "monarch of the universe." As with the expansion of the Crusades to the New World, the competition between the Spanish and the Ottomans to be the early modern world's new Roman Empire crossed the Atlantic too.

BETWEEN 1492 AND COLUMBUS's death in 1506, both he and Selim served on their empires' frontiers. Comparing Hispaniola and Trabzon, two regions not often considered together, illuminates some of the key differences in the governing philosophy of these early modern states. Populations of indigenous Americans who were not obliterated by European diseases fell instead to the sword of Christianity, as instructed by the Requirement. The decimation perpetrated by Spanish rule in the Americas resulted both from the initial ethos of Crusade that sent Columbus west and a political ideology that demanded the submission of conquered peoples.

Selim was not the buccaneer Columbus was. He imposed Ottoman sovereignty not by erasing what existed before conquest, but rather by co-opting often hostile subjects and reshaping existing institutions along Ottoman lines. Surrounded his whole life by imperial administration, he was through learning and experience a bureaucrat. With an understanding of the reciprocity of rule embedded in the Circle of Justice, and having been informed by his mother's far-sighted strategizing, he understood how to navigate the choppy social and political waters around him. In many ways, his success was a matter of class and upbringing as much as temperament and interest. Above all, sage governance and provident strategy drove Selim, rather than an apocalyptic imagination or dreams of gold and unconverted souls in far-off lands.

# THE TAINO–MUSLIMS
# OF HISPANIOLA

*A native dance for courage on Hispaniola*

SLAVERY, UNWITTINGLY, HASTENED THE INTRODUCTION OF ISLAM in the New World. With conquest had come land, and this land clearly needed labor to make it productive. Given massive native resistance and the increasing ravages of disease, Spain's rulers quickly understood that they faced a labor deficit. The importation of West African slaves to the New World offered a solution—one derived not from the compassion for native oppression expressed by the likes of Bartolomé de Las Casas, but rather from economic exigency and European self-interest.

Slavery was ubiquitous in the Old World, shared alike across the centuries by large and small states in Europe, Africa, the Middle East, and throughout Asia. In the Mediterranean, Muslim slavery differed from Christian slavery in several significant respects. In Islam, slavery was temporary, not hereditary, and it did not necessarily sever ties between slaves and their own families. Most often, slaves in the Muslim world performed domestic functions rather than brute labor in agriculture, mining, transport, and the like. Fundamental to understanding slavery in the Ottoman Empire, and indeed throughout Muslim history, is the insight that in fact it served as a conduit for upward social mobility. The Janissary Corps—the empire's most prestigious military cadre—was comprised of men who had begun their lives as Christians, mostly in Balkan villages. For these men, as wrenching as their early loss of freedom was, forgetting one's origins offered a new kind of freedom—freedom from the pain of losing one's family and homeland, freedom to focus on the prospects of their current station. Slavery, as we have seen, was even a feature of the imperial family. Every sultan's mother was technically a slave, having been captured during battle, given over by her family, or acquired through the slave trade. Yet, in spite of this status, these women—think of Gülbahar— operated at the very highest levels of government, often wielding more power than their sons and sometimes even more than their owners, the sultans themselves. Despite the obvious coercion, Ottoman slavery ultimately functioned in an integrative fashion. In fact, it was far easier for a converted Christian slave born in the Balkans to become a member of the Ottoman elite than it was for a freeborn Muslim from Anatolia to do so.

European slavery was vastly different. Christians regularly captured non-Christians (most often Muslims) in war and held them as slaves—the trade in African slaves, too, had been flourishing for decades before it expanded across the Atlantic—but these human possessions were seldom integrated into their captors' society. Most often they lived out their days performing hard labor in mines, the lower decks of galleys, or other grim surroundings. Indeed, Spain frequently fought its Muslim enemies at sea with Muslim slaves in the bellies of its ships pulling the oars. In Europe, slavery was hereditary, and even though captives or their families technically were allowed to purchase freedom (a process known as redemption), most could not meet the prohibitively high cost.

Through war, piracy, and the slave trade, thousands of Muslims reached Europe as slaves. In the sun-drenched Italian coastal city of Livorno, for example, at almost the exact moment when Spain gave its final order to expel Iberian Muslims in 1614, one out of every twelve persons was an enslaved Muslim (there were also non-Muslim slaves). The situations in other large European cities were similar. As the Ottomans did with their Christian slaves, the Europeans forcibly converted the Muslims and other non-Christians they transported to their slave markets, but their conversion was in many cases questionable, if not wholly fictitious. Thus, even as Spain expelled its freeborn Muslims, it replaced them with increasing numbers of Muslim slaves, mostly from North and West Africa. Because of slavery, Muslims—albeit in far different circumstances—retained a place in the heart of Christendom.

AMONG WEST AFRICA'S LARGEST Muslim populations were the Wolof people. The first contact between the Wolof and the Portuguese occurred in 1446, when Nuno Tristão, one of Henry the Navigator's mariners, sailed inland along the lush banks of the muddy Gambia River. He and most of his crew were killed on this expedition. Several years later, in 1452, Europe secured papal sanction for the enslavement of West Africans with the bull *Dum Diversas* that Henry received from Pope Nicholas V.

A fierce zeal to fight the Moors and extend Christianity's global Crusade spurred the expeditions of Henry and his men. These forays were organized mostly from the largest of the Cape Verde islands, Santiago—tellingly, named for the patron saint of Moor-slayers. A little more than four hundred miles due west of Dakar in present-day Senegal, the rocky island was settled by the Portuguese in 1462. Safely offshore yet within easy striking distance of Senegambia—the region of West Africa between the Senegal and Gambia rivers—Santiago proved the perfect perch from which to raid and trade along the African coast. Indeed, a robust commerce soon emerged, in which Portuguese iron, weaponry, and finished goods were exchanged for African slaves. When the Spanish entered the West African slave trade a few years later, hoping to displace the Portuguese, they came to rely on the routes and contacts established by their Iberian rivals.

The first African slaves arrived in Iberia almost immediately after the papal bull of 1452, and their numbers quickly ballooned. In fact, the slave trade was a crucial element of early modern European society and the continent's economy. Between 1489 and 1497, for example, Spanish traders sold 2,003 West Africans in Valencia, one of the largest slave markets in Iberia and indeed in the entire Mediterranean. Valencians constituted about a third of Iberia's slave dealers in the fifteenth century, and the city's government imposed a hefty 20 percent tax on all sales of slaves. When the frightened Africans arrived in the harbor, haggard and disoriented, they were first allowed to rest—with Valencia's famous ramparts functioning as their prison walls—before being displayed for sale on its thoroughfares.

The majority of the slaves transported from West Africa in the late fifteenth century were Wolof Muslims. Buyers in Valencia and throughout Iberia paid the lowest prices for Wolofs, because they were perceived as requiring more training and acculturation than others. Black slaves who had lived in Christian or Muslim kingdoms in North Africa or the Iberian peninsula were more expensive, because they were seen as more knowledgeable about slave life in Spain than those arriving directly from West Africa. Adult males were usually more expensive than women and children, and those with particularly coveted skills drew higher prices.

During this period, the Wolof Empire split into smaller rival states that took up arms against one another. This internecine warfare provided an enormous boost to the slave trade. Most of the men captured during wars in West Africa became soldiers in the armies that captured them, but those deemed less useful were sold to the Portuguese to subsidize the ongoing conflicts. These human beings for sale included not only those eliminated from the soldiering ranks but also "criminals, witches, outcasts, and perhaps, enemies of the chief." West Africans thus used the slave trade, in part, to eliminate "undesirables" from their own societies.

Given their growing need for manpower across the Atlantic after 1492, the Spanish soon realized that the Wolof and other West African slaves arriving in Iberia constituted a ready labor pool. But having just defeated Iberia's last Muslim polity in Granada, they did not want to inadvertently take Islam to their colonies in the New World, so they were at first wary of dispatching West Africans, even those who had ostensibly converted to Christianity.

The Americas represented new territory, a tabula rasa that became a promised land of sorts, where Catholicism could be imposed completely, wholly free of Islam—very different from the situation that greeted Europeans in West Africa, where Islam was thriving even in regions where it was not the majority religion. Shock at the geographic spread and strength of Islam only compounded Catholic notions that Muslims were advancing all around them. The Spanish fantasy that Native Americans might somehow be linked to Muslims was a major reason for the European dread of importing Islam to the Americas through slavery.

The Spanish Crown expressly forbade the direct transshipment of slaves from Africa to the Americas as too risky, because government representatives could not directly verify that these Africans were not Muslims. Instead, it required that all West African slaves be first taken to Spain, where they would be baptized and monitored, in a kind of religious quarantine, for any lingering signs of Islam. These converted slaves were known in Spanish as *ladinos*. Only once they had been certified as Christian were they deemed safe to export to Spain's early Caribbean colonies. Spaniards carried the first *ladino* slaves to the New World in 1501.

With the devastation of Taino populations in the Caribbean, the Spanish need for massive numbers of slaves collided with the Crown's desire to keep Muslims out of the Americas. Many in Spain and its colonies advocated for direct shipments from Africa, causing no fewer than five decrees to be issued expressly banning such commerce. In the words of one of the decrees, "In a new land like this one where faith is only recently being sowed, it is necessary not to allow to spread there the sect of Mahomet or any other." But economic pressures soon forced the government to compromise. A major sticking point was the stipulation that Muslims could only become *ladinos* by living in Spain or one of its eastern Atlantic island possessions for two years in order to de-Islamize. This long wait proved a massive impediment to the operations of Hispaniola's plantation owners—even though colonists regularly complained that their *ladino* slaves still behaved like full-fledged Muslims. To satisfy demand, the Crown occasionally, and increasingly frequently, gave official sanction to individual direct transshipments of slaves from West Africa to the Caribbean. Thanks to both these royal decrees and the illegal trade, by 1513 most of Hispaniola's incoming slaves arrived directly from Africa. Thus, Spain initiated one of the most centrally formative, though never complete, geopolitical processes of the last millennium: the demographic replacement of indigenous Americans with Africans in the New World.

In so doing, it also exported the Old World's major civilizational battle across the Atlantic. Islam is not thought of as central to the history of the New World; however, the realities of slavery, which is obviously critical to any understanding of the history of the Western Hemisphere, cannot be separated from the conflict between Islam and Christianity. In fact, as we will see, Muslims led the first ever revolt against European slavery in the Americas.

BEGINNING WITH COLUMBUS AND continuing well into the 1500s, gold was the prime motivator for Spanish exploration throughout the lands bordering the Caribbean and provided the initial justification for slavery. In Hispaniola, the Spanish forced the Taino to mine as much of the island's modest deposits as they could. But when the first West African slaves reached the Caribbean in 1501, the Spanish learned that these captives were more productive than the Taino, since many had worked the mines of West Africa. Natives were assigned to the auxiliary tasks, such as sifting and hauling. Side by side, Africans (mostly Muslims) and Taino spent long hours under the boiling tropical sun, searching for glimmers of gold in the dark silt. In the crucible of this backbreaking coerced labor, the two communities quickly recognized a shared interest against their common Spanish enemy. As early as 1503, some Spaniards took notice of this budding alliance, fearful that their African slaves were teaching their Taino slaves what they termed "bad customs"—a standard Spanish euphemism for Islam.

Soon, sugar would replace gold as the primary economic engine of the Caribbean colonies. As with other Old World crops (and animals) taken to the Americas as part of what is now known as the Columbian Exchange, the history of sugar cultivation betrays a deep Islamic influence. The cane first arrived in Iberia and the rest of the Mediterranean via Central Asia and Mesopotamia, following the Islamic conquests. It reached Spain in the tenth century, when Spaniards—as they would later do with naval technology—adapted Muslim irrigation techniques and olive presses to construct their first rudimentary sugar mills. The Portuguese took sugar and its associated production processes to Madeira, the Azores, and the Canary Islands, along with a novel technology that Muslims had never used in their cultivation of sugar: slavery. Madeira would prove the most profitable of the eastern Atlantic sugar islands, serving as a kind of dress rehearsal for the slave economies of the Caribbean. The Portuguese clear-cut the island, established a monocropping culture of sugar, built plantations with their own and some Genoese investment capital, and created a slave society. Most of the slaves who worked in the cane fields of Madeira were Moroccans, Berbers, West Africans, and other Muslims. On his second westward voyage, in 1493, Columbus made scenic, mountainous Madeira his last stop before crossing the Atlantic, and it was then that he transported the first Muslim slaves and sugar cane to the New World—two imports which forever transformed the Americas and the world.

During the first years of sugar cultivation in the Caribbean, the Spanish used both native slave labor and some of the few African slaves they had at the time. Between 1492 and 1517, however, the Taino population of Hispaniola plummeted due to European diseases and the harsh conditions instituted by the Spanish. At the same time, the sugar plantations demanded more and more hands, especially in 1517, when Selim's conquests in the eastern Mediterranean would temporarily disrupt Egypt's sugar trade, thereby boosting the development of the Caribbean economy.

Sugar cane's heft and the crushing and pressing needed to extract its juices make it a labor-intensive crop. To undertake this grueling work, in their first quarter century in the New World, the Spanish progressively and soon insatiably replaced Caribbean natives with African slaves, mostly men but some women as well, making black Africans the majority of the population of Hispaniola. According to one Spanish writer on Hispaniola in the early sixteenth century, "There are so many [blacks] in this island because of the sugar mills that the land appears a copy or image of Ethiopia." Indeed, within a few years, the

*Caribbean sugar plantation*

Spanish represened a tiny minority, perhaps just a twentieth of the African population.

ON CHRISTMAS MORNING 1521, a group of twenty "bellicose and perverse" Muslim Wolof slaves on a sugar plantation in Hispaniola owned by Diego Columbus—the appointed Spanish governor of the island, and son of Christopher Columbus—rose before sunrise to put into motion a plan they had been hatching for weeks. They grabbed the machetes they used for clearing trees and brush and began a "wild and bloody expedition under dawn's early light," dismembering their blindsided white masters and slaughtering livestock throughout the settlement. The rebels torched the thatch-roofed houses and sugar cane fields of the estate—named La Isabella after the queen who had made it all possible—before fleeing to the mountains, where they met up with other Muslim Wolof slaves from nearby plantations who had waged coordinated insurrections. Neither the Spanish nor the Taino understood a word of Wolof, so the slaves enjoyed the advantage of secret communications while planning and executing their rebellion.

The day after Christmas, the rebels attacked the estate of Melchor de Castro, the Spanish royal notary of mines. Just one day into the rebellion, their ranks had already doubled to forty. They destroyed Castro's cattle ranch, seizing some of his animals as food. They killed a Spanish carpenter with his own tools and murdered a few other Spaniards as well. They grabbed all the provisions they could carry, then burned buildings and any remaining supplies. Most importantly, they also liberated thirteen of Castro's slaves—twelve Indians and one African. Thus, the group of rebel slaves now included both Wolof Muslims and Tainos, united in hatred of their Spanish masters.

On the third day, the group headed for the sugar plantation of the colonial judge Alonso de Zuazo, located about twenty miles from Santo

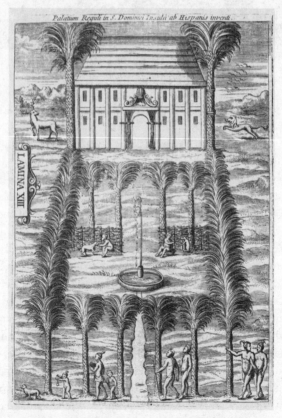

*Typical Spanish colonial estate in the Caribbean*

Domingo, the Spanish capital of Hispaniola. There they slaughtered eight to ten Spaniards and recruited to their cause another 120 African slaves, mostly Wolof. The rebels' plan seemed to be working perfectly. They had incited a wave of slave anger in the countryside and were now surging toward the ultimate prize, Santo Domingo. As if with the force of the hurricane that had destroyed many European structures on the island in 1502, the Wolof and Taino rebels sought to level the capital. As had occurred many times before on the other side of the ocean, a Muslim army—in this case, interspersed with Taino allies—marched to capture a Catholic Spanish city. If these Muslims had succeeded, the entire European venture in the New World would have been dealt a serious blow, perhaps even a mortal one, and the subsequent course of world history might have been very different.

Instead, Melchor de Castro, who had escaped his ransacked estate, along with a few other plantation owners who had heard about the revolt but had not been affected, raced ahead of the slaves on horseback to beat them to Santo Domingo. These colonists, many of whom were veterans of the battle for Granada, met with Diego Columbus to draft a plan to quell the rebellion. Twelve horsemen from a cattle ranch were dispatched to meet the oncoming rebels outside Santo Domingo. The horses—animals that had arrived in the New World with the Spanish—tipped the advantage, as they charged back and forth through the crowd of about two hundred slaves, who were weary from having been on the march for three days. Six slaves were killed in the charges, and dozens were wounded. A few Spaniards also died, and a Wolof machete nearly severed Melchor de Castro's right arm.

Spanish reinforcements from Santo Domingo streamed down the road behind the horsemen, chasing the slaves as they fled. Diego Columbus, determined to send a message to any other would-be rebels, ordered the ultimate punishment to be meted out; the roadside near the scene of the battle was said to be "planted with gallows and the hanged." The Spanish believed they had successfully projected their superior power. As one of them wrote, "The blacks were punished as befitted their daring and madness, and all the others were scared thereby and shown what would happen with them if such a thing crossed their minds." Of the nearly two hundred rebels, however, most successfully escaped the battle and subsequent reprisals by fleeing to the relative safety of the densely forested Bahoruco Mountains.

Thus, within just a few short decades after 1492, Muslims and Christians were slaughtering each other in the Caribbean, playing out a very old script that had been staged in the Old World countless times before.

⊠

AS THE SPANISH SUGAR economy progressively undercut the native elite of Hispaniola, creating a subject population of mostly African slave labor, the Taino intermediaries who had attempted to work with the Spanish invaders by providing them with food, support, and labor in return for some European wares and recognition of their authority were deemed dispensable. This Taino elite joined the community's common classes by turning on the Spanish as well, helping to organize pockets of rebellion in the mountains.

In 1519, just two years before the Wolof slave rebellion on Diego Columbus's plantation, a Taino leader dubbed Enriquillo by the Spanish led a series of raids. Born around 1500 into a prominent Taino clan, he and his family, like most of the native elite, had lost out in the island's changing demographics. From a line of caciques, or indigenous chiefs, he and his large extended family had lived for centuries in houses of straw and palm leaves at the center of several villages, the area reserved for a community's leadership. As a youngster, he was taken from his home to Hispaniola's newly established Franciscan monastery in Verapaz, where he was baptized and educated in Catholicism and Spanish culture. Following his schooling, he was assigned to work on an estate as the overseer of a group of Taino slaves—a position of relative distinction but still one of subjugation to Spanish authority. Here Enriquillo experienced the abuse that ultimately transformed him into a rebel leader. Las Casas relates the story: "Among the few and poor goods that he [Enriquillo] had, he owned a mare"—a particularly rare and prized possession for anyone on Hispaniola, let alone an Indian—"which was taken from him by the tyrant of a young man whom he served. After this, not content with this robbery and violent act, he managed to violate the marriage of the cacique and force his wife. . . . [When Enriquillo] complained of this to him, asking why he had done him such an injury and insult, it is said that he beat him." After these violations of his family, person, and property, Enriquillo recruited a group of slaves on the estate—"probably mostly men," according to one historian—to flee with him up into the Bahoruco Mountains, where they joined other runaway slaves.

Given his status among the Taino and his knowledge of the Spanish, Enriquillo earned respect within the growing maroon world in the Bahoruco. (Maroons were runaway slaves who formed independent communities away from the plantation economies of Europeans.) Ever since the arrival of the Spanish, the native people of Hispaniola had been fleeing into the mountains, depleting the labor pool, which contributed to the Spanish importation of slaves—first, Tainos and other natives from nearby islands, and then Muslim and non-Muslim Africans. Many of these slaves escaped into the Bahoruco as well. In this humid tropical landscape so similar to the land the Wolof had left behind, Muslims and indigenous Americans—Old World and New World enemies of Spanish Christians—gradually forged new political, social, cultural, and familial relationships.

From these mountainous outposts, Enriquillo regularly led his followers in raids on Spanish settlements—killing animals, seizing supplies and weapons, and sometimes liberating slaves. These diverse rebels were able to sustain themselves in the mountains because they knew how to grow and collect food, what to hunt, where to find fresh water, and how

*The Bahoruco Mountains*

to remain undetected in the thickly forested Bahoruco. As one Spanish official in pursuit of them wrote, they "know the land, and so they mock the Spaniards." While the maroons thrived, the Spanish complained that the terrain was so rough that "for each day a pair of sandals is needed." The rebels survived on spiders, crayfish, snakes, and roots. "The island is large and full of cows, wild hogs and other staples," wrote Melchor de Castro of some of the animals that proliferated on Hispaniola after 1492, "and so the blacks in revolt have security and food."

Seizing the opportunity presented by the diversion of Spanish forces to Mexico beginning in 1517, Enriquillo and his men conducted their most daring operations in 1519. Raid after raid brought them weapons, recruits, and supplies. Although it is unlikely that they provided material support for the Wolof Rebellion two years later—and, as it lasted only three days, there was no time for Enriquillo to organize support for it—there is overwhelming evidence that, after the Wolof fled into the mountains, the Taino and the Muslims joined forces. Throughout the 1520s, the Spanish sought to eradicate these renegades. Accounts refer to the rebel guerrillas as both natives and African Muslims. In October 1523, for example, the governor of Hispaniola wrote to the Spanish Crown that he and his men had declared war on the "rebel Indians and Negros," the latter here clearly referring to Wolof Muslims.

In addition to such textual evidence, recent archaeological finds indicate that Africans and natives shared a Bahoruco cave complex known as El Limona. These caves open in the rocky hillside like a series of gaping mouths. Inside, tight passageways and steep drop-offs lead into open spaces and lookout points. The identifiable skeletal remains found in the caves are those of African adult males. A number of other skeletons cannot be definitively identified, but there were indigenous Taino ceramics alongside them, suggesting strongly that these were natives living together with their African partners. El Limona seems to have been the upland rebel headquarters of the joint African Muslim–Taino resistance to the Spanish of Hispaniola.

The Wolof Rebellion of 1521 and Enriquillo's insurgency in 1519 set the stage for several more Indian–African uprisings over the next two decades. In many of these—including in 1523, 1525, 1526, 1529, and 1533—Enriquillo led the charge.

⬢

THE CHRISTMAS DAY REVOLT in 1521 may have been sparked by some of the large number of Wolof slaves who had been transported to Hispaniola earlier that year—confirmation of the Muslim threat the Spanish had always dreaded. Changes in policy were implemented immediately. Thirteen days after the revolt, Spanish authorities instituted new laws making mutilation the punishment for a slave's flight and deeming rebellion a capital crime. They further stipulated that slaves could not carry weapons and could leave their plantations only if accompanied by their master. These laws, meant to tighten the grip of the minority whites over blacks, would remain essentially the same over the course of the next few centuries in both South and North America—shaping, for example, laws such as the Fugitive Slave Act in the nineteenth-century United States. This is a further testament to the significance of the Wolof Rebellion as a watershed moment in the history of the Americas—one that historians have mostly ignored.

From a slaveholder's perspective, the Wolof were the most inapt choice for the role. Having come from a powerful empire in West Africa, they were politically sophisticated, resented Spanish domination, and spoke a language understood only among themselves. The Wolof who arrived in Hispaniola could read and write (in part because of their Muslim education); many were skilled warriors; and they were consummate traders. They were also master horsemen, having used the animals in warfare for centuries. Since horses in the Americas were novel weapons, knowledge of their use was a strategic asset. Furthermore, because the Wolof had traded with the Portuguese and then the Spanish for decades, they had a sense of how these European cultures functioned. Thus, being cosmopolitan, educated, and powerful, they were able to adjust better than most other slaves to their difficult circumstances in new places with new peoples.

For the Spanish, the absolute worst aspect of the Wolof was, of course, that they were Muslim. But, in desperate need of labor, they continued bringing Wolof slaves to Hispaniola, against their own best interests and despite numerous efforts to stop the importation. In 1532, Isabella of Portugal, the Queen Regent of Spain thanks to her marriage to Charles V, issued one of her many decrees outlawing the transport of Wolof to the Caribbean. In her words, they were "prideful, disobedient, rebellious and incorrigible" Muslims who killed Christians and corrupted "more pacific Africans from other lands." This order, like the others, did little to curb the transport of Wolof slaves to the Americas.

Advocating, once again, for a halt to the importation of West Africans, a judge on Hispaniola wrote to the Crown in 1544 of the alarming influence of the "bad customs" of Muslims on the Taino. "It would be preferable that there weren't so many *ladino* slaves born in this country," he announced in his letter, "because they are a bad nation, very daring and badly inclined, and they are the ones who mutiny and make themselves captains. . . . The same was seen in the business of Enrique [Enriquillo]."

Muslims continued to stream into the Americas over the course of the sixteenth century. Economic pressure easily overwhelmed caution. Between 1533 and 1580, for instance, the majority of the slaves taken to gold-rich Cartagena, Colombia's largest port, were Muslims. Although they came from a broad range of ethnic and social groups in Africa—some were mutual enemies—once landed in places such as Cartagena, these Muslims found common cause against the Spanish. The Spanish thus laid the groundwork, unintentionally of course, for a novel brand of supra-ethnic Muslim solidarity in the New World that allowed Muslims to become a major force in the Americas. Indeed, as the scholar Sylviane A. Diouf explains, "if counted as a whole, on a religious basis rather than on an ethnic one the Muslims were probably more numerous in the Americas than many other groups of Africans." In Cartagena, Wolof, Mandingo, Berbeci, and Fulani Muslims came together, thanks to their common allegiance to what one of the city's Jesuit priests termed "the cursed sect of Mahomet." After 1521, Muslim slaves from different backgrounds united to lead insurrections in Puerto Rico and Panama. In many of these cases, as in the Christmas Day revolt, Muslims aligned with non-Muslim indigenous slaves and maroons. Ultimately, it was not Islam that bound Muslims together and bound Muslims with others, but rather these individuals' shared status as slaves or otherwise subjugated peoples—all enemies of the Spanish.

Given their Old World enmities, Spanish colonists nearly always scapegoated Muslims as the instigators of these revolts—in Mexico in 1523, Cuba and Colombia in 1529, Honduras in 1548, and Venezuela in 1550—even when they were not remotely involved. In all these locales, the Spanish continued to accuse their Muslim slaves of prose-

lytizing Islam to indigenous Americans. It became almost a knee-jerk
reaction for the Spanish to ascribe all their New World problems to
their Old World foe.

Toward the end of the sixteenth century, Islam expanded throughout the Atlantic world. The number of Muslim slaves from around the
Mediterranean—variously described as "Moors" and "Turks," most
likely North Africans—being imported to the New World increased
at a higher rate than that of Muslim West Africans. This demographic
shift was the result of the Spaniards' greater reliance on galleys for
transport in the Caribbean. Mediterranean Muslim slaves had long
experience working the oars of these large vessels, since this was one
of their primary functions in the slave economy of the Old World. In
the early 1580s, for example, a galley commander in Cartagena wrote
to Spain requesting that more enslaved "Moors and Turks" be sent as
oarsmen because they "prove to be the best." Records from 1595 of a
galley in Havana show that nearly 30 percent of its crew was made
up of Muslims from Africa, the Ottoman Empire, and Morocco. As
with West African gold miners and the Muslim sugar slaves of Madeira,
these predominantly North African Muslims possessed the technical
expertise needed in the New World and thus, despite deep-rooted fears
among the Christians, were sent in large numbers to the Americas.

"THE CONQUEST OF THE EARTH," wrote Joseph Conrad in his 1899
novella *Heart of Darkness*, "which mostly means the taking it away from
those who have a different complexion or slightly flatter noses than
ourselves, is not a pretty thing when you look into it too much. What
redeems it is the idea only." Although Conrad wrote these words about
the Belgian Congo in the nineteenth century, he could just as easily have
been describing the first few decades of Spanish rule in the Americas. It
was certainly "not a pretty thing." It is estimated that 90 percent of the
native population of the Americas died between 1492 and the middle
of the seventeenth century—a decline from sixty million people to six
million—and that about thirteen million Africans were brought to the
Americas as slaves. Never before in world history had genocide occurred
on the scale of continents, obliterating languages and cultures, cities and
histories. More than anything else, Spanish and other European *ideas*
of the New World propelled these irredeemably wrenching conquests.

After this genocide, the "necessity" of slavery in a place like Hispaniola stoked the kinds of fantasies that had initially pushed Columbus across the Atlantic and into the horrific and complicated realities of colonial rule in the Americas. As history nearly always reveals, reality trumps fantasy. Thus, despite the Spaniards' apocalyptic fears, Islam arrived in America and left its influential mark, paradoxically brought there by the Spanish themselves in their quest for land and riches. Melchor de Castro, who was wounded during the 1521 Wolof Rebellion, later designed a coat of arms for himself that featured a right arm clenching a sword above six severed black heads dripping blood—a motif he borrowed from *Reconquista*-era Spanish seals featuring the severed, bleeding, turbaned heads of Muslims. Later, a whole generation of Europeans in the New World would borrow the symbolism of severed Muslim heads for their iconography. This sort of continuity between Old World and New—continuities observed both in the Requirement and in Spain's colonial land-tenure system, continuities forged by the extension of the war between Islam and Christianity to the Caribbean, continuities made relentlessly tragic through the decimation of native populations and the imposition of the transatlantic slave trade—affirm that 1492 did not separate the New World from the Old, the Americas from Islam.

Quite the opposite: it bound them together, through blood and violence.

# FINDING OTTOMAN
# JERUSALEM

*Expulsion of Jews from Spain*

THE YEAR 1492—IN WHICH COLUMBUS "DISCOVERED" AMERICA and Spain completed its *Reconquista*—marked another major geopolitical event as well: the expulsion of the Jews from Spain. Jews had lived there far longer than either Christians or Muslims; indeed, Jews had called Spain their home before those two religions were born. The year 1492 was thus a turning point of epochal significance for world Jewry—a moment of loss but also a beginning. The dispersion of one of the Mediterranean's deepest-rooted Jewish communities opened another chapter—their Ottoman story. Thus began Sephardic history; indeed, the term *Sephardi* refers to those Jews who trace their origins back to the community exiled from Spain in 1492. After often harrowing journeys across land and sea, most of these Jews eventually settled in the Ottoman Empire, joining its already significant and longstanding Jewish population.

The largest Jewish city in the world after 1492—indeed, the only Jewish-majority city for two thousand years—rose in the Ottoman Empire. This was the humming port of Salonica (now the Greek city of Thessaloniki), on the hilly northwest coast of the Aegean Sea. Over the next four centuries, Salonica, "the Jerusalem of the Balkans," became the global center of Jewish culture. Jews from all over the world were drawn there by opportunity, stability, and the city's cosmopolitan character. Under Ottoman Islam, Jews mostly thrived—not just in Salonica but throughout the empire, even in an outlying city like Selim's Trabzon. Remnants of these populations lived in Iraq, Yemen, Egypt, and throughout the Middle East as late as the mid-twentieth century. Selim's personal physician, some of his most trusted advisers, and his munitions experts during his wars of conquest were descendants of Spain's Jews. Thus, in the very moment that Europe exiled its Jews and Muslims, while enslaving Africans and decimating indigenous populations in the Americas, the Ottomans welcomed Jews (and Muslims) from across the Mediterranean world, integrating them into their empire—which, importantly, still had a Christian majority.

FOR COLUMBUS AND THE Spanish regime he represented, the *Reconquista* and the search for a way to defeat Islam by heading west connected seamlessly to Spain's efforts to cleanse itself of its Jews. "Your Highnesses ordained that I should not go eastward by land in the usual manner," wrote Columbus, "but by the western way which no one about whom we have positive information has ever followed. Therefore having expelled all the Jews from your dominions in that same month of January [1492], your Highnesses commanded me to go with an adequate fleet to those parts of India." The fall of Granada and its annexation to Castile following years of war represented the culmination of the Inquisition that had been raging in Spain, and throughout Catholic

Europe, for hundreds of years. Both Judaism and Islam were regarded by Christians as diseases plaguing Europe. From Amsterdam to Venice, laws prohibited Jewish and Muslim religious practices, stipulated that these communities could live only in specific neighborhoods, and sanctioned periodic outbreaks of anti-Jewish and anti-Muslim violence. Pogroms targeting "Christ's crucifiers" had occurred throughout the course of Spanish history, one of the most significant coming in 1391, when Christian mobs massacred scores of Jews across Spain's major cities. Next came waves of expulsions from neighborhoods and even whole towns, and then a flood of forced conversions. Like former Muslims, former Jews remained under suspicion. Indeed, a whole arm of the Inquisition was devoted solely to determining whether Jewish and Muslim converts—*conversos* and Moriscos respectively—were truly Catholic in their hearts or were dangerous, conniving impostors.

The historic triumph at Granada served as the staging ground for the final eradication of Judaism and Islam from Spain. Even though the enemy on the battlefield was a Muslim kingdom, there was a widespread belief that Jews had materially aided Granada's Muslims and that some had even taken up arms alongside them. What is more, the fall of Granada proved a huge economic windfall for the Spanish Crown. Not only did the victory release funds that had been tied up by the war, but the subsequent seizures of Jewish (and Muslim) money and property swelled the state's coffers further (Spain's expulsion decree, echoed five centuries later by the Nazis, expressly forbade Jews from taking gold and silver with them). Funds for Columbus's journey across the Atlantic thus came from both these sources: the war chest Spain had accumulated to battle Islam, and the confiscated assets of Jews and Muslims.

On March 31, 1492, nearly three months after the fall of Granada and six weeks before Columbus left the city after having received royal sanction in the Moorish-turned-Catholic citadel of Alhambra to begin his preparations for crossing the ocean, Spain promulgated its official decree of expulsion. It began by summarizing the underlining logic:

[I]t is evident and apparent that the great damage to the Christians has resulted from and does result from the participation, conversation, and communication that they have had with the Jews, who try to always achieve by whatever ways and means possible to subvert and to draw away faithful Christians from our holy Catholic faith and to separate them from it, and to attract and pervert them to their injurious belief and opinion, instructing them in their ceremonies and observances of the Law, holding gatherings where they read unto them and teach them what they ought to believe and observe according to their Law, trying to circumcise them and their children. . . . This is evident from the many declarations and confessions, [obtained] as much from the Jews themselves as from those perverted and deceived by them, which has redounded to the great injury, detriment, and opprobrium of our holy Catholic faith.

The decree then detailed how the expulsions were to occur:

We . . . having had much deliberation upon it, resolve to order all and said Jews and Jewesses out of our kingdoms and that they never return nor come back to any of them. . . . [W]e command all Jews and Jewesses of whatever age they may be, who live and reside and are in the said kingdoms and seignories, natives and non-natives alike, who by whatever manner or whatever reason may have come or are to be found in them, that by the end of July of the present year, that they leave the said kingdoms and seignories with their sons and daughters, male and female servants and Jewish domestics, both great and small, of whatever age they may be, and that they dare not return unto them, nor be in them, nor be in any part of them, neither as dwellers, nor as travelers, nor in any other manner whatsoever, upon punishment that if they do not thus perform and comply with this, and are to be found in our said kingdoms and seignories and have come here in any manner, they incur the penalty of death and confiscation of all their belongings for our treasury, and such penalties they shall incur by the very deed itself without trial, sentence, or declaration.

In just four short months, from April to July of 1492, the Jews of Spain—a community that had persevered if not prospered for more than a millennium—faced a bleak choice among three repugnant alternatives: conversion, flight, or death. The expulsion decree rehashed many familiar themes permeating the anti-Jewish sentiment that had intensified in Spain over the previous few centuries: the corrupting influence of Jews on Christians, the threat posed by their laws to Christian law, and the larger falsity that they held vast amounts of property to the detriment of Christians. The Spanish Crown's ultimate goal was the total Christianization of Spain by the excision of such cancerous tumors as Jews and Muslims, and so, after the fall of Granada and the anti-Jewish expulsion efforts, many Muslims were expelled as well, mostly to North Africa, and the violence against them would continue until their final expulsion in 1614. But in the immediate aftermath of 1492, Jews bore the brunt of the fanatical vision of a pure Spanish Catholic state.

Death was clearly the worst of the three options. The majority of Spain's estimated 275,000 Jews chose flight, but some 100,000 opted for conversion. Becoming Catholic allowed Jews to keep their property, homes, and trades, sparing them the agony of uprooting themselves and starting over in an unknown place with an uncertain future. Perhaps not surprisingly, most of these *conversos* came from the upper echelons of Spanish Jewish society. With the most to lose, they had the greatest incentive to convert and remain. Given the heightened hostilities of the Inquisition and the *Reconquista*, however, stipulations about conversion proved more stringent than ever before. In its most generous assessment, the Crown regarded conversions under threat of death or expulsion as insincere and thus suspicious. More sinisterly, they viewed these conversions as part of an infidel plot to embed unbelievers in the very heart of Christianity in order to corrupt it from within.

Despite their apprehensions about *conversos*, the Spanish nevertheless gained several advantages from Jewish converts. First, they swelled the ranks of the Christian flock. Second, they kept any remaining Muslims from finding allies against the surging Christian majority. Finally, and quite practically, conversion helped to lessen the potentially massive social and economic disruption caused by thousands of departing Jews. It preserved the social fabric of Spanish cities by maintaining many of the same individuals, now conveniently Catholic, in their important positions in the Spanish economy and bureaucracy.

For the majority of Spain's Jews, though, conversion was a step too far. They believed in God's plan for them—and if that meant flight, then so be it. For these devout souls, abandoning Spain was less painful than abandoning Judaism. One could toil in a foreign land or strive in

a new line of work, but one could never find a new God or a new identity. As the prominent Iberian rabbi Isaac Abarbanel, victim and chronicler of the expulsions, put it, "If [our enemies] let us live, we will live;
and if they kill us, we will die. But we will not profane our covenant,
and our hearts will not retrogress; we will walk forward in the name of
the Lord our God." This walk forward led them out of Spain.

The Catholic priest Andrés Bernáldez watched with evident sympathy—albeit, perhaps, with an eye to proselytizing opportunities—as
his country's Jews began their journeys:

> In the first week of July they took the route for quitting their
> native land, great and small, young and old, on foot or horses,
> in carts each continuing his journey to his destined port. They
> experienced great trouble and suffered indescribable misfortunes
> on the road, some falling, others rising, some dying, others being
> born, some fainting, others being attacked by illness. There was
> not a Christian but that pitied them and pleaded with them to
> be baptized. Some from misery were converted, but they were
> the few. The rabbis encouraged them and made the young people
> and women sing and play on pipes and tambours to enliven them
> and keep up their spirits.

None knew what the future held, and, given the anti-Jewish posture
of nearly all European states, most had no clear sense of where they
might go. France and Britain had banished their Jewish communities in
the thirteenth and fourteenth centuries. In Germany, many towns had
blamed Jews for the scourge of the Black Death and had subsequently
expelled them. And Italy, given the viciously anti-Semitic attitudes of
a succession of popes and secular rulers, was all but closed off to Jewish
immigration.

With its geographic and cultural proximity, Portugal received
the largest number of Spain's Jews, about 120,000. But King João II,
Moor-slayer and sponsor of several of Portugal's West African expeditions, was as hateful and fearful of Jews as his Spanish counterparts,
and quickly enacted policies to push out the refugees. He required that
they purchase extortionate entry and residence permits valid for only
eight months, after which they were forced to flee again. Those unable
to meet the border fees were sold into slavery. And, in an inexplicably

cruel move, the king forcibly separated more than a few refugee parents from their children, whom the king sent to the Atlantic island of São Tomé, off the West African coast. This recent Portuguese acquisition, right on the equator, was "inhabited by lizards, snakes, and other venomous reptiles, and was devoid of rational beings." The children were tossed mercilessly from ships onto the desolate island's beaches, where "almost all were swallowed up by the huge lizards on the island and the remainder, who escaped these reptiles, wasted away from hunger and abandonment."

After Portugal, Muslim states in North Africa received the second largest number of Spanish Jews—about 20,000 of the 175,000 who fled. Many of the Jews later forced out of Portugal by King João also escaped to Morocco. In effect, then, tens of thousands of Spanish Jews followed their Muslim neighbors across the Mediterranean to Morocco, where, thanks to the "kindness of the King," a large Jewish settlement that had long thrived in Fez enthusiastically welcomed the Judeo-Spanish community. Given the zealotry in Spain, the mendacity of King João,

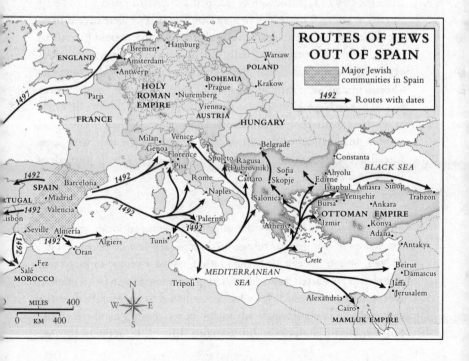

ROUTES OF JEWS OUT OF SPAIN

and the anti-Jewish politics of most of Europe, Jews were much safer in a Muslim polity than they were in any Christian state.

As in Portugal, in other Christian domains such as Navarre, Naples, and Marseille, Jews' first attempts to secure new homes only lengthened their decades of upheaval. In the decades around 1500, Sardinia, Apulia, Calabria, and Naples all expelled their newly arrived Judeo-Spanish refugees and even their older local communities of Jews. Sicily, which was controlled by the Crown of Aragon, expelled its Jewish community—numbering between 25,000 and 30,000—in 1492 as well, as part of Ferdinand and Isabella's initial decree. Many refugees, from both Spain and Italy, settled in Dubrovnik on the Adriatic—until they were banished once again in 1515. In the desperate search for freedom and safety, these exiles floated on ships around the Mediterranean, moving from one hostile port to another, usually eastward. Many died from accident or disease, while others succumbed to pirates or rapacious ship's captains.

The tragic tale of a boatload of Jews escaping persecution in Pesaro, a fishing town on the eastern Italian coast, typified the situation. Driven from the city in 1558, these Jews boarded a ship with promises of being ferried to safety. They sailed first to Dubrovnik, but were barred from the fabled walled city. Unable to find any port that would give them berth, the ship's captain eventually sold his Jewish passengers into slavery in Apulia, the olive-rich southeastern region of Italy that forms its "heel." In another example, a group of Judeo-Spanish refugees were forced to flee Naples in 1540 on a ship homeported in Dubrovnik. Once at sea, the captain robbed his vulnerable passengers of their meager possessions and abandoned them in Marseille, from where they were soon forced to flee once more. Luckily for this group, they made it to safety in Ottoman Syria.

THE OTTOMAN EMPIRE WAS the only Mediterranean locale where, in the words of one Jewish refugee, "their weary feet could find rest." Indeed, Sultan Bayezit II, Selim's father, issued a decree in July 1492, just after Jews started leaving Spain, that welcomed them to his empire. Recognizing how much Jews had contributed to the empire over the centuries, he saw a strategic advantage in welcoming members of the Spanish Jewish diaspora to his domains. In fact, he actively courted

Spain's Jews, going so far as to send ships to the Iberian coastline to bring Jewish refugees to the shores of the Bosphorus. He ordered all his provincial governors to welcome and protect any Jewish refugees who arrived in their territories—and some Jews journeyed as far east as Selim's Trabzon.

After his father's conquest of Constantinople, Bayezit had been an eyewitness to the arrival of Jews from Salonica and other merchant centers who came to take advantage of the opportunities the city offered after the conquest and helped to rebuild it after the enormous destruction wrought by the Ottoman siege. Once settled in the Ottoman capital, these Jews quickly established connections with the ruling elite and merchant classes and developed commercial interests around the Mediterranean, including with their former homes. After 1453, Istanbul was unquestionably the best place in the world for Jews to live; nowhere were Jews as prosperous and free as they were in Istanbul. Immediately after capturing Constantinople, Mehmet made the city's chief rabbi a member of his imperial council, offering him the same level of administrative power as the empire's grand mufti. Accordingly, the chief rabbi collected Jewish taxes (including the *jizya*), appointed rabbis in all the empire's cities, and generally managed his community's internal affairs. He also oversaw Jewish civil law courts and the criminal punishment of Ottoman Jews. The Ottoman Empire was, thus, "a paradise for the Jews," where they could live and trade freely in relative autonomy, with no restrictive sartorial laws and no fear of the regular pogroms that occurred in Europe.

In 1454, Isaac Sarfati, a Jew of French descent born in Germany, wrote a letter from Istanbul to the Jewish communities of the Rhineland, Swabia, Moravia, Styria, and Hungary. Having recently arrived in Istanbul, he contrasted his experiences with his earlier life in Germany, which he called the "great torture chamber," and encouraged his fellow Jews to abandon Europe for the Ottoman capital. Many did so, swelling the city's German Jewish population by thousands. Thus, even before 1492, the Ottoman Empire had already earned a deserved reputation among Europe's Jews as a place of refuge and prosperity. When Spain scattered its Jews, it was not surprising that many headed for the Ottoman Empire.

Beyond safety and an opportunity to rebuild their lives, many refugees believed that moving to the Ottoman Empire portended the fulfillment of God's divine plan to gather all of the world's Jews in Jerusalem. The fifteenth-century rabbi Moses Capsali—a scholar who was born in Crete, studied in Germany, arrived in Istanbul around the time of the conquest, and eventually became chief rabbi of the Ottoman Empire—had this to say: "our righteous Messiah will come ... because ever since the expulsion from Spain, God has started to gather the exiled from Israel and Judea in the lands of the dispersion and he is assembling them from the four corners of the earth." In the final analysis, however, most Jewish refugees settled in the Ottoman Empire for reasons of security rather than scripture.

From an Ottoman perspective, Jewish immigration proved very advantageous. First, although the Spanish refugees were generally not as wealthy as the Jewish merchants who came to Istanbul from Salonica in 1453, many maintained strong familial connections throughout the Mediterranean region, which afforded important trading opportunities and allowed the Ottomans to bypass the usurious Italian merchant families who still dominated trade in the Mediterranean and the Black Sea. In a commercial hub like Trabzon, for instance, the opportunity to replace Italian Christian merchants with Ottoman Jewish traders bolstered Ottoman enthusiasm for Jewish immigration. Spanish Jews joined older Jewish merchant communities in Trabzon, helping to expand their commercial enterprises to the west. Spain's Jews came to influence other economic sectors across the empire as well. In Ottoman Bulgaria, for example, Sephardic Jews became important in the tanning industry. In North Africa, they cornered the markets in gold- and silversmithing; in Palestine, silk production; and in Istanbul, banking. Given this vast infusion of economic power at Spain's expense, Bayezit was said to utter, "You call Ferdinand a wise king, he who impoverishes his country and enriches our own!"

The Sephardim also greatly aided the Ottomans' diplomatic agenda throughout the Mediterranean. Spanish Jews' linguistic skills and their familiarity with the tessellated principalities of Europe made them key brokers for the Ottomans in their dealings with other states. Perhaps even more important, though, European politicians generally preferred to deal with Jewish Ottoman diplomats. Even though they were representing an enemy Muslim state, Christian Europeans viewed them as less untrustworthy than Muslims and, because religion and politics were so intertwined in the early modern world, the fact that Jews were

not representing a Jewish state aided the perception that they were honest brokers. Throughout the sixteenth century, Jewish diplomats helped
the Ottomans reach several vital trade agreements, with France for
example. This so-called shuttle diplomacy also furthered the Sephardic community's interests. Ottoman Jewish diplomats often smuggled
crypto-Jews—*conversos* who had converted in name only—from Iberia
to the Ottoman Empire. Beyond such daring clandestine operations,
Jewish diplomacy allowed Ottoman Jews to maintain ties with family
members and business partners throughout the Mediterranean.

Spain's Jews also brought to the Ottoman Empire much useful technical knowledge. In the early fifteenth century, a European observer
of the empire's Sephardim noted: "Not long since banished and driven
from Spain and Portugal, who, to the great detriment and damage of
Christendom, have [they] taught the Turk several inventions, artifices
and machines of war, such as how to make artillery, arquebuses, gunpowder, cannonballs and other weapons." The Ottomans had long
employed artillery in war, but the Sephardim taught them new techniques in munitions and gunmaking. Indeed, during his conquest of
the Mamluk Empire in 1516 and 1517, Selim took with him to Syria
and Cairo a group of Jewish gunpowder makers to help with ballistics.

Along with guns, the Jews brought new medical expertise. One
family in particular distinguished itself; Spanish refugee Joseph Hamon
became the chief palace physician for both Bayezit and Selim, and, after
his death in 1518, his son Moses took over as Selim's and then Suleyman's doctor. So trusted was Moses Hamon that he served the sultans in
other capacities as well, such as helping to negotiate Suleyman's peace
treaty with Venice in 1540. He also pressed the sultan's court on matters
of interest to Ottoman Jewry, helping, for example, to secure an imperial decree condemning a blood libel accusation in Amasya in 1545 and
founding several schools in Salonica and other cities. He would eventually lose some favor because of a dispute over the best treatment for
gout; Moses recommended rubbing the sultan's legs with opium, but
other imperial physicians viewed this as only a temporary alleviation
of pain and not a true cure. Despite this row, Moses remained a trusted
medical adviser, passing on the position to his son.

In 1493, the Sephardim established a Hebrew printing press in
Istanbul, almost fifty years after Gutenberg's, and soon thereafter one
in Salonica as well. The first Hebrew-language printed books had

appeared in Italy in the 1470s, and the technology had quickly spread to congregations in Spain and Portugal. Istanbul's Hebrew press was the first printing press in any language in the Ottoman Empire. Eventually, Salonica would become the global center of Jewish print culture, underpinning the city's thriving intellectual and religious life. The most ambitious project of the Salonica press was to print the entire Talmud, an undertaking that required years of fundraising and five years just to typeset. Very few complete Talmuds existed in the sixteenth century, and merely owning one heightened a congregation's distinction. Jewish communities around the world soon looked to Salonica for intellectual, cultural, and economic leadership. For example, when Rome's only Talmud was publicly burned during a wave of anti-Jewish rioting in 1552, the Ottoman city's press printed its replacement.

Numbers attest to the success of Jewish life in the post-1492 Ottoman Empire. In 1430, Salonica, the "Jerusalem of the Balkans," had

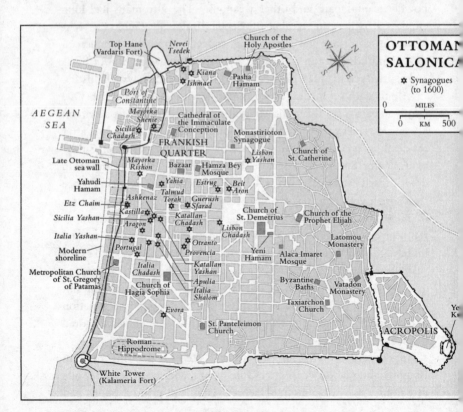

about 2,500 Jewish families. By 1519, that number had grown to 4,000. In 1553, a German traveler estimated that there were 20,000 Jewish males in the city. If we assume that each of these men had a family of five (a conservative estimate), then the Jewish population would have been 100,000—dwarfing the city's Muslim or Greek population and representing nearly 40 percent of the Ottoman Empire's Jewish population of 250,000. Other anecdotal evidence relates that, for example, Salonica ground to a halt on the Sabbath.

In many ways, Salonica became a microcosm of the immense diversity of global Jewish life. Greek-speaking Jews; Jews from Germany, Bohemia, and Hungary; Turkish and Arab Jews; Sephardim; and exiles from Italy and France all shared Salonica's streets, where one could hear Greek, Turkish, Yiddish, German, Arabic, and increasingly Ladino throughout the city. Eventually, Ladino—a mix of Old Spanish and Romance and Semitic languages, written in the Hebrew script—would triumph as Salonica's lingua franca. Although sharing a common faith, each of these émigré groups observed distinct sets of traditions and customs. As one of Salonica's rabbis wrote of the city's Jews, "each congregation appears to be an independent city." Dozens of different synagogues and competing interpretations of Judaism—as well as the city's diverse communities of Muslims and Christians—helped to forge Salonica's urban topography, creating social and artistic mélanges and exotic and piquant cuisines that would make Salonica a center of cosmopolitan life for centuries. At the turn of the sixteenth century, Salonica distinguished itself as the only place in the world where a Syrian Jew could wear a tailored Italian suit, eat souvlaki, and play backgammon with a Jew from Spain, all while speaking Hungarian.

Human nature being what it is, all was not perfect, of course. Problems inexorably arose due to the comingling of these diverse communities, leading to conflicts among Jews themselves, on subjects such as inter-community marriages and Sabbath practices, as well as between Jews and non-Jews. The Spanish Jews posed a particularly knotty problem. Rabbis debated how to determine the "Jewishness" of Jews who had converted to Christianity but now claimed to be Jews again. How would the Jewish law courts of Salonica rule, for example, on matters of inheritance or divorce for two *conversos* married by Christian rite? Was this even a legal marriage? One rabbi would regard conversion to have been a temporary survival strategy; another would consider it

*Jewish man in Salonica*

genuine and now being repudiated. Some rabbis insisted that there had to be consequences for giving up one's Judaism, whatever the reason had been.

When more mundane disputes emerged over property, crime, or even custom, the empire's Jews usually resorted to Islamic law courts. For example, newly arrived Sephardim observed far more lax kosher meat laws than Salonica's indigenous Jewish community. This was largely a function of their old need to be flexible in order to maintain their religious practices under the harsh restrictions of Catholic Spain. In Salonica, however, which kosher observances should be upheld? Unable to resolve this difference of interpretation among themselves, Salonica's Jews took the issue to the city's Islamic court. Any case involving a Muslim, whether a mixed marriage or a criminal proceeding, had to be adjudicated in an Islamic court, but in cases involving only non-Muslims, Jews and Christians could choose to go to their own community's religious law courts instead. Since Muslims could only use Islamic courts, the empire's non-Muslims thus enjoyed more legal options.

Although Salonica was the preferred destination for Spain's Jewish exiles, Jewish populations elsewhere in the eastern Mediterranean burgeoned as well. In Istanbul, the number of Jewish households rose from 1,647 in 1477 to 8,070 in 1535, an increase of nearly 500 percent. (In 1638, the number was reported to be 11,000.) By the end of the sixteenth century, twice as many Jews as Greeks lived in Istanbul, comprising as much as one-fifth of the city's total population. Many of Spain's Jews also went to Cairo, which became an important center of Sephardic religious training, as did the comparatively minor towns of Safed and Jerusalem, both in Palestine. Safed alone boasted twenty-one synagogues and eighteen Talmudic colleges.

THEOLOGICAL, DEMOGRAPHIC, AND POLITICAL factors explain the profound difference between the treatment of Jews in Europe and their treatment in the Ottoman Empire. Within Christian theology, Jews stood as deniers of Christ's message, as well as his assassins. They adhered to the laws of the Old Testament rather than to those of the new kingdom that Christians believed Christ brought to earth. Lovers of the flesh, they rejected the spirit. No authoritative Christian text attempts to reconcile Jews within the faith. As for Islam, as the last of the Abrahamic faiths it is absent from the Bible, so scripture provided no guidance on how Christians should treat Muslims. In the realm of Christian doctrine, then, Jews rejected and killed Christ, while Muslims did not even exist.

Islam, the latecomer, had to address and adapt itself to the other two religions. Islam understands itself as the culmination of the monotheistic traditions, tracing its lineage from Judaism and Christianity and seriously engaging with them as parts of its own family tree. Abraham, Isaac, Moses, and Jesus are all prophets within Islam and accorded reverence and devotion. Unlike the Bible, the Qur'an stipulates how adherents of other religions should be treated, and how a Muslim leader should rule over non-Muslims, especially Jews and Christians—who, as People of the Book, are accorded an elevated status over other non-Muslims. Since Islam grew as a minority faith surrounded by Judaism and Christianity, it had to work within existing parameters. Muslims—political rulers and all others—are duty-bound to protect Jews and Christians and to allow them freedom of worship and practice, although in times of war, of course, Muslims could kill Christian and Jewish combatants, enslave them, and attempt to convert them. However, this fundamental, indeed foundational, difference between Islam and Christianity forever shaped how the two religions, and the states that ruled in their names, dealt with nonadherents, both doctrinally and politically.

For more than two hundred years, Muslim sultans were members of a religious minority, ruling over a majority Greek Orthodox population. Only after Selim's conquests of 1516 and 1517 did Muslims come to represent the majority of the population of the Ottoman Empire. Therefore, before those years, it was crucial that the numerically dominant Christian subject population accept and support Muslim rule. Europe's Christian rulers never faced such an imperative, as they always shared the same faith as the majority of their subjects. As, gradually, the Ottomans replaced the Orthodox Byzantine Empire, they won over the conquered Christians with various inducements: security, fewer taxes, basic autonomy. Had they imposed harsh taxes or discriminatory laws, or tried to forcibly convert Christians to Islam, they likely would have faced stiff resistance, which would have spelled disaster for the empire. In Europe, where the demographic dynamics were almost completely reversed, rulers had no need to placate their minority populations; if Jews and Muslims revolted or refused to pay taxes, they would pose no catastrophic risk to a Christian polity.

Finally, in the centuries during which Europe persisted in bloodying its hands with the Inquisition while the Ottoman Empire fostered a pluralistic society, the Ottomans increasingly came to dominate the Mediterranean. Over the course of the fifteenth century, but especially after 1453, Europe recognized its own weakness and feared not just Ottoman power, but all Muslims everywhere. This sobering development would shape European literature, religious thought, and propaganda for centuries. Given the global balance of power around 1500, the Ottomans did not perceive Christianity, and certainly not all Christians everywhere, as their enemy. European fragmentation meant that the Ottomans faced only a variety of small Christian enemies—the kingdom of Hungary, Ferdinand and Isabella in Spain, Venice, Genoa, and so on—rather than a unified, territorially gargantuan, foe. More-over, being a Muslim numerical minority in a sea of Christians, the Ottomans had no fifth-column anxieties about their own Christian subjects, since they had to cooperate with Christians to maintain their rule. Given these realities, the Ottomans did not think in civilizational terms about a clash between Islam and Christianity; they did not see Europe as an existential threat; and, therefore, they did not demonize their religious minorities as Spain and other European powers did.

Still, the historical record cautions against exaggerating inter-faith harmony in the Ottoman Empire. The experience of both the Sephardim and older communities of Jews in Selim's Trabzon bears this out. The small number of Spanish Jews who made it that far east arrived in a period of both political stability and demographic change. In the globally precarious decade of the 1490s, Selim's governorship bestowed relative calm on the port city as it began its steady transfor-mation from being a majority Orthodox city to a majority Muslim one. During Selim's reign, more than 80 percent of Trabzon's population was Christian; Islam did not become the city's majority religion until decades after his time there. For centuries before and after 1492, Jews remained a tiny minority in Trabzon—a few dozen highly skilled doc-tors, artisans, and merchants among a total urban population of around 1,500—and were generally unmolested. However, violence periodically interrupted the tranquility. According to one account, both Christians and Muslims in the city regularly "kill them [Jews] if they see them." Indeed, such was Trabzon's reputation in some circles that, "if someone suggests to a Jew that he go to Trabzon, the Jew tells him to go to hell." This same account goes on to relate a specific instance, most likely fic-tionalized, of anti-Jewish violence during Selim's governorship.

The story begins when two young Muslim brothers went missing in the city. Despite a thorough search, neither the boys' family nor city officials could determine their fate. One day in the market, years later, a dervish examining two pieces of fine leather, one red and the other yellow, noticed some strange writing deep in the skins. With difficulty, he deciphered the message: "You who wish to learn of our condition should know that we have been held captive under ground for the past twenty years by Jewish tanners. Rescue us, for God's sake and for the sake of God's messenger, and you will see wondrous things." The der-vish went directly to the governor's court, and Selim dispatched soldiers to the Jewish tanneries on the outskirts of the city. They found the missing boys deep in a cave used by the tanners for storing dyes. "The backs of the two young victims," the story continues, "had been flayed, then the two brothers had been attached back to back and put to work tanning. When one stood up to work, the other was left helpless loaded onto his back." Although the story does not state this specifically, the two pieces of leather were presumably the sections of skin that had been removed from the boys in order to fuse them together. When Selim's men further inspected the tanneries, they found "several hundred other young boys named Muhammed." Word spread through the city that Jews were enslaving and flaying Muslim boys. A riot ensued and several Jews were killed.

Trafficking as it does in tropes that were commonplace in medieval and early modern Europe—the capture of Gentile children and the emphasis on bloodletting—this almost certainly apocryphal story demonstrates that anti-Semitism existed in the Ottoman Empire and often led to anti-Jewish violence, in narrative form and in reality. Unlike in Europe, however, Jews in the Ottoman Empire did not represent a threat so dire that they needed to be excised from the realm. Hyperbolic phantom fears about blood purity, corruption, and deceit—not the real-world politics of military strategy and global territorial conquest—ultimately led to Europe's expulsion of the Jews. Although occasional outbursts of anti-Jewish violence did occur, the 1490s witnessed a Jewish renaissance in the Ottoman Empire, and, for centuries afterward, the empire remained the center of global Jewish culture.

VIOLENCE, EXPULSIONS, FORCED MIGRATIONS, the expansion of religious war, the annihiliation of New World peoples, and increased slavery dominated the early modern world in the decades around the paroxysmal year of 1492. In the middle of this cyclone of conflict, conquest, and mass death, the Ottoman Empire stood like the eye of the storm—its central axis, and yet a place of surprising calm and refuge.

Still, its leaders were mobilizing for war. For Bayezit, Selim, and their empire, the most potent civilizational threat came not from Jews or Christians, but from other Muslims—the Shiites of Iran. Islam's greatest challenge at the beginning of the sixteenth century emanated not from outside but from within its abode.

# PART FOUR

# ENEMIES NEAR
# AND FAR

*(1500–12)*

IMAGE ON PREVIOUS PAGE:
*Selim*

CHAPTER
12

# HERESY FROM THE EAST

*The Prophet Muhammad visits Safi in a dream*

As EUROPE CHASED THE SPECTER OF ISLAM IN THE CARIBBEAN
and scattered Muslims and Jews like pollen across the Mediterranean,
a new Muslim power was stirring in the east. In eastern Anatolia, the

immediate hinterland of Selim's Trabzon, chaos reigned throughout the 1490s, following the breakdown of the Ak Koyunlu Confederacy. In the Caucasus and northern Iran, tribal warlords, religious upstarts, and political pretenders all saw their chance to capture territory, soldiers, and money. Selim grew increasingly anxious as these forces intensified their violence against one another and encroached ever deeper on his territories, raiding for resources and preparing the way for rebellion wherever their horses trampled. Nonetheless, he waited, seeking the perfect moment to strike.

One of the strongest factions to emerge was a religious order that had been founded by Shaykh Safi al-Din in the 1320s as a collection of wandering ascetics in and around the town of Ardabil, near the western shore of the Caspian Sea. Members of this order would, by 1501, become the Ottomans' major rivals in the east: the Safavid Empire. Safi and his successors evangelized about the power of intense devotional prayer and the mystical elements of God; they believed in holy men, jinns, and the charisma of their inspired leaders. Not surprisingly, political upheaval and social uncertainty tend to spur the growth of heterodox religious communities whose adherents come from the disenfranchised, maligned, and otherwise marginalized. Thus, in the fractured landscapes of eastern Anatolia, the Caucasus, and northern Iran, Safi's order found fertile ground for its message and expanded steadily over the course of the fifteenth century and into the sixteenth.

As they accumulated territory and followers, the budding Safavids developed a robust ideological foundation from which to challenge the most dominant force in their immediate zone of operations, the Ottomans. Shiism formed the groundwork for this ideological program. The rupture within Islam between Sunnism and Shiism had first emerged in the seventh century, over the question of who should lead the early Muslim community. While Shiites held that the political and religious leader of Islam should be a descendant of the Prophet Muhammad, Sunnis considered that the leader should be the person deemed most capable of ruling, regardless of his lineage. From the origins of Islam to the present day, Sunnis have always claimed more adherents than Shiites, yet both have coalesced into various political states battling for territory and ideological preeminence. Much of Selim's time as governor of Trabzon, like much of his later reign as sultan, was focused on facing down the threat of Shiite rebels in east-

ern Anatolia and the growth of the early modern world's major Shiite power in Iran and the Caucasus.

Shiism came slowly to the Safavids. Safi and his descendants initially practiced the kind of "frontier Islam" that thrived in areas beyond the control of empires. Around the year 1300, when they were still merely a tribal principality, the early Ottomans similarly developed a kind of flexible frontier Islam that reconciled distinct religious ideas and cultures, allowing them to thrive in an atmosphere of rival beliefs and intermittent war. As the Safavids' growing clout brought them into more regular and sustained contact and confrontation with the Ottomans and the Ak Koyunlu Confederacy, their Shiism strengthened as an oppositional counterweight to both empires' Sunni orthodoxy. The Shiism of Safi's followers eventually solidified as a source of political legitimacy and stability in the face of the turmoil that followed the disintegration of the Ak Koyunlu. For Selim, Shiism put up a target for the arrow of his violent ambitions.

BORN IN THE CITY of Ardabil in 1252, Safi grew up in a wealthy family with large landholdings. Ardabil, which is today located in Iran, close to the border with Azerbaijan, was during Safi's youth a sleepy town nestled in a mountain valley. Winter was harsh there, but spring arrived with radiant yellow buttercups, delicate red poppies, and vibrant pink roses. One of Safi's cherished pastimes was visiting the shrines of local saints; this pampered son wandered in search of something beyond this world— something deeper, more meaningful, transcendent. He spent hours in meditation, experiencing visions of angels and departed saints, and sought a spiritual guide to interpret his visions and offer him direction.

From among the Sufis who gathered around the holy shrines of Ardabil, the mystic who proved most adept at interpreting Safi's visions was a charismatic sixty-year-old named Zahid, founder of an order that took his name, the Zahidiyya. Distinguishing himself as a curious and perceptive interlocutor and loyal follower, Safi soon became Zahid's star pupil and the order's most trusted disciple. As the scion of a wealthy family, Safi also supported the order financially, which of course only served to ingratiate him further. Zahid loved his pious and munificent acolyte so much that he married his daughter to him. After Zahid died in 1301, Safi—a short, stocky man nearing fifty—was his obvious successor. On his deathbed, the Sufi master whispered to his son-in-law, "Ṣafī, God has shown you to the people, and His command is that you obey His call. . . . I have broken the polo-stick of all your adversaries, and cast the ball before you. Strike it where you will; the field is yours. I have been able to live the life of a recluse, but you cannot. Wherever you are bidden, you must go, to make converts and give instruction. It is God who has given you this task." Having received this worldly and otherworldly charge—elegantly couched in the language of a sport that had originated in Iran—Safi set out to proselytize, to reveal to others the truth he had found for himself. He forswore being a recluse, and utilized his family's resources to advance the order's political and economic influence in and around Ardabil. With the polo-stick of power firmly in his grasp, Safi whipped his horse forward to chase and then strike the ball Zahid had thrown before him. He married prominent members of his order into influential families across northern Iran, thus increasing the number of his followers and solidifying his political clout. He also bought land in order to raise revenue. Expanding its reach beyond Ardabil, Safi's order forged alliances with local powers, built new devotional sanctuaries, and worked to increase its resource base—all with the express aim of supporting its religious mission. The order soon adopted Safi's name as its own, becoming the Safaviyya instead of the Zahidiyya—and, eventually, the Safavid Empire.

Safi died in 1334, by which time his mystical sect found itself on very solid footing. For the next century, his followers built on the gains he had made. They focused on maintaining their shrines, winning adherents, and carrying out daily exercises of prayer and ritual. By the 1450s, their numbers had swollen, making them a formidable force in northern Iran and the Caucasus. During this decade, the Safaviyya made two fateful, if seemingly contradictory, political moves, the second necessitated by the first: they intermarried with the Sunni Ak Koyunlu Confederacy, and they made a deliberate, though very gradual, transition toward the formal adoption of Shiism.

As they grew in numbers and influence, the Safaviyya came into closer contact, and sometimes direct conflict, with the Ak Koyunlu, which was still the region's most dominant force. Since it was in neither group's interest to pitch battle against the other, the most expedient means of defusing that possibility was for the two groups to ally by intermarrying, even as each sought to maintain its independence from the other. As the weaker of the two groups, the Safaviyya felt this need especially acutely. Since the more powerful and more heavily militarized Ak Koyunlu were Sunnis, like the Ottomans, the Safaviyya embrace of Shiism served as an assertion of difference, autonomous identity, and sovereignty over its internal affairs, even after the marriages of convenience were accomplished. Despite their best efforts to maintain this precarious balance, however, the Safaviyya adoption of Shiism eventually led to a split with the Ak Koyunlu.

In 1478, when the formidable Ak Koyunlu leader Uzun Hasan died after nearly twenty-five years in power, his son and successor struck out at the rising power of the Safaviyya, whom he saw as both an easy target and a threat to his young reign. Seeking to purge what he regarded as their infiltration of his family and especially their disgraceful Shiism, he seized several of their shrines and much of their landholdings and imprisoned many of the order's leaders far to the south, near the Persian Gulf. In one of their major victories during a decade of many setbacks, the Ak Koyunlu captured Ardabil from the Safaviyya in 1494, forcing most of its ranks to flee. A group headed south along the western coast of the Caspian Sea—including a seven-year-old boy, a direct descendant of Safi named Ismail.

By 1499, the exiled Safaviyya had begun plotting their return northward. Over the course of the 1490s, two parallel processes had enabled the Safaviyya to recapture areas of northern Iran in the valley between Tabriz and Ardabil. First, instability gripped the Ak Koyunlu when a series of succession crises broke out, spreading violence throughout the region, even as far west as Selim's Trabzon. At the same time, the expulsion of the Safaviyya from Ardabil in 1494 actually proved advantageous, as they were able to develop relationships and alliances all along the southern Caspian coast. Seizing upon the dissatisfaction of local populations with Ak Koyunlu raids and violence, the Safaviyya galvanized men willing to fight to oust the Ak Koyunlu from their villages and towns. The Safaviyya promised to lead them north to fight the Ak Koyunlu and then to let the villagers enjoy autonomous rule. The Safaviyya wanted Ardabil and its surrounding territories, not the whole of Iran or even the southern Caspian coast.

By late 1500, the Safaviyya were ready to deliver a deathblow to the Ak Koyunlu. With some seven thousand men drawn from tribes throughout northern Iran, villages on the southern Caspian coast, the Caucasus, and even eastern Anatolia, the Safaviyya moved on the strategic Ak Koyunlu stronghold of Sharur, sited northwest of Ardabil at the crossroads of multiple trade routes. Despite being considerably outmanned, the Safaviyya and their allies fought with inspiration and abandon. Within a few days, they had killed eight thousand

Ak Koyunlu soldiers and pushed the remnants back toward Tabriz, where they slaughtered everyone they could find, subduing this historic Silk Road city that had seen both Marco Polo and Tamerlane enter its gates. By the summer of 1501, the Safaviyya had captured Tabriz.

In Tabriz, the triumphant Safaviyya military leaders gathered to decide their next moves. Out of that meeting came the decision to crown fourteen-year-old Ismail as the first shah of the Safavid Empire. A left-handed redhead with a sonorous singing voice, Ismail represented both continuity with the line of Safi and a new beginning for a new state. As a direct descendant of the Safaviyya's revered founder— who, more than a century after his death, had achieved mythic status— Ismail perfectly combined oppositional Shiism and a Sufi lineage. The

*The newly crowned Ismail hears the Friday sermon*
*said in his name in Tabriz*

Safavid leadership invested their hopes in him as both political ruler and spiritual guide.

Although it is difficult to separate myth from truth, tales of the new shah's legendary strength circulated widely. On one occasion, Ismail supposedly directed that a ram be killed and the fresh carcass be buried with only the horns showing above the dirt. He then set off on horseback at full gallop, reached down to grab the horns with one hand, and pulled the ram out of the ground. He then lifted it over his head, swung it around three times, and tossed it forward.

As they had done all along, the Safaviyya order-turned-empire strategized about how to harness their oppositional spiritual message—now embodied in the young, strapping Ismail—to win people to their cause. Infinitely more significant than everything else, they declared that the official religion of the Safavid Empire would forever be Shiism, making the Safavids the most potent Shiite power in the early modern world.

In the Safavids' early years, their Shiism seemed questionable (much like the Sunnism of the Ottomans centuries earlier), with its mélange of ancient Persian notions of kingship, Sufism, Sunni Islam, and frontier tribal heterodoxy. However, in an early modern world in which religion stood as the foremost marker of identity, the proclamation of the Safavid Empire as a specifically Shiite state was a means of projecting independence, sovereignty, distinction, and opposition to the powers surrounding them. Moreover, when Ismail claimed leadership of the global Shiite community after 1501, he would count the Shiites of the Ottoman Empire as *his* subjects.

Ismail's poetry proved one of his empire's principal means of attracting adherents. The Turkic tribal peoples of northern Iran, the Caucasus, and eastern Anatolia were mostly illiterate, so rhythmic, easily remembered verses served to draw them in. In small towns and on the plains, Safavid officials would gather among the shepherds, riveting their attention with the shah's verses. One poem goes as follows:

> *I am the faith of the Shah ['Ali].*
> *In flying I am a parakeet, I am the leader of a mighty army,*
>     *a companion of Sufis.*
> *Wherever you sow me, I will grow; whenever you call me,*
> *I will come up. I shall catch the Sufis by the hand.*

*I was on the gibbet with Mansur; with Abraham in the fire*
  *and with Moses on Sinai.*
*Come from the eve, celebrate the New Year [Nau Ruz], join the*
  *King.*

In just a few short lines, Ismail managed to invoke prophets from the Middle East's monotheistic religions (Abraham and Moses), Persian cultural traditions (New Year), Shiism ('Ali), and Sufism (Mansur and the parakeet). It was a heady mix. Ismail's target audience was varied, inchoate, and complicated, and the poetry he used as the vehicle for his message proved similarly complex, fusing messianic Sufism, Turkic cultural forms, and militancy.

As the Safavids grew more confident in their Shiism, potent and sometimes eccentric Shiite themes came to dominate the shah's poetic propaganda. Instead of claiming that he merely represented the faith of 'Ali, or that he somehow knew the prophets, Ismail asserted that he was God himself:

*I am Very God, Very God, Very God!*
*Come now, O blind man who has lost the path, behold the Truth!*

To further distinguish his new adherents from the Ak Koyunlu, the Ottomans, and everyone else, Ismail awarded a bright red hat to military recruits who pledged their allegiance to the Safavids. The helmet had twelve points sticking straight up, signifying the Twelve Imams of Shiism. As a result, Ismail's forces came to be known as Red-hats (*Kızılbaş*), a term the Ottomans would soon adopt to refer pejoratively to all Shiites, their own subjects included, whether or not they were linked to the Safavids.

※

SAFAVID CLAIMS TO SOVEREIGN adversarial power sent an unambiguous challenge first and foremost to the world's greatest Sunni power, the Ottoman Empire. In sizing up their enemy neighbors to the west, the Safavids undertook a strategy similar to that which had proved so successful against the Ak Koyunlu—they made overtures of alliance to Shiite, Sufi, and other non-Sunni populations in Ottoman eastern Anatolia in an attempt to weaken the empire from within. These forays brought them into direct confrontation with Selim. Looking south and east from Trabzon, Selim saw the eastern Anatolian theater of ideological and military battle as his sphere of authority, and he would let no threat stand.

In 1505, Shah Ismail's brother Ebrahim set off with an army of three thousand to pillage Selim's province. Selim and his motley army of mercenaries, disgruntled Janissary contingents, minority fighters, and tribal warriors chased these Red-hats for about a hundred miles from south of Trabzon as far as Erzincan, just north of the Euphrates, massacring many and seizing their arms and munitions. He then sent a separate retaliatory force to raid the western territories of the Safavids in the Caucasus.

In doing all this, Selim demonstrated clearly to both foreign adversaries and domestic onlookers that not only would he defend Ottoman soil, but he would also fight to capture new territory for the empire. He overwhelmed force with superior force, seizing every opportunity to strike preemptively or retaliate against the Safavids. He also raided Shiite villages within the empire's borders. As the Ottomans and the Safavids increasingly adopted the role of defender of their own branch of Islam, Selim saw it as his right, indeed his duty, to subjugate Shiites no matter where they were. He and Ismail waged a lively propaganda war as well—Ismail through his poetry, Selim through proclamations that were read aloud before battle. The "infidel dog" Ismail, as one of these missives read, deserved the beating his master Selim gave him.

Selim's confrontations with the Safavids exposed the vast gulf between his military philosophy and that of his father. For some time, Selim had been requesting military reinforcements from Istanbul to defend the empire's eastern flank, but had received nothing. After the battles of 1505, Ismail sent an envoy to Bayezit's court to complain about Selim's overly aggressive raids and to demand the return of his captured soldiers' weapons. Not surprisingly, Bayezit refused to return the armaments, but he did receive the envoy with full diplomatic pomp and circumstance and sent him back to Tabriz with gifts and promises of friendship. Seeing his son as a hothead, and viewing his empire holistically, he preferred to pursue a path of nonaggression and reconciliation with the Safavids. He anticipated imminent challenges from west and south, and had no interest in doing battle on the eastern front— which would require the transport of massive numbers of troops and supplies over vast distances and difficult terrain. Selim, naturally, saw things differently. So far from the Mediterranean, he did not regard the Venetians, Spanish, or Genoese as threatening. For him, the Safavids were the Ottomans' paramount enemy.

The Safavids loomed as a threat not simply because of their grow-ing military capabilities, but because they offered an existentially dev-astating alternative vision of Muslim power. More than Christianity or Judaism, the ideological challenge of Shiism struck the Ottomans' Sunnism close to the bone. The Ottoman–Safavid confrontations in these years were far from the full-blown inferno of Islamic civil war they would soon become, yet they smoldered. Watching the Safavids chip away at the ideological and territorial base of the empire he hoped to rule, Selim seethed with anger. For him, violence was the most effective—perhaps the only possible—form of diplomacy.

This divergence in outlook led to internal strife and outright polit-ical conflict in the House of Osman. Selim chased and killed Safa-vids; Bayezit gave them gifts and made overtures toward peace. Selim favored attack; his father advocated restraint. Selim believed that a weak response to the Safavid threat would only encourage them; Bayezit feared that his son's actions and rhetoric would exacerbate ten-sions between the empire and its thousands of Shiite subjects. When the sultan rebuked his son and ordered him to relinquish the terri-tories and prisoners he had captured, Selim refused. Already resent-ful of his father for privileging his older half-brothers and relegating him to the farthest reaches of the empire, Selim saw his father's policy toward the Safavids as a sign of incompetence. He resolved to stand up to the empire's enemies and ruthlessly defend Ottoman territory. In 1510, Shah Ismail sent a military contingent to the same area that Selim had successfully defended in 1505. Once again, Selim beat back Ismail's soldiers and then made inroads into Safavid territory, launch-ing a miniwar to the east of Erzincan. Much to Selim's chagrin, Bayezit intervened to settle the confrontation through a conciliatory diplo-matic process with the shah.

THE GROWING FAMILIAL RIFT over the Safavid problem—a difference in visions of imperial power and how it should be exercised militarily— would prove to be one of the major features of the succession battle between Selim and his two half-brothers, Ahmed and Korkud. Bayezit had given Ahmed, his favored son, the plum provincial governorship, in the family's old stronghold of Amasya, was helping him develop relationships with the top administrators and military commanders of the empire, and included him in all the important decisions of his sultanate around the turn of the sixteenth century. Ahmed thus represented continuity with his father's reign—including Bayezit's conservative, nonconfrontational stance toward the Safavids.

Selim set himself up in the east as the militarily aggressive option to succeed his father. He was adamant that enemies like the Safavids had to be faced down with force, not diplomacy, and was thus able to win supporters in the military, who distrusted Bayezit's reliance on restraint and patience. As son increasingly opposed father, the empire tilted toward war.

# ENEMIES EVERYWHERE

*Selim battles the Safavids while governor of Trabzon*

A T THE TURN OF THE SIXTEENTH CENTURY, AS EUROPEANS TOOK
the first West Africans—Muslims and non-Muslims—to the New
World as slaves, the importance of the Caucasus for the Ottoman slave
trade increased markedly. The Ottomans' peculiar brand of slavery had
long encouraged the connections between the Ottoman east and the

Caucasus—where many of its slaves originated—but as the empire's western borders momentarily solidified in this period, the Caucasus replaced the Balkans as the empire's major frontier zone, a porous boundary that enabled regular military raids, thus yielding large numbers of Christian boys for the Janissary Corps. With Trabzon serving as the primary conduit of these slaves into the empire, Selim held a privileged position over most other governors as a champion of the imperial military, winning him further support among the empire's soldiering classes. He exploited this advantage by exacerbating what he saw as the widening gap between the rank-and-file Janissaries and their top commanders. The latter, he felt, had grown increasingly distant from the battlefield in favor of comfortable posts in the Ottoman administration, leaving average soldiers as the staunch guardians of the empire.

Selim regularly led the raids that brought Caucasian slaves—mostly Christian, mostly white—into the empire. From Trabzon's markets, slaves were dispatched all over the empire and even well beyond. Venetian and Genoese merchants, for example, regularly bought slaves in Trabzon, along with silks and spices. Taxes from the slave trade represented as much as 30 percent of the annual income of some Black Sea cities. Thus, Selim spent a hefty portion of his time managing the slave trade—sourcing slaves, collecting taxes on sales of slaves, rooting out corruption in the marketplace, and keeping the flow of bodies moving through his city.

Selim's evolving relationship with the Janissaries shaped his decision to undertake one of his most aggressive military ventures as governor of Trabzon. In 1508, he marched a fighting force northeast into the Caucasus and attacked Georgia. This invasion opened a decade of expansionist military ventures. Christian Georgia, with its ancient churches and soaring peaks, had become an ally and sometime vassal of the new Shiite empire to its south. It was an easy target: small, no match for Ottoman might. Selim's forces were familiar with the mountainous terrain, thanks to their many raids for slaves and booty, and his call to arms promised a lightning-fast, nearly cost-free victory: "I am making a raid against the Georgian infidels who are in my vicinity; let those young men and brave fellows who delight in plunder come." In an indication of how successful Selim's coalition-building over the years had been, thousands heeded his summons and trekked to Trabzon, "from the cities, towns and villages which lay in the Divinely-protected dominions, and from among the nomadic tent-dwellers, brave and lion-like men of battle, who delighted in *cihād* and *ġazā* [holy war]."

It took less than a week to cover the 150 miles into southern Georgia, where Selim's composite force decimated a disorganized, stunned foe, "the people of unbelief and hatred," as the *Selimname* described them. According to the embellished prose of this nearly hagiographic account of the Georgia expedition, Selim "caused a vast area, throughout its length and breadth, to be trodden underfoot by horses swift as the wind, and trampled over by speed-increasing chargers; he made its inhabited places waste and desolate, and its prosperous regions the home and nest of the owl whose power is death."

The text goes on to relate that Selim's forces captured an estimated ten thousand Georgian women and children destined for slavery. The description of these raids emphasizes the riches and pleasure Ottoman soldiers derived from their foray into Georgia; they were "spoil-laden and satiated through looting and plundering all its riches, goods, chattels and farms." Their mission accomplished, Selim's forces turned their military encampment of discipline and decorum into an orgiastic scene of coerced sex with their piteous and defenseless Georgian captives:

> Into the possession of the *ġāzīs* [soldiers], the guides of the *ġazā*
>   [war], the army of mail-clad warriors, came gratuitously
> Beautiful, graceful and rosebud-mouthed creatures, and elegantly-
>   walking, cypress-statured, rose-scented idols.
> Many jasmine-complexioned girls were taken, girls who imparted
>   gladness and whose beauty was a delight.
> [They were] fairy-faced and houri-featured [a houri is a virgin
>   of paradise], with curling locks and with ambergris-fragrant
>   ringlets.
> The inside of the camp became full of [these] fairies, like a sky full of
>   moons, suns and Jupiters.

Such flowery language cannot mask the reality. Rape nearly always accompanies war.

As a military leader, Selim gave his loyal fighters what they most wanted: a fierce battle, plunder, and a license to sexual violence. This time, soldiers kept more of the spoils than was usual, as Selim relinquished the quota of a fifth of all slaves and booty that was his personal right

as commander. As portrayed in the *Selimname*, Selim was motivated by
purity of thought and action, ambition and resolve. We would say he was
single-minded, focused on his goal. He did not want money or pleasure
or slaves or even territory. His rewards would be coming.

Selim's Georgian foray was a calculated political move—a war he
could manipulate for his larger personal, political, and strategic goals.
First, he was sending an unambiguous message to the Safavids that he
was the strongman of the region. More importantly, he was establishing a stark distinction between himself and his father—and by extension his father's favorite, Ahmed; this preemptive attack would serve as
evidence to the empire's military elite that he was the most aggressive
of Bayezit's sons, and should therefore be their favored choice to succeed him. The speech Selim delivered to his soldiers made his intentions clear. On a Georgian battlefield, far off in enemy territory, Selim
was speaking to listeners far beyond those present: his father, his fraternal rivals, and all the empire's power brokers. He offered a diagnosis of
the ills that plagued the empire along with his proposed remedies, and
threw down a challenge to his domestic enemies for the throne:

> The incompetent people, the purse-snatchers, the men greedy
> for wealth and possessions, who are at my father's court, make
> gifts and presents their gods, and worship them; they are suffer-
> ing from an affliction. They have given up advancing the free-
> men, the capable and distinguished champion warriors and the
> renowned young heroes, who have constantly served our court
> since the times of my great ancestors. Their promotions and
> beneficence are always confined to the slave class, and, because
> they do not give office to anyone other than slaves, the capa-
> ble men among the people of our country and realm are, I have
> heard, inclining towards the Kızılbaş [Shiites].

The Ottoman Empire was thus, in Selim's rendition, directionless
and morally bankrupt, a condition which, he asserted, led inevitably
to political and military weakness. The ruling elite had deviated from
the pious path set down by his and Bayezit's "great ancestors," to the
point that the Ottomans could no longer defend their state. (This was
misleading, if not an outright lie; the empire was, arguably, stronger
than it had ever been.) The slave classes that made up the Ottoman mil-

itary and administrative establishment—those young Christian boys captured from the Balkans and the Caucasus, converted to Islam, and raised with every advantage—now cared more about monopolizing power, worldly authority, and wealth than the well-being and defense of the empire. Instead of becoming warriors, they had become petty, self-serving bureaucrats. In contrast, Selim presented the men who had fought with him in Georgia as the empire's true defenders. Passed over, as freeborn Muslims, and denied the countless allowances given to the elite slave classes, his armed mercenaries, peasants, and nomads, and some disaffected Janissaries too, had volunteered to risk their lives against the Ottomans' existential foes, and fought valiantly against the empire's real enemies: the nepotism, cronyism, selfishness, and greed that had decayed the state from within.

Selim thus offered an alternative to his father's rule. He proposed to return the empire to its lost moral uprightness and military security via the sanctification of pure struggle—an impassioned defense of the empire motivated not by greed for riches or worldly power but by a love for the House of Osman and respect for its luminous history. Selim pressed his case that only he could wake the empire from its slumbering demise, speaking now directly to his fighting men:

> It was for that reason that I chose to make a raid on the Georgian[s], and my aim in bringing you here was this. My regard, the effect of which is auspicious, is towards your class. Since the times of our forefathers, the counsels [given] to us have been to this effect, that our true slaves at our court are those who, in loyal devotion, risk life and head in our cause, and who give us companionship and service. If God (praise be to Him, He is Exalted) bestows upon me, His slave, sovereign power, my beneficent regard is towards freemen, and my good favour is towards capable and distinguished, sword-wielding champion warriors. . . . To make good-for-nothing people one's [trusted] servants, merely because they are slaves, is not a mark of sovereignty. It is never right to turn one's face away from freemen. If God, Who is Exalted, so wills, I am firm in this resolution.

Selim's "firm" resolution now pivots to winning the throne of "sovereign power" for himself. "Go, each one of you to your own

202 || GOD'S SHADOW

place," he continued, "and, in your [own] district, proclaim and make known to the capable and brave men that I have this pure conviction." Charging his soldiers with the dissemination of his political message, Selim sought to build an alternative power base distinct from and indeed diametrically opposed to what he called the "good-for-nothing" power elite—his father, the palace, and the top brass of the Ottoman military. From among the "freemen," the "capable and distinguished, sword-wielding champion warriors"—those his father had ignored and derided for far too long—Selim would resurrect what he regarded as the *real* Ottoman Empire.

The soldiers for whom Selim had provided plunder, booty, and slaves proved a willing audience for his ambitious plan to continue his conquests. When they returned to their homes and relayed Selim's words to their families and friends, we are told, all "became, with heart and soul, the slaves of that court." In using the carefully chosen words "slaves of *that* court" (my emphasis), this devotedly pro-Selim chronicle shoots an arrow directly at Bayezit's administration, casting Selim as a sultan with a court of his own. The *Selimname* goes on to relate that as people throughout the empire learned of Selim's message, they took to composing verses extolling his splendors and virtues and the glories of the day when he would finally become sultan, describing him as, for example, "the world-conquering monarch of glory and resolute endeavour" and "lord of a fortunate conjunction of the planets." Thus, after the Georgia campaign, if we are to believe the *Selimname*, Selim began emerging as sultan.

Selim's father was, of course, still the reigning sultan. He and his entourage watched nervously from Istanbul as Selim built a power base in the east. In the *Selimname*'s rendition of their fears, these men became "afflicted with great distress, . . . envy and jealousy," thanks to Selim's "valour and his laudable disposition for consummate bravery, manliness and skill." With Selim's rise, Bayezit and his retinue came to realize "that the courageous men of zeal who had been sick and ill with the diseases of lack of esteem and degradation had revived and gained fresh vigour." Moreover, "with the emergence of that monarch [Selim, viewed here as sovereign] whose state was dominion and whose mark was prosperity, they [Selim's soldiers] had come together and reassembled." With his own personal army, Selim surged in power. The *Selimname* goes on to say, rather prematurely, that "the people at [Bayezit's] court became aware that the sun of their prosperity had passed into eclipse and come near to setting."

As sultan of the empire, not to mention Selim's father, Bayezit refused to tolerate such insolence and escalated his support for Ahmed. As both camps grew more bellicose, it became clear that the succession battle would be bloody. The pro-Ahmed faction at Bayezit's court, again according to the *Selimname*, "began to strive eagerly, incessantly, and as much as possible, for the discrediting of the bravery and erudition of His Majesty Sultan [Selim], whose home is in heaven, and for the increase of Sultan Ahmed's grandeur and glory. In that matter they showed no lack of exertion and diligence." Meanwhile, Korkud, who had by now developed a serious interest in the throne, had begun to assemble his own retinue of supporters as well. Thus, as Bayezit aged and his three sons prepared for what might come next, their subjects girded themselves for the looming internecine battle.

SOON, A MAJOR CRISIS fanned the flames of this smoldering fraternal struggle. The Safavid capture of Tabriz in 1501 had emboldened Shiites throughout the Ottoman Empire, promising them powerful support against the Sunni empire that had often subjugated them. The imperial administration endeavored to stave off any attempts at a Safavid–Ottoman Shiite alliance that might undermine the empire from within by forcibly resettling Shiites away from the zone of Safavid influence. From eastern Anatolia, they were sent wrenchingly vast distances—to southwest Anatolia, even to the Balkans—to get them as far from the Safavids as possible. This plan, however, completely backfired. Instead of destroying what they perceived to be a threatening stronghold of Safavid sympathy, Ottoman officials spread the threat to every corner of the empire. They now had to chase the Safavid challenge all the way from the Balkans to Syria.

The province of Teke—the bulge of southwestern Anatolia just to the west of Antalya, lying between the Taurus Mountains and the Mediterranean Sea—received one of the largest populations of resettled Shiites. In 1511, a charismatic leader emerged from among them and threw the empire into crisis. His *nom de guerre*, Şahkulu, revealed his Shiite political program: with sword in hand, he rebelled against the Ottoman state as a slave (*kul*) of the Safavid ruler Ismail (*Şah*, or shah). Like so many other upstarts in early sixteenth-century Anatolia, Şahkulu began his career as a roving mystic proselytizer with a small band of followers. As did the early Safavid shahs and numerous other Muslim, Jewish, and Christian parvenus, Şahkulu began gaining more and more followers, forcing local Ottoman officials to pay him increasing attention. In line with the empire's policy of co-optation, Şahkulu, whose roots were among the tribal Turkmen, initially even received an allowance from Bayezit's imperial administration—a fact that would later be used against the sultan as evidence that he had, knowingly or unknowingly (which was worse?), aided an enemy of the state.

Increasingly emboldened, Şahkulu ratcheted up his claims, to the point of asserting his own divinity as a Shiite prophet. Some of his supporters claimed he was the Messiah. His oppositional and inspirational message found willing ears among a wide swath of those disgruntled with the Ottoman state—which seems to support one of the more bombastic assertions of Selim's speech in Georgia: that many of the empire's Sunnis were converting to Shiism. Accounts of Şahkulu's impact describe his followers as "the people of Anatolia," suggesting a large and varied base of support not only in Teke but also farther afield. Indeed, he sent letters as far as Greece and Bulgaria to drum up support for his intended rebellion. In 1510, newly arrived Jews in Salonica received letters inviting them to join him against the imperial state (few did). Inevitably, Şahkulu's attempts to foment rebellion received a military response.

Just after Bayezit resettled the eastern Shiites in Teke, he appointed Korkud governor of the province, charging him to become the "majestic and strong commander" required to defend against any Shiite challenge in the region. By the time Şahkulu launched his rebellion, on April 9, 1511 (the Shiite holy day of 10 Muharram, commemorating the martyrdom of Imam Hussein, son of 'Ali), it was patently clear that Korkud had failed in this charge. Already consumed by the impending succession battle, Korkud had abandoned Teke and taken to the road to win support around the empire for his own bid for the throne. In the spring of 1511, he was in Manisa, an important economic hub and one of the major cities in western Anatolia—and strategically located close to the Aegean coast, should a run on the capital be necessary.

Korkud's absence from Teke empowered Şahkulu, not only tactically but also rhetorically, by reinforcing Şahkulu's propaganda about the ineffectiveness and failure of Ottoman rule—that it did not serve the interests of the people, that its days were numbered. Şahkulu posited that Korkud had deserted Teke because the sixty-three-year-old Bayezit was near death—the death of a sultan always being a time of major chaos in the empire—and painted a picture of Ottoman bankruptcy and ineptitude, cowardice and selfishness, of an empire in tumult and decline.

In 1511, Şahkulu and his men were on the march, notching important victories against Ottoman forces in Teke and around the picturesque port city of Antalya. Much like the contemporary tactics of the Taino and Wolof half a world away in Hispaniola, Şahkulu and his rebels found ideal hiding spots in the forested mountains of southwestern Anatolia. From their upland locations, these forces would charge down onto Ottoman strongholds, burn military barracks, steal food and provisions, and decimate livestock. When reports reached Bayezit that the rebels had made inroads into the Ottoman military, even convincing some soldiers to switch sides, the sultan knew an immediate mobilization was needed. He dispatched one of his strongest military leaders, Karagöz Pasha, the governor-general of Anatolia, to smash the Shiite upstarts.

Karagöz Pasha pursued Şahkulu out of Teke and through western Anatolia. In town after town, he witnessed the carnage the rebels left in their wake. Some twenty thousand strong, Şahkulu's marauding Shiite forces even burned Sunni mosques and Qur'ans. Townspeople recounted tales of murder and rape, pillage and destruction. For instance, in the hilly, landlocked town of Kütahya, more than two hundred miles north of Antalya, the rebels "destroyed everything— men, women, and children—and even sheep and cattle if there were too many for their needs; they destroyed cats and chickens. They looted all the valued possessions of the [villagers] of Kütahya province—their carpets and whatever else they could find—and collected them up and burned them." At the end of April, a judge in Bursa, a hundred miles north of Kütahya, implored the head of the Janissaries to send soldiers immediately to protect his city, writing that if reinforcements did not arrive "within two days, the country was lost." Fortunately for the people of Bursa, Karagöz Pasha caught up with Şahkulu in Kütahya. Distressingly for the empire, though, Şahkulu's rebels far outnumbered the Ottoman troops. Outmanned and uninspired, the imperial army was easily routed from Kütahya, and Karagöz Pasha fell into the rebels' hands. On April 22, 1511, in front of the citadel of Kütahya, they impaled him for all to see, then beheaded him and burned the body.

For Bayezit, the situation was both terrifying and intolerable. The lack of strong leadership in Anatolia had allowed a rebel thug to run roughshod across the heart of his empire. A Shiite apostate had destroyed property, murdered imperial subjects including a prominent governor-general, and was now spreading his vitriolic heresies across the realm. In an attempt to stop him, Bayezit turned to his grand vizier—Hadım Ali Pasha, originally from Bosnia, now the second most powerful man in the empire—and ordered him to annihilate Şahkulu and his rebels. While Bayezit, of course, wanted to end the rebellion and make an example of Şahkulu as a warning to all potential enemies of his state, he understood that his response to Şahkulu offered opportunities to further other interests as well.

Of Bayezit's three possible successors—Selim, Ahmed, and Korkud—the empire's military men now rightly saw Selim as the most aggressive: chasing down Safavid raiders and Anatolian Shiites, invading Georgia, offering soldiers his own share of the spoils of war. Bayezit and the pro-Ahmed faction thus felt obliged to prove that the sultan's favorite son was as engaged and proactive a military commander as Selim—demonstrating just how successfully Selim had manipulated the debate over the empire's use of force. Grand Vizier Hadım Ali Pasha headed the palace's pro-Ahmed faction, so appointing him to be the one to destroy Şahkulu would further Ahmed's military reputation. In a deft smoke-and-mirrors operation, Ahmed remained in Amasya, far from any fighting, but it was widely reported that he was in constant contact with Ali Pasha—thus giving the impression that he was the tactical mastermind of the empire's fight against the rebels, even as he avoided any exposure to danger. This piece of political theater was a direct response to the threats Selim had issued to Ahmed and their father during the Georgian campaign. Bayezit was well aware that many in the Janissary Corps, commanders and common soldiers alike, remained skeptical of Ahmed's military chops; unforged by the fire of combat, he was considered weak, inexperienced, and even uninterested in defending the empire. In this regard, he was very much his father's son, preferring Bayezit's path of diplomatic engagement with the empire's enemies.

Unfortunately for Ahmed and Bayezit, and much more unfortunately for the grand vizier, things did not go as planned. When imperial forces confronted the rebels near Kütahya, Şahkulu and his men escaped eastward toward Safavid Iran to gather needed supplies and men from their Shiite allies. Ali Pasha, still "in coordination" with Ahmed, gave chase and met Şahkulu's forces near the mineral-rich central Anatolian mountain town of Sivas. The attrition of Ottoman troops on the long march eastward, a lack of supplies, and possibly even the treason of some of his own soldiers put Ali Pasha and his men in a highly compromised position against the already-restocked Shiite rebels. When the fighting began in July, the imperial army suffered heavy losses. A few weeks later, word reached Istanbul that Ali Pasha had been killed. The Ottomans, however, did capture some of the Shiite rebels and eventually forcibly resettled most of them in the Peloponnese, very far from the Safavid frontier. Meanwhile, the majority of the Shiite fighters fled back toward Safavid territory. When they reached Ismail's court in Tabriz later that summer, they were welcomed as heroes. The list of those arriving at the court, however, does not include Şahkulu, suggesting that he died either in the battle at Sivas or during the march to Iran.

Whatever Şahkulu's end, it does not much matter for his legacy. He had rocked the edifice of the Ottoman Empire, exposing its frailties and leaving a trail of destruction throughout its heartland. It was Şahkulu who laid the groundwork for future Safavid challenges to the Ottomans. He killed the sultan's most trusted confidant, gained supporters for Shiite interests in towns and cities throughout Anatolia, exposed Korkud as selfish and inept, and dealt a major setback to Ahmed's ambition for the throne. In the domestic game of imperial succession, Selim clearly benefited from Şahkulu's rebellion. It confirmed what he had felt for years and what he had asserted in his speech to the troops in Georgia: his father and his father's administration were weak, his half-brothers even weaker. Factionalism and nepotism, power and money motivated them, rather than the well-being of the state and its people. Korkud, having departed Teke for Manisa, had proved his fecklessness. The power vacuum he had left in southwestern Anatolia allowed the Şahkulu Rebellion to break out in the first place, and Ahmed's fearful, tepid machinations only bolstered its success. As the heir apparent, Ahmed had the most to lose from the Şahkulu Rebellion, and lose it he did. His (and Ali Pasha's) thunderous failure reverberated like a cannon blast through the mountain passes of Anatolia.

A deep sense of crisis gripped the ruling elite as they tried to fathom how such a catastrophe could have happened. Ahmed, who had been publicly projected as the leader of the empire's response to the rebellion, took most of the blame. Some observers offered critiques of his military strategy, insisting that Ali Pasha and his men had died because Ahmed had not sent reinforcements quickly enough. Others pointed to weaknesses in Ahmed's personality, suggesting that he was simply too uninspiring and timid to galvanize the empire's soldiers. When Ahmed had demanded an oath of allegiance from the Janissaries during the rebellion, they refused on the grounds that he was not personally leading them into war. By keeping himself safe, he lost the respect and even the allegiance of soldiers who were risking their lives to defend his family's empire. Obviously, none of this boded well for his bid to attain the Ottoman throne.

Ahmed suffered another blow when reports surfaced that his own son, Murad, the sultan's grandson—himself a potential future sultan—had defected to the Safavid side, donning the distinctive red helmet of the *Kızılbaş*. If Ahmed, as it appeared, could not even impose his will on his own children, how could he rule an empire? For critics of Ahmed, and by extension his father, this only confirmed their view that the two were failures at defending the integrity of the Ottoman Empire, watching helplessly as Shiism infiltrated not only their empire but even the dynastic family. Under Bayezit's rule, the empire had become soft and vulnerable. If Ahmed's conduct during the Şahkulu Rebellion was any indication, he would only make matters worse should he become the next sultan.

SELIM, THE RUTHLESS FIGHTER who had for decades battled the empire's enemies from a remote province on the border with Iran, was the clear alternative to Ahmed. Where his father had chosen to negotiate with the empire's Shiite enemies, Selim had overwhelmed them with devastating violence. Where Ahmed had cowered in his Amasya palace during the Şahkulu Rebellion, Selim had ridden out to war with his men in Georgia and Safavid territory. Selim was strong where the rest of his family was weak. As the least advantaged of his father's sons, the least likely to win the throne, he had to become more brutal and resolute than the rest. He had to prove himself against his half-brothers and their supporters, against his own father, against the Safavids—all of whom would resist him.

Selim longed to restore the empire to its former glory and strength, to inspire soldiers and subjects alike. He would reject palace intrigue, factionalism, and greed. He wanted to return the military to the days when the privileged slave classes fought for the empire before themselves; at the same time, he built a fighting force of comparatively disadvantaged freeborn Muslims, ethnic minorities, and others. Whoever they were, Selim wanted men who would fight with zeal and inspiration, soldiers who were willing to sacrifice. He had demonstrated his good intentions by giving his troops all the booty, praise, and slaves earned in the Georgian campaign. The only prize Selim wanted was the throne.

# SUMMER IN CRIMEA

*Selim meets with Mengli Giray
in Crimea*

Every sultan in the more than six-hundred-year history of the Ottoman dynasty descended from one man—Osman, the first sultan. Bayezit was the eighth link in this imperial chain; the transition from link eight to link nine proved to be one of the most wrenching for the dynasty. Selim pushed circuitously toward his father's throne— from Trabzon across the Black Sea to the Crimean peninsula in the far north of the empire, down through the Balkans and eventually to

Istanbul. Along the way, he showed himself to be a duplicitous son and a shrewd political strategist, a violent brother and a doting father. Balancing all of these identities on his shaky branch of the dynasty's family tree proved precarious, to say the least.

IN 1511, WHILE THE Şahkulu Rebellion roiled the empire, Selim's only son, Suleyman, turned seventeen, the same age as Selim was when he assumed the governorship of Trabzon. Selim at seventeen had been as stern as Suleyman was coddled. Still, the time had come for Suleyman to leave the confines of his palace home and enter the venomous world of imperial administration. The *Selimname* described him, as he entered adulthood, as "the straight-grown sapling of the orchard of success, and the fruit of the tree of world-government." As we have seen, the sons of sultans nearly always became governors, usually in the most strategic post available. The sons of these princes often became governors also, although not always, and certainly not in desirable locales. Positioning Suleyman in the right governorship—one that would advance the cause of both father and son—was a key component of Selim's grand strategy to outwit his half-brothers.

Even before the boy turned seventeen, Selim had tried (and failed) to have him named governor of Şebhane Karahisarı and Bolu, two small provinces close to Trabzon, the only home Suleyman had ever known. This would have allowed Selim to train him in government, thus preparing him for a much better post. Bayezit rejected both requests, which Selim took as evidence of his father's desire to ensure that Ahmed would inherit the throne.

In 1511, still smarting from those denials, Selim tried a different tactic. He requested that Suleyman be given one of the provinces in the Balkans—some of the most prized governorships in the empire. As Bayezit aged and Ahmed and Korkud openly declared their intentions to claim the throne, Selim knew he would need a power base closer to Istanbul. Though Selim confidently expected rejection, he persisted, for two reasons. First, the request was a negotiating strategy; it maintained pressure on Bayezit. Second, it served to expose his father's biased support for Ahmed.

When every appeal for a Balkan governorship for Suleyman was met with refusal, Selim moved on to request other postings, first in

provinces close to Istanbul and then in those increasingly distant. Finally—probably because Bayezit deemed it far away enough from the capital—Selim's bid for Kefe, in the southeast of Crimea, received approval. Kefe (later known as Kaffa, now known as Feodosia) put Suleyman at some distance from Istanbul, but at least it was a straight shot across the Black Sea—and closer to the imperial palace than Trabzon was. With the Şahkulu Rebellion still raging and the three princes jockeying for advantage, Selim accepted Kefe as the best possible posting for Suleyman. At the same time, an ominous message leaked out from the palace. Within a matter of weeks, Selim learned, Bayezit would abdicate in favor of Ahmed, who, it turned out, had already been instructed to prepare his march on Istanbul from Amasya. Korkud, still in Manisa, also got wind of this message and began making arrangements to set out for the capital, in an effort to get there first. Sensing their opportunities waning, Selim and Suleyman sprang into action to organize their affairs, their men, and the ships they would need to cross the Black Sea. Selim would go first to Crimea to drop off Suleyman, and then head southwest, to Istanbul.

Because of the modest size of their ships, Selim opted to avoid open water and take a slower but safer course, sailing around the Black Sea's rugged eastern coast for about two weeks before docking in Kefe. When he and Suleyman stepped ashore for the first time, they were immediately impressed by the city's strangeness. Crimea's long history of being ruled by outsiders—from the Scythians to the Greeks, Romans, Byzantines, Mongols, and Genoese—made the arrival of a new governor a rather unremarkable event. Though nominally in possession of the peninsula, the Ottomans kept their touch light, generally deferring to Crimea's entrenched rulers at the time, the Tatar khans. Suleyman and his father stuck out in Crimea as clear outsiders. As they dropped anchor, these were their first impressions:

> The protected city of Kaffa is the glory and crown of the regions of the happiness-befriended Tatars, and the shelter, refuge and highway of the inhabitants of the Kıpçak Steppe and of vast territories stretching all the way to the country of the church-bell-accustomed Russians and, on another side, as far as Gog and Magog, whose lantern is sedition. [It is] a massive bulwark at the edge of the sea, an impregnable stronghold, which adjoins the apogee, and a great fortress, which is the pivot of the celestial globe. . . . Inside it [is] an extended wall, famous as "the Frankish castle," whose battlements reach the sky and which is fitted out, in places, with towers rising to the heavenly sphere. [The city has] a beautiful palace, towering above its harbour, which gives joy and imparts gladness; it overlooks the horizons of the world, and its like is not to be found, or rarely, in the inhabited part of the earth.

Suleyman's mother, Hafsa, had been born in Crimea, so he knew something of the region from her, but he nonetheless felt it to be alien, perhaps even dangerous, dominated by ethnicities, languages, and cultures he did not understand. "Gog and Magog" denoted a place that existed beyond the inhabited earth, an imaginary realm of monsters

*Three Ottoman ships at sea*

and spirits. Although Selim and Suleyman considered their time in Crimea to be a mere stepping-stone to their ultimate goal, they found Crimean society as impenetrable as the high walls of the fortress that greeted them on the shoreline.

The Tatar khans, who counted Genghis Khan as one of their ancestors, descended from a long line of rulers of Central Asian origin who had steadily migrated westward to escape the Mongols. They had ruled Crimea since the early fifteenth century, and would continue to control it until the end of the eighteenth century. Selim and Suleyman understood that they would have to ingratiate themselves with the khans in order to rule effectively. Therefore, after getting their bearings in Kefe, Selim left Suleyman in the city and set off to meet the leader of the Crimean Tatars, Mengli Giray Khan, in his ornate palace in western Crimea, a complex complete with a mosque, harem, cemetery, and gardens. Mengli—short, stocky, and with a wispy beard—had distinguished himself by defeating the last remnants of the Mongol Empire in Crimea and securing the khans' independent rule over the peninsula. Once in charge, he quickly established the slave trade as one of his major sources of revenue. Between 1450 and 1586, for example, his armies led eighty-six slave raids, or about one every eighteen months, into Ukrainian territory alone. In 1520, the year of Selim's death, slavery poured a stunning 10,000 gold ducats into Crimea's coffers. Mengli used the income from slavery to build several fortresses, including the one that had greeted Selim and Suleyman on the coast.

Though Mengli and Selim had never met, they were already connected, as it was Mengli who had gifted Hafsa, Selim's concubine and Suleyman's mother, to the Ottoman court in the 1490s, in the hope that his gift would forever link the House of Giray to the House of Osman. Should Hafsa become the mother of a sultan, she would be one of the most powerful people—man or woman—in the Ottoman Empire, and this would elevate the status of the Girays. Thus, she was the figure who bound the two ruling families together—again evincing the central role of women, even concubines, in early modern imperial politics. Although this was never mentioned in the correspondence about Suleyman's posting to Kefe, Hafsa's personal ties to Crimea probably played a part in Bayezit's decision to send her son there, as Bayezit had long sought to deepen his relations with the Crimean khans. When Selim paid a visit to Mengli, he was therefore both smoothing the path for Suleyman's governorship and meeting his concubinal "father-in-law" for the first time. Selim respectfully referred to Mengli as his uncle, a term of deferential endearment for his son's "grandfather." As with much else among the Ottomans, family was politics and politics family.

Mengli served as protector and patron for both Selim and Suleyman, so Selim did his best to act the part of both dutiful "familial" relation and humble guest. As relayed in the *Selimname*—first composed decades after Selim's death, though still credible—Selim described Mengli as "firm and honest, pious and a true Muslim . . . his character sound. . . . He was a Sunni, holding the correct doctrine, a successful monarch, and a saintly-natured, well-bred person." For Mengli, meeting a potential Ottoman sultan (perhaps two) proved a moment pregnant with opportunities for himself, his family, and his state. He therefore spared no expense in spoiling Selim during his visit. According to the *Selimname*:

[Mengli] came to meet him with the army of the happiness-scattering Tatars, with all his attendants and followers, whose

*Hafsa*

distinguishing mark was grandeur, and all his children and princes, his chief subjects, his sons and his noblemen. As far as the ceremonies of hospitality were concerned, he rendered [Sultan Selīm] all such services as were due, showing him, in many different kinds and forms, the respect and honour befitting an emperor and the esteem and deference proper to a world-ruler. He provided him with food in abundance, and was not remiss in showing consideration and deference. Their meeting became a source of tranquillity and joy, and a cause of all kinds of gladness.

All of this happiness-scattering and gladness could not, however, dispel the pall of anger and resentment hanging over Selim. He had sailed to Crimea not to meet Mengli but to put in motion his plan to take over the empire, kill his half-brothers, and perhaps even commit patricide into the bargain. However this plan turned out, Selim had embarked on a path that might forever reforge the Ottoman Empire. No amount of Tatar hospitality could overcome such acrimony.

WHEN NEWS REACHED AHMED that his half-brother was in Crimea and plotting an advance on the palace, he became enraged. Ahmed had pressed Bayezit to deny Suleyman any governorship at all; and Crimea, though remote, was still dangerously close to Istanbul. Several overland routes led westward into the Balkans, and many of its ports were within easy striking distance of the capital. Growing increasingly impatient as he waited for final word from his father that he should begin his march toward the palace, Ahmed lobbied Bayezit to order the governors of all the provinces between Crimea and the capital to monitor their roads to prevent Selim from making a move southward. Bayezit issued the orders, adding that any soldier found to be aiding Selim or Suleyman would be summarily executed.

At the same time, and with his father's blessing, Ahmed devised further subterfuge. Acting the part of sultan-in-waiting, he drafted a letter to Mengli offering him independent sovereignty over the province of Kefe in exchange for imprisoning Selim and Suleyman in Crimea. Along with the letter, Ahmed sent a royal rescript officially granting Mengli the province.

As it so happened, the emissary carrying Ahmed's message arrived at Mengli's court while Selim was enjoying his visit with the khan. Seeing Selim, the emissary ordered him to return to Trabzon at once. Selim scoffed. That this man, a mere emissary, could treat a prince so rudely only further proved the corruption of his father's rule—and, by extension, the rule of Ahmed if he should gain the throne. Selim declared that he would never accept such an order, "even if Gabriel descended from the sky and the Messenger [that is, the Prophet Muḥammad] wished it," and gave the emissary a message to take back to the sultan: he demanded an immediate face-to-face audience with his father, along with the governorship of the province of Silistra on the flat plains of the Danube valley, in what is today Bulgaria. The city of Silistra, strategically located along one of the major north–south axes through the eastern Balkans and controlling access to the sea, is about three hundred miles north of Edirne, the former Ottoman capital, where Bayezit had temporarily moved his court in 1509 after an earthquake damaged the palace in Istanbul. With his demand of this posting for himself—one he knew would be refused—Selim was sending his father a clear message that he would not stop his march toward the throne. Selim further instructed the emissary to tell the sultan that the face-to-face meeting would be to discuss the pressing issue of the empire's decline. Selim's couching of his threats and insults in the formal language of a request added to the ignominy of his affront, in effect saying: "Dearest Father, I humbly ask for the honor of a meeting with your excellency to confer about how your many faults and weaknesses have led to the deterioration of our empire and how I, your dutiful son, might overthrow you to become sultan in your stead."

As Selim berated the emissary, Mengli opened Ahmed's letter. When he read it, "a tumult beset the Khan's heart, and he became troubled in mind." The offer of independent rule was of course very attractive—independence is, needless to say, the goal of all political leaders—but Mengli struggled to weigh the dividends and costs of such a deal with Ahmed. Regardless of his connections to Selim, through Hafsa and now Suleyman's governorship, Mengli wanted what was most advantageous for himself and his family: to cast their lot with whichever half-brother would win the Ottoman throne. In the summer of 1511, it was impossible to determine who that would be.

As the various possibilities surged through Mengli's anxious mind, one of his sons, Mehemmed Giray, who was present at this meeting, was unconditionally ecstatic. The Girays finally would have the chance to acquire all the lands of Crimea, to impose their sovereignty over its peoples, ports, and fortresses. Putting Selim and Suleyman in prison or under house arrest seemed a small price to pay for so much in return. Young, ambitious, and impetuous, Mehemmed, who shared his father's looks but not his personality, pushed him to accept the offer immediately and unequivocally. Imploring his son to be more circumspect, Mengli managed to convince Mehemmed that they should at least ask Selim if he would make them the same offer of independence should he become sultan. Wisely, Mengli did not want to pick a side at this point in the princes' fraternal struggle.

The following night, the khans hosted a lavish banquet in honor of Selim and Suleyman. Bathed in warm candlelight and digging into mounds of mutton, rice, and okra, the guests became increasingly inebriated as the night wore on and, as the evening's jovial mood floated from meats and vegetables to sherbets and fruits, took turns standing to toast Mengli and their visitors. After dark, Mehemmed stood up. He turned first to Selim, offering him exaltations and the most superlative flattery. Everyone cheered and drank after each solemn tribute that Mehemmed made to Selim, Suleyman, and the unity of their families. Mehemmed then raised his cup again and, as the *Selimname* relates, said, "Sultan Selim, your father has little time left, and the sovereignty of the throne of Rūm [the Ottoman Empire] is yours. Your accession to the seat of empire is close at hand. At that time, I shall ask something from you as a favour."

Selim responded: "Prince, what is it that you aim for and desire?"

Mehemmed glanced at his father, who gazed at his son knowingly. Mehemmed then said to Selim, "Give us possession of the territories of Kaffa, with the fortresses and seaports which are situated within them, and let us have free disposal of them in the days of your reign." Everyone in the room froze; the dinner's boisterous conviviality dissolved.

Selim took a moment to measure his words. "Prince," he replied, "we are sovereign monarchs. In the practices and laws of sovereign monarchs, and in their customs which have been observed from of old, the giving away of regions and countries has no place. Monarchs take countries, [but] they do not give countries to anyone. Whatever you ask for in the way of jewels, silver, gold, rubies and other precious stones, all kinds of gems and money, goods and chattels and royal estates, it will not be refused; let it be given. Only do not make fortresses or countries the object of your desire."

Flummoxed, Mehemmed sat down without uttering another syllable. Selim—calculating and politically hungry—would not accept insolence, and would never facilely surrender the power and territory his family's empire had won with flesh and fire—especially not to an upstart like Mehemmed. Years of plotting and torment, the blood of war, and a steely determination had delivered Selim closer to the sultanate than ever before, but much danger still lay ahead. His detour through Crimea, with all the challenges it posed for his war preparations, was at best an annoying necessity.

At the end of the long evening, after Selim had retired, Mehemmed stormed over to his father, yelling, "Did you pay attention to the words of this scoundrel?" While Ahmed, anticipating his own ascension to the throne, had promised the khans territory, fortresses, sovereignty, and power, Selim, who was enjoying their hospitality and protection, refused even to consider making the same offer. Mehemmed took this not only as an insult and a sign of disrespect but as a declaration of war. By this point in the evening, Mehemmed was embarrassed, livid, thoroughly drunk, and determined to teach Selim a savage lesson. Despite his father's protestations, Mehemmed marched out to collect his troops.

Realizing that only ill could come of this, Mengli summoned his other son, Sa'adet. Despite being younger than Mehemmed, "of a tender age and beardless, with rosy cheeks, a rosy face and well-arched eyebrows," Sa'adet had something his brother did not: "intelligence and sense." Fearing the potentially dire consequences for the House of Giray if Mehemmed attacked Selim, Mengli ordered Sa'adet to accompany the Ottoman prince in order to protect him from Mehemmed, and to do whatever Selim asked of him. Thus, ironically, in order to keep his own imperial family from being involved in another family's deadly fraternal struggle, Mengli created a fraternal struggle between his sons.

Sa'adet and his men set out at once for Selim's camp to help the Ottoman prince and his retinue make their escape from Crimea. Gathering their possessions, they boarded boats waiting to ferry them across the northern Black Sea to Akkerman, a port on the Dniester River estuary just north of the Balkan peninsula, which the *Selimname* termed their "skirt of safety." At daybreak, Mehemmed, still enraged, arrived at Selim's camp with thirty thousand soldiers in tow. They found the Ottomans' tents empty and abandoned. Mehemmed spat in disgust at the deserted camp and dispersed his soldiers.

SELIM HAD USED HIS time in Crimea to ready his forces for the march southward to overthrow his father. For more than a decade, he had been preparing for the summer of 1511. Now, his efforts to cultivate relationships among the Janissaries and to build alliances with disgruntled soldiers, mercenaries, and other potential soldiers coalesced. As the battle for the throne neared, Selim was eager to spend all the political and military capital he had accumulated during his years in the east. As well as his network of armed men distributed across the empire, he needed a concentrated force in the Balkans. Thus, he dispatched some of his most trusted lieutenants to the military commanders of provinces between Kefe and Istanbul, making them promises of cash and future political appointments in exchange for their support in a war against his father and half-brothers. His track record against the Safavids, as well as in Georgia, demonstrated to these potential Balkan allies that he was a military leader they could trust, one who would succeed at all costs and fulfill his promises, just as he had in the east. Selim's victories would also be theirs.

Over the summer of 1511, Selim built up his coalition in the Balkans and collected provisions and matériel in preparation for the move on Istanbul: a fleet of approximately a hundred ships, a vast array of supplies and weapons, and three thousand soldiers. Now that his son was accompanying Selim, Mengli Giray Khan ramped up his support for him too, instructing Sa'adet to assist Selim and contributing three hundred of his own soldiers, along with an additional one thousand Crimean Kazaks.

After their departure from Crimea and a few days at sea, Selim and his men, and Sa'adet and his, arrived safely in Akkerman on June 1, 1511. The city had been conquered by the Ottomans in 1484, one of the last Black Sea ports to fall. From Akkerman—ever closer to Istanbul—Selim wrote to his father. "For such a long time," he began, "I have been deprived of the sight of the happy, noble beauty of your face. Visiting one's relations is one of the obligatory duties [of men]. It was with that hope that your humble servant set out in the direction of Kaffa, and he has now come to the environs of Akkermān. It is hoped that, from among the exalted imperial favours, permission may be granted." Via Ahmed's emissary, Selim had previously demanded an audience with his father. Now Selim tried a softer tone, playing the dutiful son who longed to see his father to offer him the proper respect—an emotional ploy for political gain. A father himself, Selim understood the power of a father's love for his son, and despite the obvious suspicions his message would elicit, he hoped to be able to pluck the right tune on the strings of his father's heart. If the most expedient road from Akkerman to Istanbul was duplicitous emotion, Selim stood ready to tread that path.

As part of his strategy, Selim continued to send flattering letters to his father while he allowed time for his troops to assemble. He wrote that his sole desire in going to the Balkans was to kiss his father's hand and accord him the respect he deserved. He again requested the governorship of the Danubian province of Silistra in order to, he said, be close to his father in his old age. Bayezit and his advisers easily saw through these declarations of filial piety, sending an emissary to inform Selim that he would never again be allowed to enter the sultan's presence. Selim responded in a tone more legalistic than any he had tried before. "My lord," he asked his father's representative, "if one of God's servants has not seen his noble father for ten or fifteen years, since visiting one's relations is one of the obligatory duties, if that servant, in order to comply with the sublime Divine commandments, sets out to visit his father, is it permissible, according to the *şerī'at* [holy law], to prevent him? I ask you for a *fetvā* [legal opinion]."

The emissary answered, "According to the *şerī'at*, no-one may prevent him."

Pleased with this response, Selim retorted, "Since this act is prescribed by the *şerī'at* and, according to the *şerī'at*, may not be prevented, why [then] have they sent you, and for what purpose have you come?" He sent the man back to his father.

THE YEAR 1511, in which Selim made his push toward Istanbul and the Şahkulu Rebellion continued to sow chaos across the empire, saw other political realignments and long-distance military expeditions that would forever reforge the world. In the decades around 1500, empires across the globe countered one another's encroachments and expansions with their own wars and invasions, leading to a global race for territory and control of strategic sea-lanes and overland trade routes. In 1511 alone, the Portuguese captured Malacca in Southeast Asia, the Spanish invaded Cuba, the Taino revolted in Puerto Rico, and Henry VIII built his navy's largest-ever warship, the *Mary Rose*, a reflection of England's growing overseas ambitions.

Selim stood closer that summer than ever before to seizing the Ottoman throne. Not only was he within striking distance of the capital, but he also had a formidable fighting force and the backing of the Crimean khans, as well as some of the Janissary Corps. Yet, impressive as his support was, Selim's army paled when compared with the quality and size of the imperial army and military resources his father could muster at a moment's notice. Even more daunting than his deficit on the battlefield was the towering wall of precedent Selim sought to surmount. To become sultan, he would likely have to kill a sultan, his own father, an unprecedented act in the dynastic history of the Ottoman Empire. Selim knew that should he fail, he would surely die, one of the forgotten vanquished of the global political struggles of the early sixteenth century.

CHAPTER
15

# BOUND FOR ISTANBUL

*Selim battles his father*

As selim's uncertainties and fears quickened, so did the drumbeat of war. By the end of July, Selim had begun his march southward, along the western shore of the Black Sea from Akkerman toward the outskirts of Edirne, the former imperial capital at the bend of the Meriç River. Further men and supplies accompanied him by boat. The time for letters and emissaries had passed.

Bayezit, informed by a cascade of messengers of Selim's steady advance, dispatched one of his highest-ranking and most able confidants in an attempt to intimidate his rebellious son. Hasan Pasha, the governor of Rumelia—perhaps the most important province in the whole of the empire, as it included the former capital, Edirne, and much of the empire's lucrative lands in the Balkans—rode toward Selim's camp with a dozen or so soldiers. But Selim refused to meet him. He let the size of his own military force speak for itself, impressing upon Hasan the gravity of the threat to his father's throne. Without pursuing the matter further, Hasan returned southward. This pusillanimous retreat only added to the defiant prince's menacing reputation, both as a formidable military commander and as the son who would most readily resort to violence against his father.

Despite Selim's earlier fawning missives, his forces on the outskirts of Edirne demonstrated—if any doubt remained—that he was not there to fulfill a filial duty. Bayezit now dispatched fifteen thousand of his own troops to intercept Selim. Only with their armies face to face did Selim and his father, through their representatives, begin talking. Instead of wasting lives in a chest-puffing battle, both hoped to save their soldiers for the ultimate confrontation that surely lay ahead. They negotiated a rapprochement whereby Bayezit would grant Selim a governorship in the Balkans in exchange for his withdrawal from Edirne. Selim was given his choice of three governorships: Bosnia, the Peloponnese, or Smederevo in what is today north-central Serbia. He chose Smederevo, the former Serbian capital conquered by the Ottomans in 1439.

More significantly, Bayezit swore he would not abdicate in favor of any of his sons. This promise represented a major victory for Selim; it bought him time and forestalled the threat of the imminent enthronement of Ahmed. When Bayezit died, Ahmed would be left to fend for himself. Self-confident, self-reliant, and well-armed, Selim was convinced that without their father's support behind Ahmed, he would have the advantage in any all-out war among the three half-brothers, particularly since he had the most military experience and the most imposing fighting force.

FROM THE START OF the negotiations, both Bayezit and Selim knew that whatever agreement they reached would last about as long as the proverbial tea after baklava—and, indeed, both immediately broke it. Bayezit had offered a truce only as the most expedient means of keeping Selim away from Istanbul; he never had any intention of honoring his word. In fact, just after the agreement was finalized, Bayezit began mobilizing his forces to strike Selim—initiating the process of turning over the empire to Ahmed. Ungrateful and always fearful of his half-brother, Ahmed resented the fact that his father had even considered negotiating with Selim. He wrote an angry letter to his father complaining about the perils of granting Selim a Balkan governorship and asking mockingly why he did not just go ahead and have coins minted in Selim's likeness and the Friday prayer said in his name.

For his part, Selim never had any intention of going to Smederevo to claim his governorship. His encampment north of Edirne was much closer to Istanbul, and he had no interest in ceding this position. Rumors of Bayezit's mobilization efforts, moreover, did not inspire trust. His troops' return to Istanbul did, however, provide Selim with a useful opportunity to make inroads in Edirne, since the city was now exposed. So he lingered on its outskirts, dispatching troops on occasional raids for food and other supplies. He also persisted in his recruitment efforts across the empire and sent spies to Istanbul and beyond to monitor the moves of his father, his half-brothers, and the imperial army. Meanwhile, Selim's continued encampment near Edirne angered his father, who sent progressively more threatening orders to Selim to go immediately to Smederevo. Selim procrastinated, citing, for example, the need to stay near Edirne to assist in the ongoing fight against the few Şahkulu rebels who remained in the area.

As both an exasperated father and an increasingly perturbed sultan, Bayezit decided personally to march a regiment back to Edirne to expel his stubborn son from the city. At first, Selim continued to stall; then he rode out of Edirne toward Smederevo with a contingent of soldiers. This was a charade—but Bayezit believed the flexing of his military might had succeeded in intimidating his son. Convinced of his temporary victory, he turned back to Istanbul. As soon as Selim was informed of this, he circled his forces back to Edirne. The only definitive moves he would make would be toward Istanbul, not away from it.

This time, Selim entered Edirne in earnest. He forcibly removed his father's representatives, set free his supporters whom his father had imprisoned, and proclaimed himself ruler of Edirne. With the city and its environs securely in his hands, he chased after his father with thirty thousand soldiers, described in the *Selimname* as being "[fierce as] lion-hunters." Quickly covering the flat terrain of Thrace, he caught up with his father ninety miles to the east, in the nondescript town of Çorlu, which is notable only for being a convenient halfway point between Edirne and Istanbul.

When the armies of father and son met in late July 1511 on the road between the empire's current and former capitals, combat immediately ensued. Bayezit's forty thousand troops, their war drums beating out a steady cadence, trounced Selim's thirty thousand. The imperial army had more men, more organizational acumen, and more cannons than Selim's composite force of decommissioned Janissaries, Karamanids, and armed pastoralists. After only a day of battle, it disintegrated. Most of his soldiers were captured or killed; others retreated to their homes, abandoning Selim's cause altogether. Only about three thousand of his men stayed by his side. Selim himself was almost killed when, near the end of the day, he and the small contingent flanking him were surrounded, and then charged, by the sultan's troops. In the melee, Selim's soldiers sneaked him off the battlefield and whisked him quickly northward to the picturesque Black Sea town of Ahyolu (now Pomorie, Bulgaria). Were it not for the 10 percent of his soldiers who remained loyal, Selim would have died.

The prince and his cohort spent a few days recuperating in Ahyolu, with fresh fish and the region's sweet peaches their main solace. About a week later, Selim boarded "such vessels as were ready at hand" and sailed back to Kefe to regroup and plot his next move. "The fish held that monarch in great esteem," the *Selimname* declares, betraying some of its shortcomings as a historical source. "They [went] before him, showing the right way." Some of Selim's military commanders accompanied him, while the bulk of his men marched overland. In Kefe, although happy to be reunited with Suleyman, Selim wallowed in self-pity and doubt. A substantial portion of the fighting force he had been building up his whole adult life—a group whom he believed would provide a comparative advantage in the battle for the throne—had collapsed at Çorlu. The Giray khans promised support but it was nothing close to what he had lost, and he was wary of becoming too beholden to them.

The Battle of Çorlu represented the first time in Ottoman history that a prince warred against his father the sultan. The unprecedented nature of this conflict is why we know of its outcome but not the details of the fighting itself. Such a story necessitated suppression, an observation that prompts caution when relying on accounts such as the *Selimname*. Within Ottoman political culture, raising an army against a sultan, the divinely endowed leader of the Ottoman realm, was by definition inherently illegitimate, not to mention illegal and immoral. Even some of Selim's own supporters, as much as they despised Bayezit, found it challenging to justify the war with his father. Prince fighting prince ensured the strongest successor, but prince fighting sultan struck at the majesty and sanctity of the sultanate. The sultan was to be unassailable, untouchable, and invincible, so violence against him had to be unthinkable. Thus, Ottoman historians, and the sultans who patronized them—both at the time and afterward—systematically attempted to prevent reports of the ferocious patrilineal wars between Selim and Bayezit from entering the historical record.

AFTER ÇORLU, BAYEZIT RETURNED to Istanbul, confident that his superior military capacities had restored order to the realm. He sent word for Ahmed—finally—to come to the capital as soon as possible. It was time to crown him sultan. Despite all that had transpired over the previous few years—Selim's threats, Ahmed's consternation, several armed confrontations—Ahmed, it seemed, was at last poised to don the mantle of Osman, and he dispatched one of his most trusted advisers to arrange the details of his entrance into Istanbul. As the ornate language of the *Selimname* described it, "the hope of acceding to the seat of the Sultanate became the adornment of his consciousness, and the expectation that the Caliphate-accustomed throne would be made attainable [to him] became the engraving on the signet-ring of his desire-catching mind."

Selim, sequestered across the sea in Crimea, would not acquiesce so easily. Now, at the eleventh hour, the time had arrived for him to utilize his most potent weapon. Since his earliest days in Trabzon, he had been maneuvering for the support of the common soldiers of the Janissary Corps. Unlike the irregulars he had led to Çorlu, or for that matter the upper echelons of the military he had derided in his speech in Georgia, these troops would not dissolve in the fire of war. They were committed and ever eager for confrontation. They had access to weapons and could coordinate their military forces across the entire imperial domain. For over a decade, since the late 1490s, Selim had been giving these soldiers money, respect, and power in exchange for their support. The Janissaries, in turn, understood that their future would shine brightest with Selim as their sultan. He would put them at the center of his sultanate, advocate for their interests, and support them materially. Even though some Janissary factions remained loyal to Bayezit, Selim's resolve stiffened with the knowledge that most were now behind him and would support him over Ahmed.

As a result of the Janissaries' intelligence-gathering capabilities, Selim—even in Kefe—was able to keep close tabs on events throughout the empire. When news of Ahmed's move on the capital reached him, he mobilized quickly. He sent men to shadow Ahmed as he snaked his way through Anatolia toward the capital, while finalizing his plans with the Janissaries. Publicly displaying this armed advantage in Istanbul, in plain view of Bayezit and the pro-Ahmed faction, became a key factor in Selim's strategy to counteract his father's plan to install Ahmed on the throne.

Thus, in late 1511, the Janissaries and Selim's supporters flooded the streets of Istanbul, loudly proclaiming that they would accept no one other than Selim as their new sultan. Bayezit set pro-Ahmed thugs loose in response. The situation quickly deteriorated. Scuffles broke out in the market when soldiers started stealing food and other supplies. Pro-Ahmed and pro-Selim factions seized whole neighborhoods as their competing turf, and guerrilla warfare gripped the city. As tensions rose, a simple sideways glance could end in a raucous brawl with several dead bodies. At one point, a rumor spread that Ahmed's men had referred to the pro-Selim Janissaries as treasonous dogs. This led to days of all-out street war, in which five thousand Janissaries attacked the homes and businesses of known Ahmed sympathizers. They killed some, burned their houses, and tried to expel every pro-Ahmed supporter they could find. The *Selimname* described it this way:

> [This] vast company and [these] troops whose grandeur was auspicious made the interior of Istanbul full of a happiness-purporting sound, with shouts of "Allah! Allah!" They split up into detachments, and each detachment raided the house of a [pro-Ahmed] pasha. They arrived like a dazzling flash of lightning and despoiled and ravaged both the inside and the outside

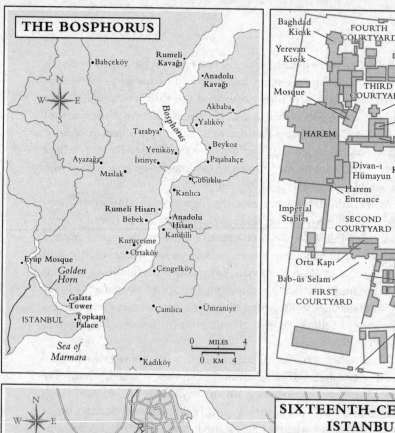

# THE BOSPHORUS

- •Bahçeköy
- •Rumeli Kavağı
- •Anadolu Kavağı
- •Akbaba
- •Yalıköy
- •Tarabya
- •Beykoz
- •Yeniköy
- •İstinye
- •Paşabahçe
- •Ayazağa
- •Maslak
- •Çubuklu
- •Kanlıca
- •Rumeli Hisarı
- •Bebek
- •Anadolu Hisarı
- •Kandilli
- •Kuruçeşme
- •Ortaköy
- •Eyüp Mosque
- •Çengelköy
- *Golden Horn*
- •Galata Tower
- •Topkapı Palace
- ISTANBUL
- •Çamlıca
- •Ümraniye
- *Sea of Marmara*
- •Kadıköy

Bosphorus

0 — MILES — 4
0 — KM — 4

# TOPKAPI PALACE

- Baghdad Kiosk
- FOURTH COURTYARD
- Yerevan Kiosk
- Treasu
- Mosque
- THIRD COURTYARD
- Libra
- Thr Roc
- HAREM
- Bab-Saad
- Palace Kitchens
- Divan-ı Hümayun
- Harem Entrance
- Imperial Stables
- SECOND COURTYARD
- Orta Kapı
- Bab-üs Selam
- Court of Janissaries
- FIRST COURTYARD
- Bab-ı Hümay (Imperial Gat

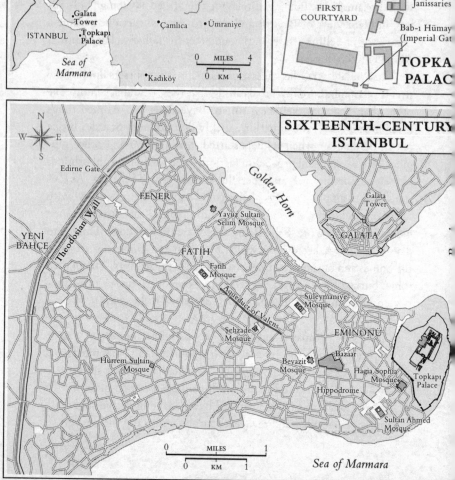

# SIXTEENTH-CENTURY ISTANBUL

- Edirne Gate
- FENER
- *Golden Horn*
- Galata Tower
- GALATA
- YENİ BAHÇE
- Theodosian Wall
- Yavuz Sultan Selim Mosque
- FATİH
- Fatih Mosque
- Süleymaniye Mosque
- Aqueduct of Valens
- Şehzade Mosque
- EMINÖNU
- Hürrem Sultan Mosque
- Beyazit Mosque
- Bazaar
- Hagia Sophia Mosque
- Topkapı Palace
- Hippodrome
- Sultan Ahmed Mosque

0 — MILES — 1
0 — KM — 1

*Sea of Marmara*

[of the houses]. Whatever there was in the way of goods, furniture and wealth, of jewel-inlaid objects of silver and gold, they looted and plundered [them]. [The pashas] themselves fled by night from this attack, the marks of which were auspicious, into the inner part of the city, and hid.

When Selim's faction threatened more destruction and rioting should preparations go forward to bring Ahmed into the city, Bayezit capitulated. Selim's strategy, organized from across the Black Sea in Kefe, had succeeded. His spectacular mobilization of his own empire-within-the-empire begged the question of who really was in charge.

AHMED RECEIVED THE NEWS, in the sleepy coastal town of Maltepe, about fifteen miles east of the Bosphorus Strait, and seethed with rage. "His disposition, which, through hope of the Sultanate, had been a flower-garden, became full of thistles." Already on the road to Istanbul to claim what he considered his birthright, he had been ignominiously halted by the actions of a group of rabble-rousing soldier-thugs. He killed the messenger who delivered the news on the spot, lending truth to the cliché about messengers.

Bayezit had brought Ahmed to the edge of the throne, but the sultan's most favored son now felt his father could do no more for him. It was time to take matters into his own hands. He decided that his best option was to raise his own army and conquer as much territory in Anatolia as possible, then move against the Janissary contingents who were conspiring with his half-brother. In essence following Selim's lead, Ahmed turned on their father too, determined to "become an independent sovereign," to forge *his* own empire-within-the-empire as well.

Ahmed pillaged the towns and cities around Maltepe before retreating into the relative safety of Anatolia. In an attempt to supplant his father's imperial administration, he appointed his own men as governors in Anatolia. Ahmed's invasion and capture of the important city of Konya—a possession he had long coveted, and one his father had always refused him—represented his final major victory. Breaking through the imperial defenses, he entered Konya, killed the governor (his nephew), took control of the city, declared himself its new sovereign, and began issuing orders in his own name. From this stronghold, Ahmed co-opted a number of pastoral groups as he planned to continue his conquests across central Anatolia.

Ahmed's insurrection conveniently aided Selim's grand strategy. From his base in Kefe, Selim had successfully convinced his Janissary supporters to prevent Ahmed from entering Istanbul, thus goading him into a direct confrontration with their father. Ahmed rejected Bayezit's orders to halt his advance, as well as his commands that Ahmed bide his time. Not surprisingly, Ahmed's impetuous fury helped to torpedo his bid for the throne; he looked more like an untamed rebel, "his thought and discernment . . . [fixed upon] pleasure and drinking," than a judicious statesman. Just weeks before, he had been within miles of the palace gates; since then he had killed a provincial governor, destroyed vast tracts of agricultural land, and was behaving like a brigand. Moreover, by ignoring the threat still posed by Shiite rebels in Anatolia, Ahmed was actually aiding their cause by wreaking even more havoc across the region.

Particularly advantageous from Selim's perspective was that Ahmed now aimed his torrent of violence against Korkud, who was still in Manisa, unable to raise the troops he needed for an advance on Istanbul. His two half-brothers' steady weakening of each other represented the perfect movement in a symphony of civil upheaval that benefited Selim. Ahmed attacked Korkud in Manisa, completely stunning him. Korkud had no idea his half-brother would launch an attack so far from the capital—indeed, no rationale for it existed other than Ahmed's near delusional plan to build a new empire in Anatolia. Woefully unprepared, Korkud's forces were disadvantaged from the start and were easily annihilated. Korkud fled to Istanbul, seeking his father's protection from a man they both now viewed as a mortal enemy. Arriving at the palace, he told his father, "I came because I was afraid of Sultan Aḥmed."

Through their own actions and reactions, Ahmed and Korkud essentially delegitimized themselves as viable claimants to the throne. Ahmed appeared deranged and overly aggressive, ignoring the established laws of state and religion; Korkud looked tepid and weak. While the two brothers tore the empire apart, Selim and his Janissary supporters projected strength, calm, and unity. In a situation verging on civil war, the backing of elements of the empire's longstanding military force was, of course, a powerful advantage. At the same time, many of the military's top brass as well as imperial administrators who had been supporters of Ahmed lost patience with him as he rampaged across Anatolia, so Selim's base of support within both the Janissary and bureaucratic establishments was growing. Amid the disorder their father had allowed Ahmed and Korkud to create, Selim stood out as the leader the empire needed, a captain who could navigate the Ottoman ship of state through these storms.

FROM KEFE, SELIM DIRECTED his Janissary allies to voice ever louder public criticism of Bayezit's failures and to press him ever harder to quell the disorder raging in Anatolia. Eventually, Selim's military backers presented Bayezit with an ultimatum: rein in your mutinous son or give up your throne.

The noose around Bayezit grew tighter. Above all, he was determined not to become the first Ottoman sultan to be forced to abdicate. Hoping to appease Selim and buy himself more time, on March 27, 1512, Bayezit appointed Selim, in absentia, commander-in-chief of the Janissaries. Important as this post was, it had little meaning on the ground at that moment. As Selim was already the de facto leader of most of the Ottoman military establishment, Bayezit's "concession" represented not so much a promotion as a simple recognition of the existing state of affairs. More importantly, the title of commander-in-chief of the Janissaries did nothing to bring Selim closer to the title he ultimately sought, that of sultan.

Although it failed to placate him, the appointment did offer Selim a justifiable path back to Istanbul, with no need for a display of his military might. Imperial representatives traveled to Kefe to escort Selim to the capital to take up his new post. While Bayezit hoped Selim's arrival in Istanbul as an administrator would save his sultanate from complete dissolution, Selim—though always wary of a trap—viewed his return as the first step in the process of his coronation. Thus, his journey back to the capital functioned more like a victory parade, with drummers and horn players leading the way. In an Ottoman version of a Potemkin march, his supporters gathered large crowds of soldiers and commoners alike to applaud him in all the towns through which he processed, tossing flowers and sweets at his horse's feet. Needless to say, this angered

Bayezit's representatives, but they could do nothing to stem the tide. As the ever-laudatory *Selimname* described the prince's return to Istanbul, "the dust of his happiness-promoting feet was desired at the exalted court, so that it might be applied to the inflamed eye of the state as collyria [eye balm] of antimony and zinc."

When the cavalcade reached the outskirts of Istanbul, Bayezit's men left Selim and his retinue to set up camp in an area outside the city walls known as Yeni Bahçe. This part of the city stood over the channel of a forgotten ancient river and boasted numerous vegetable gardens and orchards (*yeni bahçe* means "new garden"). Having spent six years in the imperial palace as a child, Selim was returning to the capital for the first time as an adult. He had lived with his mother in the harem of Topkapı Palace, overlooking the Bosphorus; he had undertaken his daily lessons there and run around its cobblestoned courtyards. Standing outside the capital now, at the age of forty-one, Selim was eager to return to the elegant imperial residence of his youth—as sultan.

# ONE AND ONLY SULTAN

*Selim's coronation*

T HE DECISIVE WEAPON THAT WON MEHMET II, SELIM'S GRAND-
father, Constantinople in 1453 was a cannon that could shoot a projec-
tile of over a thousand pounds more than a mile. Cast in Edirne, then
the Ottoman capital, the cannon required two hundred men and a hundred oxen to pull it, and two months to make the journey from Edirne

to Constantinople—a distance that normally took two days on horse-back. A group of engineers preceded the cannon, preparing the road for the weight of the enormous wheeled contraption. Mehmet positioned the cannon just outside Constantinople's western wall. When he gave the order to commence the attack, the cannon fired its one shot, exploding the ancient stones like a pile of dirt. Ottoman troops then streamed unrestrained into the beleaguered city as its hungry and terrified residents scattered in all directions.

Selim's camp at Yeni Bahçe stood several hundred meters to the south of the spot where the wall was destroyed by his grandfather nearly sixty years earlier (it had since been rebuilt). After taking a night to recover from his long march from Crimea "in a tent whose height was as that of the heavenly sphere," Selim arranged for a visit with his father. His entrance into the city proved far easier than Mehmet's. Accompanied by a group of palace attendants, Selim and his entourage walked into the walled city that afternoon, past Istanbul's bakers and butchers, across squares dominated by fountains and others shadowed by mosques. He proceeded through the capital—the Abode of Felicity (*Dersaadet*), as it was known—as though he had already become the sultan of the seven climes, "with thousands of manifestations of majesty, splendour and good fortune." In the light of early evening, as he approached the palace—no doubt with expectant dread, and suspicious still that this might all be a trap—and passed through its three gates, Selim focused his thoughts on strategy. While he would not need to smash through Istanbul's walls to seize the palace, capturing it would nevertheless shake the whole edifice of the Ottoman dynasty and cause the world to tremble.

At his first meeting with his father, Selim lavished deferential respect on the man who was still sultan, showing him "excellent kindness and perfect compassion and tenderness." He bowed before Bayezit and kissed his ruby-encrusted gold ring, which was engraved with his imperial signature. These ceremonial formalities, though, quickly turned to business. Speaking quietly, Selim presented his father with a dramatically insolent choice: either abdicate now—willingly, peacefully, and with dignity—and discreetly leave the palace for a comfortable retirement, or watch Selim's Janissaries seize the palace and the empire by force, ravaging the city on their way. Should Bayezit choose the latter path, Selim added, he could not guarantee his father's safety—or even his life. Bayezit glared down from his throne and scoffed at the insult. He had summoned Selim to Istanbul to make him head of the military, not to forsake the empire. Furious and disheartened, he dismissed Selim from his presence.

Holding on to his belief that he could appease Selim with something other than the sultanate, and and perhaps hoping that their father–son bond might still carry some weight, Bayezit summoned his son again the next day to discuss a strategy for dealing with "the evils" of Ahmed in Anatolia. Selim yearned for war against Ahmed, but he wanted to lead the imperial army against his half-brother as sultan, not as another sultan's commander-in-chief. This second meeting proved as disastrous as the first, with father and son trading insults and outright threats. For about a week, they continued their meetings, each more acrimonious than the last. From Selim's perspective, the end of his father's sultanate was already a *fait accompli*, obvious to all. Whether or not Bayezit was willing to admit it, his empire had fractured and essentially turned on him. Would he have to be removed by force, or would he cooperate and abandon his throne peacefully? Not surprisingly, Bayezit refused to countenance such disrespect. "As long as I am within the sphere of good health," he declared, "I shall not give [the] Sultanate to anyone."

Interpreting his father's answer as a clear rejection of the offer to avoid armed conflict, Selim felt he had license to use force. A few days later, he stormed into the palace with an enormous retinue of Janissary soldiers and commanders—his allies, who had long wished for an aggressive sultan on the throne. Slaughtering the guards at the palace gates, they threatened and killed their way into and through the various quarters of the palace. After securing each section, they marched into the inner throne room, the *sanctum sanctorum* of Ottoman power. Never before had such violence entered that domain. As Bayezit sat enthroned on the dais, underneath a portico of dark marble and gold filigree, Selim drew his sword, threatening the life of the sultan, the most powerful man in the empire, one of the world's leading political figures, his own father. Frail and eminently powerless in that moment, Bayezit scanned the room, hoping for solace and direction in the eyes of anyone there. He saw none. In that elegant chamber where he had, until now, welcomed only pliant advisers and bowing servants, Bayezit saw his own impending death. The sultan, the *Selimname* relates, wept. Dropping his chin to his chest in anguish and resignation, Bayezit surrendered his empire to Selim.

⚉

ON THAT DAY, SATURDAY, April 24, 1512, the Ottoman Empire ineradicably changed. As Selim's men led a despairing, enervated Bayezit out of the palace, he became the first sultan in Ottoman history to relinquish his throne before his death, while Selim became the first non-eldest, non-favored son to succeed his father as sultan. According to the *Selimname,* "everyone was flying, like birds and winged creatures," with "delight-filled pleasure at the news" of Selim's capture of the throne. A gamut of emotions raced through him: relief and excitement, satisfaction and consternation. As never before, the empire had both a sultan and a living former sultan. One had deposed the other, with no clear precedent as to whether or not such an act was legitimate, or how the two men should now behave with regard to each other, or how the imperial elite and the empire's subjects should view them. It was far too early to grasp the enormous implications of what had happened. On that mild spring evening, the only certainty was that Selim held the throne.

As news of what had occurred inside the palace spread beyond its walls, Istanbul erupted into celebration. "The most brilliant sun rose over the world; grief departed from the world entirely. . . . Happiness invaded [people's] hearts." The capital had been in dire straits for months, with grave uncertainties about the future of the empire, the Janissaries in open revolt, and people mostly locked down in the relative safety of their homes. The streets had become military zones as pro-Selim and pro-Ahmed forces battled to control neighborhoods—torching buildings, stealing limited resources, and causing general havoc. Although the existential questions facing the empire remained unsettled, and clearly not everyone supported Selim, Istanbul's residents could at least exhale as the tumultuous month of April 1512 finally ended.

The ascension of a new sultan had always been a time of celebration, but now, a sultan's ascension came with another's descension. There was, as well, no imperial death to commemorate. Neither bureaucrats nor commoners knew whether to mourn or celebrate. Perhaps mourn *and* celebrate?

Any celebration Selim enjoyed had to be brief. From the perspective of some contemporary imperial officials, as well as some later historians, Selim's actions amounted to an unlawful coup. (A work like the *Selimname* sought to dispel such notions.) The natural death of a sultan or his demise on the battlefield had always stood as the only legitimate reasons for the accession of a new sultan. Therefore, Selim's most pressing concern was what to do with his reviled father. Execution seemed gratuitous, unbecoming to a royal, and a dangerous precedent. Nevertheless, Selim needed to remove Bayezit from the imperial stage. Realizing that he would have to face accusations of illegitimacy throughout his reign, Selim wanted to avoid criticism as far as possible. He could get rid of anyone who raised questions, of course, but that would only cast further suspicion on his bona fides. The least problematic solution would be to dispatch his father to some distant locale. After keeping Bayezit imprisoned in the palace for a few weeks, Selim's advisers selected the city of Dimetoka—"a charming town with a pleasant climate," just south of Edirne (and today in Greece)—as the ideal spot for the deposed sultan's comfortable but forced retirement.

There were, of course, inherent risks. Selim had to consider seriously the possibility that his father might try to regain the throne. Bayezit would, Selim knew, retain widespread support throughout much of the empire, and he still had solid connections with some military officials and imperial administrators. He might easily raise an army against his son, especially from the area around Edirne, where he had spent many years residing in the city's imperial lodgings. Thus, Bayezit's "retirement" would have to function as a form of secure and serene house arrest. Selim organized an entourage of servants to accompany his father to Dimetoka and to attend to his well-being in his new home, instructing them to be kind and deferential but never to allow him to converse with military men or imperial officials. As a public relations ploy designed to dispel any notions of impropriety, and perhaps even to suggest that Bayezit had willingly transferred his sultanate to Selim, the ninth sultan rode on horseback alongside the enclosed carriage that carried the eighth sultan out of Istanbul. At dawn, in what must have seemed a surreal procession, vanquished father and victorious son moved slowly through the city for all to see. At the gate that led to the road to Edirne, Selim bade farewell to his father, embracing him before watching him disappear—a polite, if odd, gesture, rather like seeing off a guest at the threshold of one's home.

It remains an open question as to whether or not Selim knew it then, but this was the last time he would see his father. On May 26, 1512, Bayezit died en route to Dimetoka. In its characteristic locution, the *Selimname* says of Bayezit's death that "the provisions for the remainder of his existence had fallen to the lot of the beggar of death." Given the circumstances, Bayezit's death seems suspicious. Perhaps Selim instructed the men he sent with his father to kill him in a way that made his death seem natural. Some contemporary sources assert that Selim had his father poisoned. But perhaps Bayezit did indeed die of natural causes, his spirit broken from having lost his throne to a reviled and defiant son. Whatever the truth, Bayezit's death on the road to Dimetoka surely pleased Selim, particularly since it occurred outside Istanbul, providing him with plausible deniability. Later historians, hoping to avoid the suggestion that any sultan's reign could be illegitimate—even the first to involve the overthrow of a sitting sultan—were loth to assign blame for Bayezit's death to Selim.

Bayezit's body was wrapped and transported back to Istanbul for burial in the mosque, "paradise-like in form," that he had constructed for himself years earlier. Selim spared no expense on an elaborate funeral and a luxurious burial, bestowing upon his father all the respect and riches appropriate to a sultan. He ordered a high, vaulted, exquisitely adorned mausoleum to be erected over his father's tomb. He made the celebration of his father's life a public affair, with prescribed mourning hours, Qur'anic recitations, great processions, and countless ostentatious commemorative rituals. All of this, of course, was shrewd calculation; Selim hoped that such extravagance would bury with the body any rumors that he was somehow implicated in his father's death.

SELIM NEXT TURNED HIS attention to the far more exigent threat of his half-brothers. Although he had outfought and outwitted them to gain the throne, Selim would never feel completely safe in the palace with Ahmed and Korkud lingering somewhere beyond the city walls. In an empire that determined succession by pitting half-brothers against one another, fratricide made eminent sense. Once the fittest won the throne, he killed his rivals to ensure that no bitter also-ran would seek revenge and thereby disrupt the stability of the state. Of Selim's two enemy siblings, Ahmed was by far the more potent militarily and hence

TOPKAPI PALACE

MEHMET II'S
CAPTURE OF
STANTINOPLE

AK KOYUNLU LEADER UZUN HASAN'S SON
MEETS MEHMET II

BAYEZIT HUNTING

NEAR PLOVDIV

OTTOMAN CIRCUMCISION CEREMONY,
LATE SIXTEENTH CENTURY

MENGLI GIRAY
AND BAYEZIT

SELIM HUNTING A TIGER

BATTLE OF CHALDIRAN, OTTOMAN RENDITION

BATTLE OF CHALDIRAN,
SAFAVID RENDITION

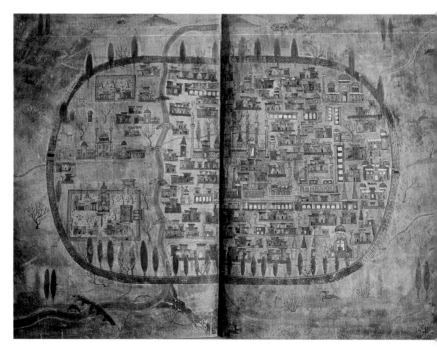

SIXTEENTH-CENTURY OTTOMAN PAINTING OF TABRIZ

SIXTEENTH-CENTURY OTTOMAN PAINTING OF ALEPPO

SELIM RECEIVES THE HEAD OF
AL-GHAWRI AFTER MARJ DABIQ

SELIM HUNTING CROCODILES IN EGYPT

SELIM IN THE PORT OF ALEXANDRIA

A MORISCO FAMILY

THE EXPULSION OF THE MOORS FROM SPAIN

TAINO COOKING

BOABDIL SURRENDERS GRANADA
TO THE SPANISH

OTTOMAN COFFEEHOUSE

MONTEZUMA'S DEATH

*The funeral of Bayezit*

the more worrisome. In the summer of 1512, marauding across Anatolia in an attempt to carve out an independent state, he posed an abiding threat to the empire.

Selim decided to start with Korkud, the easier target. Before setting out for Anatolia, however, Selim summoned Suleyman from Crimea to manage the empire's administrative affairs while he was away doing battle. Several months into his reign, Selim had only a few seasoned and trusted advisers, so he still relied mainly on those who had helped him gain the throne—none more so than Suleyman, who was now almost eighteen. Moreover, having his son watch over imperial affairs in the palace would serve as useful training for the time when Suleyman followed him as sultan. And, in the worst-case scenario, if Selim fell in battle, his only son and successor would already be in the palace to accede to the sultanate.

With ten thousand troops behind him, Selim set out for Manisa, southwest of Istanbul. Korkud had resided in Manisa since his arrival there at the time of the Şahkulu Rebellion the previous year. One of the wealthiest towns in western Anatolia, Manisa excelled in olive oil production and also exported leather goods and cotton. Korkud had made repeated requests to Bayezit, as he did now to Selim, for the governorships of Lesbos or Alanya instead of Teke, a post he had lost thanks to Şahkulu's rebels. Both were refused, mostly for fear that he sought direct access to the Mediterranean in order to flee the empire, as Bayezit's half-brother Cem had done before him, with the goal of pursuing an alliance with a foreign power. (Indeed, a few years earlier, Korkud had briefly absconded to Egypt to seek help from the Mamluks to gain the throne, just as Cem had done.) So Korkud was stuck in land-locked Manisa, close to the sea but not itself a port city. When Selim reached the city's modest palace after a ten-day march, his troops over-whelmed Korkud's guards and quickly secured the complex. Somehow, Korkud managed to escape. Before Selim set off in pursuit, he took the opportunity to himself kill Korkud's son in his palace bedroom.

Selim and his forces fanned out into the forested foothills of the Taurus Mountains south of the city. It was rough, rocky terrain, stud-ded with ravines—perfect for hiding, difficult for surviving. After about half a day of searching, one of the soldiers yelled that he had found Korkud squirreled away in a dank cave. Selim ran to the cave to find his half-brother secured by a sword on his neck, exhausted from his flight, well aware of his impending fate. Selim insulted Korkud, calling him a traitor and a dog. Korkud begged for his life. Selim said nothing, stepped out of the cave, and ordered his men to seize Korkud. They would strangle him a few months later, at the age of forty-six, on March 13, 1513.

⊠

ELIMINATING AHMED WOULD PROVE far more difficult than chasing down Korkud. He had built a strong power base around Konya, the seat of his own veritable mini-empire. Across large swaths of ostensibly imperial territory, he—not the Ottoman bureaucracy—collected taxes and raised troops. He cut deals with local power brokers and the leaders of pastoral confederations to provide him with soldiers, support, and safety. Still, when news of the death of Bayezit and then the capture of Korkud spread eastward, many of Ahmed's backers grew nervous

*Selim and Ahmed clash*

and flipped their allegiance to the new sultan. Selim was master of the empire and its resources, and Ahmed had been deemed a rebel against the state. Most recognized the fate awaiting the prince at the hands of his equally ruthless but far more competent half-brother. Others chafed under the heavy hand of Ahmed's rule (and that of his sons who served as governors), so they were more than ready to reject his frantic calls for support.

In mid-June 1512, Ahmed had sent his second son, Alaeddin, to seize the former Ottoman capital of Bursa, and in November 1512, Ahmed captured his, Selim's, and Korkud's birthplace: Amasya, northeast of Konya. For his part, after seizing and imprisoning Korkud, Selim had secured Manisa. In December, he moved north again toward Bursa, overwhelming Ahmed's forces in the city, capturing Alaeddin, and executing him along with the sons of some of his other half-brothers who had taken refuge in the city. Selim's men then pushed east, driving Ahmed and his diminished forces farther and farther away from the Ottoman capital.

In these months in early 1513, the rebel prince and his followers grew so desperate that they discussed the possibility of an alliance with the Ottomans' sworn enemy, the Safavids. An alliance never materialized, but some of Ahmed's men—as his son Murad had done during the Şahkulu Rebellion—did indeed flee over the border to seek protection at the Safavid court. Selim, of course, loathed the Safavids, having spent so much time in Trabzon warring against them and their allies. For Selim, Ahmed's treachery in even considering an alliance with the Safavids further established his obvious unfitness for any leadership role in the Ottoman Empire.

While in Bursa, Selim devised a plan to trap Ahmed, who still had some small pockets of support in the city. Masquerading as one of Ahmed's still-loyal Bursa followers, Selim wrote a series of letters flattering him, showering him with praise, and assuring him that he still enjoyed widespread support throughout the city. Bursa's "allies of Ahmed" encouraged him to return to the city, guaranteeing that they would aid him in retaking it. The letters promised troops and supplies and even listed some of the city's most vulnerable entry points. Fantasies of recapturing Bursa proved too much for Ahmed to resist, and he took the bait. In the early spring of 1513, Ahmed started moving westward from Amasya with his small number of remaining troops. When, in April, they reached Yenişehir, an agriculturally rich town about thirty-five miles east of Bursa, Selim and his forces were lying in wait. Unprepared for battle, Ahmed's men were slaughtered. Ahmed was captured alive after falling from his horse.

Cowering in shame and dread, Bayezit's favored son faced a pitiful end. Selim took the opportunity to confront his half-brother one last time. Four years apart in age, they had been pitted against each other as long as either could remember, despite their days of Persian lessons and chess games together in the Amasya harem. Their lifelong war was nearly over. In this victory—one that a fourth son never should have enjoyed—Selim gloated. Entering his half-brother's prison cell, he insulted Ahmed and chastised him for his rebellious actions, for his ties with the Safavids, for undermining the glorious Ottoman state. Ahmed, silent, fixed his eyes on the cold ground on which he languished. Selim left the cell in disgust. At the end of April 1513, a little more than a month after having finally ordered Korkud's execution, Selim had Ahmed strangled too.

FOR SEVERAL WEEKS AFTER Ahmed's death, Selim stayed in the east. His forces streamed into eastern Anatolia, killing Ahmed's supporters, pursuing his sons and some of Selim's other nephews, and retaking territory for the empire. All of Ahmed's sons who were captured were killed. Two who managed to flee into the arms of the Safavids—and were rumored to have converted to Shiism—were the only ones who survived.

By the summer of 1513, Selim had returned from the plains of Yenişehir back to Istanbul, having eliminated his rivals and secured the empire for himself. His mother had died in 1505—how joyful she would have been to see her one son gain the throne; and now his father was gone too. For the first time in his forty-two years, he stood as the undisputed head of his family and its possessions. Despite his disadvantages, Selim had triumphed.

Selim spent most of that summer in the luxurious calm of Topkapı Palace, tackling the intricacies of his new mandate—making appointments to key posts, organizing his palace administration, ensuring the proper provisioning of the army, and restoring safety and tranquility after the violent chaos of the succession crisis. He brought his consorts and daughters to the palace harem and dispatched Suleyman to a new and more prominent post, as governor of Manisa. During the long summer days, Selim strategized with his military advisers while they meandered among the roses and lilies of the palace gardens. He liked to trace the patterns formed by the blue and white tiles that lined the harem and his throne room. Above all, he reveled in the opulence of the palace—the many fireplaces and pavilions, the immense library, the kitchen's endless variety of foods, the gratification of his every whim. In his quiet moments alone—a far cry from the mayhem of the many battles that had delivered him to this point—he pensively looked out over the Bosphorus from the perfect perch of the palace, almost the same view that had enraptured him as a boy.

In an accident of history, Niccolò Machiavelli, who admired and feared the Ottoman Empire, completed his famous treatise of political philosophy, *The Prince*, the same year—1513—in which Selim defeated his half-brothers to secure the sultanate that he had gained in 1512. Selim was the archetypal Machiavellian politician, and, indeed, Machiavelli esteemed Selim over the two other Ottoman sultans he witnessed, Mehmet and Bayezit. Provided no advantages in his quest for power, from birth order to the location of his governorship, Selim had strategized and fought ruthlessly, eventually to prevail over daunting odds. Now, as sultan, he finally had the resources to strike with overwhelming force one of the chief foes of his life so far, the enemy that had troubled him over the past decade of his governorship of Trabzon: the Safavid Empire.

# PART FIVE

# SELIM'S
# WORLD WARS

## (1512–18)

CHAPTER

17

## "THEIR ABODE IS HELL"

*Ismail receives intelligence from an Ottoman captive*

THE WARS SELIM WITNESSED AND WAGED DURING HIS LIFETIME remain with us today. The legacies of the Spanish voyages to the Americas help to explain the demographics of the modern Western Hemisphere, our ideas about bondage and freedom, current geopolitics, and the history of capitalism. The eventual American eclipse of Europe, the

Middle East, and Asia began during Selim's age. In the first two decades of the sixteenth century, Babur, the founder of the Mughal Empire—the most significant empire in South Asia before the British—began the wars that would win him northern India, even as the Portuguese, who had rounded Africa in 1497, seized several ports in southern India. Like those of European rulers, Babur's actions were taken in response to Ottoman power. He had reached out to Selim to help him in his wars in Central Asia, but Selim refused to come to his aid, backing his enemies instead. In part or in whole, all of these global military ventures occurred in reaction to the Ottomans. Selim, likewise, personally led a series of wars in the Middle East that have left a lasting mark on the world. Today's competition between Sunni and Shiite powers over regional hegemony in the Middle East began during Selim's day, with his wars against the Safavids.

More than Catholic Spain, Portugal, Venice, or other European Christian powers, more than Jews, the Mamluks, Moroccans, the abject Taino, the Mali Empire, the rising Mughals, or any other Muslims, the Safavids represented the greatest military and ideological threat both to Selim personally and to the future of the Ottoman Empire. Thus, after vanquishing his half-brothers and eliminating his domestic troubles, Selim turned eastward for the first major war of his sultanate, in hopes of dealing a death blow to his suspect Shiite subjects in eastern Anatolia and their conniving Safavid patrons.

WHEN SELIM ACCEDED TO the Ottoman throne, the Safavid shah Ismail was in his twenties, with his empire on solid footing in and around the major cities of the Caucasus. Ismail was, according to an Italian visitor to his court, "fair, handsome, and very pleasing; not very tall, but of a light and well-framed figure; rather stout than slight, with broad shoulders. His hair is reddish; he only wears moustachios." His mustache indeed proved one of his hallmark features, prominent in every depiction of him. As with the presumably apocryphal tale of his having unearthed a ram while at full gallop, nearly all accounts of Ismail describe his impressive strength and inspiring courage. As the same Italian account continues, he was "as brave as a game cock, and stronger than any of his lords; in the archery contests, out of the ten apples that are knocked down, he knocks down seven." In addition to his military acumen, Ismail also enjoyed poetry, song, and dance and even composed his own *divan* (anthology) of Persian and Turkish poetry. In short, he was hardly a boor.

Selim and Ismail, of course, had a history of bloody antagonism. With no clear or natural border between the states in eastern Anatolia, the two empires conducted constant tit-for-tat strikes as each tried to establish regional hegemony. The adoption of Shiism as the Safavids' state religion had raised the stakes by infusing an ideological current into the conflict, and the Şahkulu Rebellion had stunned the Ottomans by making clear the immense threat of Safavid-sponsored Shiism within their empire. Şahkulu was the tip of a long spear wielded from Iran; to forever end the Shiite threat, the Ottomans would have to wrench the weapon from the Safavids' hands and shatter it into a thousand pieces.

In the succession battle for Bayezit's throne, the Safavids had thrown in their lot with Ahmed, because he had seemed to them, as to nearly everyone, the likely winner, as well as the most sympathetic, if not pliable, of the three half-brothers. Like his father, Ahmed strove to avoid military action whenever possible (at least, before his rampage through Anatolia), which suggested that he might be less antagonistic toward the Safavids and the Ottoman Empire's Shiites than Selim. The Safavids had sheltered Ahmed's sons during the succession battle and, at strategic moments, had even dispatched some of their forces to aid Ahmed.

Despite the setback of Ahmed's demise, the Safavids continued their support of Ottoman Shiites during the early years of Selim's reign in an attempt to weaken the new sultan. Furthermore, they refused to observe the standard early sixteenth-century diplomatic protocol—even for one's enemies—of sending an embassy to recognize the ascension of a new sovereign, busy as they were making plans for Ahmed's son Murad to overthrow Selim. Murad had fled to Iran from Sivas, but the Safavids' plans for him ultimately failed to galvanize support among Ottoman Shiites and would eventually dwindle away. Yet Murad was still enough of a threat in the winter of 1513–14 that Selim sent a delegation to the handsome seasonal residence of the Safavid court in Isfahan, an oasis town in central Iran, demanding he be sent to Istanbul. Shah Ismail mocked Selim's envoys, deriding their clothing and their faulty Persian and declaring that Murad was a favored guest of the Safavids and would remain such.

Selim's envoys also demanded that Ismail return the city of Diyarbakir and its surrounding province in southeastern Anatolia to the Ottomans. Selim claimed it as part of the hereditary lands of the House of Osman, although there was no historical precedent for Ottoman control of the city or province. Diyarbakir, a mostly Kurdish city on the banks of the Tigris River, was of the utmost strategic importance as a gateway to Syria, Iraq, and the Arabian peninsula, and stood at the intersection of several overland trade routes to the East. The Ottomans and the Safavids had waged a tug-of-war over the province during the previous decade, yanking it back and forth several times. Selim calculated that the Safavids would rebuff him, thus providing a further *casus belli*. As expected, Ismail obliged, goading Selim by stating that if the Ottoman sultan wanted the territory, he would have to take it by force. At the end of 1513, Selim's envoys departed Isfahan, insulted and empty-handed.

After a momentous year, Selim spent that winter of 1513–14 in the palace at Edirne, where he and his men enjoyed daily hunts and relaxed by warming fires in the evening. When his emissaries returned from Isfahan, Selim was unsurprised by their news. The Safavid refusal to surrender Murad and to retreat from Diyarbakir added a few more logs to the fire that had simmered inside Selim for years, a blaze now burning hotter than any in the Edirne palace. He considered that he now had sufficient political justification to declare war. He had wanted to move against the Safavids from the moment he seized the throne, but convention dictated an official declaration of intention. According to the rules of early modern diplomacy, Selim had acted correctly: he had offered Shah Ismail a means of avoiding war, and it was rejected.

In addition to the political niceties, and to further strengthen his sanction, Selim sought religious backing for his impending military venture. Although the Safavids were Shiites—equivalent to heretics, in the eyes of most Sunnis—they were still Muslims. A Muslim declaring war on another Muslim was not a simple proposition. According to Islamic law, Muslims could wage war against non-Muslims at any time, for almost any reason, but the legal threshold for initiating a confrontation against a fellow Muslim was vastly higher. Over centuries of Islamic history, Muslims had regularly fought other Muslims with little concern for the technicalities of religious law, but Selim, in his endeavor to become the world's most powerful Muslim, strove to follow the Islamic rules of war to the letter in his first major military operation as sultan. He portrayed himself consistently as a pious Muslim; he did not want to be accused of disobedience to holy law. And, since he had gained the sultanate by questionable means, Selim felt an added imperative to broadcast his piety and adherence to the laws of state and religion.

Thus, Selim turned to the empire's religious establishment to sanctify his plans for war against the Safavids. In early 1514, he succeeded in securing *fatwa*s (rulings on religious law) from two of the empire's most prominent muftis—Hamza Saru Görez and Kemalpaşazade—who deemed Shiites to be infidels and endorsed their slaughter. Hamza Saru Görez stated unequivocally in his Ottoman Turkish *fatwa* that Shiites were indeed "unbelievers" and "heretics" who should be killed; all their possessions, including their women and children, could be seized as booty for the Ottoman Empire. As an indication of just how much of an abomination Shiites were, he added that even a Shiite who "converted" to Sunni Islam should be killed. In short, Shiites should be considered as worse than Jews and Christians; they did not enjoy the safeguards to which members of those communities were entitled. The other mufti, Kemalpaşazade, later grand mufti, continued in the same vein in his Arabic-language *fatwa*, asserting that Shiites were not just non-Muslims but anti-Muslims. As sultan, Selim had the right and, what is more, the duty to destroy the Safavid unbelievers. Kemalpaşazade invoked a Qur'anic verse in his *fatwa*: "Strive hard against the unbelievers and hypocrites, and be firm against them. Their abode is hell, an evil refuge indeed" (9:73). With his simmering anti-Shiite fury now reaching a boil, a political justification on offer, and religious sanction secured, Selim girded himself to make a conclusive move against the Safavids.

He set out from Edirne on March 20, 1514. Like the change of seasons, Selim's plans for war represented a complete, if temporary, transformation of his state. This would be total war—a cataclysmic clash of exclusionary visions of universal sovereignty and of militarily committed states with diametrically opposed political agendas. Selim's preparations thus moved simultaneously on several fronts. Foremost, of course, were his battle plans and strategies of engagement. A military man for decades, he devoted himself to every logistical detail and committed every possible resource to the enterprise. His forces would far outmatch

Ismail's, both in number and in armament technology. In fact, he had what most historians consider the largest army assembled in the Middle East up to that point—as many as two hundred thousand soldiers at its peak. Alongside these vital military considerations, Selim also moved to squeeze the Safavids economically by curtailing their main source of revenue, the silk trade.

As indicated by the *fatwa*s he secured, Selim viewed this conflict as an epic confrontation between two rival ideologies, a test of who should lead the Muslim world—a war that would leave only one survivor. Both sides, however, knew that God was on *their* side. Thus, this first Ottoman–Safavid war was set to become one of the fiercest and most important battles in the history of the Middle East—indeed, in all of Islamic history. It was the first time a Sunni empire fought a Shiite empire for regional hegemony of the Middle East.

Selim reached Istanbul on March 29. In Topkapı Palace, he checked up on his daughters and consorts, who had stayed behind while he was in Edirne, and met with his military commanders and other advisers under the great dome of the imperial council room to discuss strategy and the mobilization of resources from across the empire. For Selim, in this first major military test of his sultanate, the only acceptable outcome was—of course—a crushing victory.

Selim also worked with his administrative council on the details of the economic blockade. By outlawing the export of Iranian silk from the Ottoman Empire, he could directly manipulate the trade that drove the Safavid economy and supported nearly every facet of the state, because Iranian silk merchants had to pass through Ottoman territory to access the Mediterranean and the lucrative European market. Selim established checkpoints on the major roads between the two empires, dispatched teams of inspectors to Ottoman markets to ferret out Iranian silk, and monitored all ships passing through Ottoman ports and using Ottoman sea-lanes. Denying the Safavids access to Trabzon, Bursa, Istanbul, and Antakya would sap them economically and eventually militarily. The blockade, which was up and running by the early summer of 1514, proved so effective—save for a few smugglers—that Selim maintained it throughout his reign.

Having choked Iran economically, Selim worked to win the support of other major powers for his impending war. His biggest concern was the Mamluk Empire, to the south—the third of the Middle East's major states at the time. Ottomans and Mamluks shared a long history of both cooperation and enmity. On the positive side, the two Muslim powers had partnered in the realm of commerce, working together to erect a powerful trade wall against European merchants seeking to go east from the Mediterranean. On the negative side, the Ottomans clashed with the Sunni Mamluks—as they did with the Shiite Safavids—over claims of universal sovereignty in the Muslim world. The Mamluk sultanate had arisen about fifty years before the Ottomans, and they were the protectors of Mecca and Medina, the holiest places in Islam. Also within their empire were several other historic centers of Islamic thought, such as Damascus and Cairo, giving them an ideological edge in the rivalry over leadership of the global Muslim community. More-over, the Mamluks regularly harbored domestic rivals for the Ottoman throne, including Cem and Korkud. The Mamluks, ever fickle, could tip the balance in an Ottoman–Safavid war, so Selim had to carefully consider the Mamluk position in his looming conflict.

The Mamluks had previously favored the Safavids in order to check the rapid expansion of the Ottomans. To stave off another Mamluk–Safavid alliance, and to avoid fighting two empires on two fronts, Selim sent an envoy to Cairo in 1514 to inform the Mamluk sultan Ashraf Qansuh al-Ghawri, who was in his mid-seventies, of his plans to invade Iran and to invite him to join the war on the Ottoman side. Selim knew the Mamluks would refuse, so his message, composed in the flowery language of deference and fraternity, served as a thinly veiled threat—namely, that if the Mamluks would not support the Ottomans, they should stay out of the conflict altogether. If they chose to ally with the Safavids, the message intimated, Selim would unleash his impressive military against them. In a calculated demonstration of Ottoman power, Selim also dispatched one of his most trusted naval commanders to the Red Sea to support the Mamluk navy against the encroaching Portuguese.

Selim reached out to other regional powers too, widening the scope of the impending war. The Uzbeks of Central Asia controlled territory to the east of the Safavids, so Selim sent a letter to the leader of this enemy of his enemies, 'Ubayd Allah Khan, suggesting that they might join forces to attack the Safavids simultaneously, in a pincer movement. 'Ubayd Allah expressed interest, but he was too involved with fractures within his own empire, including a war against Babur, the eventual

Mughal emperor, to be able to mount an effective offensive. Closer to home, remnants of the Ak Koyunlu still held territory in remote areas of the Caucasus between the Safavids and the Ottomans. Since it was mostly the Safavids who had displaced the Ak Koyunlu, Selim easily won their allegiance. He also recruited other tribal groups and principalities in eastern Anatolia. Foremost among these were the Kurds, whom he had cultivated as supporters during his governorship of Trabzon, defending their right to their ancestral lands and offering them some degree of local autonomy in exchange for troops and their recognition of Ottoman sovereignty.

IN APRIL 1514, WITH an economic embargo in place, the Mamluks more or less sidelined, and other powerful interests at his back, Selim marched out of Istanbul at the head of a 140,000-man army, setting up his first camp at Yenişehir, the town where he had killed Ahmed a year earlier. Eastern Anatolia had forged Selim as an administrator and military commander, providing him with the tools he needed to win the

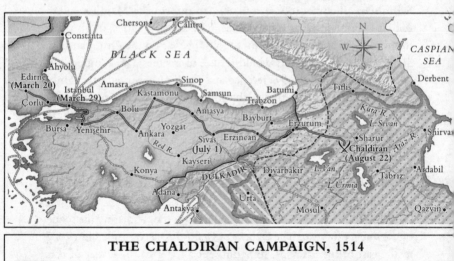

## THE CHALDIRAN CAMPAIGN, 1514

Ottoman Empire | Mamluk Empire | Ak Koyunlu Confederation | Safavid Empire | Trade route

0  MILES  400

0  KM  400

throne. It was both logical and symmetrical that Selim would head east on the first campaign of his sultanate.

As protocol dictated—but other rulers routinely ignored—en route to the battlefield Selim sent Shah Ismail an official declaration of war. The letter was written in Persian, so that Ismail would have no uncertainty about his feelings. Styling himself the "slayer of the wicked and the infidel, guardian of the noble and the pious; the warrior in the Path, the defender of the Faith; the champion, the conqueror; the lion, son and grandson of the lion; standard-bearer of justice and righteousness," Selim addressed Ismail as "the possessor of the land of tyranny and perversion, the captain of the vicious, the chief of the malicious." He went on to enumerate the abominations Ismail and his Shiite coreligionists had carried out against Islam: their destruction of mosques, the Shiite practice of temporary marriage, their contradictions of the Qur'an, and, worst of all, their massacres of Sunnis, the world's true Muslims. In the face of this loathsome tyranny, and with the sanction of his two *fatwa*s, Sultan Selim was fulfilling his duty to defend the one true faith against Shiite depravity: "The ancient obligation of extirpation, extermination, and expulsion of evil innovation must be the aim of our exalted aspiration. . . . [T]he lightning of our conquering sword shall uproot the untamed bramble grown to great heights in the path of the refulgent Divine Law and shall cast them down upon the dust of abjectness to be trampled under the hooves of our legions."

Selim offered Ismail one final chance to save himself: surrender; turn over the entire Safavid Empire—its territories, resources, and peoples—to the Ottomans; confess the glory of Sunnism and convert; and profess allegiance to the majesty and wonder of Selim. In an age of eradications—the Jews from Spain and the Taino from Hispaniola, for example—Selim's letter echoed some of the same language the Spanish used against their enemies. In all these cases, neither expulsion nor extermination was ever completed, of course. Selim included a verse of his own poetry in his letter to Ismail:

*He whose face touches the dust of my threshold in submission*
*Will be enveloped in the shadow of my favor and my justice.*

Thus, should Ismail choose the wicked blindness of his own bright light over the gloriously stark clarity of contrasts effected by Selim's shadow, the Ottoman sultan promised to "crown the head of every gallows tree with the head of a crown-wearing Sûfî [Shiite] and clear that faction from the face of the earth."

As the messenger carrying his letter raced ahead of the Ottoman army to Ismail's court, Selim embarked on his slow march out from Yenişehir, deliberately snaking through all the major towns of north-central Anatolia, including Bolu, Ankara, Kastamonu, and his birth-place, Amasya. The march provided a prime opportunity for him to impress upon his subjects the stability inaugurated by his reign, to demonstrate the power and majesty of their new sovereign and his army, and to quash any possible thoughts of sedition. Before they saw anything, people would hear the pulsating booms of the drummers beating out a cadence. Then, thousands of troops would begin stream-ing into view and march past, instilling awe at the empire's military might. Finally, Selim himself, cloaked in his finest silks and wearing a tall white turban, would appear, surrounded by his military entourage. Such a procession could easily last an entire day. For most in Anato-lia, this was the first and only time they saw their sultan. Thus, still only two years into his reign, Selim's war against the Safavids not only advanced his foreign policy, but also furthered his efforts to win over the people of his empire.

Selim's foreign and domestic programs intertwined in an even bloodier way during his march, when he led one of the largest domes-tic massacres in Ottoman history, killing as many as forty thousand of the empire's Shiite subjects. Early in his reign as sultan, he had created a register of all Shiites "age seven to seventy" living in the towns of Tokat, Samsun, Sivas, Amasya, and Yozgat. Now, as his army passed through these cities, they rounded up and executed every Shiite they could find—an echo of other military ventures such as the medieval Crusades, when Christian soldiers regularly killed Jews as they marched east from Europe to the Middle East. Most of the Ottoman Shiites were beheaded, although some were stoned or drowned to further terrorize the communities. Even though as governor of Trabzon Selim had mur-dered Shiites during the Şahkulu Rebellion, and at other times too, now as sultan he possessed military resources of exceptionally violent capac-ities. Of the vastly diverse populace he ruled—the majority of whom, we should remember, remained Christians—Ottoman Shiites were the most politically suspect and potentially dangerous. Unlike Christians,

Jews, Kurds, or any other group in the empire, Ottoman Shiites had a foreign state actively claiming their allegiance and encouraging them to turn against their overlords. Driven by his passion to destroy the Safavids, Selim strove to eliminate the threat of what he saw as a Shiite fifth column arising in his army's wake. He had learned this lesson from previous Shiite rebellions in the east and from his father's failed efforts to relocate the Ottoman Shiites—which, rather than diluting their resistance, made the Şahkulu Rebellion only the more wide-ranging and hence potent. Selim's massacre of the Shiites stood until the end of the nineteenth century as the largest domestic population purge in Ottoman history, and it is remembered and mourned to this day.

THE EASTERN ANATOLIAN TOWN of Sivas on the Red River boasted a thriving cotton economy and several Armenian monasteries and churches. At an elevation of over 4,000 feet, its winters were cruel. Selim and his troops arrived there on July 1, after three months of marching through central Anatolia, the summer's beating sun making winter seem like a mere rumor. In Sivas, Selim rested, reviewed his battalions, restocked and reprovisioned, and met with his advisers to discuss the war plans. After a few days, the army started toward Erzincan, 150 miles to the east. Almost directly south of Trabzon, Erzincan represented the easternmost extremity of full Ottoman sovereignty in Anatolia. Although the city was squarely Ottoman, the territories to its east were rather fuzzier in their sovereignty, falling in a zone of overlapping Ottoman and Safavid control. Safavid dominion was more pronounced—the Safavid capital, Tabriz, was much closer than Istanbul—with the balance tipping more firmly toward the Safavids the farther east one went.

Just before Selim reached Erzincan at the end of July 1514, he received an envoy from Ismail's court with the Safavid ruler's response to his declaration of war. Striking a tone of mocking irony and insult, Ismail began his message by nostalgically longing for the days of Selim's father, when the Ottomans and Safavids lived in peace and harmony (which they rarely ever had). In another insult couched as praise, Ismail lauded Selim's remarkable accomplishments as governor of Trabzon. Then, relentless in his braggadocio, the Safavid shah wrote that he could easily have invaded eastern Anatolia long before, but he thought it unnecessary since most of the people in the region were for all intents and purposes already his subjects. In fact, he even found this response to Selim's letter an enormous waste of his time, an annoyance that he had postponed until after a hunting trip. The bellicose tone of Selim's letter, Ismail added, clearly indicated just how ill-prepared and unworthy he was to be the leader of a state; perhaps the letter was, he suggested, "the mere fabrications of the opium-clouded minds of certain secretaries and scribes." Taunting Selim—indeed, daring him to invade—Ismail ended his message with a threat couched in verse:

> Bitter experience has taught that in this world of trial
> He who falls upon the house of 'Ali [the Shiites] always falls.

Furious, Selim ordered Ismail's envoy to be slain on the spot.

Selim's response to Ismail's churlish letter, written in Erzincan in early August 1514, offered fresh insults and threats. With this message, Selim also sent Ismail a few "gifts"—a rag, a staff, a toothbrush, prayer beads, and a begging bowl: the accoutrements of a Sufi—implying that Ismail was no better than the mendicant mystics who were his ancestors. Ismail answered the challenge of Selim's obnoxious gifts with a present of his own—a box of opium, insinuating again that the leaders of the Ottoman Empire were drug addicts whose reason was clouded by hallucinations.

After this *pas de deux*, Selim and his soldiers marched out of Erzincan. Before leaving, he ordered forty thousand of his troops to retreat west to secure the area between Kayseri and Sivas, where a Shiite uprising had broken out in response to his massacres—exactly the type of internal rebellion he had hoped to avoid. He continued eastward with his main force toward Erzurum, where he dispatched to Ismail yet another barbed, aggressive message. Selim's innovation this time was to dub Ismail a woman, recommending that on the battlefield he wear a *chador* (veil) instead of armor.

Near Erzurum, far from the Ottoman heartland, Selim's army entered territories only recently deserted by the Safavids, who had sacked and burned everything before making their retreat. This scorched-earth policy succeeded in weakening the Ottoman army and drawing it farther east, into regions of Safavid strength. By the late summer of 1514, Selim's troops had thinned from 140,000 to around

120,000, and they were running low on supplies. His soldiers were weary from almost six months of marching through the blasting heat of a long summer, unsure of what lay before them.

To boost their spirits and reinforce the supply lines, Selim ordered a fleet of provisioning ships—which he had organized before he left—to sail from Istanbul to Trabzon. From there, pack mules transported the supplies 150 miles to Erzincan and then another 150 miles to Erzurum. But the routes challenged the burdened mules and their handlers, as the terrain was roadless, mountainous, and slow. Ultimately, it proved impossible to supply so many soldiers this way. The men grew increasingly disgruntled. Selim, realizing that he could not sustain his soldiers' bodies or spirits much longer, wanted—indeed, needed—war. Moreover, if he failed to deliver his men to the battlefield quickly, the season's window for war would close.

Word reached Selim in Erzurum that the Safavid army had encamped on the plains of a high valley named Chaldiran, another 250 miles to the east (in what is now northwestern Iran). Chaldiran floated in the mountains between the two empires at an elevation of 6,000 feet, an island of green in the rugged territory between the Sunni and Shiite states. Selim assumed that this camp served as Ismail's frontier headquarters, a way-station through which to funnel men and matériel to the west. Thus, instead of waiting for their two armies to meet somewhere between Chaldiran and Erzurum, Selim resolved to march his forces as quickly as possible to strike the Safavids at Chaldiran itself. He rallied his troops to prepare for this one last push to begin the war they all craved. It took a week—longer than Selim would have liked—to collect the military supplies and food the army needed to carry to the battlefield.

Despite being pummeled by August's scorching heat, Selim's men covered the rocky terrain on the steady climb from Erzurum to Chaldiran in good time, leading pack mules and towing cannons. Morale rose and fell, with only the excitement of impending battle pushing them forward. A few days away from Chaldiran, the heavens intervened to bolster the men's spirits. On the afternoon of August 20, a solar eclipse—always an auspicious harbinger—halted the Ottoman forces in their tracks.

Astronomers from around the Muslim world had flocked to Istanbul after its conquest in 1453, producing dozens of learned treatises on topics as varied as the earth's rotation, the nature of time, the planetary system, and, indeed, eclipses. Some of this work anticipated and even influenced later theories by the likes of Nicolaus Copernicus and Tycho Brahe. Even if he had encountered some of these astronomers or their works in Istanbul, Selim, now far off in eastern Anatolia, did not concern himself with such celestial matters. He focused singularly on the worldly challenges before him, the looming war with his rivals of old. But Selim's men basked in the ethereal light of this cosmic omen, inspired now to cover the remaining few days toward their goal.

THE FERTILE PLAINS OF Chaldiran must have seemed a mirage, after the trek through vast stretches of drab terrain, when the Ottoman army reached the valley on August 22. Having crossed the whole of Anatolia, Selim spotted his enemy's forces only a few thousand meters away. Making his arrival imposingly obvious, he sent detachments to take up positions on the western edge of the valley floor, and he ordered others to move into the hills to the north and south. Selim had guessed, and now confirmed, that his forces far outnumbered those of the Safavids—he had more than a hundred thousand soldiers to Ismail's roughly forty thousand. Perhaps most significantly, Selim had some twelve thousand musketeers and three hundred wheeled-cannon carriages, while the Safavids only had cavalrymen and foot soldiers. Given their strategic advantages, Selim and his commanders resolved to strike quickly, before the Safavids could muster reinforcements.

War began the next day, August 23. At sunrise, the men in the hills charged down to the valley floor. This, combined with the might of the Ottoman soldiers already on the plains, drove most of the Safavids up into the parched eastern hills. Now on the higher ground, Ismail's troops fanned out to surround the Ottomans in the bowl beneath them. With Selim's soldiers encircled and exposed, Ismail believed he had seized the upper hand. A signal from him would release his men to flow down and squeeze the Ottomans in a death vise. To loosen their inhibitions as they surged downhill, Ismail distributed wine to his soldiers just before the attack.

The Ottomans' advantage in firearms proved the battle's decisive factor. In a tight formation of their own inside the Safavids' constricting ring, the Ottomans positioned their cannons facing outward, with musketeers behind them. As the Safavids' slightly inebriated cavalry-men spurred their horses down onto the valley floor, with foot sol-diers charging behind them, Ottoman gunners—following the cadence of the drummers beating out their war anthem—fired their cannons and muskets, easily picking off their enemies. From above, the scene would have looked like a stone dropping into water—ripples of bullets emanating out in concentric circles. Safavid bodies began piling up. As bursts of gunpowder puffed black smoke into the air, elements of the two sides' cavalries collided elsewhere on the valley floor. Ismail himself hacked to death several Ottoman soldiers before sustaining a wound to his hand and eventually evacuating the battlefield. Even in this fighting on horseback, at some distance from the direct reach of cannon fire, the Ottomans maintained the advantage. Selim's warhorses had been trained around gunfire, whereas the Safavid horses were easily startled by the blasts. "The Persian horses," according to the second-hand report of a Venetian ambassador, "hearing the thunder of those infernal machines, scattered and divided themselves over the plain, not obeying their riders' bit or spur any more, from the terror they were in. . . . [They] had never before heard such din."

By that afternoon, the soil of Chaldiran gurgled with blood. Thou-sands of soldiers had died, along with many high-ranking generals, sev-eral of Ismail's closest advisers, and a number of provincial governors who had joined the fight. Ismail led the ragged remnants of his army back to the east, but Selim did not immediately pursue them. Stung by his previous experience with the Safavids' scorched-earth policies in eastern Anatolia, he feared the retreat might be a trap, so he held his victorious troops in Chaldiran for a few days. As they contemplated their next move, they solemnly buried their dead.

AFTER THEIR DEVASTATING DEFEAT, Ismail's remaining forces fled all the way to the city of Qazvin, south of the Caspian Sea and the Alborz Mountains, where, as a boy, Ismail had plotted his triumphant return north. The mood in Qazvin was considerably more somber in 1514 than it had been in his youth. He made plans to regroup, dispatching letters across the world seeking alliances against the ascendant Otto-mans. Spain, Hungary, Venice, the pope, and the Knights of St. John all ignored his entreaties. Only the Portuguese—who were establishing settlements around the Indian Ocean and Persian Gulf and looking for allies against the Mamluks—responded, and then only rather meekly. They sent Ismail two small cannons and six arquebuses, barely enough for a hunting trip.

Meanwhile, in Chaldiran, Selim received two envoys from Tabriz. Presuming that the Ottoman sultan, with his overwhelming army, would next march on the Safavid capital, the city's governors decided to betray their imperial overlords. Preemptively they professed their loyalty to the Ottoman Empire, promising Selim safe passage and even inviting him to enter and take the walled city. Selim remained cautious, in case the message was a ruse, but decided to send some of his advisers back to Tabriz with the envoys to investigate the matter. The leaders of Tabriz welcomed Selim's men extravagantly, offering them control of the city's markets, showing them the ramparts and stockpiles of armaments, and touring them around the palace they planned to prepare for Selim and his retinue. The envoys reported back that the proposition seemed genuine: Tabriz's residents indeed wanted Selim to take their city.

Needless to say, occupying the Safavid capital would pitch the final shovel of dirt on that empire's buried corpse, and so—though remaining vigilant—Selim advanced on Tabriz. He and his troops entered the surrendered city on September 5. As they quietly filed through the gates, residents peered from windows and doorways at the strangers crowding their streets, curious about their green and red uniforms, intimidated by their long guns. This influx of Ottoman soldiers more than doubled the city's population.

As a mark of his sovereignty in place of Ismail's, that week's Friday sermon in mosques throughout Tabriz was delivered in Selim's name. Selim instructed his advisers to send letters from Tabriz to the Crimean khan, the Mamluks, and the doge of Venice, informing them of his conquest of the Safavid capital. At the same time, Selim's men secured the city and celebrated in its streets. After months of marching and stress, exhaustion and homesickness, the capture of Tabriz provided the Ottoman soldiers with an opportunity for an exuberant saturnalia. This city of great culture boasted a magnificent library of books from Central Asia, the Caucasus, and the Middle East; dueling schools of poetry; a unique style of miniature painting reflecting Chinese influences that had come with the Mongols; and a cottage industry of fine

*Scenes of Tabriz*

luxury carpets. The majority of Selim's men were much more interested in less high-minded endeavors, however, choosing to pursue equestrian sports, wrestling, polo, and archery, as well as gorging themselves on Tabriz's famous carrot stew and kabobs and, of course, guzzling wine. As in most occupied cities, the soldiers also committed acts of sexual violence against Tabriz's women and men.

Selim dispatched some of the city's riches and a group of its finest artisans, poets, and intellectuals back to Istanbul. As a sign of the breadth of his victory, he even transferred to Istanbul Ismail's favorite wife, Tajli Khanum, who was said to be exquisitely beautiful. There, she was married to the chief judge of the Ottoman army, Ja'far Çelebi. Later, Ismail would send four of his most trusted men with lavish gifts and—in stark contrast to their previous correspondence—complimentary statements and offers of riches to try to retrieve his wife. Selim responded to the appeal by cutting off the noses of the four men and sending them back to Ismail damaged and bloodied, much like his empire.

It was already September, and northern Iran, the Caucasus, and Anatolia would soon turn frigid and snowy, making it nearly impossible for the Ottoman soldiers to trek back to Istanbul. So Selim decided to winter in Tabriz. More significantly, this would allow him to continue his fight against the Safavids in the next military season. Resting, reprovisioning, and strategizing that far east, Selim calculated, would allow the Ottomans to attack Qazvin the following spring, and from there attempt the invasion and subjugation of the whole of Iran. However, when word reached his troops that he planned to keep them in Tabriz through the winter in order to fight again in the spring, they nearly mutinied. In the previous nine months, they had marched more than a thousand miles from Istanbul, fording rivers and climbing mountain passes, carrying supplies and dragging heavy weapons through torrential rain and roasting heat—all with the looming imperative of remaining ever-ready for war. Physically battered and emotionally drained, they wanted only to return home. Selim thus had no choice but to retreat. After just eight days in Tabriz and with the change of seasons approaching, a disappointed Selim and his impatient soldiers packed up to begin their long march back to Istanbul.

In late 1514, Selim stood closer than ever before to his dream of extinguishing one of the Ottomans' primary ideological and military foes. The repugnant Safavids had pestered him and his empire for years. From Tabriz, he believed, he could have destroyed them forever with one more concerted thrust into the heart of Iran. Abandoning the city now indefinitely deferred that ambition.

DESPITE THE FRUSTRATION OF his forced retreat from Tabriz, Selim's defanging of the mangy Shiite dog—his favorite epithet—allowed the

Ottomans to focus on other enemies and other interests. Most immediately, neutralization of the Safavids solidified the Ottomans' authority on their eastern border as never before, especially in the rural areas between the cities of Bayburt, Erzincan, and Erzurum. By far the most important development, however, was the imposition of Ottoman sovereignty on the southern city of Diyarbakir—long a territorial ambition of Selim's, as we have seen—which paved the way for later victories that would prove infinitely more significant and enduring than any gratification that could have come from moving farther east into a crumbling Iran.

Shah Ismail's defeat at Chaldiran was, to him, an utterly devastating psychological blow. Never having lost on the battlefield, his ego and aura of invincibility had ballooned, as his letters to Selim amply suggested. In the fall of 1514, instead of trying to pick up his military and emotional pieces, the Safavid shah entered a period of mourning, wearing only black robes and a black turban. He ordered all his military standards dyed black as well. Despite the very real threat the Ottomans still posed to his west, and the encroachment of the Uzbeks and the emergent Mughals to his east, Ismail would never again lead his troops into battle. He allowed his state to slip into disarray as he took to the bottle and the comforts of the flesh. In the words of one of Ismail's official chroniclers, "most of his time was spent in hunting, or in the company of rosy-cheeked youths, quaffing goblets of purple wine, and listening to the strains of music and song." Word of Ismail's sorry state soon spread far beyond his court. No doubt with considerable satisfaction, one of Selim's chroniclers wrote that, after Chaldiran, Ismail was "always drunk to the point of losing his mind and totally neglectful of the affairs of the state."

Ismail's personal crisis soon became a political one. Before Chaldiran, the Safavid shah had led his men as a divinely endowed and protected spiritual teacher who directed each soldier on the battlefield and in the mosque. Selim's thrashing of Ismail made faith in the shah impossible. No longer the invincible messenger of God, Ismail became instead a fallible human. As the Safavid military elite saw their leader defeated and drunk, they responded with skepticism and disrespect, followed ultimately by outright sedition. After Chaldiran, they realized that only a combined Safavid–Mamluk force could match the overwhelming military capabilities of the Ottomans, so they pressed Ismail to reach out to the Mamluks to attempt to establish such an alliance. The Mamluks were wary. Given Ismail's parlous mental state, his own military's loss of respect for him, and the Ottoman disruption of the Safavids' southern military routes, the Mamluks were dubious that Ismail would, or even could, deliver on his pledges. Better to go it alone against the Ottomans, concluded the Mamluk military commanders, than to forge an alliance with a divided, unreliable Safavid state.

⌘

THE BATTLE OF CHALDIRAN and the resultant weakening of the Safavid Empire allowed a new power to rise in the Middle East. In March 1515, the Portuguese captured the strategic island of Hormuz, a tiny speck of land at the entrance to the Persian Gulf, just off the Iranian coast. They would hold it for another century, making it the earliest European possession in the Persian Gulf. From the days of Henry the Navigator and Columbus exploring the west coast of Africa and the islands of the eastern Atlantic to Vasco da Gama's rounding of the Cape of Good Hope in 1497, the Portuguese had steadily been building a global maritime empire of coastal forts and fortifications. In the early decades of the sixteenth century, their major theater of war was the Indian Ocean. To add to their holdings in India, they captured Malacca on the Malay peninsula, on the ocean's far side. They also notched important victories in Brazil, and Newfoundland and Labrador in Canada.

Portuguese ships had first appeared in the port of Hormuz in September 1507, and had been booted off the island a few months later by locals acting in concert with the Safavids. But the diversion of Safavid forces away from the coast after Chaldiran enabled the Portuguese to invade the island again, and this time they held it. The capture of Hormuz won the Portuguese control over the strait through which all shipping from Persian Gulf ports had to pass, as well as a key way-station on the sea-lanes to their colonies on the west coast of India.

The imperial powers of the Ottoman Empire, Spain, and Portugal had consistently butted heads in North Africa and the western Mediterranean. And it was, of course, the commercial blockade of the Ottomans and Mamluks that had forced the Portuguese and the Spanish to seek out novel ways to reach Asia. In the years after Chaldiran, as the Ottomans and the Catholic powers continued to clash in North Africa, and the battle between Christians and Muslims crossed the Atlantic, the Portuguese and the Ottomans would also intensify their struggle for global power on the other side of the world, in the Indian Ocean.

Portugal's empire consisted almost entirely of isolated coastal holdings. While it had established colonies on the five continents of the New and Old Worlds, when taken together, the total amount of territory the Portuguese controlled was, in fact, quite small. The Ottoman Empire was the exact opposite—a contiguous terrestrial whole concentrated in one region. While the equation would change later, in the sixteenth century land equaled power. Selim held more of the earth's surface than any European power and more than most of the globe's other states. After Chaldiran, he would tip the global territorial balance even more in his favor.

# FRATERNAL EMPIRES

*The chainmail of the Mamluk sultan Qaitbay*

IN THE EARLY SIXTEENTH CENTURY, ALL THE WORLD'S MAJOR empires made religiously-tinged claims to universal sovereignty. The Safavids chose to tie their state to Shiism to distinguish themselves from other Muslim states, insisting that since this was God's true religion, they were destined to take over the world and rule over Muslims everywhere. The Spanish and the Portuguese similarly projected their Catholicism into and onto the world, claiming they were the world's divinely ordained religious rulers. Thus, they cleansed Iberia of all non-Christians and carried Christianity to the pagans in North America, the infidel Muslims in North and West Africa, and the uncouth unbelievers in India. A few decades later, in an act that might be compared to the Safavid embrace of Shiism, various European states would adopt Protestantism as their official creed, in part as a direct challenge to Catholic assertions of universality.

Unlike these powers, Selim could never claim to be the foremost defender of his religion on earth. The Mamluks, as guardians of the holy cities of Mecca and Medina, stood in his way. Thus, to prove himself the world's leading Sunni Muslim, to affirm that God had chosen *him* to cast his shadow over all of creation, and finally to fulfill the prophecy at his birth that he would hold all of the seven climes, Selim had to conquer the Mamluk Empire. Only then could he claim preeminence in the Muslim world and unleash his ambitions for Sunni Ottoman global domination. Above all, Selim wanted to become the caliph—a designation reserved only for the ruler of Mecca and Medina, and a title that no previous Ottoman sultan had been able to claim.

The increasingly bellicose Ottoman–Mamluk competition for the caliphate manifested itself, perhaps oddly at first glance, through gift-giving, one of the primary tools of early modern diplomacy. Around the world, sovereigns used gifts not only as markers of alliance between states but, even more so, as missives of one-upmanship in a politics of rivalry and threat. Two gifts from the middle of the fifteenth century reflect how the unmatched prestige of the caliphate figured prominently in the increasingly acrimonious relations between the Mamluks and the Ottomans. In 1440, the Mamluk sultan sent to his Ottoman counterpart a Qur'an purported to have belonged to 'Uthman, the third leader of the early Muslim community after the death of the Prophet Muhammad in 632. 'Uthman is a figure of monumental stature in Islamic history. Not only is he one of the four leaders known as the Rightly Guided Caliphs, who personally knew and immediately succeeded the Prophet, but he also produced the first canonical written text of the Qur'an. Because the revelations Muhammad received from the angel Gabriel and then taught to his followers remained an oral tradition for several decades, a number of divergent versions emerged. 'Uthman reconciled these into a standard edition, destroyed all of the previous ones, and then distributed this text, known as the 'Uthmanic codex, as the only sanctioned

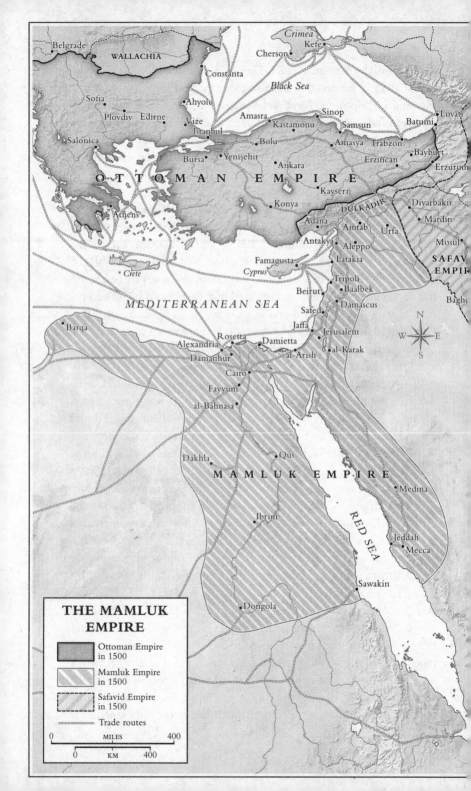

THE MAMLUK EMPIRE

- ■ Ottoman Empire in 1500
- ▨ Mamluk Empire in 1500
- ⬚ Safavid Empire in 1500
- ∷∷∷ Trade routes

0 — MILES — 400
0 — KM — 400

Belgrade

WALLACHIA

Crimea
Kefe
Cherson

Constanta

Black Sea

Sofia

Ahyolu

Sinop
Amasra
Kastamonu
Samsun
Batumi
Lovat

Plovdiv  Edirne

Vize
Istanbul

Bolu

Amasya  Trabzon
Bayburt

Salonica

Bursa  Yenişehir
Ankara

Erzincan
Erzurum

OTTOMAN EMPIRE

Kayseri

Konya

DULKADIR

Diyarbakir

Mardin

Adana

Aintab  Urfa

Mosul

Athens

Antakya
Aleppo

SAFAV
EMPIR

Famagusta
Cyprus

Latakia

Crete

Tripoli
Baalbek

Baghd

Beirut
Damascus

MEDITERRANEAN SEA

Safed

Jaffa

Jerusalem

Barqa

Rosetta
Alexandria
Damanhur

Damietta
al-Arish
al-Karak

N
W    E
S

Cairo

Fayyum
al-Bahnasa

Dakhla

Qus

MAMLUK EMPIRE

Medina

Ibrim

RED SEA

Jeddah
Mecca

Sawakin

Dongola

version of the Qur'an. In sending such an obviously precious and sacred object to their rival, the Mamluks sought to impress upon the Ottomans their wealth and power as the caliphs of the Muslim world and possessors of the heritage of Islam. Clearly, the price of gifting this object was well worth making the ideological point that something as valuable even as the 'Uthmanic codex was an object with which they could part, given their vast collection of treasures.

A few years later, after the Ottoman seizure of Constantinople in 1453, Mehmet II retorted with a gift of his own. As part of his imperial embassy to the Mamluks to relate the news of his glorious conquest, he sent an emissary directly to Mecca with a personal message to the custodians of that city's holy sites. Mehmet wrote, "We have sent to you personally two thousand florins of pure gold, taken as booty from the conquest, and another seven thousand florins for the poor . . . in Mecca and Medina." In bypassing, and thus disrespecting, the authority of the Mamluk sultan to engage directly with the rulers of Mecca, Mehmet hoped to win over these important leaders by impressing upon them the Ottomans' wealth and grandeur. Having defeated Byzantium, one of history's most powerful empires, a descendant of Rome, the Ottomans now uniquely combined the legacy of Rome with Islam and hoped soon to solidify their Islamic credentials by adding to their state the most important places in the Muslim world.

The ideological antagonisms that shaped this diplomacy of gift-giving stood alongside more mundane modes of imperial interaction. For more than two hundred years, the Mamluk and Ottoman empires had shaped each other. While the Safavids had only recently emerged in the region—and after Chaldiran seemed to have a questionable future—the Mamluks and the Ottomans had risen to power with and against each other, their conflict and collaboration in part determining their military structures, regional politics, and economic policies. Founded within fifty years of each other, the Mamluk and Ottoman empires, as that era's most powerful Muslim states, essentially divided up the eastern Mediterranean. In the fourteenth and fifteenth centuries—depending on the period, the geographic location, and the issue at hand—the two powers toggled back and forth between enmity and alliance, relentlessly vying for and sometimes sharing authority and territory.

In a teetering world of rapidly shifting geopolitics and rival claims

to universal sovereignty, it often proved of enormous mutual benefit for the two empires to work together. They held the Middle East,
Balkans, and North Africa as two Sunni Muslim empires fending off
Christian polities to the west and the descendants of the Mongols
and other Central Asian powers to the east. Together they controlled
trade between East and West, and cooperated in their regulation of
commerce, security, and transportation. The Ottomans supplied the
Mamluks, in forest-free Egypt, with wood from Anatolia; in return,
Mamluk merchants carried spices and textiles from the Indian Ocean
and the Red Sea north to Bursa, Izmir, and other major Ottoman trading cities. The Ottomans furnished the Mamluks with slaves from the
Caucasus, many of whom eventually became the elite of Mamluk society, much as the Janissaries did in the Ottoman Empire. The Mamluks,
for their part, delivered to the Ottomans slaves from their holdings in
Sudan. The two empires' common objective of maintaining the free
flow of commodities, cash, slaves, and agricultural products between
their markets created a shared interest in preventing the encroachment
of Europeans in the eastern Mediterranean, and, as we will see, in the
Red Sea and Indian Ocean.

In addition to their shared political strategies and fraternal ideological worldviews, the two Sunni empires had soldered their relations
with several intermarriages. For instance, the Mamluk sultan Barsbay,
who ruled the empire between 1422 and 1438, married an Ottoman
princess related to the Ottoman sultan Murad II, Mehmet II's father.

※

AFTER HIS DEFEAT OF the Safavids at Chaldiran, Selim redirected his
military focus southward. He became convinced that full control of
the Ottomans' eastern holdings could come only with the elimination
of the Mamluks, who now posed the greatest territorial and ideological
challenge to his empire. As long as they ruled in the Middle East, he
would never be able to claim leadership of the global Muslim community. His confidence surging, Selim shifted the established Ottoman
policy of uneasy coexistence with the Mamluks to one of direct military confrontation.

Beyond his generally warlike character, several factors motivated
Selim to move on the Mamluks. First, of course, he viewed the Mamluks' protection of his rivals during the succession crisis—Korkud, and

one of Ahmed's sons—as a personal and political betrayal. Because Selim's succession battle was bloodier and more complicated than his father's had been, he took the Mamluks' support of his half-brothers much more seriously than Bayezit had taken their support of Cem. Any friend of Selim's enemy became his enemy, too.

Additionally, in the realm of global geopolitics, Selim presumed that the Mamluks and the Safavids would always align against him, since they had a common interest in checking the Ottomans' exploding power throughout the Mediterranean and Middle East. The Mamluks mourned the outcome of the Battle of Chaldiran, for, were it not for Ismail's wretched condition after 1514, the two empires might have led a joint military campaign against Selim. Breaking with established practice, the Mamluks sent no embassy of congratulation to Istanbul after Chaldiran, and the Mamluk sultan banned celebrations of the Ottoman military victory (by contrast, the Ottoman conquest of Constantinople had led to days of festivities in Mamluk Cairo). And a few years later, when the Ottomans invaded Mamluk territory, the Safavids planned to send troops.

The joint Mamluk–Safavid interest against the Ottomans was particularly pronounced in southeastern Anatolia, the three empires' only point of territorial contiguity, which made it effectively the region's landlocked navel. Ever since the Ottomans first emerged as an empire in mid-fourteenth-century Anatolia, a string of buffer states along the Mamluk–Ottoman border in northern Syria and southern Anatolia had helped to sustain the long peace. Along the west–east line that included the cities of Adana, Aintab, Urfa, Diyarbakir, and Mardin, large tribal principalities had managed to remain largely independent by skillfully playing the Ottomans and Mamluks against each other, raiding and trading, cutting deals, switching allegiance easily and often, but always maintaining the balance of peace. Because this buffer zone was far from both the Ottomans' and the Mamluks' loci of power, neither had invested the colossal resources that would have been needed to exercise direct sovereign control over the region. In all likelihood, such an effort would have been a spark for confrontation.

In 1466, nearly fifty years before Selim won control of Diyarbakir (however shaky that control was immediately after Chaldiran), the Ottoman–Mamluk buffer zone had begun to erode. In that year, Mehmet moved to annex part of the region around the town of Aintab.

In response, the Mamluk sultan Qaitbay seized an old Byzantine hill-top castle far to the north, near the town of Kayseri. As both powers chipped away at their territorial buffer, they raised the imperial stakes. After Mehmet died on campaign in 1481—a campaign, it was rumored, intended to face down the Mamluks in northern Syria—Qaitbay took advantage of the temporary chaos that the Ottoman succession struggle caused to extend Mamluk power further into the rapidly shrinking buffer zone. Then, in 1485, after he had secured the sultanate, Bayezit struck back, sponsoring an invasion of the territory the Mamluks had just seized in the now increasingly militarized region between the two empires. He sent arms and other resources to the Dulkadir dynasty, one of the local tribal principalities, who seized the opportunity to push southward and conquer land in northern Syria, before the Mamluks retook it. Thus began a period of indeterminate border wars between the Ottomans and Mamluks. In the years between 1485 and 1491, both empires led raids against the other—directly and through proxies— gaining and then losing territory, killing and capturing each other's soldiers.

That this region was the point of greatest distance from the Mamluk, Ottoman, and later Safavid capitals suited its dominant pastoral groups. That said, whichever empire could dominate the rocky landscape of southeastern Anatolia would achieve a distinct tactical advantage. The Mamluks and the Safavids rightly saw the region as the Ottomans' most vulnerable point of attack, its largely undefended soft underbelly. Although the area was almost as distant from the Mamluks' capital, Cairo, as it was from Istanbul, they already held the region's major city, Aleppo, giving them a military staging point. As for the Safavids, the general lawlessness in southeastern Anatolia offered them opportunities, even after Chaldiran, to move both Shiite propaganda and Shiite troops into the region.

Selim understood his vulnerability in the Middle East's "navel," especially the opportunity it presented for the Mamluks and the Safavids to launch a joint military operation against him. This explains in large measure why he made Diyarbakir a focus of attention during the Chaldiran campaign. Diyarbakir functioned as the gateway southward from Anatolia into Syria, and controlling it allowed Selim to contemplate the possibility of other strategic victories. Solidifying Ottoman sovereignty over Diyarbakir, along with much of the Kurdish territory around it, fortified his frontier against the pacified Safavids and extended his border with the Mamluks to the south and east. As was the case with earlier raids into this buffer region, the 1514 annexation of Diyarbakir shrank the space between the empires, drawing them closer to direct contact and thus vastly increasing the potential for military confrontation.

Selim's determination to invade and destroy the colossal Mamluk Empire and take over all of its territories in the Middle East, in North Africa, and on the Red Sea would be the largest military venture any Ottoman sultan had ever attempted. But Selim, the eternal underdog, knew what it meant to face a much more powerful opponent— one more lavishly resourced and historically advantaged. Far beyond the plotting, intrigue, and violence of his succession battle, Selim's war against his Sunni sibling would demand that he overcome earth-rattling odds.

AS HE HAD DEMONSTRATED before, Selim understood the virtue of patience and the need for exceptional reconnaissance before war. To secure information about the Mamluks' on-the-ground resources, troop numbers, and positions, he enlisted a veritable army of spies from within the Mamluk Empire. The use of spies and double agents was, as we have seen, nothing new in the Mediterranean and the Middle East, but increasing geopolitical tensions made covert intelligence gathering a vital component of early sixteenth-century imperial politics. Venice led the way, with the world's most extensive and robust network of spies. The espionage agents Selim had inherited as sultan kept him constantly abreast of the current state of rivals' and enemies' military circumstances, preparedness, and supply chains. He knew when the Mamluks repositioned armaments, when infighting occurred among their military commanders, and when they maneuvered funds to free up cash for war. The Mamluks—and of course the Ottomans too—always worried about spies in their midst, and as the two empires lurched closer to war, both sides did all they could to ferret out and purge those they suspected of being in the pay of the other side.

One of the most prominent, and most useful, of the Ottomans' spies in the Mamluk Empire was Khayr Bey, the Mamluk governor of Aleppo and the highest official in this enormously important city, which had been repeatedly pummeled over the past decade. Like all the Mamluk elite and much of the Ottoman elite, he had begun his career as a slave. Given his origins in Abkhazia on the Black Sea, Khayr as a youngster was likely funneled via Ottoman slave markets to Mamluk territory. He had worked his way up through the imperial bureaucracy and was by all accounts a gifted representative of Cairo—efficiently collecting taxes, ensuring the protection of foreign merchants, and maintaining order throughout the city.

After Istanbul and Cairo, Aleppo, with its iconic hilltop citadel, was the third largest international trading center in the Middle East. At the crossroads of all overland trade routes to and from the Mediterranean, it was effectively a landlocked port city. Aleppo's exquisite covered bazaar, the largest in the world, with more than thirteen kilometers of internal streets, offered wares from China, Spain, and all points in between. Holes in its vaulted stone roof allowed light to flood into the market and provided air circulation as customers and traders haggled over furs, leather, metalwork, shoes, textiles, and endless foodstuffs. Abutting the buffer zone between the Ottomans and the Mamluks, Aleppo was a frontier city between the empires, a Mamluk bulwark against their enemies to the north. Well aware that he would have to seize this walled entrepôt in order to achieve any success against the Mamluks, Selim did whatever he could to make inroads into Aleppo and the surrounding region. He had the perfect mole in Khayr Bey.

Because of Aleppo's relative proximity to Istanbul, in September 1497 Khayr was tasked with journeying to the Ottoman capital as the Mamluks' official representative to inform Sultan Bayezit of the death of Sultan Qaitbay and the accession to the throne of his young son, Muhammad al-Nasir. Khayr ended up staying in Istanbul for more than a year, during which time he was awed by the city's riches and pleasures and deeply impressed by the effluence of imperial soldiers returning from raids or battles with seemingly endless spoils. On just one day in late 1498, for instance, Bayezit received two high-ranking military men. The former privateer and now imperial admiral Kemal Reis was reporting on a mission to Khayr's very own Mamluk court. On his return voyage from Egypt, Kemal had been attacked by a flotilla of the Knights Hospitaller of St. John from Rhodes, but he successfully defended his ship against them, even taking five of their vessels. From these ships came vast treasures and hundreds of captives that Kemal delivered to Bayezit in Khayr's presence. Later that day, one of Bayezit's most trusted frontier warlords, Malkoçoğlu Bali Bey, returned to Istanbul from a campaign in the Balkans, where he too had seized vast amounts of cash, property, and slaves. Khayr Bey, overwhelmed by all this wealth, the lavishness of the Ottoman court, and the hegemonic power of the sultan, was easily bribed with cash, slaves, and promises of further wealth and power to flip his allegiance.

While there is no information on the details of the deal, what is clear is that once Khayr returned to Aleppo, he began a secret correspondence with Bayezit's court, conveying useful information about Mamluk affairs. This crucial reconnaissance continued when Selim assumed the throne. Both Ottoman sovereigns sent Khayr a steady stream of gifts and money in exchange for the espionage he provided. Khayr's treason would eventually be revealed, and he would forever be known derisively in Mamluk historical sources as Khain Bey instead of Khayr Bey—a play on words, as *khain* means traitor.

IN THE SPRING OF 1515, having wintered in Amasya after their retreat from Tabriz, Selim and his soldiers arrived back in Istanbul just as his palace gardeners began planting that year's tulips: magenta and blush, canary and garnet. Joyous news came of the birth of his second grandchild, a boy named Mustafa, who was described, even in his youth, as possessing "extraordinary talent." Born in Manisa, where Suleyman now served as governor, Mustafa and his father would eventually partake of the well-worn Ottoman tradition of filial animosity. After fathering several more sons, Suleyman would have Mustafa, his most potent rival, strangled in 1553.

In order to ramp up for war against the Mamluks, Selim had to rebuild morale and support among the Janissaries after their yearlong campaign on the eastern frontier. To achieve this, he deployed the power of pomp and a martial *esprit de corps*, lavishing riches and ceremonial honors on his soldiers as rewards for their victory at Chaldiran. They were celebrated with royal processions and banquets extolling their bravery and strength against the Safavid enemy. At the same time, Selim ordered the rearming of his forces: bullets and armor were stockpiled, new cannons were cast, new swords were forged. Even more important, he worked to retool the forces who would wield these weapons. As he had done throughout his career, Selim expanded the ranks of the army beyond the elite of the Janissaries, seeking out irregular fighters who would be loyal to him alone. He had always despised soldiers who spent their lives rising through the ranks, men who excelled more at administrative bickering than they did on the battlefield. He cleared the imperial forces of many of these men—executing some, discharging others—and replaced them with faithful companions from earlier operations, men who had proven themselves bloodthirsty and committed to the empire above all else, even their own careers and lives.

The same summer that the Portuguese secured their hold on Hormuz, Selim set out to strengthen his navy. The Chaldiran campaign had revealed the weakness of the Ottoman fleet, as the ships that sailed to Trabzon to reprovision the army had proved wholly inadequate, and, after this long venture in the Black Sea, they were now even more desperately in need of attention. A successful invasion of the Mamluk

*Selim's forces attack 'Ala' al-Dawla*

Empire would require a steady line of ships based in eastern Mediterranean ports, to provision the army as it marched south and to support
its attacks with cannon fire from the sea. The ultimate prize—Cairo—
was much farther overland from Istanbul than Chaldiran was, and
Selim was determined that his army should not grow as disgruntled,
tired, and low on supplies as it had on that campaign.

With his war preparations moving on apace, Selim sent a warning shot across the Mamluks' bow. Acting on reconnaissance from
Khayr Bey in Aleppo, Selim dispatched a small battalion to attack one
of the Mamluks' proxies in the buffer zone of southeastern Anatolia.
In June, Ottoman forces easily seized the territories of a group they
had previously armed, the Dulkadir tribal confederation, capturing
'Ala' al-Dawla, its leader. As a not-so-subtle message of aggression, and
a continuation of the imperial gift-giving tradition, Selim sent 'Ala'
al-Dawla's head to Sultan al-Ashraf Qansuh al-Ghawri, in Cairo. To
leave no room for misinterpretation, and to follow proper diplomatic
protocol, Selim pinned to the severed head a formal declaration of war.

NOW THAT SELIM'S INVASION was clearly a question of *when* rather than
*if*, al-Ghawri bolted into action. Like Selim, he organized his troops
and readied their weapons; he also sent a mission to Shah Ismail's court
to raise the possibility, which he had so recently rejected, of a Mamluk–
Safavid alliance against the Ottomans. A year after the ignominy at
Chaldiran, Ismail was able to stay sober long enough to outline plans
for a joint military force; however, the envoy al-Ghawri sent to the
Safavid court happened to be another of Selim's spies. Even as Ismail
prepared to dispatch troops to al-Ghawri in the spring of 1516, Selim
sent another threatening letter to the Mamluk sultan, informing him
that he knew all about his "secret" plans with the Safavids, calling him
a stupid coward, and adding for good measure that he would soon
destroy the Mamluk Empire.

Startled by the letter, al-Ghawri resolved to move his troops north
toward the border as soon as possible. The sooner he reached the theater of war, he wagered, the more advantageous a position he could
stake out. Preparations proved complicated, however, which stalled
his departure from Cairo. To raise the huge army that war in Syria
would demand, al-Ghawri required every village to supply men for

the expedition, with peasants and merchants alike conscripted. Not surprisingly, such coercion spurred many to flee, which sowed chaos across the empire and exacerbated shortages in the rural labor pool needed for food production. And, even as less food was being harvested, al-Ghawri demanded a larger share of it than usual for the state. On the rampage, soldiers seized horses from government mills as well as from those owned by villages. Without horses, the mills could not turn, leading to a scarcity of flour throughout Egypt and Syria. And without flour, there was no bread. All of this contributed to a situation of near-famine that devastated towns from Cairo to Anatolia.

Moreover, given general mismanagement and the massive outlay required to combat the Portuguese in the Red Sea and the Indian Ocean, the Mamluk treasury in those years was starved for cash. This meant that most soldiers were paid with promissory notes—clearly not a recipe for inspiring a loyal fighting force. Conscripts regularly mutinied, deserting their camps and often seizing food to take back to their villages.

Next came distressing news from Iran. The Safavid forces that Ismail had promised to al-Ghawri's envoy—the one who doubled as Selim's spy—would not be arriving after all. Morale was simply too low after Chaldiran to muster an adequate number of troops, and the few soldiers who did begin the march southward could not make it past the Ottomans' fortified line at Diyarbakir. After centuries of uneasy rapprochement, the Mamluks—underresourced and undermanned— would have to go it alone against their far more formidable Ottoman adversary.

# CONQUERING THE NAVEL

*Battle of Marj Dabiq*

**D**ESPITE ITS ENORMOUS RELIGIOUS AND HISTORIC SIGNIFICANCE for all of the Middle East's major faiths, Jerusalem in the early decades of the sixteenth century was a minor town with a minuscule population of fewer than six thousand souls. Over centuries of attempted Crusades, European Christians had only briefly been able to control the city, which had been ruled by Muslim powers since 638, a mere six years after the Prophet Muhammad's death. Although the Crusader Columbus ultimately never set foot in Jerusalem, he had long sought to seize the holy city—a project he pursued with not inconsiderable zeal, but as it turned out, on the far side of the Atlantic. Selim would soon succeed where Columbus and nearly all other Crusaders had failed—he conquered Jerusalem.

AFTER SEVERE DELAYS, THE Mamluk sultan al-Ghawri led his army out of Cairo on May 17, 1516, aiming for Jerusalem as his first major encampment in Syria. Before leaving the capital—which was gripped in those years by a series of plague outbreaks, on top of the food shortages and fiscal crisis—al-Ghawri had designated one of his senior advisers, Tuman Bey, as regent during his absence.

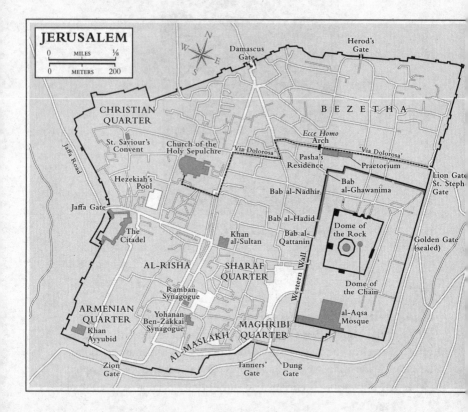

Trying to minimize the effects of the blazing hot early summer sun, al-Ghawri and his troops crossed the Sinai peninsula's landscape of orange sandstone and tawny gravel mostly at night, and mostly along the Mediterranean coast, away from the region's treacherous canyons and quicksand, and its notorious bandits. By the middle of June they had arrived at Jerusalem and were camped outside its walls.

As rulers always did when passing through Jerusalem, al-Ghawri took the opportunity to pray at the Dome of the Rock and other mosques in the city, and to visit its historic sites. Meanwhile, his men gathered all the provisions they could, and enjoyed the cool waters of the ponds and streams nearby. After what the troops probably felt was too short a respite, al-Ghawri continued the push north toward the Ottoman border. Along the way, he maintained a policy of forcibly seizing food, resources, and men. As in Egypt itself, this of course did not endear him to the local population. Still, he deemed brutal coercion his most effective means of raising an army quickly and then supporting it.

His next stop was Damascus, a rich city of soaring arches featuring expensive designs of alternating black basalt and white limestone. Damascus, with its estimated ten thousand households, had always been loyal to the Mamluks, and mounted massive ceremonies to welcome al-Ghawri—although the festivities failed to lift the somber fog of looming war wafting through the city's narrow, curving streets and tunneled thoroughfares. When, as was the custom, the city's European merchants threw gold and silver coins at the feet of the sovereign, some of al-Ghawri's underpaid and starving conscripts lunged at the money, almost toppling the Mamluk sultan from his horse. Like the soldiers, the people of Damascus felt the desperation of that ruinous summer too, as al-Ghawri monopolized resources and manpower for his total-war preparations.

On July 10, nearly two months after departing Cairo, al-Ghawri finally arrived at Aleppo, where he planned to set up his headquarters. One of the oldest cities in the world, founded in the third millennium BCE, Aleppo is strategically located between the Mediterranean and the Euphrates. Its most prominent religious site, the Umayyad mosque, dates to the eighth century and claims to house the remains of the father of John the Baptist. (Its famed minaret, once one of the highest points in the city, was constructed in 1090 and destroyed in 2013 during the Syrian Civil War.) The weary Mamluk soldiers ran amok through the twisting lanes, commandeering and looting houses, stealing from the marketplace, monopolizing vital resources, raping and killing. Thus, Aleppo felt more like an occupied city than one hosting its imperial army before triumphantly sending it off to war. As they prepared for battle, al-Ghawri and his officers had no inkling that the governor of the city had turned on them and aligned his fortunes with the Ottomans.

While the Mamluks were making their way north, Selim began his own undulating march south. He instructed one of his top generals in the east—a trusted military adviser from his Trabzon days—to mobilize as large a contingent of troops as possible and to rendezvous with him at Elbistan, a former stronghold of the Dulkadir confederation about 180 miles north of Aleppo. Selim reached Elbistan, on the banks of the churning Ceylan River, on July 23; the auxiliary forces materialized a week later. Now on opposite sides of the buffer zone, Selim and al-Ghawri dispatched embassies trading offers, insults, and threats. Each had the same message for the other: surrender or die. Neither sovereign, of course, was particularly eager to do either, and both killed several of the other's envoys. Now, in late July 1516, far from their capitals, after months of mobilization and back-and-forth vitriol, war was imminent.

On July 30, word arrived in Selim's camp that the Mamluk army was on the move toward his position. The departure of al-Ghawri's troops for the battlefield was decidedly inauspicious. The people of Aleppo cursed and jeered the Mamluk sultan and his army as they marched out through the gates, berating the soldiers for the havoc they had caused. As Aleppo faded behind them, rumors began swirling among al-Ghawri's advisers that Khayr was a traitor, supplying information to the Ottomans and providing safe haven to Ottoman sympathizers. Could this explain why the residents of Aleppo were allowed to treat the Mamluk army with such disrespect, unchecked by the city's authorities? Al-Ghawri was unsure what to believe, but he could not allow this to distract him from the unstoppable momentum toward war.

On August 5, Selim delivered a rousingly inspiring speech before leading his army out of Elbistan. From his campaign in Georgia through to his victory at Chaldiran, he had learned that the key to success on the battlefield was keeping his soldiers motivated and fortified. Thus, he rode back and forth through the ranks, looking into the eyes

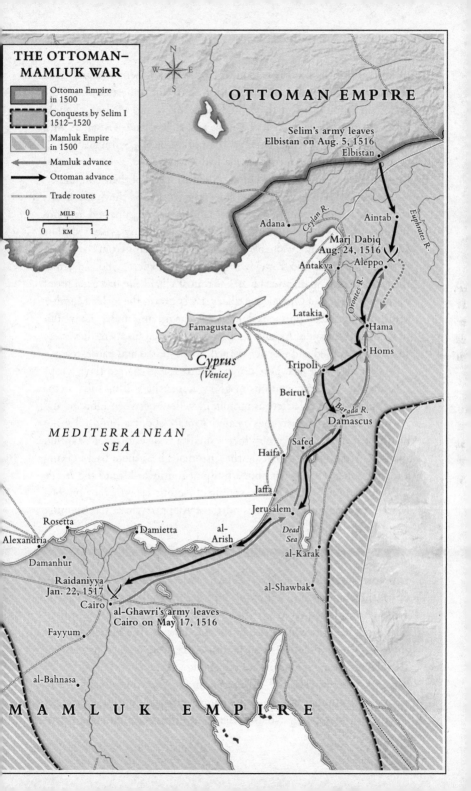

THE OTTOMAN–
MAMLUK WAR

- Ottoman Empire in 1500
- Conquests by Selim I 1512–1520
- Mamluk Empire in 1500
- Mamluk advance
- Ottoman advance
- Trade routes

0 MILE 1
0 KM 1

N
W E
S

OTTOMAN EMPIRE

Selim's army leaves Elbistan on Aug. 5, 1516
Elbistan

Adana

Ceylan R.

Aintab

Euphrates R.

Marj Dabiq
Aug. 24, 1516
Antakya
Aleppo

Orontes R.

Latakia

Hama

Homs

Famagusta

Cyprus
(Venice)

Tripoli

Beirut

Barada R.
Damascus

MEDITERRANEAN
SEA

Haifa

Safed

Jaffa

Jerusalem

Rosetta

Damietta

al-Arish

Dead Sea

al-Karak

Alexandria

Damanhur

Raidaniyya
Jan. 22, 1517
Cairo

al-Shawbak

al-Ghawri's army leaves
Cairo on May 17, 1516

Fayyum

al-Bahnasa

MAMLUK EMPIRE

of as many of the men as he could. God, he told them, wanted them to crush the Mamluks, wanted them to seize his holiest cities for the Ottoman Empire. Before they could reach Mecca and Medina, though, Syria awaited them, with its beauties and riches, and Jerusalem with its mosques and spiritual blessings. Mamluk subjects, Selim assured his men, wanted Ottoman rule. As he had always done, Selim promised his soldiers not only victory but also the full spoils of their conquests.

He also told his professional soldiers the truth, and they took heart: they were better equipped than the Mamluks, their guns and cannons technologically superior to the armaments the enemy possessed. The Ottomans had gained valuable knowledge of firearms from their wars in the Balkans, and also from Jewish gunpowder experts who had fled to the empire from Spain after 1492. The rout at Chaldiran had been proof of the supremacy of Ottoman artillery. By contrast, the feeble Mamluk army, debilitated by previous failures, was staggering under the weight of its own ineptitude. Against them, Selim assured his men, they were supremely focused and sharply trained, battle-tested and battle-ready.

As the crushing heat bore down, Selim's forces carried their weapons, morale, and expectations of glory across the rolling hills, occasional plains, and treacherous mountain valleys between Elbistan and Aleppo. In mid-August, they neared Aintab, about a hundred miles north of Aleppo, where they met a small advance force of Mamluk soldiers. After a brief skirmish, the Ottomans beat them back, taking a few prisoners. Selim continued pushing southward, onto the fertile soils of northern Syria. On the evening of August 23, 1516, they reached Marj Dabiq, about thirty miles north of Aleppo, where the Mamluk army awaited them.

❈

THE NEXT MORNING, a Sunday, the two armies collided on the flat plains of Marj Dabiq, with metal biting into flesh, blood dripping to earth. The fighting lasted from first light to late afternoon. Although both sides brought approximately sixty thousand men to the battlefield, only about fifteen thousand of the Mamluk force were trained professionals. The rest were conscripts: a hodgepodge of merchants, disgruntled peasants, mercenaries, and townsmen, many with questionable commitment. A number of them did whatever they could to shirk combat altogether—deserting, avoiding the front lines, even maiming themselves. Those who did fight were woefully untrained, with no idea how to load a musket or align in battle formation, or even how and when to retreat. As Selim had predicted, the Ottomans' superior technology carried the day, supporting waves of cavalry as they mowed down the Mamluks' pathetic forces. As had happened at Chaldiran, the blasts of the Ottomans' cannons and guns spooked the Mamluks' horses, which bucked and bolted in every direction. The horsemen, too, lacked training and experience. For the Mamluks, the scorching August day was nothing less than grisly chaos.

Around noon, with battle raging, the duplicitous Khayr requested entry to Sultan al-Ghawri's tent. Beyond all of the extremely valuable information Khayr had fed to the Ottomans over the years, it was in this moment that his treason best served Selim and his army. Khayr informed the Mamluk sovereign—technically still his own sovereign—that the Ottomans had surrounded the Mamluk army and would soon be closing in. According to Mamluk sources, Khayr recommended surrender as the only way for al-Ghawri and his commanders to survive. Given his suspicion of Khayr's loyalties, al-Ghawri viewed this information warily. But whether or not Khayr told the truth, and whether or not al-Ghawri believed him, was irrelevant. Word of Khayr's message spread quickly. Rumors swirled: the Mamluks were trapped; a massive bloodbath was about to occur; escape was now impossible. The troops—professionals as well as irregulars—panicked, and most fled for their lives. By early afternoon, the Mamluk army had been devastated; the few soldiers who managed to stay alive into the late afternoon then cleared out as quickly as they could. As the ascending gunsmoke mingled with the kinetic light of a summer evening, what had been a day of screams and explosions on the Marj Dabiq battlefield dissolved into a night of eerie quiet. In the crepuscular haze, all that remained were Mamluk corpses and the moans of the mortally wounded.

One of the corpses was that of their leader, Sultan al-Ashraf Qansuh al-Ghawri himself. When his soldiers first started to desert the fight, he had tried to stop them. "This is the moment to take heart!" he implored them. "Fight, and I will reward you!" But his attempts at inspiration failed. Nearly alone on the battlefield and exhausted by the relentless August heat, the seventy-five-year-old al-Ghawri recognized that his empire was slipping away. According to the most detailed account of his death, by the Mamluk chronicler Ibn Iyās, al-Ghawri "was gripped by a sort of paralysis [perhaps from a hernia] that affected the side of his body, and his jaw dropped open. He asked for water, which was brought to him in a golden goblet. He drank some, turned his horse to flee, advanced two paces, and fell from his saddle." His body hit the ground and lay motionless. As the Ottoman cavalry galloped forward, celebrating the victory Selim had promised them, their horses' hooves trampled the Mamluk sultan—just another anonymous, half-buried body in the dirt.

The next day, August 25, as the sun rose shimmering in the east, the extent of Selim's victory proved stunning. Al-Ghawri had met an ignominious end; his fighting force was gone; most of his empire's top administrators had been killed, including the governors of Damascus, Tripoli, Safed, and Homs. Now, all of Syria, with its rich markets, agricultural lands, and strategic significance, lay before Selim, undefended. The tattered Mamluk Empire, alive though it remained, had been pummeled and injured, mortally so.

THE MAMLUK ARMY'S HUMAN shards dragged themselves back to Aleppo from Marj Dabiq. Towing their weapons, their maimed, and their frayed spirits, they approached the city's outskirts starving and battered. Their clothes hung from them like Spanish moss; some had no shoes. Spotting the bedraggled soldiers in the distance, the people of Aleppo—led by Khayr Bey, who was now openly professing his allegiance to the Ottomans—closed the city's nine massive wooden gates against them. The hapless soldiers would have to beg for refuge elsewhere. Aleppo had become an Ottoman city.

After years of depredations under Mamluk rule, the residents of Aleppo eagerly recognized Selim as their legitimate ruler. On August 28, the gates were thrown open so that he could make his triumphant entrance: a parade of exuberant soldiers, drummers, and cannons. That week, Friday prayers in the city's mosques were said in the Ottoman sultan's name.

In Aleppo's central citadel, Selim received Khayr, his spy, and a key to his victory. Perched on a hill and surrounded by its own moated wall, and with only one entrance, the citadel was the city's crown jewel and one of the oldest continuously inhabited structures on earth. Whoever controlled the citadel controlled Aleppo. Selim thanked Khayr in front of the city's elite and welcomed him into the imperial administration as the first Ottoman governor of Aleppo. The two then sat down with Selim's military commanders to review the Ottomans' current war footing, plot future strategy, and appoint officials to root out any lingering Mamluk supporters in the city. All of Aleppo's vast wealth—its long-distance trade connections from West Africa to Southeast Asia, its rich bazaars dealing in textiles, spices, and metalwork—now came under Ottoman control. Selim also took possession of the gold, silver, food, arms, and supplies that al-Ghawri had commandeered on his way to Aleppo and stashed in the citadel before he set off for battle, and distributed it to his soldiers as a reward for their victory and motivation for what lay ahead.

Before leaving Aleppo, Selim put into place the bureaucratic and legal structures of Ottoman governance that would bring the city and its neighboring regions squarely under the empire's rule. Governors, judges, tribal chieftains, and notables from surrounding towns and villages arrived by horse and mule and on foot to pay their respects to the forty-five-year-old sultan. In return for their promised loyalty, Selim allowed most of them to keep their positions. Kurdish and Turkmen tribes in the area, and the rulers of cities such as Malatya, Aintab, and Raqqa, all recognized Ottoman sovereignty and agreed to pay tribute to the empire in exchange for protection. Selim also sent a military detachment to the Safavid border as a show of force, to dispel any

*The citadel of Aleppo*

notion that the Ottoman–Mamluk conflict somehow rendered Syria or Anatolia vulnerable to attack.

Although the Mamluks had suffered tremendous losses at Marj Dabiq, including the death of their sultan, they still controlled massive amounts of territory and enormous resources in the Middle East and North Africa. Before marching on Cairo, Selim would need to fortify his control over the key Syrian cities and towns left exposed in the wake of the ignominious Mamluk retreat. Aleppo was merely the critical first step. On September 16, Selim left Aleppo and arrived at Hama four days later. Straddling Syria's longest river, the Orontes, Hama boasted seventeen large ancient waterwheels and several aqueducts. Selim and his troops stayed there for two days before moving on to Homs, about thirty miles due south on the Orontes. After reprovisioning his army from Homs's rich fields of rice, grapes, olives, and other staples, Selim continued south to the Levantine port city of Tripoli, a key locus of Mediterranean silk production. The townspeople put up some initial resistance, as they would have to any outsider, but Selim overcame that quickly.

As in Aleppo, once he had secured control over Hama, Homs, and Tripoli, Selim brought the administrative and judicial bureaucracies under Ottoman governance. He was content, per established imperial policy, to keep most of the old order in place, provided those in power recognized his sovereignty. After conquest, exchanging the maintenance of precedent for loyalty made imperial transitions easier on everyone. Urban administrators wanted to keep their positions, and Selim needed to be confident in the trustworthiness and ability of his officials to uphold order while he waged war.

From Tripoli, Selim led his army inland toward Damascus, Syria's most important city. News of his victories and the imposition of Ottoman hegemony had already reached the city, along with reports of his comparative largesse and the leniency of his rule. As in Aleppo and the other northern towns, the Mamluks had won no friends in Damascus, having seized the city's cash, men, and food for their war effort, so the city's residents stood ready to exchange the Mamluks for the Ottomans. On October 9, Selim entered the city quickly and painlessly. One of his first acts was to call a meeting in which he assured Damascus's leaders that he would protect their authority as long as they recognized the sovereignty of their new Ottoman governor. Proving the desirability of Ottoman rule—especially when compared to the despoliations of the Mamluk army's stay there—Selim made sure that his soldiers did nothing to harm the city's residents or disrupt its robust trade. Indeed, he went so far as to pay his soldiers extra so as to diminish any incentive to plunder. And in a move that made Damascus's many foreign merchants especially enthusiastic about the onset of Ottoman rule, Selim reduced customs duties from 20 percent to 5 percent.

Selim's general policy of maintaining the existing local order while demonstrating the virtues of Ottoman hegemony often took on a religious dimension, alongside his overriding economic, legal, and political concerns. After seizing a territory, he would make a point of praying in iconic religious sites such as the Umayyad mosques of Aleppo and Damascus, after which he would visit the shrines of local saints and the residences of living holy men to publicly express his respect. Not only did this ingratiate him among the believers who venerated their holy men of old and revered their living spiritual guides, it also evinced his own piety, as he called on otherworldly power to aid him in his current and future endeavors.

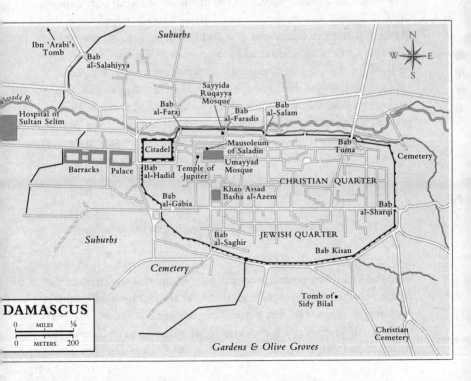

A local legend from the southern Anatolian town of Aintab confirmed the vital importance of gaining local spiritual sanction for imperial political acts—and the potential perils of not doing so. When Selim took this city, one of its religious leaders punished the sultan by inflicting on him a severe case of constipation. The holy man only lifted the curse when Selim, after days spent writhing in discomfort, visited him to offer the proper respect, apologizing for any suffering he had caused, kissing the man's hand, and promising to provide material support for his spiritual order. This and similar tales made clear to the Ottomans—and, indeed, to other imperial powers—that they would have to adjust to the customs of the places they sought to rule, deferring to local authorities and institutions.

In Damascus, this reconciliation of the Ottomans' new imperial authority with longstanding local religious practice played itself out in dramatic fashion. After taking control of the city, Selim committed himself to discovering and reviving the tomb of Ibn 'Arabi, a prominent thirteenth-century religious thinker, philosopher, and poet known simply as "the greatest master." One of the most significant scholars in all of Islamic letters, the author of more than a hundred texts, Ibn 'Arabi was born in Spain and died in Damascus in 1240, after a life of writing, teaching, and travel in the pursuit of knowledge. Because he lived his last years in Damascus, he was considered a local saint, a Damascene spiritual intercessor. According to the *Selimname* and other laudatory texts, the spiritual bankruptcy and political corruption of previous rulers in Damascus had led to the disappearance of Ibn 'Arabi's grave. The scholar's body had been lost—whether by theft or because a structure had been built over the grave, no one knew. Before his death, the seer had predicted the loss and rediscovery of his own gravesite with the following cryptic couplet:

> *When the sīn enters the shīn, then will emerge the tomb of Muhy al-Dīn.*

Muhy al-Dīn is Ibn 'Arabi's proper name. *Sīn* and *shīn* are letters of the Arabic alphabet that share the same shape but are distinguished by three dots over the *shīn*. The first letter of Selim's name is *sīn*, and the first letter of the Arabic name for Damascus (*Shām*) is *shīn*. The couplet can therefore be interpreted as, "When Selim enters Damascus, the tomb of Ibn 'Arabi will emerge." Thus, the first of the couplet's prophecies seemed to have been fulfilled, suggesting that Ibn 'Arabi's tomb would be found before too long.

One night soon after Selim took Damascus, Ibn 'Arabi visited him in a dream and ordered him to mount a black horse first thing in the morning. Ibn 'Arabi instructed Selim not to hold the horse's reins, but to allow the animal to guide him. The next day, Selim followed the instructions. The steed carried him through the city and eventually meandered into a refuse dump. After wading through piles of trash, it began to dig with a front hoof in a nondescript spot. Selim dismounted and started to dig alongside the animal. There, buried under garbage, they found one stone and then another. Eventually, it became obvious to Selim that this was the grave of Ibn 'Arabi. He ordered the site cleared and cleaned and spared no expense in building an ornate mausoleum for the Muslim saint.

According to this likely apocryphal account, one of the holiest men in all of Islamic history had predicted Selim's entry into Damascus nearly three hundred years before it happened. Selim was therefore not a foreign conqueror but the rightful inheritor, even restorer, of Damascus; his arrival was the fulfillment of a blessed medieval prophecy. Selim's recovery and reestablishment of Ibn 'Arabi's grave symbolized a centuries-old relationship, Selim's respect for Damascus and its people, and the appropriateness of his rule.

Some accounts take the story a step further, claiming that the spiritual adviser of Osman, the progenitor of the Ottomans, had studied under Ibn 'Arabi. This tied Ibn 'Arabi to the very origins of the Ottomans. Leapfrogging back in time, Selim thus could draw an unequivocally direct connection between himself and the founder of the empire. This conveniently furthered one of Selim's favorite suggestions: that all the sultans before him had strayed from the essence of Osman and that he represented a renewal of the empire's true nature.

As we have seen, as much as conquests required armaments, they also needed legends and heroes. On the other side of the world, at almost the exact moment that Selim discovered Ibn 'Arabi's tomb, Hernán Cortés employed the power of stories and legends to explain his own conquests in Mexico—the Seven Cities of Cibola, tales about God favoring Christians over all others, the Aztecs welcoming light-skinned Europeans as gods. Creative narrative constructions, like Cortés's in Mexico, and historical reconstructions, like Selim's in Damascus, were crucial components of nearly all of the early modern world's imperial conquests. In Aintab, Damascus, and indeed in each town along Selim's route toward Cairo, such fables helped to rationalize and justify the violence of war and to integrate new territories into the imagination and reality of the Ottoman Empire.

As a large and demographically diverse city, Damascus demanded more from Selim than any other city in Anatolia or Syria. He spent two months there, from the middle of October to the middle of December 1516. During that time, he met with officials from throughout Syria in order to effect its complete transition to Ottoman rule—cutting deals, doling out favors, and generally doing whatever he could to shore up his territorial gains and preserve peace. He remained committed to chasing down the old regime's holdovers, publicly executing thousands of Mamluk loyalists in the last few months of the year. Significantly, from Damascus he also finalized the renewal of a peace treaty with Hungary, thus avoiding the complications of a potential war on the empire's western front. Resolutely focused on Cairo, and confident that Syria was now largely secured, Selim led his forces at year's end toward the third holiest city in Islam, Jerusalem. As his army marched out of Damascus, snow began to fall. He considered this an auspicious sign.

SELIM ENTERED JERUSALEM IN mid-December 1516, again with little incident as the city's residents, like those of Damascus, expected his arrival. As one of his first acts in the city, he pledged to protect Jerusalem's Christians and Jews. Had Columbus ever succeeded in conquering Jerusalem, an equivalent act of protection seems unimaginable, given his interests in destroying Islam. Selim also met with representatives of the Armenian, Coptic, and Abyssinian churches in Jerusalem, as well as with the heads of the Rabbinate, to assure them that Ottoman rule would not alter their ritual practices, property holdings, or community affairs. In fact, he increased the stipend of the Franciscan friars in the Church of the Holy Sepulchre and reduced the visa fees for Christian pilgrims visiting the city.

During his brief but pleasant respite in Jerusalem, Selim, like al-Ghawri a few months earlier, visited all of its holiest places: the Church of the Resurrection, the Mount of Olives, and the Temple

Mount. His entourage secured the winding streets of the Old City
so that he and his closest advisers could roam as sightseers in this cra-
dle of the three Abrahamic religions, temporarily free of any military
concerns. We know they enjoyed the city's marketplaces; Jerusalem's
famous sweets of honey, dough, and nuts; and the cool but salubrious
breezes of December. The city's cobblestone streets felt familiar to Selim
from Istanbul, Aleppo, and Damascus. As he climbed the stairs up to
the courtyard of the Dome of the Rock, the third holiest site in Islam,

*The Dome of the Rock*

he surely felt the sanctity of the place from which Muslims believe the Prophet Muhammad ascended to heaven.

Constructed in the seventh century, the imposing mosque—with its distinctive turquoise, azure, and cobalt blues—seemed to hover above the city, like a portal to heaven. Up close, the façade, detailed with bone-white calligraphy, was mesmerizing. Pious Muslims believe their prayers in the Dome of the Rock count five hundred times more than a normal prayer. Indeed, before Mecca was established, all Muslims in the world faced Jerusalem—specifically, the Dome of the Rock—during prayer. Inside the mosque, Selim bowed his head, no doubt asking God to protect his realm and begging for safety and victory as he marched his forces onward from Jerusalem.

All preceding Ottoman sultans had governed as Muslims over a mostly Christian population, but as Selim conquered the Middle East that winter, gaining vast swaths of new territory, he steadily changed the demographics of the empire, bringing more and more Muslims under Ottoman rule. But in order to achieve his long list of military desiderata—destroy the Mamluks, gain access to Africa and the Indian Ocean, win Mecca and Medina, protect the Red Sea from the Portuguese, capture North Africa, and unite the entire eastern Mediterranean under the Ottoman flag—he still had to seize the Mamluk capital, Cairo. That would require an enormous outlay of force, will, and cunning.

Selim and his army set out from Jerusalem in late December 1516, exiting the Old City via the southern Tanners' Gate. Before departing, he sent word back to Istanbul to make arrangements for his prized, reprovisioned fleet to meet him in Egypt with new arms and additional troops. It would take this enormous convoy of 106 ships several months of winter seafaring to reach the Egyptian coast. If all worked according to plan, Selim's army and navy would rendezvous in Egypt for the final push to defeat the Mamluks. Despite having rested in Jerusalem, Selim's soldiers were weary, having fought and marched continuously since the summer, and they were running low on many basic supplies. Just before the new year, however, they secured the fertile coastal plains of Gaza, on the southeastern corner of the Mediterranean, which provided them with enough food to reach Cairo.

Now Selim's army faced a daunting logistical problem: how to cross the Sinai Desert—the mountainous, stark, and punishing continental

hinge between Syria and Cairo—the site of the ancient world's first turquoise mines, and the place where Moses, during the flight from Egypt,
purportedly received the Ten Commandments. Using established overland routes that mostly followed the coastline, and shipping lanes in the
Mediterranean and Red seas, the Mamluks had been able to manage
the challenge posed by this desolate region in the very heart of their
state. To Selim and the Ottomans, though, Sinai must have looked like
a moonscape. They had never encountered such an environment; there
were few obvious resting places or oases, only a few small streams, and
the constant threat of Bedouin raids. Fortunately, it was winter, so at
least the desert temperatures were tolerable. Every winter, even in the
twenty-first century, migratory birds from the northern Mediterranean
make their way south to nest in Sinai. The sight of golden eagles with
seven-foot wingspans and swooping falcons trawling for mice surely
added to the foreboding oddity of the region.

A reliable supply of water was the most pressing need facing Selim's
men. Thus, before leaving Gaza, Selim assembled a veritable second
army of fifteen thousand camels carrying thirty thousand water bags.
These beasts of burden were, he knew, essential if he was to cross Sinai;
without them, he would be unable to attack Cairo. Their wide feet
allowed them to walk on sand without sinking too deeply, almost as
though they were floating over the landscape. Their long eyelashes,
unlike those of horses, protected their eyes from windswept sand. They
could go weeks without water, losing close to 40 percent of their body
weight, and still carry enormous loads. He bought some from local
Bedouin in Gaza and commandeered others.

Thus, with his convoy of cocoa-colored camels, horses, guns, and
twelve large cannons, Selim and his troops set out across the desert.
Aided by winter rains that firmed up the sandy terrain, the entire army
covered the two-hundred-mile trip across Sinai to the outskirts of
Cairo in just five days in mid-January 1517.

A WORLD AWAY IN his comfortable palace in cultured Cairo, Tuman
Bey—now the Mamluk sultan, by dint of Sultan al-Ghawri's death—
dreaded what he knew was coming. He had heard the reports of the
Ottomans treading on al-Ghawri's body with their horses; he saw
his empire dissolving before his large, almond-shaped eyes. Now the

Ottomans were marching on the capital. That battle would be decisive: either the Ottomans would take Cairo, and then North Africa and the Hijaz (the territory on the other side of the Red Sea that contains Mecca and Medina, now western Saudi Arabia), thus ending the reign of the Mamluks forever, or Tuman and his troops would repel them and reclaim the upper hand.

At the end of 1516 and into 1517, Tuman had devoted himself exclusively to raising troops, amassing provisions and arms, and constructing fortifications around Cairo. He built his main line of defense at Raidaniyya, a town about ten miles northeast of the capital on the road from Sinai. In an enormous encampment, Tuman assembled Egyptian soldiers from the south, his elite security forces, and a regiment of North Africans stationed in Egypt—in truth, anyone he could compel to fight. Although several of his battalions were decimated and others exhausted from the failed six-month campaign in Syria, he forced them to Raidaniyya. At this point, the Mamluk army had lost almost half the empire, thousands of troops, and massive amounts of provisions, weapons, and money. Morale was as depleted as the matériel. Nevertheless, remarkably, Tuman managed to assemble at Raidaniyya a force larger than the one al-Ghawri had taken into Syria, armed with cannons and muskets, supplied with armor and wagons as well as three Indian elephants that had been presented to the Mamluks as a diplomatic gift.

Tuman ordered a stone wall to be constructed, from behind which the Mamluk forces could shoot at the approaching Ottoman army. In front of this barrier was a ditch embedded with vertical spears, to impale the Ottomans' horses and camels. Tuman himself carried heavy stones to help with the construction of the wall—which perturbed his men. Never before had they seen a sovereign doing the work of a common soldier. A sultan should not carry his own dinner, let alone the building blocks of a fortification. If his soldiers had any remaining doubts, they surely now understood that times were dire indeed.

Cairo's bustling markets emptied as merchants gathered up everything from eggplants to copper plates, transferring their goods to storehouses for safekeeping. As is usual at the beginning of a war, the wealthy hid their belongings outside the city or in cemeteries, in the structures accompanying family burial plots. Meanwhile, refugees from the countryside—some avoiding conscription, others escaping food shortages—flooded into Cairo, assuming that once war erupted, they would be safer within the city walls. Cairo's streets thus emptied of their normal traffic: merchants and water carriers, market overseers and judges, peddlers and urban residents on their way to work, the mosque, or the bazaar. Instead, soldiers preparing for war and beleaguered, homeless peasants took over Cairo's wide thoroughfares and public squares. Overwhelming the call to prayer and the yogurt seller's invitation to sample the day's offerings, horns sounded to organize the movement of troops and enforce a citywide curfew. As these piercing calls sporadically interrupted the city's eerie silence, a sense of inevitable calamity gripped Cairo's half a million residents.

Tuman and his military advisers huddled in their camp at Raidaniyya. Figuring that the Ottomans, far from home, were probably running low on food and supplies, and that their camels would be drained after the trek across Sinai, Tuman wanted to rush forward and attack them before they had a chance to rest and reprovision in the villages on the way to Cairo. His advisers argued against this on the grounds that they had invested enormous resources in constructing a fortified position at Raidaniyya, that their supply lines from Cairo were operational, and that they had amassed a formidable force of soldiers and weapons behind their wall. Mamluk commanders saw great advantage in drawing the Ottomans into their secure position of strength, and Tuman finally conceded the point. The army held at Raidaniyya.

Selim's forces loomed closer. Once they emerged from Sinai's mountainous, sandy terrain onto the flat expanses of eastern Egypt—now marching on the third continent of their long journey—the Ottomans' progress was swifter. Without uneven footing to worry them, Selim and his soldiers could concentrate on the fighting to come. Each man began to prepare himself in the ways soldiers always did before battle—thinking of his family and his fate, readying his weapon and his soul. Once the rival armies were close enough, each sultan tried to gauge the strength of the other side. Under cover of night, Tuman dispatched spies to the outskirts of the Ottomans' encampment to assess their forces: more than he had initially thought, but, in his estimation, still far below the number of troops he had at the ready.

Selim wrote a letter to Tuman, inviting him to surrender in exchange for recognition as an Ottoman vassal. The Ottomans had often engaged in this politics of threat and compromise in order to gain territory without war. The tactic might succeed with the prince of a small city-state in Bulgaria, for example, but Tuman scoffed and spat at Selim's "offer" of vassalage. He was the head of a grand Muslim empire, one of the world's most significant states. He was the caliph, overseer of Islam's holiest places. He would never let Selim, sultan of a lesser empire, bully him—or, worse, rule him.

To leave no doubt about his position, Tuman attached his hate-filled rejection note to the head of an Ottoman soldier his forces had earlier captured and now killed for the express purpose of conveying this message—a decapitated rejoinder to the war declaration Selim had sent to al-Ghawri pinned to the head of 'Ala' al-Dawla. On the road to Cairo, the stage was now set for war.

# CHAPTER
## 20

# CONQUERING THE WORLD

*The Battle of Raidaniyya*

THE BATTLE FOR CAIRO FINALLY COMMENCED ON JANUARY 22, 1517—and it ended astoundingly quickly. After barely an hour, the Mamluk army was shattered, and in full retreat toward Cairo.

Tuman Bey himself was partly at fault. He had almost no military experience, and had been sultan, and thus leader of the imperial army, for only five months at this point. Perhaps his military advisers should have known better, or perhaps the Mamluk army should have attacked early, as Tuman had suggested. Selim, a master tactician, took note of the fortification at Raidaniyya and turned the Mamluks' strongest defensive weapon against them. Outflanking the Mamluks, he trapped them against the impregnable wall they had constructed to keep the Ottomans at bay. Furthermore, the Ottoman guns outperformed the outdated and decrepit artillery of the Mamluks; the occasional mis-firing of the Ottomans' own muskets probably cut down more of their soldiers than the Mamluks did. The Ottomans killed more than twenty-five thousand Mamluk soldiers at Raidaniyya. Thus, the battle for Cairo was over before the Ottomans had even glimpsed the city.

The Mamluk capital now lay completely exposed. Most of the inhabitants of the villages between Raidaniyya and Cairo had fled, so provisions stored in these villages were freely available. Although it would be weeks before the Ottomans fully secured Cairo, and months before a full transition of government was effected, what remained of the Mamluks' territories after their defeat in Syria now also belonged to Selim. Within weeks of the Spanish seizing a city in Mexico they christened *El Gran Cairo*, Selim had conquered Egypt's Cairo for the Ottomans. The Mamluk Empire was dead.

It is no hyperbole to state that Selim's victory at Raidaniyya changed the world. With the Mamluks obliterated, Selim united portions of three continents under his rule, nearly tripling the size and population of the Ottoman Empire. As he and his forces marched toward Cairo at a steady, gentle cadence, after nearly half a year of campaigning, Selim surely reflected on just how much he had accomplished. He had spent his early life developing the skills and relationships he needed to capture the imperial palace, and conquered the odds in becoming sultan. Now he had vanquished his state's foremost enemy, and had journeyed farther to expand the empire than any sultan before him (and, in fact, no sultan after him would expand the empire as much as he did). Selim now con-trolled more territory than any other human alive, two of the largest cities in the world—Istanbul and Cairo—and an army that rivaled any military force on earth. With the addition of the Mamluk territories, an Ottoman sultan for the first time ruled a majority-Muslim popula-tion. Soon Selim would take command of Mecca and Medina, becom-ing the first true Ottoman caliph (previous sultans had claimed the title, without merit), moving ever closer to fulfilling the prophecy made at the time of his birth that he would possess the world's seven climes. After 1517, Selim held the keys to global domination in the sixteenth century—control of the middle of the world, monopolization of trade routes between the Mediterranean and India and China, ports on all the major seas and oceans of the Old World, unrivaled religious authority in the Muslim world, and enormous resources of cash, land, and manpower. Selim had become the world's most powerful sovereign, God's undefiled shadow on earth.

CAIRO, HOWEVER, PROVED NO place for self-congratulatory daydreaming. Lingering resistance in the former Mamluk capital and the surrounding region made Egypt much more difficult to subdue than anywhere in Syria. The city was vast, with nearly half a million people, its skyline punctuated by domes and minarets. From late January through the spring of 1517, Tuman and a handful of his men who had escaped the bloodbath at Raidaniyya began a campaign of guerrilla warfare against the Ottomans, supported by many of Cairo's denizens who, frightened by the recent mayhem, offered them shelter, food, and arms. Selim, sensibly, avoided entering Cairo for weeks, preferring the safety of his garrisoned military encampment outside the city's walls. At the same time, Selim allowed his soldiers to loot Cairo. After the fall of a city, Selim sometimes decided, as we have seen, to authorize pillage, in order to reward his men for their fortitude and to strengthen their fidelity; it depended on the message he sought to send to his enemies and his loyal soldiers alike. As a later historian wrote of Selim's defeat of the Mamluks, the war of 1516–17 proved more pivotal for the empire than the conquest of Constantinople in 1453. Selim's grandfather had allowed his soldiers to plunder Constantinople. It seemed only fitting, then, at least to Selim, that his soldiers should be allowed to revel in their conquest of Cairo.

Selim's endorsement of his soldiers' plundering served another strategic aim: it would strike fear in the hearts of those who opposed Ottoman rule and offered safe haven to the Mamluk resistance. In the early weeks of February 1517, Ottoman forces chased down and killed many Mamluk sympathizers and succeeded in driving Tuman and his men into hiding deep in the south of Egypt. Despite the Ottoman destruction of the Mamluk army and seizure of their capital city, low-level

*Fighting the Mamluks in Cairo*

violence would continue for months—the Ottomans pursued some in the Mamluk resistance for many years—and it was April before Tuman was finally captured and killed. His body was strung up on one of Cairo's gates, where it remained for three days for all to see.

Selim entered Cairo on Sunday, February 15, 1517, in a formal procession attended by enormous celebrations marking the return of peace. After years of tension and hardship, fighting and chaos, Cairo could again enjoy some modicum of normalcy. Many bowed their heads as Selim rode his horse slowly and regally through the city, dressed in a deep blue robe, his bejeweled white turban towering over the crowds lining his route. A long stream of advisers in full military uniform walked in two stately rows behind him, impressing upon the assembled crowds the arrival of the Ottomans' new imperial order. "Long live the victorious Sultan Selim!" shouted many along the parade route.

In the city's central square, in the shadow of the Citadel, the city's largest and most important mosque, Selim promised to instill order

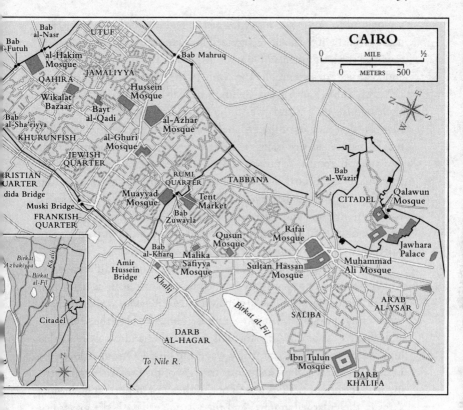

and prosperity across his empire. From this point on, no soldier would molest a citizen or unlawfully seize property, trade would return to Cairo's markets, and security would be ensured throughout all the newly acquired territories. His administration would fairly assess and collect taxes, inspect roads and public works to make needed repairs, and outlaw forced labor and military conscription practices. Huzzahs erupted across the city. The next Friday, following custom, preachers in all of Cairo's mosques delivered their weekly sermons in Selim's name.

WITH THE MAMLUKS DETHRONED, order restored to Cairo's streets, and commerce once again beginning to flow, Selim commenced the arduous work of organizing the governance of the vast new territories he had just conquered. War was one thing, administration quite another. Throughout his life, Selim had excelled at both, and he now introduced to Egypt the many lessons he had learned in Trabzon, and more recently in Syria: he recognized longstanding property holdings, renewed the assignments of market inspectors and other vital officials, and kept tax rates essentially the same. In the North African provinces of Libya, Tunis, and Algeria, Selim recognized the sitting governors in exchange for their allegiance to the Ottoman Empire. The sharifs of Mecca—descendants of the Prophet Muhammad who were responsible for the maintenance of Islam's holiest sites—also accepted Selim as their new ruler. In return, he promised them whatever resources they needed to manage the annual pilgrimage and maintain the many imposing and ornate buildings they oversaw. In all of these areas—Syria, Egypt, North Africa, and the Hijaz—Selim followed the proven Ottoman strategy of essentially retaining the status quo, making it painless and palatable for the governed to accept the new regime.

Still, the situation in Egypt itself required a slightly different tack. Khayr Bey, the Ottomans' spy in Aleppo who had been instrumental in their victory over Sultan al-Ghawri at Marj Dabiq, was made governor of Egypt. Khayr had proven himself both loyal to the Ottomans and effective as an administrator; this assignment handsomely rewarded him for his years of patient, risky wagering on the Ottomans over the Mamluks. As the richest and most strategic of the provinces the Ottomans added after 1517, Egypt was one of the most important governorships in the enlarged empire, and the Ottomans lavished a great deal of attention on their new and prized possession. Its vast agricultural wealth generated more tax revenue than any other Ottoman province, and it would soon provide about a quarter of all the food consumed in the empire—from Algeria in the west to Trabzon in the east. Egypt was the most populous of the empire's recently acquired provinces and the outlet that allowed the Ottomans access to the Red Sea, the Indian Ocean, North and sub-Saharan Africa, and the Arabian peninsula. Entrusting such a vital territory to Khayr reflected Selim's supreme confidence in him.

Khayr, however, proved as cruel in Cairo as he had been shrewd in Aleppo—perhaps not surprising in a man who earned his position by being a traitor. In one instance, he ordered the hanging of a peasant who stole a few cucumbers from one of his fields. Many accounts of his governorship mention his miserliness, his love of the bottle, and his obvious drunkenness in front of his advisers. Even inebriated, though,

Khayr could be effective as a ruler, since his main task was merely to uphold the administrative structure of Egypt as it existed at the time of the conquest.

❄

OF ALL THE TERRITORIES the Ottomans acquired in 1516 and 1517, one clearly distinguished itself from the rest: the Hijaz. The Ottoman take-over of Mecca and Medina did not simply represent more land and rev-enue for the empire. It made Selim the "Protector of the Holy Cities," the caliph—the undisputed leader of the Muslim world.

The ceremony to invest Selim with the caliphate occurred in the spring of 1517, in Cairo. Precedent dictated the symbolic trans-fer of caliphal power from one sovereign to another in a "public ser-vice" before the governing elite of the two states. As a recognition of defeat and conferral of the caliphate on Selim, the Mamluk sultan was to sanctify the Ottoman sultan as "servant of the two sacred cities, the victorious King Selīm Shāh." Because Tuman, the previous sul-tan and caliph, was no longer alive, his oldest living relative, a man named al-Mutawakkil III, stood in for him. Given that such trans-fers of worldly and religious power usually occurred after war, it was often the case that others had to represent a fallen caliph. As Cairo still lacked an official Ottoman residence, and to avoid using his ene-my's palace, Selim convened his political and religious advisers with al-Mutawakkil under the magnificent dome of the Citadel. In the quiet ceremony, Selim knelt to accept the sword and mantle of the Prophet Muhammad from al-Mutawakkil, one of the few times in his adult life he prostrated himself—in deference not to a human, but to his God. These sacred objects connected the political leader who held them to the Prophet himself, who was not only the world's first Muslim but also the first caliph. As Selim rose with the white goat-hair coat on his shoulders and the simple steel sword in his hand, he fused religious and political power, joining the line of Osman and the line of the Prophet for the first time in history. Selim stood proudly, beaming his delight, and casting the long shadow of God.

With his heavenly mantle and manifold earthly powers, Selim, now forty-six, ruled the Mediterranean coastline continuously from the Adriatic to Algeria—the whole eastern half of the sea. Not since the days of the Roman Empire had the Black, Red, Caspian, and Mediterranean seas been governed by a single polity. Selim had become the early modern Caesar.

⊗

ONE NIGHT IN THE spring of 1517, in the tent that served as his headquarters in Cairo, Selim was deep in discussion about Egypt's taxation system when a visitor was announced. Though the hour was late, Selim agreed to see the man. Piri Reis, a former pirate turned captain in the Ottoman navy, walked slowly forward, holding something in his hands. He had sailed to Egypt just after Selim invaded, on one of the first Ottoman ships to dock in Alexandria. With his tightly wrapped white turban and thick beard making him look more scholar than sailor, Piri riveted his eyes on the carpeted floor in front of Selim. No subject of the empire was considered worthy enough to look directly into the face of the shadow of God.

Selim and Piri had met a few years earlier in Istanbul, when Piri arrived at the palace as a representative of the navy to report on recent expeditions in North Africa. Selim had forgotten this meeting, but naturally Piri remembered it. One of Selim's secretaries removed the object from Piri's fidgety hands. It was a scroll. Selim unfurled the drab gazelle-skin parchment and was transfixed by the vibrant colors inside. Purples and oranges, silver and crimson inks, perfectly straight lines and jagged squiggly ones created a map of the entire known world—the result of three years of careful labor. Selim had heard of the Americas and the West Indies, but this was the first time he had seen their shape (as it was then thought to be) and their distance from the Mediterranean and Middle Eastern worlds he knew so well—the worlds he had just conquered.

As his eyes bounced from coasts to castles, oceans to islands, Selim—according to Piri's account of the meeting—plied Piri with questions. Piri described the years he had spent poring over dozens of maps as he sailed the Mediterranean. Arab and Italian cartographers had long depicted the outlines of the Mediterranean's craggy coastline, and Piri had also learned a great deal from Portuguese maps of West Africa. The great innovation of his map, though, was to make the world whole—to add the New World to the Old. Piri's was the first world map ever to include the Americas.

Piri delighted Selim with the story of how he had acquired Columbus's Atlantic maps from his uncle Kemal Reis, whose capture of the five Knights Hospitaller ships had so impressed Khayr Bey during his visit to Bayezit's court. During a raid off the coast of Valencia in 1501, Kemal had seized a group of Christians, one of whom had sailed on three of Columbus's four voyages across the Atlantic. When Kemal's men searched his belongings, they discovered several maps from those voyages. They also found a feather headdress and an odd black stone (perhaps obsidian), which the captive said he had carried back from the New World.

Inspired by these discoveries, Kemal apparently sailed west from Valencia in August 1501 through the Strait of Gibraltar, which would have made his ship the first Ottoman vessel to enter the Atlantic. He and his men were said to have raided ports along the Iberian coast and then to have veered southwest toward the Canary Islands, before heading back along the Moroccan coast and returning to the Mediterranean.

Combining his expertise in Old World cartography with the maps his uncle passed on to him (he may have even interviewed his uncle's Spanish captive), Piri gave shape to the world from China to the Caribbean. According to his notes on the map he gave Selim and later writings about it, Piri combined elements from more than a hundred maps into this one—among them the maps used by Columbus (Piri refers to him as the "Genoese infidel Colon-bo"), Arab maps of China and India (the best resources then available about those regions), Portuguese maps of West Africa and parts of India, and earlier Turkish and Italian maps of the Mediterranean. As Piri wrote, "I have made maps in which I was able to show twice the number of things contained in the maps of our day, having made use of new charts of the Chinese and Indian Seas which no one in the Ottoman lands had hitherto seen or known." Borrowing from Spanish and Portuguese accounts of the New World, the translations of which he had likely secured from fellow sailors, the text accompanying Piri's map speaks of the Americas and their peoples. It relates, for example, that people in the New World possess "four kinds of parrots, white, red, green and black. The people eat the flesh of parrots and their headdress is made entirely of parrots' feathers." He mentions the Spanish interest in finding gold in the New World and Columbus's efforts to secure a patron for his voyages. The map's text also notes that "the Portuguese infidels have written in their maps" of "white-haired monsters," "six-horned oxen," and "oxen with one horn." Piri remained true to the place names given by Columbus, rendering them in Ottoman Turkish, and also true to the shape of the New World shown on Columbus's maps, in which Cuba is attached to mainland North America and Hispaniola is oriented north–south. Ottoman Turkish text surrounds depictions of Native Americans, and West Africa seems remarkably close to South America. Uniting worlds that had always been kept separate, and infinitely more comprehensive and detailed than anything Columbus, or anyone else for that matter, had had at their disposal, Piri's map was the most complete world map ever created.

That late night in Cairo, Selim—his shadow now falling over three continents—was mesmerized by how much of the world was his, but equally entranced by what might one day become his. He pondered the land across the western ocean, then looked to the map's east, contemplating whether or not the Ottomans could march an army across Central Asia to the ancient cities of China. Just a year earlier, as he advanced through Syria, he had received the firsthand account of an Ottoman merchant who had journeyed from Iran to China, and his curiosity was piqued. He saw also how far south Africa extended, and the enormity of the Atlantic. Even as Piri's map delineated the impressive breadth of Selim's intercontinental power, it revealed clearly just how many challenges the Ottomans still faced if they wanted to dominate the entire world.

Selim noticed that Piri had labeled the islands of the Caribbean, as well as sections of the American mainland, *Vilayet Antilia*. *Vilayet* was the generic Ottoman term for an administrative province, such as Vilayet Aleppo or Vilayet Trabzon. Thus, quite stunningly, Piri seemed to be designating the Caribbean and parts of the American continents as a province of the Ottoman Empire. Was he imagining that the New World would eventually, inevitably, become part of Selim's expanding empire, reifying the very worst of Spanish and Portuguese fears? Perhaps he meant to issue a daring challenge to Selim— a suggestion that he attempt to follow Kemal Reis's lead by extending the empire westward out of the Mediterranean into the Atlantic, even to the New World?

Selim, despite his excitement, was becoming tired. In one swift motion, he ripped the map in half and handed to the stunned mapmaker the portion depicting the New World. Walking out of his tent,

Selim tucked the other half—that showing the Mediterranean, Africa, and Asia—into the pocket of his robe and retired for the evening.

It remains impossible to know why Selim ruined the map Piri had so painstakingly put together, retaining only the eastern half—the portion of the map that has never been recovered. It was obviously within his purview to *consider* an Ottoman venture across the Atlantic to the New World. But why should he? He had never met with defeat on the battlefield and now possessed nearly unrivaled expanses of territory and unparalleled access to trade routes and economic resources. The Ottomans' unmatched successes in the Old World gave them no compelling reason to cross the ocean. With his conquest of Cairo, Selim had in his hands all the keys to world dominion in the sixteenth century.

This, then, would seem to answer the question of why Selim tore Piri's map. The New World floated out across the ocean—risky, unknown, unproven in its wealth. Unlike weak European powers, Selim had no reason to gamble so desperately. The Spanish went to the New World—unintentionally, of course—because the Ottomans and Mamluks forced them to do so. By contrast, no polity could push the Ottomans, now the dominant power of the Old World, out of the Mediterranean. Consolidating Ottoman hegemony in areas of known resources and proven strategic importance—the areas depicted on the eastern half of Piri's map—was a far better geopolitical tactic than chasing an expensive and treacherous phantom into the largely uncharted Atlantic.

WITH THE CONQUEST OF the Mamluk Empire, Selim took nominal possession of Yemen, on the southeastern shore of the Red Sea. Yemen, with its access to the Indian Ocean, would open up a vast new horizon for Ottoman trade. It was also a strategic chokepoint in protecting the areas around the Red Sea, including the newly acquired prizes of Mecca and Medina. Selim knew he would need to move quickly to seize Yemen before the Portuguese could exploit the political transition and establish a strong base on the Red Sea.

After Vasco da Gama (notably, a member of the Order of Santiago, the patron saint of Moor-slayers) reached India in 1498, clashes between the Portuguese and the Mamluks had increased in frequency and intensity, as the Europeans attempted to displace the Mamluks as the pre-

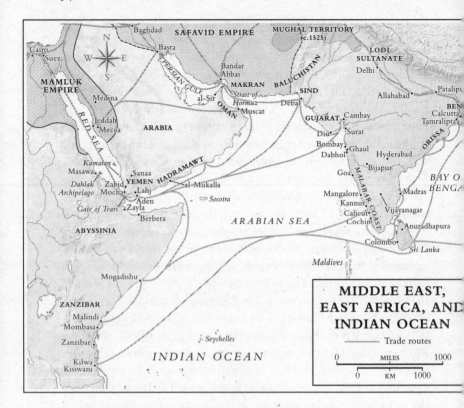

eminent trading power in the Indian Ocean. In 1500, for example, the
Portuguese burned ten Mamluk ships in the major spice trading port of
Calicut (now Kozhikode) on the Malabar Coast. The Mamluks had cultivated many connections throughout India, especially among the numerous small Muslim principalities that regularly appealed to them for help
against the encroaching Portuguese. Muslim leaders in Gujarat and Goa,
two of the major ports on India's western coast, as well as in Aden and
Muscat on the Arabian peninsula, all looked to the Mamluks for military support. To counter these Muslim alliances, the Portuguese forged
relationships of their own in India and elsewhere. In 1502, for instance,
the Portuguese reached an agreement with the Hindu ruler of Cochin
(now Kochi), near the southern tip of India, to expel the city's Muslim
merchants, specifically because of their close relations with the Mamluks.

In 1504, the Portuguese blockaded the mouth of the Red Sea, known
as the Gate of Tears because of the many ships that have sunk there over

the years trying to navigate the narrow opening. A year later, they attacked Jeddah, the maritime gateway to Mecca and Medina, and in 1507, nineteen Portuguese ships from India sailed into the Red Sea, destroying several Mamluk ships. On that same expedition, they had also grabbed the strategically located island of Socotra, just off the Horn of Africa, in hopes of making it an outpost for controlling access to the mouth of the Red Sea. Socotra, the so-called "Galapagos of the Indian Ocean," was notoriously otherworldly; a full third of the island's flora exists nowhere else on earth. Its most famous species is the dragon's blood tree, with scarlet resin and upward-turning branches that make it look more like an umbrella than a tree. Unfortunately for the Portuguese, the island's lack of water and its inhospitable conditions forced them to relinquish it after only a few months.

In 1513, an even more threatening Portuguese naval battalion, comprised of twenty-four ships and over 2,500 men, arrived in the port city of Aden, at the southwestern corner of Yemen and the mouth of the Red Sea. This venture was, in fact, yet another manifestation of Christianity's global Crusade. Like many of the Iberians who explored down the coast of West Africa and crossed the Atlantic, most of those who sailed into the Indian Ocean began their careers warring against the Ottomans and other Muslims in North Africa and around the Mediterranean. Afonso de Albuquerque, Portugal's governor in India—who himself had spent a decade in North Africa fighting against Islam—had sent a proposal to Pope Leo X, informing him that Portuguese ships could sail up the Red Sea to capture Mecca—the "Muslim Jerusalem," as he put it. Europe's Catholic powers could then ransom Mecca back to the Mamluks in exchange for the true Jerusalem, their goal for centuries. Afonso also asserted that Prester John, the wealthy Christian king of Ethiopia, would help the Portuguese attack Mecca. The myth of Prester John was cut from the same cloth as the notion of the Grand Khan of China—a spectral Christian leader, sometimes described as black, sometimes as white, far off in a vague East, with whom Europe could align to surround the Muslim world and crush it. Although there were Christians in Ethiopia, as there were in parts of East Asia, no historical evidence has ever surfaced to suggest that a Prester John actually existed. Still, Afonso assured the pope that, once allied with this African Christian king, Europeans could dig a canal in Ethiopia at the source of the Nile to drain it eastward into the Red Sea, thus rob-

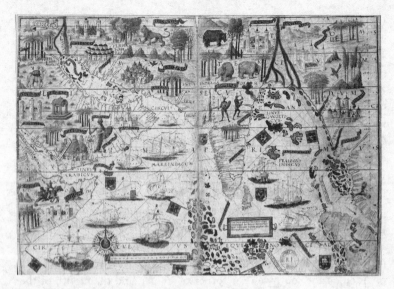

*Portuguese map of the Indian Ocean*

bing Mamluk Egypt of its major source of water. The Muslim lords of Jerusalem, starving as their fields dried up, would be compelled to relinquish the city. Afonso succeeded in destroying part of Aden in this year and even more of the port of Kamaran Island, farther north in the Red Sea and just off the Yemeni coast. As the Portuguese ships continued north, toward Jeddah, however, they were turned back by unfavorable winds.

This was obviously a lucky outcome for the Mamluks, as they were helpless against these Portuguese incursions. Their navy had been decimated a few years earlier when, in 1509, Francisco de Almeida—another veteran of Portugal's wars in Africa—burned the Mamluk fleet docked at the island of Diu, on the west coast of India. This defeat had opened the way for a quick succession of Portuguese victories in India, allowing them to develop their infrastructure of coastal holdings. On their heels against the Portuguese, the Mamluks appealed to their Ottoman brothers for support.

Even though he was in the final stages of planning his assault on their empire, Selim responded positively. In 1515, he sent one of his most experienced admirals, the Lesbos-born Selman Reis—with a flowingly long mustache and powerful tree-trunk legs—to the Red Sea with supplies and sailors to help the Mamluks rebuild their navy. This move, of course, did not derive from a sense of religious brotherhood. Instead, it was a means of protecting Ottoman economic interests by undermining the growing Portuguese trade in the East, as well as preparing for the time when, once the Mamluks had been defeated, the lands bordering the Red Sea would become part of the burgeoning Ottoman Empire.

In 1517, when Selim was in Cairo, Selman Reis sent him a feverish letter, begging for more supplies, sailors, and cash. "The Portuguese have not yet entered the sea of Tor [the Red Sea]," he warned, "but if they hear that these ships are not operational and lack crews they will inevitably come with a big armada for, apart from these ships, there is nothing here to deter them." Putting things considerably more positively, he offered that, "should it [Yemen] be conquered [by the Ottomans], it would be master of the lands of India and send every year a great amount of gold and jewels to Istanbul."

The sultan ordered fifty new ships to be constructed in Suez to vie with the Portuguese—"perfidious troublemakers"—for the Indian Ocean trade, and dispatched "numberless troops" overland, first to secure Yemen and then to confront the Portuguese at sea. Given the distances involved, as well as the massive project of imperial integration that he faced after his victory over the Mamluks, it would be several years before these goals were fully achieved. Even after Selim's death, his successors would struggle to safeguard this extreme southern fringe of the empire.

Home to fiercely independent tribes, living in famously perilous mountain terrain, Yemen has always been (and remains to the present day) a formidable challenge for any single government to control fully. With their capital a continent away, the Ottomans knew they could never exercise complete sovereignty over Yemen, but they were determined at least to hold its key port cities on the Red Sea and the Indian Ocean. Even this would prove fantastically difficult. In the interregnum between Mamluk and Ottoman rule, armed Circassian and Syrian mercenaries—initially hired by the Mamluks and Selman Reis to fight against the Portuguese—plunged Yemen into chaos as they battled each other, as well as pirates and tribal leaders, for control of the territory and its many resources. According to one local historian, Yemen in the years around 1520 was "in a state of incessant anarchy and discord, during which there was nothing but spurted blood, violated hearths, spoiled goods and spilled tears." Not until 1527 did the Ottomans muster enough naval strength to control Yemen's coast. That year, they established a permanent naval base and customs house on Kamaran Island, which the Portuguese had razed almost fifteen years earlier. Over the next century, Yemen would move repeatedly in and out of the empire's shadow of sovereignty.

※

IN 1517, AS SELIM's "numberless troops" streamed southward from Syria along the eastern coast of the Red Sea, they stumbled upon something none of them had encountered before—a bush with a strange, bright-red berry. Arguably even more than gaining Jerusalem and Cairo, assuming the caliphate, or building the largest empire in Islamic history, this plant represented the most significant outcome—and certainly one of the most lasting—of Selim's conquest of the Mamluks. What Selim's army found in Yemen was coffee.

No one, at least in the West, quite appreciates that an Ottoman sultan made coffee the global phenomenon it is today. Thanks to the intercontinental unity Selim achieved in 1517, coffee infuses our bodies, structures our day, dominates millions of agricultural acres, generates billions of dollars in corporate profits, and energizes nearly every kind of social interaction across the world. For the first time since the Roman Empire, Selim joined Yemen—where coffee had arrived from Ethiopia—to a polity that stretched from the Arabian peninsula to Bulgaria and from Iraq to Algeria. The commercial, institutional, political, and cultural connections Selim forged across the Old World allowed coffee to spread—first snaking up from Yemen across the Middle East; then to Ottoman eastern Europe, Iran, and India; and ultimately to western Europe, the Americas, and Southeast Asia. The first coffee drunk beyond the borders of the Ottoman Empire was drunk in Venice in the late 1580s.

As the bean gained popularity within the empire, the Ottomans generated foundational ideas about the drink. Many of these ideas remain with us today, most significantly in the form of the ubiquitous locale that Selim bequeathed to humanity—the café. By cultivating and distributing a consumable good and developing a culture of consumption around that good, the Ottomans led one of the world's earli-

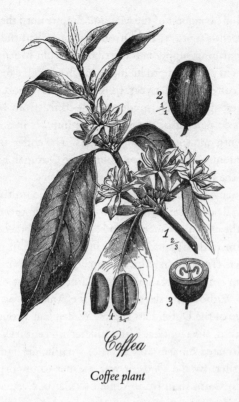

*Coffea*

*Coffee plant*

est consumer revolutions. In so doing, they diffused something of the Ottoman Empire around the world and very literally into our own individual bodies, from 1517 until today.

Coffee was the first truly global agricultural commodity. With the integration of the New World and the Old having taken place only a few years before Selim conquered Yemen, the coffee plant soon thrived in the soils of all five known continents. Linking producers to consumers across oceans, coffee formed a common market from the Americas to the Malaccas. More than spices, more than textiles, coffee drove the economy of the early modern world, and the Ottomans' dominance of the coffee trade helped them eventually to surpass their earlier rivals, the Portuguese, in the Indian Ocean economy. In addition to its geographic spread and later universality, coffee's addictive character, its material durability, and its high profit margins worked to merge capital and culture like no other commodity ever had.

From Selim's conquest of the Mamluk Empire until the third decade of the eighteenth century, the Ottomans controlled the world's coffee trade, managing supply and distribution from Mocha and several smaller Yemeni ports and producing as much as twelve to fifteen thousand tons of coffee beans per year. In Amsterdam's import market—the world's largest in the early modern era—coffee from Mocha represented about 90 percent of the total coffee imports in any given year of the sixteenth and seventeenth centuries. The coffee trade pumped enormous amounts of cash into and out of the Ottoman Empire—cash from which the state earned substantial tax revenues.

At the turn of the eighteenth century, coffee cultivators in the Americas and Southeast Asia began to take over the market from Yemen. By the end of the 1720s, Java had replaced Yemen, claiming 90 percent of Amsterdam's coffee market in that decade. In 1750, Amsterdam's imports from the Americas matched those from Java, and by 1840, Yemeni coffee had fallen to only 2 or 3 percent of the world's production. Without the slave labor of the Americas or the colonial labor regimes of the Dutch East Indies, Yemen had a comparative disadvantage, as, in the eighteenth and nineteenth centuries, most coffee was still cultivated on the same kind of smallholder family farms as centuries earlier. By the 1770s, it was cheaper to import coffee from Hispaniola to Cairo than from Yemen to Cairo. Even as the sun set on Ottoman Yemen's two centuries of global dominance in the coffee trade, coffee had become, thanks to Selim, "one of the most valuable internationally traded agricultural commodities in history." Today, coffee is the world's second most traded commodity—the first being another Middle Eastern export, oil.

# PART SIX

# FINAL FRONTIERS

## *(1518–20)*

IMAGE ON PREVIOUS PAGE:

*Selim in conversation*

# EMPIRE EVERYWHERE

*Selim hunting*

Wː HAT HAS BEEN HISTORY'S GREATEST KILLER? IT WAS NOT A
state, a weapon, or an idea. Arguably, it was plague. *Yersinia pestis* and its
bacterial cousins have for millennia crippled whole societies, brought
down empires, and marked the end of historical epochs. Extant in

rodent populations even today, plague moves from the small mammals to humans through fleas. When a flea bites an infected rodent and then a human, plague bacilli enter the bloodstream and rapidly multiply. Lymph glands filter the bacilli from the blood. In the lymph glands, these bacilli continue to multiply and accumulate, producing the telltale dark protuberances on the victim's neck and groin known as buboes. From rat to flea to human, plague has caused immeasurable pain and suffering, both for individual humans and whole regions of the globe. In the sixth century, for example, the Plague of Justinian eradicated nearly a fifth of the world's population, almost bringing down the Byzantine and Sasanian empires. The Black Death of the fourteenth century killed a third of Europe. Since antiquity, the Middle East, with its global commercial and transport links, has served as the crucial conduit of plague between the Mediterranean and Asia. Almost all of history's plague outbreaks, therefore, have a Middle Eastern story. In fact, the disease was a regular feature of the region's history.

IN JULY 1517, Selim's prized naval fleet finally arrived from Istanbul, laden with supplies to replenish the army for the long march home. He waited for the hottest part of the year to pass before beginning that march on September 13, 1517. The week before his departure, the fleet set sail on its return trip to Istanbul, carrying, in place of the offloaded provisions, a veritable intellectual army of eight hundred Egyptian scholars, artisans, religious leaders, and merchants, including a number of Mamluk dignitaries such as al-Mutawakkil, from whom Selim had received the caliphate, who lived out the rest of his days under house arrest in Istanbul.

Selim concentrated at the center of his empire not just the Middle East's agricultural and economic riches but, perhaps even more importantly, its intellectual, artistic, and cultural wealth. The Ottomans could thus absorb the traditions of places such as Cairo and Damascus, Tabriz and Aleppo, long-established hubs of Islamic learning and global commerce. This monopolization of human capital further solidified Istanbul's role as the new center of the Muslim world and the seat of the global caliphate, developments that would influence life in the Ottoman Empire for centuries to come.

After almost two years away, Selim reached Istanbul in July 1518, long after his ships had made landfall. On his way back to the capital, he passed through Jerusalem to see its holy sites one more time and spent several months in Damascus and Aleppo, overseeing administrative affairs associated with the Ottoman transition. In Damascus, he visited the recently completed shrine of Ibn 'Arabi, which pleased him greatly, and in Aleppo, he enjoyed a few days of hunting and held several meetings in the citadel, awed again by the view of the city below.

Between Chaldiran and his campaign against the Mamluks, he had devoted more than half of his six years as sultan to waging war. His first act upon his return to the city was to go to the Hagia Sophia mosque, next to Topkapı Palace. Surrounded by the exquisite marbles and gold mosaics of the former Byzantine church, Selim thanked God for his safe return and all his successes. He then entered the palace and greeted his consorts. He summoned his old barber, who cut his hair and shaved his beard, and then he took a long, hot bath.

Only two months later, Selim received reports of plague in Istanbul.

Being sultan did not give him immunity from plague, of course, but it did make him less vulnerable than most other humans. The simplest strategy to protect oneself from the disease—running away from it—was the most effective. So Selim and his retinue fled plague-stricken Istanbul for the former imperial capital of Edirne. Although he could not have known it, this would be the last time he stepped on Istanbul's cobblestones or laid his eyes on the Bosphorus.

LIKE CAMP DAVID FOR American presidents, Edirne was a favorite escape for Ottoman sultans—close to Istanbul but still rural, much quieter than the capital, far from the stresses of palace intrigue and imperial bureaucracy, and a respite from the demands of Janissary regiments and governors for attention and money. Selim loved Edirne's expansive landscape, towering trees, and tranquility. Residing there from the fall of 1518 to the late summer of 1520, he kept an official schedule to attend to pressing matters, to meet foreign dignitaries, and to monitor his troops, but he also found time to enjoy long days of relaxation. Of course, Selim realized the importance of being present in Istanbul, but, truth be told, he preferred being elsewhere. Over the course of his life, he had spent very little time in the Ottoman capital, so he still found the city rather alien and the walled palace, while opulent, almost suffocating. Thus, leaving Istanbul after only a few months did not bother him. Indeed, Edirne in many ways reminded him of Trabzon. Both were small cities surrounded by nature, where he could balance time with his consorts and advisers with time away from the palace.

Selim's primary delight in Edirne was hunting. It was not unusual for him to escape to the woods with a small coterie of advisers for as much as a week at a time. For a sultan accustomed to warfare—and one as cunning and skillful as he was—hunting was of the utmost importance. It allowed him to replicate the tactical aspects of military campaigns while avoiding the dangers of death or capture that came with real war. Unlike the crowded city or the intrigue of the palace, the forest afforded Selim space for peace and reflection on noble ideals such as wisdom, justice, and morality. Crisp air, quiet, and infinite sky focused the mind and purified the soul. The countryside offered Selim a chance to test his mind and body, maintain good health, keep his military skills sharp, and build physical stamina. Visitors, who often came from far away, might have to wait in Edirne for days until Selim returned from one of his expeditions, and some observers complained that he ignored important affairs of state and army in favor of chasing game.

Selim's passion for hunting even entered into the record of Ottoman–Venetian diplomacy. From Edirne in late 1519, Selim asked the *bailo*—the Venetian ambassador in Istanbul—to send him two Italian hunting greyhounds, dressed in full livery. He also asked the Venetian representative to send him "two small docile hairy" dogs, presumably for his entertainment at home. Selim the "warmonger," sultan of the seven climes, evidently had a soft spot for what, today, we call lap dogs.

Between 1518 and 1520, Selim implemented a series of measures aimed at solidly administering and properly defending his hugely expanded domains. Across his realms, he appointed governors and judges, updated and expanded law codes, streamlined market regulations, and issued countless orders on administrative matters ranging from taxation to mosque and church reconstruction to vegetable prices. In August 1518, for example, the prices of oats and vegetables skyrocketed in Syria, leading to protests in the markets and bazaars. That summer too, the Janissaries, who had supported Selim in his bid for the throne, came to collect on their investment—demanding higher salaries, better assignments, and more influence in the empire's economic and political affairs. Selim well understood how vital the army had been to his rise and how crucial they would be to his future, so he did all he could to appease them, lavishing on them money, appointments, and supplies. Meanwhile, visitors poured in, seeking an audience with Selim to congratulate him on his conquests, curry favor, and beg for protection and patronage. Officials from as far afield as India and Hungary traveled to Istanbul and then Edirne to meet one of the world's most powerful humans—who, by all accounts, enjoyed the attention.

Trade and economic policies had always played a central role in the empire's geostrategy. They would be decisive factors, Selim knew, in any future military ventures. Having been the globe's middlemen for centuries, the Ottomans had now extended their sphere of influence with new territories on the Arabian peninsula that allowed them to project their power into the Indian Ocean. When Piri Reis presented Selim with his world map in Cairo, the sultan, smartly, had wagered on East over West. Despite the recent opening of the Atlantic, the majority of world trade—with its attendant consequences for the movement of plague—still operated between the Mediterranean and Asia. Indeed, it would be more than a century before the Atlantic trade began to outpace Eurasian trade. Selim's newly achieved dominance of the entire eastern Mediterranean allowed him to exert almost complete control over the commerce between East and West, making the Ottoman Empire the world's primary economic geopolitical power.

Possession of Yemen allowed Selim to slash further holes in the global silk trade. He maintained the overland embargo that he had imposed just before the Battle of Chaldiran in 1514, which forced Iranian silk merchants eastward in search of other, maritime routes to Europe and overland routes to India; now, his eastern navy could directly interfere with those trade networks. An unintended consequence of this was to foster a closer alliance between the Portuguese and the Safavids, as the European maritime power began shipping Iranian silk from the Persian Gulf around the Horn of Africa and into Europe. As Selim looked more and more toward the Indian Ocean, especially after his capture of Yemen and increasing interests in the coffee trade, he quickly realized that pushing the Safavids into the arms of the Portuguese was damaging to Ottoman interests. Thus, he proposed a set of treaties with India's Muslim rulers for joint operations against the Portuguese. Lisbon's representatives in the subcontinent wrote anxiously to their king: "[The harbor of] Diu is waiting for the

Ottomans with open arms." Another Portuguese envoy, after returning
to India from Malacca, wrote of the expectations of India's Muslims:
"With the news of the Ottomans, I have returned to find everywhere
in rebellion." In October 1518, Selim—still in Istanbul before leaving
for Edirne—made Portugal's fears a reality when he received an ambassador from the ruler of Calicut, who had traveled thousands of miles
by ship and by caravan to seek an agreement of cooperation against
the Portuguese. Selim enthusiastically entered into this alliance in February 1519, dispatching from the Red Sea thirty ships and thousands
of sailors—a significant commitment for the Ottoman navy. He also
instituted high tariffs on Portuguese merchants in Alexandria and other
Ottoman port cities—thus advantaging Venetian merchants, as well
as those from Dubrovnik and elsewhere. Such machinations aimed to
keep goods from India flowing through the Mediterranean, instead of
around Africa on Portuguese ships.

In the growing global trade war of the early sixteenth century, even
the Ottomans' enemies to the west, the Venetians, lobbied Selim on
trade policy. Despite the privileges he had granted Venetian merchants
in Egypt, they suffered overall more than the Portuguese from the high
tariffs he imposed on spices and other goods moving from the East
through the Red Sea and Egypt. They continued to complain about
the Iranian silk embargo, especially since, unlike the Portuguese, they
lacked the advantage of an alternative southern route around Africa.
By March 1519, Venetian trade in Egyptian ports had all but dried up.
Eventually, the two powers managed to reach an agreement, driven
largely by the pleas of Ottoman merchants, who earned handsome
profits from their trade with Venice. Selim obliged his merchants, but
only under certain conditions. He would grant Venetians in Ottoman
ports a special discounted tariff rate if, in return, Venice would guarantee favorable prices on the goods it sold in the Ottoman Empire.

VENICE AND HUNGARY REMAINED the strongest entities on the empire's
western border, and Selim worked to neutralize both by negotiating
new treaties with each of them. He had signed a peace accord with
Venice in 1513, to prevent the island republic from aligning with Shah
Ismail. In 1517, he renewed the treaty, agreeing that Venice could retain
its control of Cyprus as a tributary colony, despite its proximity to

Syria and Anatolia. Security along the long Ottoman–Hungarian border, however, proved much more difficult to maintain than peace on the Mediterranean islands the Ottomans and Venetians regularly traded back and forth. While Selim and King Vladislaus II of Hungary had successfully reached an agreement in 1513, border skirmishes over taxation and territorial sovereignty regularly erupted, so the two sides frequently had to pump new life into their peace treaty—in the winter of 1518 and the summer of 1519, for example. In 1519, Selim also renewed the empire's peace treaty with Poland.

Stability in the relations between the Ottomans and their European enemies was, in fact, not ultimately secured by treaties, but rather driven by Renaissance Europe's internal fragmentation. King Francis I of France and Holy Roman Emperor Charles V both styled themselves Europe-wide (even universal) rulers, and their contentious rivalry divided much of the continent among their respective allies, who fought frequent proxy wars against each other. Still, glimmers of European peace began to flicker in the mid-1510s—only to be doused once more by the first stirrings of Martin Luther's Reformation in 1517. After Selim's victory over the Mamluks that year, Pope Leo X, almost as a reflex, called for yet another Crusade against the Ottomans. According to Venetian accounts, Selim laughed when he heard this. Selim—and undoubtedly the pope himself—knew full well that Europe was far too internally fractured to mount the robust, unified campaign they would need to challenge the Ottomans.

With Europe more or less neutralized, in the fall of 1518 Selim began to contemplate his first major offensive since his defeat of the Mamluks. With the addition of Egypt to the empire, the sea routes to North Africa took on greater importance and therefore so did the island of Rhodes, halfway between Istanbul and Alexandria, and still controlled by the Knights Hospitaller of St. John. This limestone fleck, with its rocky shores and forests of pine and cypress, became a priority for Selim. Ottoman ships needed a way-station between the imperial capital and the empire's largest and most lucrative province, in order to resupply and rest before venturing out of the Aegean into open sea. A base of operations such as Rhodes—at the mouth of the Aegean, and at the corner of Anatolia—would enable the empire to quickly dispatch aid to vessels in distress, control the movement of ships in and out of the Aegean, defend against the ever-present pirates, and generally project Ottoman naval power into the Mediterranean. Holding Rhodes, moreover, would provide security for the heavily forested areas of southwestern Anatolia, one of the empire's few sources of the large, tall, straight trees essential for ship construction. Given their maritime ambitions, the Ottomans, like their neighbors in Venice, closely guarded their forests as a precious asset.

At the end of 1518, between hunts around Edirne, Selim began planning an invasion of Rhodes, giving orders to ready ships, oarsmen, weapons, and supplies. Ironically, with these moves, Selim temporarily unified European powers as no European leader could. News of the preparations gave immediate concern to Venice and, of course, to the Knights who ruled Rhodes; many other states, too, sought a peace that would prevent the Ottomans from strengthening their hand in the Mediterranean so dramatically. In the spring of 1519, as Hungary, in the midst of a deep financial crisis, negotiated one of the many renewals of its peace treaty with Selim, its diplomats in Edirne attempted to insert into the document guarantees that the Ottomans would not invade Rhodes, as well as language that would secure Ottoman peace with *all* of Europe's Christian powers. Not surprisingly, given his strong position, Selim initially rejected the inclusion of such a sweeping statement, preferring to negotiate agreements with each of Europe's weaker powers individually.

As part of his effort to win the Ottoman throne, Cem, Selim's uncle, had fled to Rhodes in 1482. Unlike Cem, Selim would never see the island for himself. In the summer of 1519, he postponed his plan to invade Rhodes, because his old nemesis, the Safavid Empire, had become a threat once more, stirring up the Shiites in eastern Anatolia. Facing down an impending move by the Safavids and their Ottoman Shiite supporters was far more urgent than capturing Rhodes. Thus, Selim grudgingly signed the treaty with Hungary in July 1519, ensuring a temporary respite for Rhodes and some relief for Europe's other anxious rulers. Only in 1522 would Rhodes finally fall to the Ottomans, with Suleyman completing the project his father had begun.

THE SAFAVIDS, FAR TO the east, had recovered from the rout at Chaldiran four years previously. The Shiite threat endured; Selim had been unable to finish the job in 1514 because his troops' insistence on returning home had forced him to halt his advance at Tabriz. So, in Edirne in the fall of 1518, Selim devoted himself, once again, to preparing for a war against the Safavid scourge that had occupied so much of his life. If Selim was indeed the warmonger that a contemporary observed him to be, the Shiites of Iran and Anatolia shaped his warmongering life more than any other enemy. Ventures such as a campaign for Rhodes paled in comparison to Selim's determination to destroy the Safavids.

As before, Selim's first step was to eliminate support for the Safavids within the empire itself. This was a far greater challenge than it had been in 1514. In addition to the old pockets of Shiites in central and eastern Anatolia, there were Shiite populations spread across the Middle East who resented their new Sunni overlords. From Edirne, Selim sent orders to Aleppo to deport several rich Shiite families thought to be supportive of the Safavid shah. Also worrisome was the sizable Shiite population of Tripoli, the hilly town on the Mediterranean coast in Lebanon. Even though it was distant from the Safavid border, Selim sent two hundred troops with sixteen cannons as a preemptive show of force against any potential Shiite agitators in the city. Despite the suppression of the Şahkulu Rebellion and Selim's purges as he marched toward Chaldiran, Shiites remained numerous in the vastly enlarged territory of the empire. In 1518, six years after Bayezit's death, Selim was still cleaning up the mess his father had created when, in his attempt to suppress Shiite unrest, he dispersed eastern Anatolian populations to the west. In Bursa, for example, the empire's first capital and one of the oldest Ottoman cities, nestled in the shadow of western Anatolia's great snowy mountains, officials now purged two hundred families suspected of Shiite sympathies.

Given its proximity to Iran and many important Shiite religious sites, Baghdad presented a particularly acute challenge. In contrast to the undulating topography of Anatolia, Baghdad sprawled over the flat terrain that the Tigris and Euphrates rivers had smoothed over millennia of floods. At the far eastern edge of Selim's empire, it was the primary frontier city between Ottoman Sunnism and Safavid Shiism. Baghdad's large Shiite population proved a bulwark of resistance to Ottoman rule, helping the Safavids secure the upper hand for most of the first third of the sixteenth century. After several failed attempts to invade the city, only in 1534 would the Ottomans finally break through to capture Baghdad. Here, in the first half of the sixteenth century, began the epic military and political struggle we know today between the Sunnis and Shiites of Iraq.

In November 1518, Shah Ismail moved a rebuilt force of twelve thousand soldiers to Baghdad, in preparation for launching attacks to the west, against the Ottomans' new and still vulnerable eastern border. Selim countered by amassing his own troops in Syria—always mindful of the difficulties he faced in defending this distant frontier from his command post in Edirne. Direct confrontations between Selim's and Ismail's forces began in early 1519, despite that winter's bitter cold and heavy snowfall. In far eastern Anatolia and northern Syria, Ismail had been able to capture several abandoned hilltop castles to use as lookout points and shelters for his troops during the extreme cold. Pre-Islamic kingdoms, the short-lived medieval Crusader states, and the powerful Abbasid Empire (whose capital was Baghdad) had constructed these fortifications in order to spot enemies coming over the horizon. When, in March 1519, the weather began to improve, the Ottomans attempted to retake one of the captured castles, but Safavid forces soundly repelled them, using guns they had recently acquired from the Portuguese to kill about a thousand Ottoman fighters. Reports even surfaced of Ottoman soldiers defecting to the Safavids.

As both armies began a total mobilization, this military confrontation between Muslim empires far off in the remote navel of the Middle East steadily drew in European powers, who understood its ramifications for their trading interests in the Indian Ocean and Persian Gulf. Not only did the Portuguese arm the Safavids, but Venetian spies relayed Selim's plan to travel to the front so that he could personally lead his soldiers into Syria in June to wipe out the Safavids' gains in the region. (Venetian reconnaissance reports serve as the most complete record of the course of the war in these years.) Still regretting his hurried retreat from Tabriz in 1514, Selim, now forty-nine, hungered to chase the Safavids out of Syria and all the way back to their capital, and to seize it for a second (and final) time. He dispatched a thousand gunners and a thousand additional soldiers to the east that June. At the same time, he received reports that the Safavids had sacked Mosul, in the north of Iraq. In that ancient, fiercely independent city on the banks of the Tigris, the Safavids slaughtered every Turk they could find. They did the same in Baghdad that summer, killing some twelve thousand

Ottoman soldiers and civilians who had arrived there during one of the Ottomans' thwarted campaigns for the city. Refugees able to flee to the safety of the Ottoman Empire reported that Ismail had somewhere between sixty and eighty thousand cavalry in Iraq, many guns from the Portuguese, and about 1,500 Ottoman defectors on his payroll. He had, in addition, enlisted Georgians and Tatars to fight alongside his troops. Since Selim had raided and antagonized both of these communities when he was governor of Trabzon, they stood more than ready to take up arms in Ismail's employ.

In response to this troubling news, Selim—still in Edirne, but preparing to make his way to Istanbul—dispatched an imposing fleet of a hundred ships from the Danube to head east across the Black Sea to Trabzon with reinforcements of soldiers and supplies. He asked the empire's leading clerics to renew their *fatwa*s designating Shiites heretics and therefore sanctioning war against them. And he mobilized a force of nearly fifteen thousand troops to march east from Aleppo toward the Safavid front. Along the way, the soldiers faced jeers and harassment from disgruntled townspeople who were suffering not only from outbreaks of plague but also from lack of food—there was a drought that year—and who blamed the Ottomans for exacerbating their hardships. Retaliation by Ottoman soldiers and the commandeering of food supplies of course angered the local population even more. Recognizing an opportunity, Safavid forces campaigning in northern Syria won support by styling themselves the people's defenders against their new and oppressive Ottoman rulers—the same tactic that the Ottomans had used to co-opt discontented populations to support them against the Byzantines in past centuries, and more recently against the Mamluks.

Throughout late 1519 and early 1520, Selim's troops chased down internal enemies whom they suspected of supporting the Safavids. In March 1520, for example, a rebellion some ten thousand strong erupted in the north-central Anatolian towns of Amasya and Tokat. Many of the agitators were indeed Shiites acting in support of Ismail's cause; many others joined the revolt not for ideological reasons, but to protest against recent imperial predations in their region. The Ottoman army's monopolization of resources, and the security measures instituted because of the impending war, had made enemies out of otherwise loyal Sunni subjects.

✖

UNLIKE PREVIOUS SULTANS, Selim had concentrated his military operations almost exclusively in the east. As he wrote in verse of his own reign in these years:

> From Istambol's throne a mighty host to Iran guided I;
> Sunken deep in blood of shame I made the Golden Heads [the
>    Safavids] to lie.
> Glad the Slave [the Mamluks], my resolution, lord of Egypt's realm
>    became:
> Thus I raised my royal banner e'en as the Nine Heavens high.
> From the kingdom fair of Iraq to Hijaz these tidings sped,
> When I played the harp of Heavenly Aid at feast of victory.

But despite Selim's "feast of victory" in the east, by the spring of 1520 he had redirected his attention to one particular territory in the west: Morocco. His defeat of the Mamluks had earned him control of large portions of the North African coast as far west as Algeria, and he dreamed of going even farther. The northwest corner of Africa—opposite the Iberian peninsula—was potentially even more strategic than the continent's northeast corner, the recently conquered Egypt.

Thus, even as Selim began to wage yet another war on his far eastern border, his mind's eye kept watch on his new far western border in North Africa. Pushing west from Algeria into Morocco would give the Ottomans their first outpost on the Atlantic and put them on the threshold of the Iberian kingdoms. We can imagine Selim perched on his hunting steed in the quiet forests of Edirne, contemplating crossing the Strait of Gibraltar, like the Muslim conquerors of the eighth century, to retake Granada, or thinking back to his meeting with Piri Reis in Cairo. Perhaps, it had been a mistake to relinquish the Atlantic portion of Piri's map after all. Capturing Morocco would bring Selim closer than any of his predecessors to making *Vilayet Antilia* a province of the Ottoman Empire.

CHAPTER

22

# FULCRUM OF THE ATLANTIC

*Sixteenth-century map of North Africa*

AFTER WHAT ISABELLA AND FERDINAND INTERPRETED AS THEIR divinely scripted conquest of Granada in 1492, the end of Muslim rule on the Iberian peninsula, they understood that the only way to secure the city and their other gains along the peninsula's long southern coastline was to bring North Africa squarely under Spanish control. Otherwise, Granada and the south would forever be vulnerable to a Muslim *Reconquista*. Muslim North Africa had long been a thorn in their side, and it remained a far more immediate concern than Columbus's adventure into the still-unknown New World. During the 1490s, the Ottomans edged ever farther west in the Mediterranean, making the threat of Islam ever more pressing. After a brief military distraction in 1497, when they had to divert their forces to defend against a French invasion of their territories on the Italian peninsula, Isabella and Ferdinand launched what they described as a new Crusade against Islam in North Africa.

The first armed venture in this renewed Spanish effort, in September 1497, quickly captured the Moroccan coastal city of Melilla on the peninsula of Cape Three Forks. This almost effortless victory fueled the fire of those Spaniards who supported a more aggressive policy of penetration in North Africa. Within the Spanish court, others pressed Isabella and Ferdinand to focus their efforts on the consolidation of the peninsula rather than on foreign wars. The hawks, with Isabella at their head, carried the day, insisting that vengeful Iberian Muslims, who

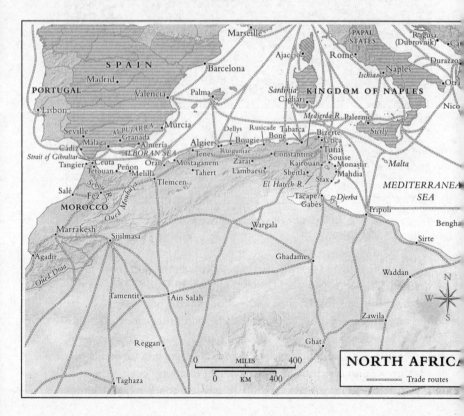

had been expelled from Spain in 1492, were collaborating with North African Muslims to launch attacks on Spain from across the sea. The only way to properly defend the Spanish mainland, they claimed, was to forge a territorial buffer zone.

For this Spanish imperialist faction, a series of domestic uprisings between 1499 and 1501, known as the Rebellion of the Alpujarras, proved the critical need for a determined North Africa campaign. In the hilly southern region near Granada, local Muslims led a series of insurrections against Spanish attempts to forcibly convert a remaining pocket of Islam to Catholicism. As the Crown worked incessantly to eradicate any lingering remnants of Islam, burning Qur'ans and other Arabic texts, forbidding the speaking or writing of Arabic, and banning Muslim garb, it was met, not surprisingly, with strident resistance. The revolt of the Muslims of Alpujarra became increasingly violent and soon erupted into full-scale war. Ferdinand himself collected some of the massive firepower the Crown had assembled during the siege of Granada and led an army to battle the rebels.

At the same time that Ferdinand headed south, Isabella's health began to decline. She would feel weak for months at a time and then recover, only to grow weary once again. In the fall of 1504, she became bedridden, suffering from dropsy (as edema was called then) and fever. On November 26 of that year, Isabella died at the age of fifty-three. Her death ended the reign of one of history's most significant royals. She oversaw the expansion of Europe to the Americas, the Inquisition, the expulsion of Jews and Muslims from Iberia, and the unification of Spain. "In all the realms," one of her sympathetic court historians wrote, "her death was mourned with such great pain and sentiment, not just by her subjects and countrymen, but commonly by all." Columbus, who had returned from his fourth and final voyage just a few months before Isabella's death, deeply mourned the loss of his patron. It was, indeed, a profound loss, as after her death, the situation in the Caribbean—from a Spanish perspective—deteriorated rapidly. In Las Casas's words, "all these island territories began to go to the dogs once news arrived of the death of our most gracious Queen Isabella."

Isabella's last testament made clear what she wanted her legacy to be: the conquest of Muslim Africa and Crusade against Islam. As part of the defense of Spain against another Muslim invasion, she instructed, for example, that Gibraltar should become part of the "permanent properties of the Crown and part of the royal patrimony," and ordered that proceeds from the sale of her properties should be used to redeem two hundred Christian captives from the hands of the infidel Muslims (she also made provisions for the poor and for the maintenance of churches and convents). Either fittingly or ironically, depending on one's point of view, Isabella instructed that she be buried in the Alhambra in Granada, the governing seat of the city's former Muslim rulers, the symbol of the *Reconquista*, the very epicenter of her defeat of Islam. Freezing rain and mud hampered the progress of her funeral cortege, but she eventually reached her desired resting place. Though, in defiance of her final commands, her body was moved in 1521 to the newly constructed cathedral of Granada, it is her instructions that are the most telling: Isabella wanted to occupy for eternity a structure built by Muslims. Even in death, Isabella would continue to wage war against Islam.

Isabella's death left the faction advocating for an aggressive policy in North Africa without one of its strongest backers. To steer that policy after her death, Ferdinand appointed a former corsair named Pedro Navarro as captain-general of Spain's military campaign. Navarro had spent most of his career fighting for the Crown of Aragon in Italy, and had participated in the siege of an Ottoman-held island off the western coast of Greece. In the fall of 1509, he began implementing Ferdinand's—really Isabella's—plans. He led an expedition of four thousand men against the independent port of Bougie on the Algerian coast, across the sea from Marseille, in a region dominated by the indigenous Kabyle people. The Ottoman admiral Kemal Reis had temporarily captured Bougie in the late 1480s as a safe haven from which to stage military operations in the western Mediterranean, and Navarro now sought Bougie essentially for the same reasons: its protected harbor and its strategic location between the sea's western and eastern halves. By the end of 1510, Navarro had captured Bougie as well as several other smaller North African coastal cities: Tenes, Dellys, Mostaganem, and Peñon.

He kept pushing east, all the way to the walled city of Tripoli in Libya, with its distinctive lookout towers. This became the watershed, the farthest eastward extension of Spanish hegemony in North Africa, as the increasing power of the Ottomans in the western Mediterranean would combine with other forces to steadily diminish Spain's influence

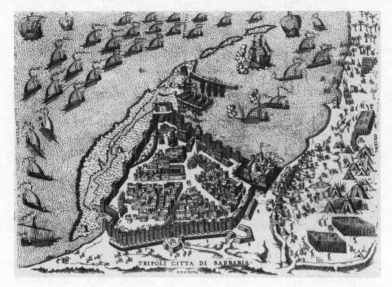

*Tripoli*

in North Africa. Ferdinand would never be able to fulfill Isabella's final wishes for the destruction of Islam.

THE PEOPLE OF SPAIN's frontier possessions in North Africa were almost all Muslims, who certainly had no love for Catholic colonial rule. These Christian dots in a sea of Islam, especially those farthest away from Spain, proved enormously difficult to defend and provision with supplies and military equipment. Even in Iberia itself, the Crown had failed to secure its rule over the Muslims who remained in the peninsula after 1492. The Alpujarra revolts, only one of many Muslim rebellions, would rage for years, despite—or, more accurately, because of—the ongoing attempts to forcibly convert Muslims, which continued until the early decades of the seventeenth century.

After Kemal Reis's missions of the late 1480s, the Ottomans monitored the status of the Muslim populations of Spain and North Africa, eventually emerging as their chief suppliers of matériel, cash, and other resources. The Ottomans also forged alliances with the leaders of the mostly disconnected and often mutually antagonistic North African Muslim principalities—both those notionally held by the

Spanish Crown and those that remained independent. Ottoman support for these Muslim city-states—or even the mere rumor of such support—deterred Spain from attempting to forcibly subjugate these communities. More than anything else, Spain did not want war with the Ottomans.

The Ottomans and the Mamluks had already forced the Spanish westward. As the Ottomans gained more and more of the Old World—territories in North Africa, southeastern Europe, western India, and elsewhere as well—Spain tried to make up for its precipitous losses in North Africa with new holdings in Mexico and the Caribbean. It proved far easier, as we have seen, for Spain to fight in the New World than in the Old. Even so, it was only with Cortés's conquests in Mexico in the 1510s that the Americas began to offer some recompense for Spain's territorial diminishment at the hands of the Ottomans.

In 1518, Cortés added two million square kilometers of Mexican land to the kingdom of the recently crowned Charles V. The gold and silver that Europeans so coveted began flowing out of the Americas to Iberia. Between 1511 and 1520, for example, 9,153 kilograms of American gold arrived in Seville alone. In the second half of the sixteenth century, close to two-thirds of the world's silver derived from the mines of Potosí, in what is today Bolivia. Some of this silver flooded the Ottoman market, leading to a catastrophic debasement of the Ottoman currency. The size of the satchels that merchants in Istanbul, Aleppo, and Sofia carried to the bazaar grew over time, as they needed ever-increasing numbers of silver coins to make basic purchases. And while it would take an additional century for New World commerce to overtake Eurasian trade, and for the concomitant upsurge in transatlantic slavery, even in the early sixteenth century Spain increasingly came to see that its "frontier of opportunity lay in the New World, not in Africa." The Crown hoped that Bernal Díaz's New World *Gran Cairo* would eventually prove more valuable than Cairo itself.

Still, even as Selim's conquests of 1516 and 1517 furthered Spain's pivot away from North Africa to the Caribbean and Mexico, the monarchy had invested too much in its Mediterranean holdings to relinquish them easily. Moreover, it understood that should Islam conquer the whole of the sea, it might then reconquer the territories it had lost in Spain and perhaps even continue marching north through Iberia into Europe. Propelled in part by its newfound riches in the Americas, Spain therefore redoubled its resolve in North Africa in the 1510s. This became the zone of confrontation between these two powerful empires, whose expanding theaters of war now stretched from the Indian Ocean to the Mediterranean and across the Atlantic. Indeed, so important was the fight against the Muslim enemy that Spain recalled many of its soldiers from the Americas—soldiers who, often, had begun their military careers in Spain's Old World wars against its infidel enemies. The two empires would collide in Morocco for their final battle for North Africa.

SELIM'S NORTH AFRICA STRATEGY relied heavily on two brothers, Oruç and Hayreddin Barbarossa. They were born in the 1470s in the town of Mytilene, on the Aegean island of Lesbos, near the Anatolian coast—almost two thousand years after the birth of Lesbos's most famous resident, the lyric poet Sappho. This hilly island of olive trees and pines has proven of strategic importance to every state that has ruled in the Aegean, from the time of Homer's *Iliad* to the present day. Very likely from Christian stock, the Barbarossa brothers—so named because of their red beards—came from a family of mariners who had built their careers as privateers in the Aegean and the eastern Mediterranean. They worked as sailors for hire in commercial transport, raiding, and war. Since the Ottomans had added Lesbos to their expanding empire a few years before the brothers' birth, they often found themselves in the employ of the Ottoman state or Ottoman merchants. Selim's half-brother Korkud had hired them to facilitate his naval ambitions against the Knights of St. John and other maritime powers, but when their patron failed in his bid for the throne, the Barbarossas fled the region, fearful for their lives. Mercenaries that they were, they always managed to find work somewhere.

In 1513, the year after Selim's accession to the throne, the brothers ended up in Tunis, which then had a population of over a hundred thousand souls, working for the sultan of the Hafsid empire. Sited on a promontory commanding the sea-lane between Sicily and North Africa, the chokepoint between the western and the eastern Mediterranean, the stronghold of Tunis grew powerful and marvelously wealthy over the years, due chiefly to its corsairing ventures all along the Barbary Coast, as Europeans often called North Africa.

(Recall that, in 1472, Columbus had sailed to Tunis in an attempt to retrieve a ship that had been captured from King René of Anjou.) The brothers excelled in their new employ as state-sponsored pirates, and their reputation as cunning and effective professional corsairs spread widely.

Given the brothers' skill and experience—as well as their extensive personal stockpile of guns and cannons—rulers of Muslim city-states across North Africa competed for their services. In 1514, for example, the elders of Bougie appealed to the Barbarossas for help against the Spanish admiral Pedro Navarro, who had captured their city in 1510. The brothers pummeled the small city with steady bombardments, eventually blasting a hole in Bougie's thick ramparts. The Barbarossas' sailors then streamed into the city, engaging the Spanish soldiers stationed there with gunfire and hand-to-hand combat. They soon had to pull back, though, having exhausted their ammunition and needing to tend to Oruç, who took a bullet in his left arm. Bougie therefore remained in Spanish hands, at least for a time. Such confrontations between Muslim and Spanish forces broke out all across North Africa in the mid-1510s, with the Barbarossas and Navarro as the primary warring protagonists. Thus, while Navarro and his men extended Spain's empire eastward along the North African coast, the brothers, in the employ of various small Muslim states, pushed westward, leading, inevitably, to direct confrontation.

As the Barbarossa brothers were drawn deeper into the Muslim fight against the Spanish in North Africa, their ambitions grew. They realized their need for a forceful and resolute backer, one that could match the resources and power of the Spanish Crown. Without such backing, they might be able to rebuff individual Spanish attacks, but they would never gain the defensible posts they needed to launch their daring forays into the sea, especially against a rival such as Navarro, who enjoyed the full weight of Spain, as well as Pope Leo X, behind him. The ruler of Tunis had offered the brothers a cut of all the booty they collected from raiding ships passing through the strait, but his limited influence meant that this could be no more than a tenuous arrangement. The Barbarossas would find a far more powerful patron in Sultan Selim.

After their failed siege at Bougie in 1514, the brothers sent one of their men to Istanbul to seek a meeting with the Ottoman sultan. The emissary was none other than Piri Reis, the mapmaker Selim would encounter again in his tent in Cairo a few years later. Piri had first met the Barbarossas when they had sailed together on his uncle Kemal's ships in the western Mediterranean—voyages during which he likely acquired the Columbus expedition maps he would later use for his own world map. After these ventures with his uncle, Piri needed work, so he occasionally joined the Barbarossas' team of corsairs in Tunis.

Piri arrived in Istanbul in late 1514 weighed down by gifts for Selim from the Barbarossa brothers, letters of support and goodwill, and apologies and pleas that Selim forgive them their treasonous foolishness in having supported Korkud for the throne before 1512. Most important, Piri carried a proposal. The Barbarossas presented themselves and their services to Selim. Rather than being a piddly city-state's corsairs, they sought to be Selim's imperial warrior-pirates, the captains of his western Mediterranean fleet. They promised their total and eternal allegiance to him and guaranteed that whatever they gained on the seas would be his. To do their work effectively for him, they asked for supplies, additional ships, and the full backing of his empire against Spain's reach in North Africa. Selim immediately and unequivocally agreed.

Thus, in early 1515, between his victory at Chaldiran and the beginning of his overland march to Egypt, Selim sent Piri Reis back to Tunis with two war galleys, two jewel-encrusted swords, vast quantities of fresh supplies, new munitions, letters of safe passage, and cash. The Barbarossas now had their imperial patron, and Selim had his long-sought strategic forward naval force in the western Mediterranean.

As the Barbarossas had hoped, Selim's backing forced a complete realignment of power in North Africa among local rulers, the Ottomans, the Spanish, and the Mamluks. Given the immense power and resources now behind them, the Barbarossas—much as Kemal Reis had done previously, on a much smaller scale—were able to forge regional coalitions, having convinced most of the Muslim rulers of North Africa that the Ottomans represented the best guarantor of their interests. They raised troops from local communities as well as from among the recently arrived Spanish Muslim refugees, and even sent ships to Granada to rescue Ibero-Muslims and resettle them in North Africa. During these missions, the Barbarossas' men observed the dire situation of Muslims in post-*Reconquista* Spain. They reported back, for example, that "the Unbelievers took young women with children and gave them to Christians—that is they could not be married to Muslims. Their desire was to cut out the Islamic population from their society." Selim's arrangement with the Barbarossas even allowed them to recruit young boys from Anatolia to fight for them in North Africa—rather like a private Janissary Corps.

The brothers' efforts to bypass the authority of the established rulers of port city-states across the western Mediterranean naturally created both intense animosities against and new opportunities for the brothers and their new patron. For a few years after their 1515 agreement with Selim, the Barbarossas danced carefully between selective alliance- and enemy-making, in the process refashioning older political and military arrangements that often stretched from North Africa to capitals across the Mediterranean. Although they enjoyed all the advantages that came with the support of one of the Mediterranean's largest empires, it would be another year before Selim would defeat the Mamluks, and even longer before he would be able to secure much of North Africa, both the Mamluks' holdings and independent regions. Before late 1517, Ottoman power in North Africa remained rather anemic, and thus the Barbarossa brothers still needed the support of local populations and at least some of the region's rulers to be able to ply the coast.

The first test of the brothers' Ottoman backing came in August 1515, when they prepared to attack the city of Bougie for a second time. Even though the deposed Muslim ruler of Bougie had, just the previous year, hired the Barbarossas to retake the city from the Spanish, he now feared that the brothers—no longer operating as mercenaries but as agents of the Ottoman Empire, with its own potentially hostile agenda—would take Bougie not just from the Spanish but also from him. This, peculiarly, resulted in an alliance between the city's Muslim rulers and their historic Spanish enemies, pitted against the Ottoman-backed Barbarossas. In the summer of 1515, the Barbarossas lost at Bougie for the second time.

In the spring of 1516, as Selim was preparing to march into Syria, a variation on the Bougie scenario played out in the much larger city of Algiers, strategically located in the center of North Africa. The Muslim ruler of Algiers, the head of the Tha'āliba tribe, sought help from the Barbarossas to eject the Spanish from his city; they agreed, and after only one day of fighting stood victorious. It was not long, however, before a dispute erupted over who should rule the city, with its enormous protected harbor. As representatives of the Ottoman state—and in a declaration of their growing personal aspirations—the Barbarossas demanded some amount of political authority in Algiers in exchange for their defeat of the Spanish. When the city's ruler refused, the brothers responded with the sword, killing him and forcibly taking his city for themselves and, ostensibly at least, for their patron, Selim.

The Ottoman capture of Algiers represented a fundamental shift in the geopolitics of North Africa: it was the first territory conquered in the name of the Ottoman Empire. No longer was the empire merely making strategic military and economic alliances and sponsoring Spain's enemies in the Mediterranean. Now, Selim's grand colonial ambitions were revealed. By the time Algiers was in the Barbarossa brothers' hands, Selim had entered Syria, allowing the Ottomans to attack the Mamluks from both the north and west.

As if proof of God's love for his shadow, Ferdinand died—on January 23, 1516, at the age of sixty-three—just as Selim prepared to move against the Mamluks, relieving Selim of any concern about interference from the Iberian peninsula in his imminent attempt to assert power over the Mamluk dominions in North Africa. After Isabella's death, Ferdinand had accomplished little of substance. He had defied her final directive, keeping the crown of Castile for himself instead of passing it to their daughter Joanna, and broke a deathbed promise by remarrying within a year, this time to Germaine of Foix, thirty-six years his junior. Despite his betrayals, he was buried next to Isabella in the Alhambra, and his body was moved along with hers to the new cathedral of Granada in 1521. Because of the complex—even byzantine—politics of European marriage alliances, his death put Castile and Aragon into the hands of the northern European Habsburgs. Combined with a succession crisis—a period of instability that eventually gave Spain to Charles V—the transfer of power north, away from the Mediterranean, meant that the reconfigured Habsburg Spanish Empire largely ignored North Africa for the next several years, directing its gaze westward across the ocean. Thus, the Barbarossas could continue to chip away at Spain's outposts, folding them into the expanding Ottoman state.

Mamluk power in North Africa had been waning during the previous few years, as the empire had been forced to focus its attention and military resources on the Ottomans in northern Syria and southern Anatolia and the Portuguese in the Red Sea. Due in large measure to the Barbarossas' balancing act of alliances, the takeover of the region progressed rather smoothly, eased by Selim's usual policy of cutting deals with local potentates. Hayreddin Barbarossa was appointed governor of Algeria—now the empire's westernmost border and a staging ground for a potential invasion of Morocco—and also governorgeneral of the entire western Mediterranean. Placing one of the Barbarossa brothers in charge of that region (Oruç would die in 1518) proved both expedient and effective, since they had had long experience in the western Mediterranean, had ingratiated themselves with many of the region's potentates, had already pledged their allegiance to Selim, and were respected and feared by their rivals. Selim supported Hayreddin with further troops, ships, and cannons, which Hayreddin used to great effect as he attempted to impose Ottoman authority in

*Hayreddin Barbarossa and Suleyman*

the interior of Algeria—even to the point of perfecting a technique for attaching sails to wheeled cannons to move them through the Sahara.

Queen Isabella of Castile would have shuddered with fear and quaked with anger to see what her feckless husband Ferdinand had allowed to happen.

※

AS SELIM CONTEMPLATED AN invasion of Morocco in 1518, he turned to Hayreddin Barbarossa for insight and advice. Hayreddin, far less enthusiastic than his sultan, explained how Morocco differed from the rest of North Africa and why it would prove enormously difficult to conquer.

Like no other territory in North Africa, Morocco's heavily populated and ecologically diverse interior was ruled by a stable, powerful agrarian state. For centuries, a series of dynasties—the Almoravids, Almohads, Marinids, and Wattasids—had successfully resisted Spanish, Portuguese, and Mamluk penetration of Morocco's stunning yet forbidding interior of soaring mountains and deep river valleys. In Selim's day, the Saadian Empire controlled the territory. They had risen to power in 1509 and would, Hayreddin reported to Selim, very likely repel the Ottomans just as they had other invaders over the previous decade. While the Ottomans, with the Barbarossas' maritime expertise, had managed to conquer the string of cities beaded along Africa's northern coast, they had failed to make inroads into the interior. Thus, much like another of the Ottoman Empire's new territorial extremities, Yemen, Africa's northwest corner was a land of stubborn geography that had historically ensured political independence.

Moreover, the Saadians—far from being small-scale upstart rulers of a tiny city-state bound to the sea—had inherited the advantages of the dynasties that ruled Morocco before them: a standing army, a loyal population, immense land resources, impregnable mountain fortresses, and plenty of cash. In several ways, their rule was similar to that of the Ottomans: in their tax-revenue-based economy, military organization, and family politics. Hayreddin also informed Selim that the Saadians had been expanding their arsenal over the past decade. Anyone who had tried to operate in North Africa in recent years understood the realities of Morocco's military power and had generally steered clear of it. As with Yemen, sending troops and supplies over such a long distance would prove an enormous challenge for the Ottomans. All of this, needless to say, boosted the Saadian leader Ahmad al-A'raj's confidence. He proved this by directing insults at the Ottomans, mocking them as a bunch of fishermen who would never be able to penetrate even a short distance beyond the coast.

Despite the warnings from Hayreddin Barbarossa, Selim began formulating a strategy for invading Morocco. He was a man driven by challenges, and he hoped to force Spain completely off the African continent and secure the mouth of the Mediterranean, which only a few Ottoman sailors—Kemal Reis foremost among them—had ever seen. The Mediterranean would, then, be well on the way to becoming an Ottoman lake. If Morocco were made Ottoman, God's shadow could stretch into the Atlantic—and perhaps even cross that ocean, an unthinkable notion only a couple years earlier—affording Selim's empire a potentially vastly different future.

Unlike those who had preceded him and failed, Selim would not commence his attack on Morocco from the sea. Rather, he planned first to secure the interior, marching his troops overland from Algeria and then north and west to capture the Mediterranean and Atlantic coasts, which would require traversing the extremely rugged terrain of the Atlas Mountains. Since the Spanish had never possessed all of Algeria, as Selim did after the conquest of the Mamluk Empire, they had never had the territorial advantage needed even to contemplate such an inside-out strategy. Selim settled on the town of Tlemcen, which lay in a valley about forty miles south of the Mediterranean, behind the coastal hills, as the most suitable border crossing. In late 1517, very soon after Algeria was secured, the Ottomans led a series of test raids west from Tlemcen. These failed. After several armed clashes, they had gained almost nothing and so pulled back.

These skirmishes demonstrated to Selim that he would need far more troops and provisions in Algeria if he was to mount a real attack into the belly of Saadian power in Morocco. Undeterred by the overwhelming challenges—the great distance from Istanbul, the landlocked location of Tlemcen itself—he began moving men and matériel by ship, and also undertook the enormous expense of transporting goods overland from Syria—across the desolation of Sinai, through Egypt's irrigated delta towns, and then across the expanse of the Sahara Desert. (Hayreddin's sail-equipped cannon technology no doubt aided in this operation.)

When the Ottomans began amassing forces in western North

Africa, tocsins rang out across Spain. Although stretched by their many new interests in the New World, Spain recognized the existential threat represented by Ottoman designs on Morocco: if Morocco fell to the Ottomans, Iberia could be next. Promptly they reshuffled their military resources. Fresh from fighting their new infidel enemies in the Americas, thousands of Crusading Spanish soldiers were quickly redispatched to battle their original infidel nemesis in North Africa. Even Hernán Cortés himself eventually returned from Mexico to wage the final battle of his long and storied military career against Hayreddin Barbarossa in Algiers in 1541. Despite their vaunted reputation as conquistadors in the New World, this generation of Spanish soldiers, of which Cortés was the most prominent exemplar, began and ended their careers warring against Muslims in the Old World.

When they returned from the Americas after 1517, these conquistador-Crusaders encountered a world vastly different from the one they had left behind. Martin Luther had announced himself as an internal enemy in the very heart of Catholic Europe, plunging Christendom into a religious civil war. The Ottoman Empire possessed immeasurably more territory around the Mediterranean than it had in 1492, and was on the very doorstep of Spain. The rounding of the Cape of Good Hope in 1497 and the establishment of European trading posts around the Indian Ocean had created a completely different geography of European imperial ambitions. And the existence of Native Americans in the New World posed a theological challenge to almost everything Christians had understood about God's creation for more than a millennium.

Morocco, therefore, was much more than a frontier between empires. It stood as the fulcrum between the past and the future, between Islam and Christianity, between Eurasia and the Atlantic world. The battle for Morocco would determine whether Catholicism or its enemies prevailed, whether the Old World or the New would prove the key to global domination, whether the Ottomans or the Europeans would shape the course of world history in the early sixteenth century and beyond.

⁂

IN THE EARLY AUTUMN of 1518, the Ottomans, the Spanish, and the Saadians stood poised for a triangular war in Morocco. On September 20, a fleet left Spain for its North African holdings, only to have high winds slam twelve of the ships into rocks on the Moroccan coast, completely destroying them. All three thousand Spanish soldiers on board six of these vessels perished, and the horses on the other six ships drowned as well. But this was just the first of several waves of Spanish military transports to cross the sea. Soon Crown soldiers were flowing steadily into Morocco.

As in Bougie, the Ottoman threat was so menacing to both the Spanish and the Muslim North Africans that it turned enemies into allies. Such Christian-Muslim alliances were rare, of course. Decades earlier, Cem had attempted to broker one between the Mamluks and the Knights Hospitaller of St. John. The adversary that motivated all of these efforts to forge unique bonds of politics over religion was the Ottoman Empire, a sign of its primacy in the early modern Mediterranean.

Aware of the partnership against him in Morocco, Selim understood that he would have to devote enormous military resources and personnel to the western Mediterranean. His preparations, like those of his enemies, therefore demanded a delicate rebalancing of many priorities. Above all, he wanted to be sure that an invasion of Morocco would not compromise his ongoing efforts against the Safavids and their Shiite allies within the empire. By February 1519, Selim had ordered sixty thousand Ottoman troops from the Balkans to head south to Nicopolis, on the western coast of Greece, a port which offered a perfect launch pad for the North Africa campaign. The Ottomans held all of the surrounding region, so the movement of men and supplies overland to the coast from Istanbul, the Balkans, and mainland Greece was expedient and safe. From Nicopolis, it was a straight shot across the heart of the Mediterranean—away from any coastline and away from Sicily, Malta, and other pirate hotspots—to the sandy shores and lagoons of Tripoli in Libya, which was by this time an Ottoman stronghold. By March, Selim had also assembled an impressive fleet in the Aegean: 120 heavy galleys, 150 light galleys, 30 transports, 68,000 guns, and enough cannons to outfit 112 galleys. At the same time, he fortified Ottoman territories all along the North African coast. In July, for example, the Ottoman navy secured the island of Djerba, at the corner of the Tunisian coast, a key hinge of control between Tripoli and Tunis.

Meanwhile, Spain continued to funnel soldiers and supplies to North Africa. In November 1519, it dispatched one of the largest fleets in its armada to collect troops on the volcanic island of Ischia, near

Naples, and also mobilized troops from its various other Italian possessions. Selim was just about to embark his forces when news of these maneuvers reached him, and decided to hold his ships in port to allow time to better assess his enemies' shifting troop levels and resources, even asking the Venetian *bailo* in Istanbul whether he had received information about Spain's forces via his Mediterranean spy networks. Selim had no interest in dispatching to North Africa any more of his precious troops than necessary, especially since he was still deliberating about reinforcements for his eastern front against the Safavids, but he knew as well that it would be dangerous to send too few. In March 1520, he finally settled on eighty thousand as the appropriate number of troops to deploy for the North Africa expedition.

Even as both sides committed vast resources and beat the drums of war, they attempted to engage each other diplomatically. Ottoman and Spanish ambassadors traveled back and forth between Selim's headquarters in Edirne and Charles's mobile court (given the attention his enormous empire required, he was always on the move, from the Low Countries to Spain, Germany to Italy). These negotiations stalled, because each side thought it held a military advantage and would therefore benefit from a war. Spain drew confidence from its historic hegemony in the western Mediterranean and its alliance with the Saadians; Selim believed that his empire's enormous resources, its recent territorial gains, and his judicious troop deployments would carry the day.

As a sign of the futility of these negotiations, the two sides spent more time discussing the rather minor issue of the travel of Christian pilgrims to Jerusalem than they did on the much more pressing matter at hand, their impending military confrontation. As part of any peace, the Spanish demanded guarantees of safe passage for Christian pilgrims to Jerusalem, while Selim retorted that he had already put such guarantees in place. After his conquest of Jerusalem in late 1516, three years earlier, he had granted Christians and Jews full autonomy over their affairs and had welcomed the world's Christians to Jerusalem as esteemed guests of his empire. This situation had changed in 1517, when Pope Leo X declared a new Crusade against the Ottomans, making Selim increasingly wary of European Christian visitors in his empire. Crusaders had posed as pilgrims before. Selim therefore imposed a quota on the number of pilgrims, and ordered mandatory inspections of their ships and lodgings. Still, confident in his military superiority over a Habsburg Spanish Empire with shifting priorities, and understanding how impossible it would be for Europe to mount a Crusade, Selim agreed, yet again, to guarantee the protection and free passage of Christian pilgrims to Jerusalem. Both sides recognized the increasing uselessness of these discussions. As the geopolitics of the moment tilted increasingly toward war, it was soldiers, not pilgrims, that would matter most.

⊗

WITH HIS EMPIRE'S RECENT expansion, Selim's Ottomans now trod the soils of Yemen, Gujarat, Algiers, and Ethiopia; they pulled their ships into ports across the Mediterranean, the Red and Black seas, and the Indian Ocean; they fought Christian and Muslim armies from eastern Europe to Central Asia; they traded goods in Baku, Oman, and Indonesia. Now they were about to push for the empire's first territory on the Atlantic.

In May 1520, as Europe convulsed with revolts in Spain against its Habsburg ruler and Luther's Protestant challenge churned the Catholic hierarchy, a man named Ali Bey, one of Selim's dragomans (interpreters), arrived in Edirne carrying a gift for his sultan: a new *mappamundi*, this one inscribed in Italian and Latin. Like the map Piri Reis had unfurled for Selim in Cairo in 1517, this new world map enchanted and amazed the sultan, as Venetian sources relate—though, unlike Piri's map, it has not survived and therefore not received the attention from historians it deserves. When Selim first saw it, he immediately rose from his throne to examine it more closely. He laid it out on a table, circled it as one would a sacred shrine, and pored over it with his advisers. He traced the coastlines with his eyes, taking in the shapes of the continents—all the world's known territories, from west to east, north to south.

This time, Selim did not rip the map in half. In the flickering candlelight of that warm evening, he instructed a secretary to cross out all of the map's Italian and Latin names and replace them with their equivalents in Ottoman Turkish (as they had appeared on Piri's 1517 map). As the man set to work, the entire world slowly transformed from Italian and Latin to Ottoman, enacting a new conquest of the imagination on parchment. Costantinopoli became Istanbul, Egitto became Mısır, Insula Hispana (Hispaniola) became *Vilayet Antilia*. On this map, in Edirne, Selim now possessed all of creation.

The comparison between Selim's reactions to these two maps reflects an important transformation in his worldview between 1517 and 1520, one most scholars have not appreciated. With his conquest of the Mamluk Empire, he had become increasingly confident that his empire was the vanguard of global power, and in 1517, he had correctly understood that world domination meant controlling the Mediterranean and the territories to the east of the sea. The lands Piri had depicted on the other side of the Atlantic had seemed negligible, the attempt to conquer them a risk worth taking only for the weaker, more desperate Europeans. By 1520, Selim seems to have decided that he wanted that "negligible" territory—he wanted the Americas. And because he now knew that his route to the Americas went through Morocco, he redoubled his resolve to conquer that territory. In the words of Abbas Hamdani, one of the few historians who has taken Selim's interest in the Atlantic seriously, "As the Ottomans were engaged in a counter-crusade in the Indian Ocean and the Mediterranean Sea against those very powers who had discovered these new lands [the Americas], they appeared ready to pursue their enemies on into and perhaps across the Atlantic. . . . Ottoman interest in North Africa and their desperate drive toward the western shores of the Maghrib [North Africa] are themselves evidence of the Porte's [i.e., the sultan's] intentions. If the Ottomans did not reach America, it is because they failed to gain the Atlantic coast."

By 1520, Selim had grown accustomed to being the ruler of the world's largest empire, sultan and caliph, God's shadow on earth. The east, and now clearly the west, too, fell within his sights. Seizing Morocco would allow him to invade north into Spain, cross the ocean to the Americas, and extend his dominion down the western coast of Africa as well. Surely, Selim now imagined that virtually all of the territories on the western portion of Piri's map—the half that survives, the half that he previously chose to ignore—could be his. Selim knew territorial expansion would be his most lasting legacy, and he therefore aspired to make reality match the vision he created by preserving the world intact, this time, and having all of its place names translated into Turkish. He intended to make the whole world Ottoman.

CHAPTER
23

# ETERNITY

*Selim on his deathbed*

IN THE CENTER OF A KIND OF VENN DIAGRAM OF GREEK, BULGARIAN,
and Turkish cultural zones, Edirne was not only the Ottomans' second
capital city from the late 1360s until 1453, but also is distinguished as the
home of the oldest continuous athletic competition in the world. Every
year since 1346, Edirne has hosted an olive oil wrestling tournament.
Exactly as the term suggests, men wearing only leather shorts lather
themselves in olive oil and wrestle on a grassy field until one either pins

the other on the muddy, slick ground or raises him above his shoulders. Wrestling is one of the oldest sports in the world, and evidence for oil wrestling exists across the ancient Mediterranean, from Greece and Rome to Assyria, Egypt, and Iran. The Ottomans continued the tradition when they entered the Middle East—yet one more way in which they inherited the legacies of the great ancient Mediterranean empires.

The figure of a wrestler fittingly symbolizes Selim. He had been a combatant his entire life—first against his own family, then against the Safavids and Mamluks, and now against the Spanish in the Mediterranean and the Portuguese in the Indian Ocean. Selim's ambitions in Morocco, however, presented him with a far more formidable test than any he had faced to this point. Part of the challenge of olive oil wrestling is, obviously, the difficulty of grasping one's opponent. Instead of simply grabbing at a slippery arm or leg, one must develop a strategy, first, to avoid losing one's own footing, and then to lure one's foe into a compromising position. Leverage, balance, and distraction prove crucial for success. In Edirne in the summer of 1520, Selim in many ways stood like a wrestler, having to weigh his multiple military engagements and trying to anticipate his enemies' maneuvers to plan his own countermoves. He had seen the European powers weaken themselves through infighting, he had amassed troops and supplies in Algeria for

*Olive oil wrestling in Edirne*

an overland offensive, and he had readied his northern Mediterranean forces to move quickly on Morocco.

If Selim had captured Morocco, he would have completely reforged the history of the world after 1520. In a Catholic European doomsday scenario, he might have allied with Spain's non-Catholic enemies on the continent, perhaps even with the surging tide of Martin Luther's nascent Protestant movement, to surround Spain and conquer the whole of Europe. Islam would prevail over Christianity, Ottoman ecumenicalism over European intolerance. The voyages of Columbus and Vasco da Gama had catapulted northwest Africa from being a tucked-away corner of the Mediterranean to serving as the strategic hinge of a new transoceanic world. Morocco was one of the keys to global dominion in the sixteenth century.

WHILE STROLLING THROUGH THE palace gardens in Edirne, discussing invasion plans with his advisers, Selim sat down to relieve his sore back. Long hours standing tall on his horse while hunting often stiffened his joints. He assumed his back pain would be temporary, as it always had been, and that he would be fine after a little rest. He sat, stretched, and thought nothing of it. He asked to see the *mappamundi* again, and requested updates on the situation in Rhodes, which he still contemplated invading. As the Aztecs and the Spanish warred in Mexico that summer of 1520, Selim dined with his consorts in Edirne, enjoying the cool breezes of the lingering evenings.

In August, he consulted one of his physicians about the pain in his back, pain that now felt different from the usual ache, more "like the prick of a thorn." His chief physician, Hasan Can, found what looked like a pimple with a whitened tip, and prescribed an ointment. After a few days of treatment, the pain remained. Growing impatient and wanting immediate relief, Selim instructed a bath attendant to pop the pustule, softened by the warm steam. The attendant obeyed, causing Selim to writhe in intense pain. Over the following days, the agony continued; after a few weeks, his back became so painful that he could no longer ride a horse. Still, he kept up his normal schedule of council meetings, consulting with his advisers, and receiving foreign dignitaries and visitors.

Selim did his best to keep his excruciating pain a secret, yet rumors started to swirl. Word spread that his eyes began to yellow. Some speculated that the boil was in fact a plague bubo and that he was close to death; he could have contracted the disease during the 1518 outbreak in Istanbul, and moved to bucolic Edirne to recuperate rather than escape. No evidence exists to support this claim.

The empire's best doctors—an ecumenical group of Muslims, Jews, and Christians—traveled to Edirne from Istanbul. They debated the proper course of action, recommending rest and suggesting various topical solutions. Nothing worked; Selim's pain intensified. His personal physicians urged him, despite his growing weakness, to return to Istanbul, where he could receive better care. He agreed, but insisted that his procession back to the capital appear as normal as possible—a simple return to the palace. However, he was so wracked by pain that he had to be wheeled on a cart.

Inside his opulent tent and surrounded by a phalanx of advisers and soldiers, the sultan stayed hidden so that no subject of the empire could see him in this ignoble state. The procession stopped in Çorlu, the nondescript halfway point between Edirne and Istanbul, to allow him a respite from the ordeal of travel. The last time he was in Çorlu, he had been leading an army of irregulars against his father the sultan. Vigorous and violent then, he was now a debilitated man. Even the simple journey to Istanbul was proving too much for him, and so he rested in Çorlu, fading in and out of consciousness, barely strong enough to summon his physicians, closest advisers, and military men to his bedside. He kept his consorts away. When he ordered his men to recite the "Yā-Sīn" chapter of the Qur'an, they dutifully obeyed what would prove to be their sultan's final command. Selim mumbled the verses along with them, surely focusing his hazy thoughts on its lessons about the hereafter and resurrection. In that moment—though we of course cannot know for certain—perhaps Selim imagined Suleyman's reign as the empire's next sultan, or remembered his beloved mother's devotion to his own success; perhaps he recalled his despised father and his dead half-brothers; perhaps he ruminated on his unfulfilled dream of world domination. He closed his eyes. His advisers crouched over their frail and immobilized sovereign. They watched as Selim's chest moved up and down and his lips twitched.

And then, a few minutes later, only stillness. God's shadow had died.

SELIM DREW HIS LAST breath early in the morning of September 22, 1520, mere weeks before his fiftieth birthday. The cause of death was most likely plague, or perhaps anthrax contracted from his horse. A few months earlier, in June, the Aztec ruler Montezuma, whom Cortés described as a sultan, also died, probably at a similar age. Coming within months of each other, these two deaths could not have been more significant for the course of world history. Montezuma's demise allowed the Spanish to march on the Aztec capital, with the empire yielding to its final destruction the very next year, 1521. This opened the floodgates of European colonization in the New World. Had the Spanish lost to Montezuma, the last half-millennium of world history would have been quite different. Similarly, a victory for the Ottoman Empire in Morocco would have redirected global history onto a completely new trajectory. Selim's death forever quieted that possibility. His designs on Morocco, his Caribbean aspirations, his war against the Safavids, his grand plans for the Ottomans in China—all screeched to a halt. Ottoman soldiers held their secure position in Algeria. Selim's naval flotilla remained in port in western Greece. No Ottoman Morocco, no Ottoman unification of North Africa, no Islamic retaking of Spain, no Ottoman outpost on the Atlantic—and no *Vilayet Antilia*.

AS THE HALF-DOZEN OR SO advisers in Selim's tent in Çorlu prayed over their sultan's corpse, they resolved to keep his death a secret until they arrived in Istanbul. They held their regular council meeting on the day after his death and sent word through the encampment to prepare to march that afternoon. Careful to keep the body hidden, they resumed their procession to the capital as though nothing was out of the ordinary. Just before leaving Çorlu, however, they dispatched a single messenger to Manisa, swearing him to absolute secrecy, to inform Suleyman, still Selim's only son, of his father's death. Ideally, Suleyman would arrive in Istanbul and safely and completely possess the realm before news of his father's death spread. In this space between sultans, the longtime loyalists feared the disorder that might arise in a leaderless empire.

Selim's chief physician, Hasan Can, oversaw the several undertakers and corpse-washers who cleaned and readied the body for transport from Çorlu to Istanbul. He reported that, on two separate occasions during the washing of the body, Selim moved his right hand to cover his naked penis. Those who saw this miraculous event proclaimed their wonder and respect for Selim, praying to God for their sovereign's eternity. The apocryphal detail, clearly, was meant to testify to Selim's modesty, piety, and uprightness, and vouch for his dominion and power even in death. Given the dubiousness surrounding the legality of his accession to the throne, such a story was designed to attest to his eternal virtue.

Suleyman arrived at the imperial palace before his father's corpse. His advisers quickly put him in a boat that would ferry him north along the Golden Horn to the Mosque of Eyüp. An estuary whose waters have served as the economic and political hub of Istanbul since the seventh century BCE, the Golden Horn lies immediately north of the peninsula on which the palace stands, where the Bosphorus meets the Sea of Marmara. Eyüp, one of the Prophet Muhammad's companions, died on the shores of the Golden Horn in the 670s, during the first Arab siege of what was then still the Byzantine capital. Given Eyüp's personal connection to the Prophet, the mosque that was built around his tomb became sacred ground, and served as the traditional location of a sultan's coronation.

Suleyman did his best to project a sultanic bearing as he stepped onto the dock. The Venetian *bailo* described him that year, at the age of twenty-five, as "tall and slender but tough, with a thin and bony face. Facial hair is evident but only barely." A procession waited to honor him as he walked up to the mosque. Inside, a deep crimson carpet embroidered with a design of ornate blue flowers covered the floor. A dome—decorated with a design of white, blue, and red, even more ornate than the carpet beneath it—towered over the huge inner chamber. Gazing up at the dome, one was meant to feel something of heaven itself. Suleyman scanned this sanctum of inspiration and awe, and saw gathered there all of the imperial elite. He was escorted to one side of the open space, seized the sword of Osman that had been placed there for him, and thrust it high into the air. The assembled advisers, dignitaries, and secretaries bowed, declaring their allegiance to Suleyman as their sovereign.

The Ottoman Empire had its tenth sultan.

*Suleyman receiving dignitaries after his ascension to the throne*

WITH THE SYMBOLS OF imperial power now safely in Suleyman's hands—the first time in Ottoman history that succession had occurred without fraternal struggle, just as Selim had envisioned—the sultan's death was announced publicly. In Europe, the reaction was pure elation. The devil who had threatened Christian power in the western Mediterranean, the Balkans, and the Indian Ocean was no more. In Selim's place, they saw a coddled and untested young prince. Christian leaders knew Suleyman had been spared his father's constant wars, and they rejoiced at the prospect that an inexperienced military strategist was now the Ottoman sultan. As Paolo Giovio, one of the Medicis' official historians and author of *Life of Leo X*, as well as a book on the Ottoman Empire, wrote, "a furious lion had left a gentle lamb as his successor."

Within the empire, critics of Selim invested profound meaning in the fact that he died in Çorlu. This was the town where he had met his father in battle, beginning the armed antagonism that would lead to the unprecedented event of a son deposing his father. Even eight years later, many considered Selim's violent seizure of the Ottoman crown an illegitimate act. For them, Selim's death at the very site of his sultanate's original sin proved God's contempt for him; it was evidence of his rule's illegality and represented divine retribution for the evil he had invited into the empire.

When Janissary commanders and officers heard of Selim's death, many threw themselves on the ground in sorrow. He had been their stalwart patron. Some pounded their heads on the earth. As the news circulated, a somber mood spread through the empire's military corps. Coming to pay their respects to their deceased sovereign and to pledge their allegiance to their new sultan, "the army flowed into the capital like a silent river."

Commoners, too, mourned their departed ruler. Large crowds of onlookers, many doleful, some merely curious, assembled at the city's Edirne gate, waiting for Selim's body to arrive. When the procession reached the walls, the new sultan stood ready to receive his father's catafalque. With his mother, Hafsa, at his side, Suleyman kneeled by his father's coffin, weeping and proclaiming his love for him. As a show of respect, he helped to carry the bier during part of the funeral cortege through the city to the Fatih Mosque, where Selim would lie in rest near his grandfather, Mehmet II. For the man who had given him so much—perhaps more than any sultan ever gave a prince—Suleyman willingly humbled himself as a sign of his love, gratitude, and devotion, sentiments not often felt between Ottoman royals.

Given the brevity of his time on the throne, and the even shorter amount of time he had spent in Istanbul during those eight years, Selim never had the opportunity to build the sort of sprawling mosque complex for himself that most previous sultans had made sure to do during their reigns. This task thus fell to Suleyman. He commissioned a mosque complex for his father in one of the city's most resplendent locations—atop Istanbul's fifth hill, in the Fatih district. Climbing the steep hill up to the mosque, one is rewarded with a sweeping view of the historic Golden Horn, the Topkapı Palace, and most of the city. On the northeastern slope lies one of the city's largest Roman cisterns, the Cistern of Aspar. Selim's granite and marble mosque boasts a hemispheric dome flanked by two slender, pencil-shaped minarets.

*Selim's mosque*

Twenty-four smaller domes stand on a forest of columns in the courtyard outside. The complex also houses a school, a hospice, a garden, and
a platform from which one can take in the expansive view.

In 1528, Suleyman had Selim's coffin transferred from the Fatih
Mosque to the garden of the new mosque, in a small, private ceremony
attended by his mother, some of his children, and his closest advisers.
Still feeling vulnerable in the early years of his reign, Suleyman did
not want public attention devoted to his father, so there was no procession, no ritual mourning, no military ceremony. Selim was interred
in an octagonal mausoleum overlooking Topkapı Palace, as if to watch
over his descendants for the next four centuries. Ironically enough,
given his lifelong battle with the Safavids, Selim's eternal home was
adorned with tiles crafted by Iranian artisans then resident in the Ottoman Empire.

Almost six years later, on March 19, 1534, Hafsa died. Beloved
within the palace as well as outside of it, "torrents of tears . . . poured
forth when people learned of Hafsa's death." Selim's death had rendered
her legally free, and she became the first in a string of powerful mothers
who governed alongside their sultan sons. For more than forty years—
from her first administrative responsibilities in Trabzon in the 1490s to
her death in Istanbul—Hafsa played a vital role in the governance of

the empire. She was described as "the mother of the monarch, refuge of the world, the great woman whose whole work was piety, the [pure] woman whose every thought was good." She had given birth to Suleyman when she was fifteen, and her one son bore her "great reverence and love," as she had remained at his side throughout his life. Suleyman buried his mother next to Selim.

Extremely close to both his parents during their lives—but especially to his mother—Suleyman remained emotionally attached to them after their deaths. He regularly visited their tombs to pay his respects, reflect, and seek their spiritual advice and stewardship. He also stationed reciters of the Qur'an at their graves and oversaw several refurbishments of the complex during his forty-six-year reign.

IT WAS SULEYMAN WHO built his father's mosque complex, and Selim who erected the imperial infrastructure that allowed Suleyman to become one of the most significant sultans in Ottoman history. Beyond ensuring for his one son perhaps the easiest succession of any of the empire's thirty-six sultans, Selim laid the groundwork for Suleyman's successes through the immense territorial expansion he achieved. More than any other single factor, Selim's tripling of the size of the empire helps to explain the colossal effects of the Ottoman Empire on global history after 1517. Much of the magnificence ascribed to Suleyman's reign—the longest of any sultan—derived, in part or in whole, from the Ottomans' geographic supremacy. Suleyman took the throne as the first sultan to inherit a world empire.

Selim's imperial expansion thrust the Ottomans into the center of early modern diplomacy and led, in turn, to the creation of vast collections of foreign documentation about the empire, as powers across the world searched for ways to counter the Ottomans' gargantuan military might. Suleyman inherited this elevated global diplomatic influence. Indeed, one of the reasons historians have devoted so much attention to Suleyman is the existence of these sources, in addition to a long record of his correspondence with European and other powers, as well as clandestine reconnaissance reports produced mostly by the Venetians, who were as likely to barter in gossip as in spices and silks. Given that many of these documents are written in European languages and preserved in European libraries, they were some of the earliest accessible sources for

European historians writing about the Ottoman Empire—thus positioning Suleyman, more than Selim, at the center of Europe's expanding knowledge of the empire and its history.

The Venetian sources draw a contrast between the personalities of father and son. At the time of his ascension to the throne in 1520, Suleyman was, according to the Venetian *bailo*, "friendly and in good humor," a young man who "enjoys reading, is knowledgeable, and shows good judgement." This stands against the much more dour picture of Selim offered by the previous *bailo*: "He reflects constantly; no one dares to say anything, not even the pashas who are there with him; he governs alone, on the basis of his own thinking." Later, writing in the 1550s, the Italian historian Giovio, who had described Selim as a lion and Suleyman as a lamb, continued in this vein with the observation that Selim "shed more blood in his eight years of rule than Suleyman has in thirty." No doubt to counter skepticism about his military acumen and aggressive character—skepticism that clearly lingered throughout his reign, as Giovio's quip shows—Suleyman led two early and successful campaigns, seizing Belgrade in 1521 and Rhodes in 1522.

Taking over his father's empire, Suleyman could have been reckless or extravagant, more Nero than Augustus, and squandered his father's gains by allowing his territorial inheritance to dissipate. Instead, he defended the empire's recent acquisitions, converting most of them

*Suleyman's siege of Rhodes*

into permanent Ottoman holdings. In addition to his early successes in Belgrade and Rhodes, he scored major new victories, in Hungary at the Battle of Mohács in 1526 and in Iraq with the Peace of Amasya in 1555. He furthered his father's efforts in the Indian Ocean against the Portuguese and fought several long wars against the Safavids. He also continued, unsuccessfully, to push westward in North Africa; Morocco remained tantalizingly close but, as always, unattained. For the most part, though, Suleyman's "magnificence" derived from simply maintaining the territories his "grim" father had conquered.

More than Suleyman—more, in fact, than any of the other thirty-five sultans over the empire's six centuries—Selim molded the Ottoman Empire into a global political and military force. Indeed, as historian Leslie Peirce observes, "Some Ottoman pundits would later call Selim's reign a golden age." In the five hundred years since Selim cast his broad shadow across the world, the contours of today's Middle East and Mediterranean world largely remain those he set; the histories of the continents he united continue to follow paths he first cleared; and, sadly, the wars he started and led between his Sunni Ottomans and the Shiite Safavids have in some ways not ended. He, much more than Suleyman, was the most magnificent sultan in Ottoman history.

# DESCENDANTS

## *(After 1520)*

CHAPTER

24

# SELIM'S REFORMATIONS

*The four schools of Islamic law*

WHILE SELIM'S MOST IMMEDIATE DESCENDANTS WERE, OF
course, his one son, Suleyman, and his six daughters, we are all, in
geopolitical terms, his heirs. Today, the world's largest religions are
Christianity and Islam, with the two faiths claiming over half of the
earth's population. Selim's place in Islamic history is clear; less obvious is his fundamental importance to the history of Christianity, especially to the Reformation, that other event of global consequence that

began in 1517, the year Selim defeated the Mamluks. Only by fully recognizing the catalytic role of the Ottoman Empire in the Reformation's history—an influence usually overlooked or ignored—can this tectonic rift in Christianity be properly understood. As the sun rose in the east behind Selim's stocky frame, it cast his shadow over a small German town on the river Elbe named Wittenberg.

In the first quarter of the sixteenth century, as we have seen, the world's Muslim and Christian empires deliberately used religion to advance their political and ideological legitimacy. The Ottoman takeover of Mecca and Medina, the empire's transformation from a majority Christian state to a majority Muslim one, and Selim's union of sultanate and caliphate, all put Sunnism at the center of Ottoman imperial identity and weaponized it against the empire's non-Sunni foes. In turn, the Safavids fused Shiism to their state primarily to distinguish themselves from the Ottomans (and other Sunni Muslims) in their rivalry for hegemony in the Muslim world. Christian Europe, similarly, made being non-Catholic not simply a subordinate status but an enemy one. After having targeted Jews and Muslims, Catholics made other Christians enemies in Europe, Native Americans enemies in the Americas, pagans and Muslims enemies in West Africa, and Hindus enemies in India.

Selim's defeats of the Safavids and the Mamluks issued both a military and an ideological challenge to Europe. The Ottomans' massive expansion in the second decade of the sixteenth century raised the pressing question of why they were able to ascend so dramatically while European powers seemed unable to stop them. Some began to wonder whether Europe's comparative political and military weaknesses stemmed from moral failings; in an eschatological worldview, reversals of fortune were expressions of God's judgment. The fear that Ottoman armies provoked in Europe prompted existential introspection, sowing fertile ground for challenges to the entrenched social, religious, and political order.

By far the most extensive and consequential of these critiques came from a young German priest named Martin Luther, who had almost become a lawyer. Islam extended to Luther vital ideological ammunition for the rhetorical guns he pointed at the Catholic Church. In targeting the Church, Luther would regularly cite Europe's "Muslim other" in comparison. Usefully for Luther, the sultan—first Selim, then Suleyman—offered a potent means to critique the Medici-born Pope

Leo X, whose moral depravity was, he suggested, what had enabled the Ottomans to spread Islam around the world. In Luther's final analysis, the evils of the pope always exceeded the evils of the sultan.

While Luther unfailingly viewed the Ottomans as enemies, and Muslims as unbelievers, still he sought to understand them. He wrote reams about the Ottomans, whom he always referred to as "the Turks." He studied Islam deeply, and even contemplated sponsoring the first German translation of the Qur'an. Many Islamic concepts, as we will see, would influence his own notions of religion. As one scholar explains it, "the 'terrible Turk' and his religion lurks in the shadows throughout all of Luther's life."

IMMEDIATELY AFTER THE OTTOMAN defeat of the Safavids in 1514, Leo X called for a new Crusade. Ever since the fall of Constantinople in 1453, any victory that expanded Ottoman power—even one far removed from Europe—had sparked concern, because an increase in Ottoman strength amplified the threat the empire posed to Europe. (Recall that, at the end of the fifteenth century, Venice had sought an anti-Ottoman alliance with the Ak Koyunlu Confederacy of eastern Anatolia and the Caucasus.) Selim's victories over the Mamluks in 1516 and 1517—news of which spread like fire in European capitals through a network of spies, diplomats, and envoys—sent an even stronger shock wave through the continent. Though Catholic Europe had been organizing, or planning to organize, Crusades against the Muslim world for centuries, there had been no serious military confrontation for several decades. The balance of power had shifted so massively to the side of the Ottomans that it deterred European rulers from any thought of sending troops against them. Indeed, apart from a small war in Belgrade in 1456, Europe had not led a major Crusade against Islam since 1453, when the loss of Constantinople all but required a European response—and that, even so, was more bluster than reality. Thus, between 1453 and 1517, Ottoman power in the Mediterranean was able to expand essentially unchecked.

In this age of the Renaissance, Europeans focused more on the Ottomans than they did on the rediscovery of the classics, architectural adornment, or the artistic perfection of the human form. As one of the foremost historians of the Renaissance, James Hankins, again reminds us, "The humanists wrote far more often and at far greater length about the Turkish menace and the need for crusade than they did about such better-known humanist themes as true nobility, liberal education, the dignity of man, or the immortality of the soul." "The bulk of humanist crusading literature," he continues, "begins only after the fall of Constantinople in 1453." The volume of work in this genre multiplied after major Ottoman victories such as the capture of Otranto in southern Italy in 1480, peaking with Selim's conquests of 1516 and 1517. It subsided in 1571 with the epic Battle of Lepanto in the Ionian Sea, one of Europe's few sixteenth-century victories against the Ottomans, immortalized in Shakespeare's *Othello* and later in Verdi's opera based on the play.

Christianity had never been so impotent. For Pope Leo and the Catholic Church, weakness soon morphed into panic and then outright hysteria. All sorts of rumors about the Ottomans and their potential military advances swirled through the Vatican. Vatican spies reported, for example, that Selim was reading the life of Alexander the Great for inspiration and direction. As the new Alexander, Selim seemed poised to unite the two Romes under the Ottoman crescent—a clear, if fantastical, end-of-days scenario for Christendom. In April 1516, several reports claimed that twenty-seven Ottoman ships had arrived off the coast of Civitavecchia, a port city near Rome with a recently completed defensive garrison, spurring a petrified Leo to flee the Vatican. No evidence exists to corroborate this purported sighting, and, given the Ottoman war effort in Syria that spring, it seems unlikely. In early 1517, at the very moment when Selim was entering Cairo, Leo interpreted lightning storms over Rome as an omen of impending doom. And, a few months later, just after the Mamluk conquest was completed, another forty Ottoman ships (almost certainly misidentified) were reportedly seen sailing through the Strait of Bonifacio, between Corsica and Sardinia. Thus, as the Ottomans occupied ever more territory around the Mediterranean, they occupied ever more of the European imagination.

In early 1518, Pope Leo, famous for his chubby cheeks and sagging chin, wrote again to European rulers—as he had done unsuccessfully after Selim's victory over the Safavids at Chaldiran nearly four years earlier—inviting them to unify in a new Crusade against the Ottomans. He sent cardinals to England, France, Spain, and the Holy Roman Empire, seeking a five-year truce among the European powers that would allow them to direct all of their energies against the Ottoman threat. As in 1514, he found no willing allies. The European monarchs preferred to plan wars against one another than to consider a huge, expensive, and potentially suicidal confrontation with their daunting adversary to the east, which had only become more powerful during the intervening years. Charles V of the Holy Roman Empire and Francis I of France were rivals; the Italian Wars at the turn of the sixteenth century had killed thousands; succession conflicts roiled Castile, Scotland, and Bavaria; and most European rulers despised Leo—who treated the papacy as his to enjoy—and hoped eventually to invade and capture Italy for themselves. In stark contrast to the mosaic of squabbling polities that was Europe, the Ottoman Empire ruled across three continents as a unified juggernaut. As the pope wrote to one of his bishops, "While we waste time in negotiating and writing, the Turk spends it in getting to work and putting his plans into effect, and he will have taken some Christian port before we have the news that he has even set out!" Even though Leo would continue to renew his calls for Crusade until Selim's death in 1520, European unity against what he termed "the diabolic Mohammedan rage" never materialized.

This same political stasis, which prevented Europe from even considering military action against the Ottomans, is what allowed an upstart like Luther to flourish without the vestige of a response to what would become an existential challenge to Europe's prevailing order. As the scholar Egil Grislis explains the contemporary political scene, "Instead of fearing the Turks, Luther had every reason to be grateful to them. It was the constant danger of a Turkish invasion that had kept the [Holy Roman] Emperor from taking severe measures against Luther's reformation. The empire needed the help of the Evangelical princes in the war against the Turks and therefore had to postpone its plans to destroy Luther. From the point of view of realistic power politics, the safety of the Reformation depended upon the strength of the Turkish armies." Europe's territorial fracture only substantiated Luther's charges about the Church's corruption, and made his message about the need for reform more exigent. Without the looming threat of the

# THE FURTHER FRAGMENTATION OF EUROPE AFTER 1517

Roman Catholic

Mixed Catholic and Protestant

Lutheran

Muslim

Calvinist

Eastern Orthodox

Shifting allegiance

Anglican

**NORWAY**

**SWEDEN**
Göteborg

SCOTLAND
Edinburgh

*NORTH SEA*

Aalborg
**DENMARK**
Copenhagen

*BALTIC SEA*

Hull
Chester
**ENGLAND**
WALES
Bristol  London
Southampton

**POMERANIA**
Danzi
Stettin
**MECKLEN-BURG**
Hamburg
Bremen
**BRANDENBURG**
Berlin
Magdeburg  Wittenberg
Leipzig  Dresden
**SAXONY**

**POLAN**

Bruges  Antwerp
Brussels  Cologne
Münster

Frankfurt
Worms  Nuremberg
**BOHEMIA**
Prague
Krakow

Paris
Strasbourg
Ulm
**BAVARIA**
Augsburg
Munich  Salzburg  Vienna
**AUSTRIA**

Nantes
**FRANCE**
La Rochelle

Basel
**SWISS CONFEDERACY**

**HUNGAR**
Mol

Lyon
**SAVOY**
Milan
**MILAN**
Venice
**VENICE**
Zagreb
Belgr

Bayonne
Aigues-Mortes
Marseille
Genoa
**PAPAL STATES**
Florence
Pisa
Spoleto
Ragusa
(Dubrovnik)
Cattaro
Durazzo
**OTTOM.EMPIR**

**SPAIN**
Barcelona
Valencia
Palma
Ajaccio
Rome

Murcia
Cagliari
**KINGDOM OF NAPLES**
Naples

Almería  Algiers
Oran  Tenes  Bone  Tabarca  Tunis
*MEDITERRANEAN SEA*
Palermo

Mahdia

*A generalized representati of the evolving confession situation in the middle deca of the sixteenth century*

0  MILES  200
0  KM  200
N
W  E
S

Ottomans, the great sweep of the Protestant Reformation would not have been possible.

※

IN 1516, AS SELIM was marching into Syria, the pontiff dispatched "an undistinguished Dominican" friar named Johann Tetzel to Germany to sell indulgences to support construction work on the imposingly ornate St. Peter's Basilica. Tetzel's pithy sales pitch became famous: "as soon as the coin in the coffer rings, the soul from purgatory springs." At the time, such purchases of absolution were almost de rigueur, but Martin Luther, then a thirty-three-year-old devout Augustinian monk and priest, started to voice extreme discomfort with the idea that blessings and forgiveness, which doctrine decreed were bestowed by God for a lifetime of good works, could be bought by a sinful human—or that sinful human's descendant—in an instant. It further disturbed him that the worldly lavishness, if not debauchery, that he saw in St. Peter's and throughout Europe's churches was apparently being subsidized by the promised absolution of the spirits of individual parishioners.

This entrenched practice would be at the center of Martin Luther's writings against the Church. Interestingly, it, too, was fueled by the fight against Islam. The idea of indulgences arose in the twelfth century, at the height of the Crusades. Before Crusaders left their homes to battle Muslims in the Middle East, priests would guarantee them absolution of their sins in advance, in case they died while fighting for the liberation of Jerusalem. Instead of financial compensation, these promises of salvation served as the soldiers' reward for their bravery in the Holy Land—thus establishing the principle that redemption could be won by something other than piety. From these origins, indulgences ballooned into a commodity that flooded the Church's coffers with cash. By Luther's time, individuals could simply pay the Church—no warring required—for the forgiveness of ordinary sins such as lying or lust. Like checking a price list in a butcher's shop, a believer could find his sin on the ledger and pay the going rate to have it excised from his worldly and, he would hope, eternal life. Even setting aside the rise of the Ottomans, then, the sale of indulgences tied Islam to the birth of the Protestant Reformation.

In 1517, Luther outlined his concerns about indulgences and other Church practices in a letter he sent to his bishop. This letter, which came to be known as the 95 *Theses*, is the familiar story of the beginning of the Protestant Reformation. Quickly translated from Latin into German and printed on one of the earliest printing presses in Europe, it was distributed widely across Germany. (It was almost certainly never posted on the door of the church of Wittenberg, as is commonly thought.) Within a month, Luther's strident critique of Leo and the Catholic Church had been further translated from German into several other European languages and was forging its way across the continent, creating nothing less than a theological tempest.

One of Luther's most blistering denunciations of the Church centered on Pope Leo's calls for a new Crusade. In large measure because of its long association with indulgences, Luther viewed the Church's history of Crusading as part of Catholicism's web of corruption and its vile obsession with worldly things. A focus on warfare betrayed an obsession with flesh rather than soul, with this world rather than the next. The Church had often waged Crusades, he observed, for no other reason than to make money, building its campaigns for holy war on foundations of false threats and greed rather than a pious desire to defend the faith and flock.

*Martin Luther*

Luther expressed his opposition to Europe's holy wars in the theological terms most familiar to him: "The 'big wheels' of the church, now dream of nothing else than war against the Turk. They want to fight, not against iniquities, but against the lash of iniquity and thus they would oppose God who says that through that lash he himself punishes us for our iniquities because we do not punish ourselves for them." The Ottomans, in Luther's view, were God's "lash of iniquity," which he used to punish Christendom for its sins—sins that Church leaders willfully ignored, even encouraged, by allowing absolution to be so cheaply bought.

Thus, even though Luther clearly regarded the Ottomans as evil—God, he explained, sometimes "punished pious people by evil men"—at that moment the Ottomans, in his formulation, represented Christians' "best helpers." They—unwittingly—motivated Christians to improve and refine their spiritual lives; in their absence, God would have used some other calamity as his instrument. Christians themselves—not the Ottomans—were Christianity's true problem. Christians should therefore recognize and willingly accept the challenging opportunity God offered them in the shape of the Ottoman threat. Only if the Church overcame its sins would God drop the Ottoman lash.

"Since the devil is a spirit, he cannot be overcome with armor, rifle, horse," wrote Luther, in a criticism of the pope's call for Crusade. Only spirit could overcome spirit. And, "since the Turk is the wrathful rod of our Lord God and the servant of the raging devil, it is necessary first of all to overcome the devil himself, the Lord of the Turks, and thus to take the rod out of God's hand. Without the devil's help and God's support the Turk will remain alone in his power." The way to establish peace and security, then, as Luther saw it, was not war against the Ottomans but a struggle *within* Christendom against its *own* sins. If Europe's Christians, each and every one, cleansed themselves of sin, God would no longer need the whip of the Ottomans to chastise them, and the Muslim empire would therefore dissolve from the earth, allowing a purified Christendom to triumph.

The space the Ottomans opened up in Europe by weakening the Catholic Church thus allowed individual Christians to flourish in their personal faith and Luther to extend the reach of his teachings. Islam, in Luther's view, served Christianity in threatening it. For the true believer, Islam was a tool which could be used to root out the corruption in Catholicism.

⸜⸝

LUTHER RESERVED HIS MOST virulent attacks for Pope Leo himself. "In the East rules the Beast," he offered, "in the West the False Prophet." Both figures presaged the end-times. "After the Turks," Luther suggested, "the Last Judgement follows quickly."

A state, a religion, a community, will always face external enemies; standing up to the heathens who persecuted Christianity from without was of course necessary and laudable. More sinister, because more difficult to recognize, was the enemy inside the gates—the one who looked like you, the one you knew, your own religious kin. Thus, the bankrupt pope always proved far more dangerous than the sultan. As Egil Grislis puts it, quoting Luther, "The Turk is the 'black devil,' rude and superficial, incapable of deceiving either faith or reason, 'who like a heathen persecutes Christianity from without.' The pope, by contrast, is 'the subtle, beautiful, hypocritical devil who sits within Christianity and retains the Holy Scripture, baptism, sacrament, the keys, catechism, marriage.'" As the Safavids were to the Ottomans, the deadliest foe was one's brother in faith, who seemed to act like you, even pray like you, but whose tenets were corrupted by corrosive wickedness and the desire for earthly power.

Instead of upholding the right and good of the faith, Luther insisted, the hypocritical Pope Leo had allowed evil to infect the Church. In the gloomy halls of the Vatican, the Catholic elite pretended to be pious and pure while engaging in one abomination after another. This failure of the pope's spirit, Luther felt, explained the Catholic body politic's weakness against the Ottomans. "The pope kills the soul," he wrote, "while the Turk can only destroy the body." Assigning Islam to the bodily, and hence fleeting, realm of this world, Luther in this passage partakes of the long Christian obsession with the supposedly lecherous sexuality of Muhammad—that "due to his lust, whatever he speaks or does is flesh, flesh, flesh"—and then uses Islam's asserted base corporeality to again castigate the hypocrisy of the Catholic Church: "The coarse and filthy Muḥammad takes all women and therefore has no wife. The chaste pope does not take any wife and yet has all women."

This core conceptual dyad of body and soul, flesh and spirit, also shaped one of Luther's other central fixations with Islam—the fate of European Christians captured by the Ottomans. He erroneously believed that the Ottomans wanted to forcibly convert *all* Christians to Islam—which, as we have seen, was never the case. Luther either did not know or did not care that the empire's population had become majority-Muslim only in 1517, after over two centuries of being a majority-Christian society. A Christian living happily, even willingly, under Muslim rule must have been inconceivable for him. He thus ignored Ottoman Christians—the various Orthodox denominations, Armenians, Chaldeans, and others living in the Balkans and the Middle East—in his thinking about Christianity in the empire.

There were two classes of European Christians in the Ottoman Empire that primarily concerned Luther: the Christian boys of the *devşirme* who had been captured in the Balkans and forcibly converted to Islam, then given every luxury while being groomed for the upper echelons of the imperial military; and Christians seized as slaves in warfare or through piracy who remained unfree, received no privileges, and represented a ready source of labor, mostly as oarsmen in war galleys.

The phenomenon of the *devşirme* raised particularly vexing concerns for some Europeans and presented Luther with a theological puzzle. If a European soldier killed an Ottoman soldier of *devşirme* origins, was he in fact killing one of Christendom's own? Even if they presented themselves as outwardly Muslim to survive, perhaps some of these Ottoman soldiers remained true Christians in their souls (an interesting parallel to Christian understandings of Jewish and Muslim conversion during the Inquisition). Luther assuaged such fears by insisting that even if, as a survival tactic, a Christian supposedly converted to Islam in flesh alone—itself a proposition of dubious possibility, in a Catholic worldview—taking up arms against true Christians represented the complete corruption of the soul and forever sealed the former Christian's fate in hell.

Luther urged those other European Christians seized by the Ottomans—combatants or civilians captured in war, never converted, and condemned to menial labor—to view their enslavement as God's rod of punishment, which they should willingly accept as a means of spiritual improvement. The slave should, in Luther's words, "as faithfully and diligently as possible, serve his lord to whom he has been sold, regardless of the fact that you are a Christian and your lord a heathen or a Turk." The Ottoman master could torture the body, rape, and break bones, but as long as the soul within that accursed body remained pure and faithful, the Ottoman devil would always lose. Such reasoning also applied to the other major class of Christian slaves in the Ottoman Empire, European women in Ottoman harems. "If the married women have been led away to Turkey, and must live with other men both as to bed and board," Luther wrote, "they must patiently submit and suffer for the sake of Christ, and for this reason not despair, as if they were damned. The soul can do nothing about what the enemy does to the body." In fact, the pain inflicted on the body would help to cleanse the believer's soul. In Luther's theology—and later, as one of the core tenets of Protestantism—worldly poverty led to heavenly riches. Thus, the converted Christian soldiers of the *devşirme* who were comparatively privileged on earth would deservedly receive everlasting damnation, while lowly Christian galley slaves and unfree concubines could, by piously accepting their suffering, earn eternal life.

IN HIS COPIOUS WORKS on the Ottomans and Islam generally, Luther developed a much more nuanced view of Muslims than has generally been appreciated. Indeed, he recognized several meaningful affinities between his own evolving philosophy and Islam. Perhaps the most powerful derived from his and Islam's shared commitment to iconoclasm. Of Muslims, he wrote, "They reject all images and pictures, and render homage to God alone." He had greater respect for Islam's singular focus on the "one only God" and its emphasis on the spirit of worship than he had for Catholicism's obsession with paintings, gilded decoration, and the lavish accoutrements of its clerical elite.

Luther saw a further formal similarity between his eventual Protestantism and Islam in their mutual anathema to strict ecclesiastical hierarchy. Religious bureaucracies, he believed, bred the venality, bribery, and political intrigue that so plagued the Catholic Church. Even more nefarious, averred Luther, was the Church's insistence on acting as a mediator in the relationship between the individual believer and God. The Church's officially sanctioned explanations of God's message prevented people from developing a direct relationship with the divine, prevented them from personally knowing God. Luther believed that each reader or hearer of scripture had the capacity—indeed, the obligation—to interpret God's word personally. No human held a monopoly over the interpretation of God's message, he contended, and therefore no human should command authority over another in his spiritual communion with God.

In this regard, Luther saw much to admire in Islam. Neither Protestantism nor Islam upholds a figure such as a pope or a body like the council of bishops; the institutions of those faiths exist to aid the believer in his life of piety and prayer, not to direct it. In Islam, even though learned men and respected theologians offer elucidations of the Qur'an, every individual is free to deduce from the text and other authoritative sources whatever he or she understands to be the truth. Obviously, not everything is deemed acceptable textual exegesis—and some readings are judged incorrect or sinful by the majority of Muslims. Still, like Protestantism, Islam upholds the ideal of freedom of individual interpretation, and no religious authority outlaws divergent readings of sacred texts. Indeed, such openness to, and even support of, differential analyses of the Islamic canon explains the extensive disagreements and contradictory points of view that permeate the voluminous writings of the tradition. In both Protestantism and Islam, doctrine exists to support interpretation—not the reverse, as in Catholicism.

Luther's assessments of the Ottomans and Islam—both positive and negative—thus ultimately reinforced his views about the irreparable error into which the Catholic Church had fallen, and his personal mission of reform. Even as the Ottomans persisted in capturing, converting, and killing European Christians, Luther saw the papacy as Christianity's greatest enemy, the insidious channel of corruption that had allowed the evil of the Ottomans to flourish in the first place.

❈

SELIM LED THE OTTOMAN EMPIRE along a similar set of dual paths, as he amplified the importance of personal piety while at the same time reformulating his society's religious institutions. His conquests of 1516 and 1517 not only made his empire a majority-Muslim state for the first time in its history, they also delivered to the Ottomans cities—including Aleppo, Damascus, Cairo, Jerusalem, Mecca, and Medina—with long and proud traditions of Muslim culture and learning. These ancient cities housed the Muslim world's most significant institutions—the mosques of Mecca and Medina, al-Azhar in Cairo, and the Dome of the Rock in Jerusalem, to name only a few—and thus challenged the Ottomans to demonstrate their own piety. Having seized mostly Christian territories to this point, and having included so many converted Christians in their imperial administration, the Ottomans, even as conquerors, had to prove their Islamic credentials if they wanted to win the loyalty of their new and mostly Arab Muslim populations.

By becoming caliph almost overnight in 1517, Selim faced the profound challenge of being the foremost defender of the faith. Embracing this new imperative, he responded swiftly by becoming more visibly Islamic in his person and actions—through his dress, his insistence on the use of the title caliph as coequal with sultan, and his patronage of religious sites, for example. At the same time, he remade one of the most widespread, centrally organized religious institutions in the Muslim world, the Islamic court system. These courts, already situated in nearly every major neighborhood of every city and small town of the empire, were extremely effective and highly visible imperial outposts, the most immediate interface between the empire and its subjects.

Muslim political authorities—in a structure somewhat akin to the American legal system—appointed judges and oversaw the function of these courts. *Sharia*—the unified body of Islamic legal prescripts that began to be formed during the Prophet's lifetime and was largely codified in Islam's first two centuries—served, in theory at least, as the basis of the rule of law. Because *sharia* was so vast and complex a corpus of legal knowledge and practice, it afforded judges enormous flexibility in exercising their personal judgment; rulings often had only the thinnest of connections to *sharia*. Thus, for centuries before 1517, local judges had exercised largely autonomous and individualized control, essentially independent of state power, based on their own interpretation of *sharia* as well as on traditional practices, legal precedent, and sometimes even coercion.

After 1517, Selim revolutionized this system, unifying under a more formal administration the network of courts spread out across both the old Ottoman Empire and the vast territories he had just conquered from the Mamluks. Decades earlier, as governor of Trabzon, he had accomplished something similar, on a much smaller scale. By expanding the administrative purview and governing capacities of the courts, he converted them into strong projections of state power, transforming institutions that were, in theory, upholders of *sharia* law into secular bodies of governance that dealt with a wide range of issues often having little to do with Islamic law. Like Luther in his attempt to reform the Catholic Church, Selim aimed to make the institution of the Islamic law court a social body that served people's everyday needs.

With his promulgation of a new imperial legal code, Selim secularized the courts to make them more accessible and relevant. Serving multiple functions, they now combined the roles of a local public records office, a police station, a forum for public shaming, and an agency for dispute resolution. Recast almost as Ottoman embassies in nearly every urban district and rural locale throughout the empire, the courts helped to win over newly conquered populations—Jews and Christians as well as Muslims—by steadily demonstrating that the Ottomans' imperial presence could improve the material and personal conditions of their daily lives. In court, one could protect major assets, adjudicate an estate, accuse a spouse of adultery, or register the costs of a new construction project. Above all, Selim's reforms allowed Ottoman subjects, for the first time, to create permanent and protected public records of their local community's affairs that they could summon during a later dispute or otherwise reference when needed. Thus, the courts came to serve as valuable repositories of communal history and memory.

Contrary to popular thinking and both recent and older assertions otherwise—by writers such as Salman Rushdie, Thomas Friedman, and Ayaan Hirsi Ali (many of whom, conveniently, are either Muslims or ex-Muslims)—Islam did in fact undergo a reformation. Selim's Islamic Reformation formulated new ways for Islam and Islamic institutions to function in a changing world. Because of the unique status he had earned for himself, Selim was the only ruler capable of leading such a program of reform, the only Muslim monarch able to adapt the civilization and institutions of Islam to stand as universal principles of governance. His retooling of the court system for worldly rule represented one of the most monumental administrative reforms ever undertaken in Islamic history, one that positioned the Ottomans at the center of a global movement of religious reformation in the early sixteenth century.

IT IS NO COINCIDENCE that Martin Luther and Sultan Selim embarked upon major reforms of their religious cultures almost simultaneously.

Both agendas were responses to the same set of global exigencies. Moreover, what each man did shaped the thoughts and actions of the other, as if in musical counterpoint. The Ottoman Empire's military successes revealed Christian weakness and exposed the corruption of its ideology; in turn, the apocalyptic fervor of the imperial rivalries of the early sixteenth century pushed the Ottomans to define themselves more vigorously and directly as the vanguard of global Islam after 1517. Luther saw affinities between his own ideas and Islam; Selim and his successors saw in the Protestant Reformation a further rift in Europe that they could exploit to their advantage. The splintering of Christendom that resulted from the increasingly violent Protestant–Catholic conflict allowed the Ottomans, under Suleyman, to win massive territorial gains, especially in southeastern Europe. Thus, even as professed ideological enemies, Luther's Christians and Selim's Muslims ultimately marched in synchronicity toward their religious reformations, each ever-mindful of the other.

As Selim and Luther sought to remake older religious institutions into practical bodies that served the needs and interests of the individuals in their charge, each fought an internecine battle that forced him to define and defend his own vision of society and the world, as well as to argue vociferously for why it should triumph over the rival worldview. All the aspirants in this struggle for world domination— Selim and Luther and their corresponding enemies, the Safavids and the Catholic Church—developed ideas of universality and proclaimed themselves the sole sovereign power that would rule the globe after the end-times. Sunnis and Shiites and Protestants and Catholics all fused religion to politics, making their wars not only about empire but also about eternity. The Ottomans, however, were singular among these states, because they *initiated* this political and religious struggle for world domination—winning territory that led their enemies to predict that the ultimate battle was nigh, proving the bankruptcy of the supposed divinity of various imperial rulers, and challenging the notion that God was on the side of anyone other than themselves.

Many Muslims today ignore the fact, or simply do not know, that Sultan Selim led a reformation in Islam almost half a millennium ago. Similarly, though the world's Protestants may not recognize or accept it, their history and success owe a major debt to the Ottoman Empire.

# AMERICAN SELIM

*John Smith's map of Virginia, with his coat of arms depicting three
severed Turkish heads*

SEEING THE HISTORY OF THE AMERICAS IN THE LIGHT OF THE RISE
of the Ottoman Empire offers an alternative narrative to the dominant
interpretation, which pretends that Islam played no role in Europe's
expansion to the New World. As we have seen, Columbus was a man
of his time, driven by the zeal of Crusade, as was his patron, Queen Isabella; and the Spanish, obsessed by the threat of Islam, imported those

fears to the New World. The notion of Islam as a specter looming over the New World has—most often, quite irrationally—coursed through the history of the Americas in an unbroken line from the period of Spanish colonization to the present day. No group has been vilified for longer in the Americas than Muslims.

⁂

AS EVERY SCHOOLCHILD LEARNS, Columbus set sail with India on his mind's horizon. Rarely, though, do schoolchildren learn *why* Columbus sought to cross the Atlantic. Hoping for an alliance with the Grand Khan of the East, he aimed to retake Jerusalem and destroy Islam; more prosaically, his voyages promised an end run around the trade monopolies of the Ottomans and the Mamluks. And when Columbus arrived in the Americas, fresh from the battle which marked Spain's final defeat of the Muslim kingdom of Granada, he saw—or, more accurately, imagined—Muslims everywhere. Spanish conquistadors would claim to see mosques in Mexico, American Indians wearing "Moorish" clothing and performing "Moorish" dances, Turks invading New Spain from the Pacific, and West African slaves attempting to convert America's indigenous peoples to Islam. Filtering their experiences in the Americas through the lens of their wars with Muslims, Europeans in the New World engaged in a new version of their very old Crusades, a new kind of Catholic *jihad*. Long after the many Matamoros—Moor-slayers—who sailed to the Americas aboard Columbus's ships were dead themselves, Islam would continue to forge the histories of both Europe and the New World and the relationship between the two.

On either side of the unambiguous watershed represented by the year 1492, Islam endured as Europe's primary obsession, its perennial rival and major cultural "other"—a spur of innovative historical change as well as an enemy on the battlefield. Throughout the seventeenth century and into the eighteenth, Europe remained far more concerned about the Ottomans and Islam than about the lands across the Atlantic. Remarkable, in fact, is the apparent *lack* of interest in the Americas among most Europeans. Spain's Charles V, for example—the leader most responsible for his empire's enormous expansion in the New World—uttered not a word about the Americas in his memoirs. What obsessed him were the Ottoman advances in Europe and his fears about the growing weakness of Christianity vis-à-vis Islam. Sixteenth-century France produced twice as many books about Islam as it did about the Americas and Africa combined. Overall, between 1480 and 1609, Europe published four times more works about the Muslim world than about the Americas. This disparity only increased over the course of the seventeenth century.

Following the lead of their Spanish predecessors in the New World, the British a century later initially understood American Indians through their own history of encounters with Muslims in Europe and the Mediterranean. Before it ever set sail across the Atlantic, that quintessential symbol of British arrival in North America, the *Mayflower*, had begun its seafaring life trading with Muslims in the Mediterranean. And before he crossed the Atlantic, John Smith, the founder of Jamestown in 1607, spent several swashbuckling years helping to beat back the Ottomans in Hungary and Wallachia (now part of Romania). The Ottomans captured him in 1602 and held him enslaved for two years before he managed to escape. Later, when he became Admiral of New England, Smith named three islands across from Cape Cod "the three Turkes heads," and he dubbed what is today Cape Ann "Cape Tragabigzanda," after a young woman with whom he had fallen in love while serving her family as a slave. Smith's personal coat of arms—like the one Melchor de Castro drew up after the 1521 Wolof Rebellion in Hispaniola—featured the severed heads of three Turks he had supposedly killed while fighting in eastern Europe. "The lamentable noise of the miserable slaughtered Turkes," he wrote, "was most wonderfull to heare." In addition to his account of his travels around the Mediterranean and works on Virginia and New England, Smith produced the first map of Virginia, with his coat of arms proudly displayed in the bottom right corner. Thus, more than a century after Piri Reis drew the first world map to join the Americas to the Old World, the Ottomans appeared yet again—in very different circumstances—on one of the first maps of North America. Beneath the three heads on his crest, Smith emblazoned his favorite Latin dictum: *Vincere est vivere* (To conquer is to live).

And conquer Smith most certainly did. He would soon add hundreds of Indian heads to his gruesome tally from the Old World. Like the Spanish conquistadors, Smith and countless other Englishmen who arrived to fight in America had already battled, traded with, or otherwise engaged the Ottomans and other Muslims in the Mediterranean. William Strachey, Virginia's secretary, had spent time in Istanbul a few years before going to Jamestown, and George Sandys, eventually the colony's treasurer, had traveled extensively throughout the Ottoman Empire—to Istanbul, Jerusalem, and Egypt—and had written a best-selling account of his adventures. Although one might assume they would have known better, these Britons repeated Spanish assertions from a century earlier about Muslim connections across the Atlantic— for example, again, that Native American dancing somehow had roots in Old World Muslim dances. They also filtered their understanding of the New World through their earlier personal experiences. Strachey drew parallels between Indian deerskin leggings and "the fashion of the Turkes." Smith wrote, "If any great commander arrive at the habitation of a Werowance [chief], they spread a mat as the Turkes do a carpet for him to sit upon."

The Ottoman Empire affected the English colonization of America in other ways as well. In the seventeenth century, many of the thousands of English Protestants who crossed the ocean would cite two evils as the reasons for their flight: the injustices and discrimination of their Catholic coreligionists and the scourge of the Muslim Ottomans. In 1621, for instance, Robert Cushman, a passenger on the *Mayflower*, wrote of the promise of America as a refuge from an Old World then in the grip of the Protestant–Catholic Thirty Years' War: "If it should please God to punish his people in the Christian countries of Europe, for their coldness, carnality, wanton abuse of the Gospel, contention, &c., either by Turkish slavery, or by popish tyranny, (which God forbid) . . . here is a way opened for such as have wings to fly into this wilderness." As Luther had done at the very start of the Protestant Reformation, Cushman here speaks simultaneously of two enemies: pope and sultan. Persecuted by papal tiara and sultanic turban, he saw America as his salvation from both.

The road to that salvation was not straightforward. Only after a century or so of abysmal living conditions, rampant death, few profits, and apparently only a fleeting possibility of permanent settlement in the Americas, did the English succeed in making some small territorial gains. Some even began to turn a profit along the western Atlantic coast. Though Native Americans were frequently—understandably— hostile to the settlers, negotiation eventually proved possible, and what settlers could not accomplish through these means they attained by subjugating those whose land they felt entitled to take by virtue of their superiority as Christians. Slow though the progress of these fledgling colonies was, when juxtaposed with their ongoing skirmishes with the Ottoman Empire and Barbary pirates in North Africa, the English experience in North America was, by the end of the seventeenth century, beginning to look like a resounding success.

In the course of that century, North Africa remained the primary locale of England's overseas operations. With its storied riches of gold, slaves, and spices, North Africa attracted more English adventurers in the seventeenth century than North America did. Some of these adventurers succeeded in earning handsome profits, but many more succumbed to the entrenched power of North Africa's numerous independent sovereigns and pirate captains. Barbary pirates regularly captured English ships in the Mediterranean and eastern Atlantic (many of them sailing to and from the Americas) and enslaved those on board. Indeed, by the end of the seventeenth century, there were more enslaved Englishmen in North Africa than free ones in North America. "Conquerors in Virginia, they were slaves in Algiers," as the scholar Nabil Matar nicely summarizes.

In 1699, the infamous Puritan minister Cotton Mather bemoaned the fate of those prospective New England settlers taken into North African slavery. "God hath given up several of our Sons, into the Hands of the Fierce Monsters of Africa. Mahometan Turks and Moors, and Devils are at this day oppressing many of our Sons, with a Slavery, wherein they Wish for Death, and cannot find it." Mather—a slaveholder himself—thus drew a direct line between the English colonial project he represented in America and the Muslims of the Mediterranean. At the same time that he attacked North African slavery, he expressed no qualms about—and, in fact, encouraged—the American and English enslavement of African Muslims and non-Muslims. Moreover, Mather believed it was the duty of all Christians to contribute to the annihilation of the Ottoman Empire, in order to precipitate the restoration of the Kingdom of Israel in Palestine, a vital prerequisite for the second coming of Christ.

By the beginning of the eighteenth century, the conquest of North America would stand as the ultimate model of English colonial warfare. Given their divergent fortunes in their two main theaters of war, success in Virginia and New England made it easier for the English to abandon their largely failed efforts at commerce and settlement in

North Africa. They would, however, return in the early nineteenth century to colonize parts of the Middle East. When the Ottomans pushed Europe out of the Mediterranean around 1500, they obviously had no inkling of the violent fury with which it would one day return.

⊠

THIS TRANSATLANTIC CRISSCROSSING OF war, cultural denigration, and colonization between Europe and Islam, Old World and New, had, as we have seen, already begun in the fifteenth and sixteenth centuries. And even as the American colonies began to assert their independence from England, phantom Muslims continued to lurk in North America. Like the Spanish and English before them, the founders of the United States saw Islam where it did not exist. The largest group of Muslims in North America in the mid-eighteenth century were slaves. While estimates vary, Muslims might have constituted up to a tenth of the African slave population of North America between the sixteenth and the eighteenth centuries. Yet, given their racial bondage and scattered demography, they clearly posed no "Islamic threat" to the burgeoning American republic.

Nevertheless, quite oddly, one of the debates that emerged during the drafting of the Constitution was the question of whether or not a Muslim could be president of the United States. Regarded as the "eternal enemy without," Muslims in this context (more so than Jews or Catholics) represented one of the primary legal limit-cases for the founders in their conversations about the ideals of citizenship and religious freedom in the young United States. In 1788, the answer to the question of whether an "imagined" Muslim could be president of the United States was a theoretical, though reluctant, yes. As Muslims were virtually absent from the United States in that period, the fact that the shapers of the Constitution even thought to consider the question of a Muslim president points to the shadow threat Islam was conceived to be—an inheritance of America's European origins.

Columbus had seen the lands across the ocean as a means of funding an apocalyptic war to "recapture" Jerusalem. The Puritans saw America as the New Jerusalem. Nineteenth-century Americans understood the western United States as an Edenic wilderness they had to redeem. The Holy Land thus always lurked as part of the European and then American understanding of the New World. In the nineteenth century, as more and more Americans traveled to the real Jerusalem for tourism, religious missions, and trade, their notions of an American Eden in North America formed much of their encounter with Ottoman Palestine.

After the Civil War ended, Abraham Lincoln and his wife, Mary Todd, discussed a trip to recuperate from the terrors and tragedies of the war. They considered first a journey "out to the West as far as California, then perhaps to Europe." The other option was "a special pilgrimage to Jerusalem, which Lincoln had often said was a city he longed to see." His assassination cut short these plans, though just before his death he and Mary had reportedly settled on Jerusalem. In Lincoln's mind, California and Jerusalem existed on a continuum. Each represented both a spiritual destiny and a geographic destination for Americans. Such a notion derived from the same mythology of Crusade that drove Columbus west—a redemptive journey to gain the promises of a Promised Land.

The nineteenth-century writers who, unlike Lincoln, did eventually cross the Atlantic to the Middle East not only shared this vision of Jerusalem but also articulated the way in which Americans in that period and later came to understand the East—by yoking Muslims to Native Americans. In a mirror image of Columbus's effort to understand the indigenous peoples of the Americas by means of the Islam of the Old World, nineteenth-century Americans fell back on what they knew of Native Americans—as derogatory and scant as that knowledge was—to comprehend what they saw in the Holy Land. Thus, on the road from Damascus to Jerusalem, Mark Twain writes in *The Innocents Abroad* (1869) that the "dusky men and women" he saw "reminded me much of Indians. . . . They sat in silence, and with tireless patience watched our every motion with that vile, uncomplaining impoliteness which is so truly Indian, and which makes a white man so nervous and uncomfortable and savage that he wants to exterminate the whole tribe." Later, he says, "These people about us had other peculiarities, which I have noticed in the noble red man, too: they were infested with vermin, and the dirt had caked on them till it amounted to bark." If for Columbus Muslims represented the ultimate other through which to understand all difference anywhere in the world, for Twain Native Americans played this role.

In his epic lyric travel poem *Clarel* (1876), Herman Melville describes pyramids in Egypt's Nile Delta as:

*Three Indian mounds*
*Against the horizon's level bounds*

Of an encounter with a group of Arab bandits on a road near the Jordan River, he writes:

*Well do ye come by spear and dagger!*
*Yet in your bearing ye outvie*
*Our Western Red Men, chiefs that stalk*
*In mud paint—whirl the tomahawk.*

Above all, neither Melville nor Twain could ever assimilate Islam to their world. The nineteenth-century American writer Washington Irving differed in this regard, as he studied the religion and the history of Islamic Spain and wrote books on these topics employing Arabic and Spanish sources. His rendering of Islam to the American public thus offered both a more scholarly take and a more sympathetic one. But for Melville and Twain, Islam was always other and only enemy, useful for literary and rhetorical purposes, but not worthy of serious or nuanced engagement. For example, the existence of Arab Christians in Bethlehem, Christ's birthplace no less, was a detail that befuddled and seemingly annoyed Melville:

*Catholic Arabs? Say not that!*
*Some words don't chime together, see*

Twain could only understand Islam by domesticating it to what he knew of America. In *Tom Sawyer Abroad* (1894), one of the sequels to his masterpiece, Tom explains to Huck that a Muslim "was a person that wasn't a Presbyterian," to which Huck responds that "there is plenty of them in Missouri, though I didn't know it before." This is, of course, satire. Embedded in the joke, however, is the historical truth that even in the nineteenth century—as it was for Columbus and his men—Islam remained beyond the frontiers of Americans' conceptual universe, a limit-case for Twain to make the point that only Presbyterians matter in Missouri. Everyone else is so beyond the bounds, they might as well be Muslims.

In the twentieth century, artistic engagements with the Muslim

The Thief of Bagdad *(1924)*

world continued to perpetuate American notions of uncivilized and evil Muslims, rapacious and licentious Arabs. In the new medium of cinema, films such as *The Thief of Bagdad* (1924), *A Son of the Sahara* (1924), and *The Desert Bride* (1928) projected these stereotypes on screen for American audiences. From the early twentieth century to today, the violent, brooding Arab villain has been a favorite of Hollywood. In twentieth-century American literature, too, caricatures of Islam continued to flourish. Consider just one example. The Beatnik writers Jane and Paul Bowles, William Burroughs, and Allen Ginsberg all lived in Morocco for a time in the 1950s and 1960s. Both in their writings and in their personal lives, these paragons of hippie counterculture adopted often racist attitudes toward Moroccans, much closer to those of the dying colonial order around them than to anything resembling the spiritually free future with which they are generally associated. Morocco for these towering American literary figures was a libertine frontier of sex and kif, empire and nostalgia, populated by people who were at best a backdrop, at worst sexual objects to exploit.

❈

AS THE UNITED STATES engaged more directly with real Muslims both in America itself, through immigration at the turn of the twentieth century, and in the Middle East and elsewhere, through travel, Christian proselytizing, expatriate residence, diplomacy, and increasingly war, the earlier, often fantastical fears of Muslims and Islam persisted. Over the course of the last half century, one figure above all others has dominated these fears—the terrorist. The deaths of Americans in places such as Lebanon, Somalia, Iraq, Yemen, and Afghanistan confirmed to many the menace of Islam, and, of course, the attacks of 9/11 brought this peril into the United States itself. These all-too-real instances of Muslims killing Americans have coursed new vitality into the centuries-long notion of a Muslim threat to the United States. Now, in the early twenty-first century, an imaginary of what Muslims are thought to be—ruthless, violent, hate-driven—has overtaken any reality of what Muslims actually are in the United States—citizens, parents, voters, Americans. This contemporary fear and demonization come easily because they tap directly into a long history of the perceived threat of Islam in the Americas—which, as I have suggested, began at the first moment Europeans set foot on these continents.

This is not to discount the fact that Muslims have attacked America. They have. The indisputable reality, however, is that Muslims are not modern America's primary domestic terrorists. That distinction belongs to white nationalists. Since 9/11, white nationalists—nearly all of whom are professed Christians—have accounted for more terrorist attacks than any other group in the United States. Yet, Muslims have received the greatest attention as potential domestic perpetrators of violence against Americans and, in turn, have been regular targets of both discriminatory legislation and hate crime in the United States.

Irrational fantasies about a Muslim threat in the contemporary United States emerge in many ways. For example, between 2010 and 2018, forty-three states introduced 201 bills aimed at banning *sharia* law as a looming danger to the West. Of course, Selim's post-1517 reform of *sharia* courts never entered these discussions. If it had, perhaps state legislators would have come to understand that the overwhelming majority of the resolutions in the millions of cases adjudicated in *sharia* courts over the centuries have had next to nothing to do with *sharia* law—either the real law itself or their caricature of it. Perhaps they would have learned that Islamic courts served Muslims and non-Muslims alike, and that Christians and Jews often preferred the Islamic court to their own. Taking a comparative perspective, they might have discerned that *sharia* courts in Selim's day provided more rights to religious minorities, especially to women in the realm of family law, than did Christian courts in Europe. Needless to say, in such polemical conversations, historical reality is usually beside the point.

Examples of this sort abound. Again tapping deep into the fantastical vein of the rhetoric of Islam-as-threat in the United States, many on the American right assert that President Barack Obama is a Muslim (or, even worse, a crypto-Muslim), in a direct echo of the founders' debate over whether a Muslim could ever be president. Far more than an echo, however, was the statement by Ben Carson—Republican candidate, one-time front-runner, and subsequently President Donald Trump's Secretary of Housing and Urban Development—during the 2016 presidential campaign: "I would not advocate that we put a Muslim in charge of this nation. I absolutely would not agree with that." With millions more Muslims living in the United States in the early twenty-first century than in the eighteenth century, the question of a Muslim president in 2016 was no longer a theoretical legal exercise but one that had enormous real-world consequences, as the post-election attempts at a Muslim travel ban made painfully clear.

After the 2016 election, one of the more extreme claims made about immigration over the United States's southern border—through towns such as Matamoros—was that Muslims were part of the "invasion" of the United States. President Donald Trump tweeted an endorsement of a "border rancher" who claimed to have found "prayer rugs" on his property. The notion of Muslim terrorists—or, for that matter, throngs of Central American criminals and drug dealers—crossing into the United States from Mexico has been repeatedly refuted by fact, but, again, fantasy does not pay heed to fact. The imaginary *moros* of 1492 have become today's imaginary border-crossing Muslim terrorists. We might do well to remember that in the last three decades, it is the United States that has invaded Muslim countries, not the other way around. As of 2020, America continues to battle the Muslim world in Afghanistan, Iraq, Syria, Yemen, and elsewhere, with the Afghan conflict holding the dubious distinction of being the nation's longest war. In these wars, Americans fly Apache and Kiowa helicopters over Muslim towns and cities and shoot Tomahawk missiles at their targets below. Black Hawk helicopters ferried the Navy SEALS in the nighttime raid dubbed Operation Geronimo that killed Osama bin Laden in Pakistan. Thus for centuries now, the American psyche has drawn a durably resilient conceptual link between violence against Native Americans and the Muslim world.

Indeed, the idea that Islam is a deep existential threat to the Americas is one of the oldest cultural tropes in the New World. Its history is as long as the history of European colonialism and disease. It must, therefore, be a part of any understanding of the history of the Americas. After 1492, European colonialism, as we have seen, folded the Americas into the long history of European–Islamic relations. Seeing American history in this way allows us to give a more holistic accounting of the American past.

The history of the United States does not begin with Plymouth Rock and Thanksgiving. The first European foothold in what would become the continental United States was not Jamestown, but a Spanish Catholic outpost in Florida. The origins of the American people must obviously include the history of the indigenous peoples of the Caribbean and the Americas, West Africans, and the Jewish and Catholic subjects of mainland European polities. This history must also include Muslims, both African slaves and Selim's Ottomans, for Islam was the mold that cast the history of European racial and ethnic thinking in the Americas, as well as the history of warfare in the Western Hemisphere.

※

ISLAM IS PROJECTED TO supplant Christianity as the world's largest religion by the year 2070, so an understanding of Islam's complex role in world history becomes ever more imperative. We must move beyond a simplistic, ahistorical story of the rise of the West or a facile notion of a clash of civilizations. Without understanding the role of the Ottomans in the history of the last five hundred years, we cannot hope to understand either the past or the present. The Ottomans stood, in 1492, at the very center of the known world. The Ottoman Empire made the world we know today.

# CODA

. . .

# SHADOWS OVER TURKEY

*Sultan Selim the Grim Bridge*

NEARLY FIVE CENTURIES AFTER SULEYMAN INTERRED HIS FATHER in the mosque complex that has been his home ever since, another head of state has become a frequent visitor to Selim's tomb: Recep Tayyip Erdoğan, Turkey's current president and former prime minister. The Turkish leader has displayed a keen interest in Selim—far more than in any other figure from the Ottoman past—and has expended enormous resources and energy in promoting the sultan's legacy.

Nowhere did Erdoğan and his associates in the Islamist Justice and

Development Party (*Ak Parti*) more clearly evidence their attraction to and respect for Selim than on the western shores of the Bosphorus Strait, on May 29, 2013. They gathered there with other government dignitaries, bureaucrats, business leaders, engineers, and local and foreign media for the groundbreaking ceremony for a third bridge across the famous waterway. The name of the new bridge had been kept secret until that day. May 29 is a date of colossal significance in Turkey; it commemorates Mehmet II's 1453 conquest of Constantinople. So important is it, in fact, that one of the two earlier bridges that span the Bosphorus bears Mehmet's name. (The other, the first to have been constructed, is known simply as the Bosphorus Bridge.) On the 560th anniversary of Mehmet's conquest, it was announced that the third bridge would be named for Mehmet's grandson: the Sultan Selim the Grim Bridge (in Turkish, *Yavuz Sultan Selim Köprüsü*).

Naming this new connector of continents after Selim serves Erdoğan's political project. He and his Islamist party colleagues regularly describe themselves as the "grandchildren" of the Ottomans, making Erdoğan unique among modern Turkish leaders. From Mustafa Kemal Atatürk, who founded the republic in 1923 in the aftermath of World War I, until Erdoğan, Turkey's political elite emphatically made a clean break between the empire and the republic. The republic was established, indeed, to correct all that was wrong with the empire and had led to its demise. Modern Turkey would replace Islam with secularism, the sultan with a parliament, the Ottoman alphabet with a Latin one, Ottomanness with Turkishness.

Turkish nationalism would, as declared by its republican proponents, excise from Turkey's political body all the "weak abscesses" that had handicapped the empire during its long history: Armenians, Kurds, Arabs, Greeks, and all other "feeble non-Turks." Turkey's leaders thus pointedly rejected the longstanding Ottoman governing principle of allowing various ethnicities and cultures autonomy within its realm in exchange for their recognition of Ottoman authority. As elsewhere, Turkey's national project would prove extremely controversial and violent. To the extent that the rulers of modern Turkey have ever admitted to having employed violence, they have defended it as vital to "correcting" the empire's "mistakes"—its multilingual, multidenominational, multicultural character. All the leaders of Turkey from Atatürk until

Erdoğan emphasized Turkish republicanism over any connection to the Ottoman past.

Part of Erdoğan's exceptionality, therefore, is his calculated embrace of aspects of Turkey's Ottoman heritage. He casts himself as a new kind of Turkish politician, one who celebrates Turkey's Ottoman lineage instead of rejecting it and one who positions himself, at least symbolically, in the tradition of the sultanate. In these and other ways, Erdoğan seeks to reconcile the republic and the empire in the service of his own political goals. One of his primary tools in this process is religion. Alternately describing himself as an Islamic secularist and a secular Islamist, Erdoğan has increased the visible markers of Islam in public life in Turkey. He regards Islam as a common cultural idiom stretching across time and space, connecting him both to the Ottoman past as well as to Muslims—albeit only *certain* Muslims—outside Turkey's borders. Thus, Selim represents the crucial fulcrum, as it was Selim who made the Ottoman Empire a majority Muslim state, won the caliphate, and preemptively attacked any power that stood in the way of Ottoman ambitions.

Erdoğan finds much to be lauded and emulated in Selim's expansionist politics and his emboldening of orthodox Sunnism. Understanding Selim first and foremost as a resolute bulwark of Ottoman—and therefore Turkish—power, Erdoğan and his ardent followers seek to aggressively project their own Turkish Islamist power. Selim's Ottoman Empire was vastly more powerful on the world stage than Turkey is today. Erdoğan seeks to revive that global influence. As he would explain it, one of the reasons the republic lost its clout in the twentieth century was its staunch secularism. Erdoğan and his supporters see Islam as a cultural and political reservoir of strength, a vital component of the glories of the Ottoman past which they seek to emulate in contemporary Turkey.

This perspective explains many of Erdoğan's actions and ideas. One of his more outlandish statements is his claim that Muslims, not Christians, discovered America. He derived this notion from some of the texts I discussed earlier—ones that mention mosques and Moors in the New World. Without the proper appreciation of the historical context of these statements—and, perhaps more to the point, because it supports his larger political agenda—Erdoğan enthusiastically invoked the idea of a Muslim discovery of America as yet another example of the magnificent accomplishments of Muslims throughout history that the West has suppressed. Why would today's Muslims, he rhetorically asks Turkey's secular republicans, want to separate themselves from such a glorious heritage by letting go of their religious identity? Are they so enamored—or duped—by Europe and the United States? For Erdoğan, Selim is the perfect standard-bearer of this grand, if sometimes imaginary, Muslim legacy, and Erdoğan himself stands as its chief inheritor and defender.

Where Selim conquered the Middle East from the Mamluks with camels and cannons, Erdoğan seeks to control the region using Turkey's military strength and political Islamism. Where Selim made the Ottoman Empire a global economic hegemon through his control of Eurasian trade, Erdoğan has encouraged Islamist-owned companies and developed Turkey's economy into the world's seventeenth largest. Where Selim captured Mecca and Medina, shaping the empire as an orthodox Sunni state, Erdoğan cultivates his own Sunni religiosity to position Islam at the center of Turkey's domestic agenda, then uses it as a force against Iranian Shiite influence and Saudi Sunni competition in the Middle East—hoping, as Selim did, that Istanbul's Sunnism will soon conquer the world. Where Selim ruthlessly eliminated his domestic and foreign enemies, Erdoğan has pursued a similar path in targeting his country's Alevis (Turkey's Shiite community), Kurds, intellectuals, elected officials, police, Christians, Saudi Arabia, journalists, ISIS forces in Syria, leftists, and even peaceful demonstrators in Washington, DC.

Thus, by choosing to name the Bosphorus's third bridge after Selim, Erdoğan very pointedly embraced a particular vision of Selim's legacy and of Ottoman history more generally—one that also, quite usefully, serves to critique Atatürk's republican secularism. Like many of Erdoğan's aggressive Islamist policies, this move elicited vocal criticism both inside and outside Turkey. Some of the loudest voices against naming the third bridge after Selim came from Turkey's Alevis, many of whom trace their lineage to the Anatolian Shiites whom Selim repeatedly massacred. The Sultan Selim the Grim Bridge thus incites feelings of intergenerational trauma, insult, and violence similar to those experienced by African Americans, and many other Americans, when faced with Confederate monuments. And, like proponents of these statues in the United States, Erdoğan used the naming of the bridge to send a message to one of his country's largest minority communities—a message about who the "real Turks" are.

Erdoğan also took rhetorical aim at Turkey's external Shiite enemies. He revealed the bridge's name during the Arab Spring, when several governments around the Middle East were collapsing, creating temporary power vacuums. Iran flexed its muscle through its nuclear program in those years, hoping to make further inroads into the Sunni Arab world. Erdoğan countered by supporting various Sunni Islamist political parties in countries affected by the Arab Spring. Symbolic though it was, Erdoğan's choice of name sent a clear message that Turkey today, like Selim's empire centuries earlier, would stand as the Middle East's stalwart defender of Sunnism and would indeed project force whenever and wherever necessary to support Sunnis against Shiites and to battle all those perceived to be Turkey's enemies.

SELIM FIGURES IN ERDOĞAN'S symbolic politics in another way, too. In 2005, thieves stole a kaftan and crown that Selim had worn during his life and that had adorned his tomb in the mausoleum Suleyman built for him in the 1520s. A few months later, baggage screeners at Istanbul's Atatürk International Airport discovered the items in the luggage of two men attempting to smuggle them out of Turkey to, it was claimed, the headquarters of Fethullah Gülen in the United States. Gülen leads a Turkish Islamist organization named Hizmet, a staunch rival to Erdoğan's party. Onetime allies, the two leaders fell out in a power struggle and soon turned on each other. Gülen fled the country in 1999 for his own safety, eventually settling in Pennsylvania to orchestrate anti-Erdoğan activities as best he could from there—perhaps, some claim, with support from elements of the United States security services. Over the years, some of Gülen's followers quietly infiltrated the Turkish military and police and were accused of being behind the failed coup of summer 2016. Selim's kaftan and crown symbolize the caliphate, so their possessor symbolically becomes Selim's successor, as both sultan and caliph. If indeed Gülen sought the kaftan and crown for himself, it would have been to impress upon Erdoğan and the world that he—not Erdoğan—was Selim's rightful descendant, Turkey's true political and spiritual leader. When the royal accoutrements were dis-covered in the airport, they were not immediately returned to Selim's tomb but rather held in safekeeping—allegedly for security reasons.

In 2017, Erdoğan won a constitutional referendum that greatly expanded his powers, removing most of the checks and balances on his rule (some of what he achieved in 2017 has since been lost due to his party's 2019 electoral setbacks and Turkey's inconsistent domestic economy). Accusations of corruption, vote rigging, poll violence, and manifold irregularities marred the highly controversial referendum. A vainglorious Erdoğan's first act after his 2017 victory—imperfect as the process may have been—was to return Selim's stolen possessions to the deceased sultan's tomb. In a highly scripted and dramatic perfor-mance, with cameras rolling and lights flashing, Erdoğan brought out from hiding the powerfully symbolic kaftan and crown, carried them to Selim's mosque, and personally placed them on the ornate coffin.

With his characteristic showmanship, Erdoğan made the most of this event; his far-from-subtle first act after winning a referendum that gave him near-limitless power in Turkey reverberated all the way to Gülen's headquarters in Pennsylvania. Selim was the first Ottoman to be both sultan and caliph, and—by showcasing his personal posses-sion of Selim's kaftan and crown—Erdoğan became the first republican

*Turkish president Recep Tayyip Erdoğan at Selim's tomb*

to profess himself the heir to both titles. Indeed, the vote confirmed Erdoğan as the closest thing to a sultan the Turkish republic has seen. Like Selim, Erdoğan has weaponized his new status to send forceful warnings to his adversaries at home and abroad. In some ways, as far-fetched as it might sound, 2017 was not so different from 1517.

THE BRIDGE BEARING SELIM'S name—one of the world's tallest and widest suspension bridges—opened in 2016. It stands as one of only three concrete connectors between East and West, Europe and Asia. "When man dies," Erdoğan said at the bridge's inauguration, "he leaves behind a monument." As combative, narcissistically grandiose, and historically selective as he is, Erdoğan is not wrong to single out Selim as a world-changing, world-connecting figure worthy of the honor—next only to his grandfather—of having a bridge over the Bosphorus named after him.

The gray line that is the bridge's shadow also now connects the continents, moving with the sun across the strait's blue waters. God's shadow forever binds the world.

# ACKNOWLEDGMENTS

. . .

A FTER YEARS OF STEADY PROGRESS AGAINST THE HEADWINDS OF daily life, always endeavoring to write and to think, arriving at the end of this book is both wonderful and frightening, inspiring and daunting. What now shall I do with myself? Ends, thankfully, are also possibilities.

My largest debt is to my editor Bob Weil, an unequaled force of passion, ability, and intellect. As editors should but usually don't, Bob read every word of this book, sometimes three or four times. He shaped it more than anyone else, always pushing me to make it better, bigger. Over years, and countless lunches and dinners, phone conversations and emails, Bob has proven much more than just a brilliant editor. Luckily for me, I now count him as a friend, interlocutor, and adviser of sorts.

That I even know Bob is thanks to my wonderful agent Wendy Strothman. She pushed me to write differently and made sure this book got to where it needed to go. Working with her on writing and conceptualizing this book has been a masterclass in genre, audience, and tone. I thank her and Lauren MacLeod, a formidable team.

I could not have written this book without the confidence and support shown me by Yale University. Yale has been my institutional home for a decade now. It has given me an enormous amount and, in turn, rightly, asked much of me. I thank Tamar Gendler, dean of the faculty of arts and sciences, and Katie Lofton and Amy Hungerford, current and former deans of the humanities, respectively, for their votes of confidence. The support of the Whitney and Betty MacMillan Center for International and Area Studies made the research and writing of this book possible. I thank its current and former directors, respectively, Steven Wilkinson and Ian Shapiro.

More crucially than its generous material backing, Yale has surrounded me with wonderful scholars and people. In the Department of History, I thank Naomi Lamoreaux, Paul Freedman, Joanne Meyerowitz, Carolyn Dean, Dan Magaziner, Anne Eller, Bob Harms, Dani Botsman, and Anders Winroth. Elsewhere on campus, I am fortunate to know Noreen Khawaja, Eda Pepi, and Jackie Goldsby. Katie Lofton—thinker, friend, leader—has supported me in deep and caring ways, in realms personal and professional. She read sections of this book and gave of her characteristically engaged and incisive intellect. Stuart Schwartz also read the chapters of this book about the Americas. I thank both of these towering scholars for helping me to cross the Atlantic.

I became chair of my department in the middle of working on this book. For allowing me to balance the writerly life of the mind with the demands of administering one of the largest departments at Yale—one of the largest history departments anywhere—I thank Liza Joyner, the department's entire staff, and especially Dana Lee.

I thank my graduate students for their commitment to scholarship and generosity of collective thinking. They always push me, and I am grateful for that. I thank in particular Ian Hathaway for reading Italian for me.

One of my closest colleagues from Yale is now, sadly, a few hours south. Francesca Trivellato is one of the smartest people I know. Getting to teach with her, talk with her, read her work, and learn from her has been one of the most formative parts of my intellectual life.

Leslie Peirce—teacher, interlocutor, friend, dinner companion—recently published a masterful book, *Empress of the East*. Sharing our projects in Ottoman history and many downtown meals has meant a great deal to me over the past few years.

For five years, Beth Piatote supported me and this book more than anyone else. Incisive reader, gifted writer, nimble thinker, she read an early version of the manuscript and helped me to see contradictions as connections and opportunities in complexity. I will always be grateful and respect her.

For its material support—manna from heaven, really—I happily and gratefully acknowledge the Anneliese Maier Research Award of the Alexander von Humboldt Foundation. This gift has made so much possible. I enjoy this largesse because of Cornel Zwierlein. I thank him for nominating me for this award and for all the energy and excitement of his collaboration over the past few years.

Colleagues far from my world, with no reason to be generous to me, have been, and for that I'm enormously grateful. Jane Landers shared with me her important unpublished work and sent me off in wholly new directions. Susan Ferber and Alex Star offered their takes on early ideas. Ussama Makdisi helped with beginnings of all kinds. For many generous gifts, I thank Jennifer L. Derr, Angie Heo, Nancy Khalek, and Nükhet Varlık. Thanks to Tom Laqueur, for his example. My colleagues in the fields of Ottoman and Middle Eastern history have always been open to me and welcoming of my slightly eccentric ideas. This book is both for them and—in many I hope productive ways—not for them.

I presented some of the ideas here—especially about Columbus—at the University of Michigan, McGill University, and New York University. My grand German tour of talks during the hottest summer then on record was made possible by the Alexander von Humboldt Foundation. I thank the audiences in all of these venues for their challenging questions and generous engagement with my work.

For a decade now, I have been lucky to be in constant fellowship with Edith Sheffer, historian, writer, friend. She has been there for me at all my lowest moments, and the high ones too, and shared in the daily intricacies of all that's on the other side of the wall. I thank her for her friendship and for sharing a sensibility about the world. Preeti Chopra has been my friend now for almost twenty years and remains a key person for me.

An author could not ask for a better team than the one at Liveright and W. W. Norton. Gabe Kachuck fielded my endless queries with grace and patience, offering solutions and direction. Anna Oler, Peter Miller, Cordelia Calvert, Steve Attardo, Dassi Zeidel, Marie Pantojan, and countless others improved this book. I was fortunate to work with Kathy Brandes and Allegra Huston on the text of this book and with Sarah Evertson on its images. The maps were made by David Lindroth, and Heather Dubnick put together the index.

One of my oldest friends in Turkey, Merve Çakır, helped to secure image rights from the Topkapı Palace Museum. I thank her and Esra Müyesseroğlu.

My parents are always there. What does one say to those who have always given him everything?

# CHRONOLOGY

· · ·

## SELIM AND HIS WORLD

### BEFORE SELIM (PRE-1470)

| | |
|---|---|
| 1071 | Seljuk Turks defeat Byzantines at Manzikert, in eastern Anatolia |
| 1187 | Saladin, founder of the Ayyubid dynasty, captures Jerusalem |
| 1202–04 | Fourth Crusade sacks Constantinople |
| 1258 | Mongols capture Baghdad, capital of the Abbasid caliphate |
| 1302 | Osman I defeats Byzantine army in western Anatolia |
| 1352 | Ottomans enter Thrace; Orhan Gazi signs treaty with Genoa |
| 1369 | Ottomans capture Adrianople, renamed Edirne |
| 1389 | Battle of Kosovo: Ottomans defeat Serbians |
| 1394–1402 | First Ottoman siege of Constantinople |
| 1402 | Battle of Ankara: Tamerlane defeats Ottomans |
| 1402–13 | Ottoman interregnum: civil war between the sons of Bayezit I |
| 1447 | Birth of Bayezit II, father of **Selim** |
| 1453 (ca.) | Birth (in Albania) of Gülbahar, mother of **Selim** |
| 1450s | Coffee likely first used in Yemeni Sufi lodges |
| 1451 | Christopher Columbus born in Genoa |
| 1453 | Conquest of Constantinople, renamed Istanbul, by Mehmet II, grandfather of **Selim** |
| 1459 | Birth of Cem, half-uncle of **Selim**; Ottoman conquest of Serbia and the Morea (Peloponnese) |
| 1461 | Ottoman capture of Trabzon |
| 1463 | Ottoman capture of Bosnia and Herzegovina |
| 1463–79 | Ottoman war with Venice |

| | |
|---|---|
| 1466 | Ahmed, older half-brother of **Selim**, born in Amasya |
| 1467 | Korkud, older half-brother of **Selim**, born in Amasya |

## YOUTH (1470–87)

| | |
|---|---|
| 1470 | **Selim** born in Amasya: October 10, 1470 |
| 1472 | Columbus crosses the Mediterranean to Tunis |
| 1474 or 1475 | Columbus sails to Chios |
| 1475 | Ottomans capture Genoese colony of Kefe (Crimea) |
| 1476 | Columbus first sails from Mediterranean into North Atlantic |
| 1477 | First printing of *The Travels of Marco Polo* |
| 1478 | Crimean Tatars accept Ottoman suzerainty |
| 1479 | **Selim**'s circumcision ceremony in Istanbul (his first time in the city); Treaty of Constantinople between Ottoman Empire and Venice; Columbus marries Filipa Moniz in Lisbon |
| 1480 | Ottoman capture of Otranto (southern Italy) |
| 1481 | Sultan Mehmet II, grandfather of **Selim**, dies; Bayezit II, father of **Selim**, becomes sultan and moves his family to Topkapı Palace in Istanbul |
| 1481 | Ottoman retreat from Otranto; Cem, half-uncle of **Selim**, flees Anatolia for Mamluk Cairo; Cem makes Islamic pilgrimage (*Hajj*), the only Ottoman sultan or prince ever to do so |
| 1482 | Columbus sails to São Jorge da Mina (West Africa) |
| 1485–91 | Ottoman war with Mamluk Empire |
| 1486 | Queen Isabella I of Castile meets Columbus in Córdoba |

## GOVERNORSHIP (1487–1512)

| | |
|---|---|
| 1487 | **Selim** becomes governor of Trabzon, in eastern Anatolia; birth of Ismail, future head of Safavid dynasty, in Ardabil (Iran) |
| 1487ff | Ottoman ships appear in Corsica, Pisa, Balearic Islands, Almería, Málaga |
| 1487 or 1488 | Ottoman privateer (and then admiral) Kemal Reis sent to western Mediterranean |
| 1488 | Sultan Bayezit II attacks Malta |
| 1490 | Death of Ya'kub, leader of the Ak Koyunlu Confederacy, sparks succession crisis |

| | |
|---|---|
| 1490–95 | Kemal Reis conducts raids along North African coast |
| 1492 | Spanish take Granada, ending seven centuries of Muslim rule on Iberian peninsula, and expel all Jews; Bayezit II welcomes Spanish Jews to Ottoman Empire |
| 1492 | Columbus lands on Bahamian island of Guanahani; two weeks later, he reaches north coast of Cuba |
| 1493 | Columbus returns to Europe, minus one ship; eight months later, he crosses Atlantic again |
| 1493 | Hebrew printing press established in Istanbul |
| 1494 | Suleyman, son of **Selim**, born in Trabzon: November 6, 1494 |
| 1495 | Cem dies in Naples |
| 1497 | Vasco da Gama rounds Cape of Good Hope, reaches Calicut in 1498 |
| 1498 | Columbus begins third transatlantic voyage |
| 1499–1501 | Muslim uprisings (Alpujarra revolts) in and around Granada |
| 1499–1503 | Second Ottoman war with Venice |
| 1501 | Safavids capture Tabriz, establish Safavid Empire with Ismail as its first shah; Ottomans disperse their domestic Shiite populations |
| 1501 | Kemal Reis conducts raids off coast of Valencia, likely capturing a sailor in possession of maps from Columbus's earlier transatlantic voyages; Spanish take first West African slaves to New World |
| 1502 | Columbus departs on fourth and final transatlantic voyage |
| 1503 | Spanish register fears that African slaves are preaching Islam to Indians on Hispaniola |
| 1504 | Queen Isabella dies; Portuguese blockade mouth of Red Sea |
| 1505 | **Selim** rebuffs Safavid raids in and around Trabzon |
| 1506 | Columbus dies in Valladolid, Spain |
| 1508 | **Selim** invades Georgia |
| 1509 | Major earthquake in Istanbul; Bayezit II Mosque, built in 1506, badly damaged |
| 1510 | **Selim** defends Erzincan from attempted Safavid raid |
| 1511 | Şahkulu Rebellion; Suleyman becomes governor of Kefe |
| 1512 | **Selim** marches from Crimea toward Istanbul |

## SULTANATE (1512–20)

| | |
|---|---|
| 1512 | **Sultan Selim I** ascends Ottoman throne after abdication of Sultan Bayezit II, who dies a month later en route to Dimetoka |
| 1513 | **Selim** kills half-brothers Ahmed and Korkud |
| Spring 1514 | **Selim** massacres 40,000 Ottoman Shiites in eastern Anatolia |
| Aug. 1514 | **Selim** wins decisive Battle of Chaldiran against Safavids and seizes Tabriz |
| 1515 | **Selim** returns to Istanbul; Portuguese capture Hormuz |
| 1516 | King Ferdinand II of Aragon dies |
| Spring 1516 | Barbarossa brothers capture Algiers for the Ottoman Empire |
| Jul. 1516 | **Selim** arrives in Elbistan (southern Anatolia) |
| Aug. 1516 | **Selim** enters Aleppo in triumph |
| Dec. 1516 | **Selim** enters Jerusalem |
| 1517 | First official European diplomatic mission to China |
| Feb. 1517 | **Selim** enters Cairo, effectively ending Mamluk Empire; Francisco Hernández de Córdoba becomes first European in Mexico, dubbing Maya city *El Gran Cairo* (later Cape Catoche) |
| Spring 1517 | **Selim** proclaimed caliph, receives world map from Piri Reis, and in September begins ten-month return march to Istanbul |
| Oct. 1517 | Martin Luther writes *95 Theses* |
| Late 1517 | First Ottoman raids from Tlemcen (Algeria) west into Morocco |
| Jul. 1518 | **Selim** arrives in Istanbul after long march from Cairo |
| Fall 1518 | **Selim** prepares for war against Safavids and their Ottoman Shiite supporters; orders construction of fifty ships in Red Sea to counter Portuguese influence |
| Late 1518 | Fleeing plague, **Selim** leaves Istanbul for Edirne |
| Feb. 1519 | **Selim** dispatches thirty ships to fight Portuguese on India's western coast and orders 60,000 Ottoman troops to Nicopolis (western Greece) in preparation for sailing to North Africa |
| 1519 | Battle of Otumba in Mexico: Spanish defeat Aztecs |
| 1519 | **Selim** renews peace treaty with Poland |
| Jul. 1519 | **Selim** signs new peace treaty with Hungary |
| May 1520 | **Selim** receives new world map |
| 1520 | **Selim** dies in Çorlu, near Edirne (eastern Thrace): September 22, 1520 |

## AFTER SELIM (POST-1520)

| | |
|---|---|
| 1520 | Suleyman, **Selim**'s only son, becomes tenth Ottoman sultan |
| 1521 | Christmas Day Wolof Rebellion in Hispaniola: first slave insurrection in the Americas |
| 1522 | Ottoman conquest of Rhodes |
| 1528 | **Selim**'s body transferred from Istanbul's Fatih Mosque to Selim I Mosque (Yavuz Selim Mosque), commissioned by Suleyman |
| 1529 | First Ottoman siege of Vienna |
| 1534 | Hafsa, former concubine of **Selim** and mother of Suleyman, dies and is buried next to **Selim**: March 19, 1534 |
| 1535 | Ottomans establish administrative control in Yemen |
| 1540s | First coffeehouses open in Istanbul |
| 1546 | Incorporation of Basra (Iraq) into Ottoman Empire |
| 1553–55 | War with Safavids, concluding with Treaty of Amasya |
| 1565 | Ottoman siege of Malta |
| 1566 | Unexpected death of Sultan Suleyman in Hungary: September 6, 1566 |

# NOTES

...

To allow as many readers as possible to follow the sources used in this book, I have, when available, cited primary sources in English translation and referenced English-language secondary materials.

## INTRODUCTION

5   **Gibbon's once canonical eighteenth-century account:** Edward Gibbon, *The History of the Decline and Fall of the Roman Empire*, 6 vols. (London: J. Murray, 1846).

5   **Matamoros, a remnant symbol of Christian Spain's brutal wars against Islam:** Abbas Hamdani, "Ottoman Response to the Discovery of America and the New Route to India," *Journal of the American Oriental Society* 101 (1981): 330.

5   **The people who would eventually become the Ottomans:** See, for example, Carter Vaughn Findley, *The Turks in World History* (Oxford: Oxford University Press, 2005), 21–92.

7   **stormed through the walls of the Byzantine capital, Constantinople:** Franz Babinger, *Mehmed the Conqueror and His Time*, trans. Ralph Manheim, ed. William C. Hickman (Princeton: Princeton University Press, 1978), 85–98.

7   **plucked out one of the eyes of Christianity:** The phrase belongs to Pope Pius II, whose birth name was Enea Silvio Piccolomini. Kate Fleet, "Italian Perceptions of the Turks in the Fourteenth and Fifteenth Centuries," *Journal of Mediterranean Studies* 5 (1995): 161.

10  **Selim:** The standard accounts of Selim's life in Turkish and English include Feridun M. Emecen, *Zamanın İskenderi, Şarkın Fatihi: Yavuz Sultan Selim* (Istanbul: Yitik Hazine Yayınları, 2010); Selâhattin Tansel, *Yavuz Sultan Selim* (Ankara: Türk Tarih Kurumu, 2016); Yılmaz Öztuna, *Yavuz Sultan Selim* (Istanbul: Babıali Kültür Yayıncılığı, 2006); Çağatay Uluçay, "Yavuz Sultan Selim Nasıl Padişah Oldu?," *Tarih Dergisi* 6 (1954): 53–90; Çağatay Uluçay, "Yavuz Sultan Selim Nasıl Padişah Oldu?," *Tarih Dergisi* 7 (1954): 117–42; Çağatay Uluçay, "Yavuz Sultan Selim Nasıl Padişah Oldu?," *Tarih Dergisi* 8 (1956): 185–200; Fuad Gücüyener, *Yavuz Sultan Selim* (Istanbul: Anadolu Türk Kitap Deposu, 1945); Ahmet Uğur, *Yavuz Sultan Selim* (Kayseri: Erciyes Üniversitesi Sosyal Bilimler Enstitüsü Müdürlüğü Yayınları, 1989); Ahmet Uğur, *The Reign of Sultan Selīm I in the Light of the Selīm-nāme Literature* (Berlin: Klaus Schwarz Verlag, 1985); H. Erdem Çıpa, *The Making of Selim: Succession, Legitimacy, and Memory in the Early Modern Ottoman World* (Bloomington: Indiana University Press, 2017); Fatih

Akçe, *Sultan Selim I: The Conqueror of the East* (Clifton, NJ: Blue Dome Press, 2016).

11 **one of the first non-firstborn sons to become sultan:** The only previous occurrence came during the period of civil war between 1402 and 1413 known as the Ottoman Interregnum, when the sons of Bayezit I fought one another to the death, with Bayezit's fourth son, Mehmet, surviving to take the throne. This exception, however, was always interpreted as a cautionary tale about the dangers inherent in imperial succession and the need, therefore, to recognize the eldest son as the legitimate successor. Even after becoming sultan, Mehmet, tellingly, was known as the "young lord." Dimitris J. Kastritsis, *The Sons of Bayezid: Empire Building and Representation in the Ottoman Civil War of 1402–1413* (Leiden: Brill, 2007); Caroline Finkel, *Osman's Dream: The Story of the Ottoman Empire, 1300–1923* (New York: Basic Books, 2006), 22–47; *Encyclopaedia of Islam*, 2nd ed. (Leiden: Brill Online, 2012), s.v. "Meḥemmed I" (Halil İnalcık).

11 **"sanguinary tyrant":** Stanley Lane-Poole, assisted by E. J. W. Gibb and Arthur Gilman, *The Story of Turkey* (New York: G. P. Putnam's Sons, 1893), 152. Also cited in Çıpa, *Making of Selim*, 132.

11 **kicked the decapitated heads:** Çıpa, *Making of Selim*, 2.

11 **"His eyes betray . . . a warmonger":** Andrea Gritti, *Relazione a Bajezid II*, serie 3, vol. 3 of *Relazioni degli Ambasciatori Veneti al Senato*, ed. Eugenio Albèri, 1–43 (Florence: Società Editrice Fiorentina, 1855), 23–24, cited in Çıpa, *Making of Selim*, 62–63.

12 **the *Selimname*:** Celia J. Kerslake, "A Critical Edition and Translation of the Introductory Sections and the First Thirteen Chapters of the 'Selīmnāme' of Celālzāde Muṣṭafā Çelebi" (D. Phil. thesis, University of Oxford, 1975).

12 **to paint the sultan in as flattering a light as possible:** Çıpa, *Making of Selim*, 140–52.

## CHAPTER 1: PERFUME OF THE WORLD

16 **"Today, at this court":** Celia J. Kerslake, "A Critical Edition and Translation of the Introductory Sections and the First Thirteen Chapters of the 'Selīmnāme' of Celālzāde Muṣṭafā Çelebi" (D. Phil. thesis, University of Oxford, 1975), 31a.

21 **"There are no ties":** Franz Babinger, *Mehmed the Conqueror and His Time*, trans. Ralph Manheim, ed. William C. Hickman (Princeton: Princeton University Press, 1978), 405.

22 **governor of Amasya for sixteen years:** Gábor Ágoston and Bruce Masters, eds., *Encyclopedia of the Ottoman Empire* (New York: Facts on File, 2009), s.v. "Bayezid II" (Gábor Ágoston).

23 **Amasya:** For a study of fifteenth- and sixteenth-century Amasya, see Hasan Karatas, "The City as a Historical Actor: The Urbanization and Ottomanization of the Halvetiye Sufi Order by the City of Amasya in the Fifteenth and Sixteenth Centuries" (Ph.D. diss., University of California, Berkeley, 2011).

24 **Topkapı Palace:** In these early years, the palace was known simply as "the new palace," to distinguish it from an older structure that Mehmet II first used as his residence when he entered the city. Gülru Necipoğlu, *Architecture, Ceremonial, and Power: The Topkapı Palace in the Fifteenth and Sixteenth Centuries* (New York: Architectural History Foundation; Cambridge, MA: MIT Press, 1991), 4–13.

25 **They did not send anybody:** John Freely, *Jem Sultan: The Adventures of a Captive Turkish Prince in Renaissance Europe* (London: Harper Perennial, 2005), 25.

27 **Bayezit seems to have tapped Ahmed:** Andrea Gritti, *Relazione a Bajezid II*, serie 3, vol. 3 of *Relazioni degli Ambasciatori Veneti al Senato*, ed. Eugenio Albèri, 1–43 (Florence: Società Editrice Fiorentina, 1855), 23–24, cited in H. Erdem Çıpa, *The Making of Selim: Succession, Legitimacy, and Memory in the Early Modern Ottoman World* (Bloomington: Indiana University Press, 2017), 62–63.

27 **"only cared for eating":** Quoted in Çıpa, *Making of Selim*, 285, n. 7.

28 **a man he deeply respected and loved:** Fatih Akçe, *Sultan Selim I: The Conqueror of the East* (Clifton, NJ: Blue Dome Press, 2016), 8.

28 **drew his last breath:** On Mehmet's death, see Babinger, *Mehmed the Conqueror*, 403–04.

29 **"This second Lucifer":** Quoted in Freely, *Jem Sultan*, 37–38.

29 **"It was fortunate":** Quoted in Babinger, *Mehmed the Conqueror*, 408.

## CHAPTER 2: EMPIRE BOYS

33 **"very melancholic":** Quoted in *Encyclopædia Britannica*, s.v. "Bayezid II, Ottoman Sultan" (V.J. Parry), https://www.britannica.com/biography/Bayezid-II (accessed February 23, 2019).

33 **a bon vivant:** John Freely, *Jem Sultan: The Adventures of a Captive Turkish Prince in Renaissance Europe* (London: Harper Perennial, 2005), 27.

33 **Konya:** *Wikipedia*, s.v. "Konya," https://en.wikipedia.org/wiki/Konya (accessed February 8, 2019).

34 **Ottomans were in the ascendancy in the Mediterranean:** Niccolò Machiavelli, *The Prince*, trans. Harvey C. Mansfield, 2nd ed. (Chicago: University of Chicago Press, 1998), 17–19, 81–82.

35 **killing the grand vizier:** Caroline Finkel, *Osman's Dream: The Story of the Ottoman Empire, 1300–1923* (New York: Basic Books, 2006), 82.

36 **the empire's elite bestowed upon Bayezit the sword:** Freely, *Jem Sultan*, 43.

36 **struck coins in his own image:** Freely, *Jem Sultan*, 46.

38 **Pope Sixtus IV wrote to Christian leaders:** Freely, *Jem Sultan*, 53–56.

39 **When Cem first reached the city:** Freely, *Jem Sultan*, 58.

39 **dined as part of the sovereign's entourage:** Freely, *Jem Sultan*, 60.

39 **long beard and spiky eyebrows:** For a picture of Qaitbay, see *Wikipedia*, s.v. "Qaitbay," https://en.wikipedia.org/wiki/Qaitbay (accessed February 8, 2019).

39 **[Cem's] Hajj:** Freely, *Jem Sultan*, 61–62.

40 **"While you lie . . . your chief aim":** This exchange is recounted in Freely, *Jem Sultan*, 62.

41 **to honor the peace treaty with the Ottomans:** Freely, *Jem Sultan*, 25, 63.

## CHAPTER 3: AN OTTOMAN ABROAD

44 **Cem's first letter was to Venice:** Nicolas Vatin, *Sultan Djem, Un prince ottoman dans l'Europe du XVe siècle d'après deux sources contemporaines: Vâkı'ât-ı Sultân Cem, Œuvres de Guillaume Caoursin* (Ankara: Imprimerie de la Société Turque d'Histoire, 1997), 18.

44 **his request . . . was refused:** John Freely, *Jem Sultan: The Adventures of a Captive Turkish Prince in Renaissance Europe* (London: Harper Perennial, 2005), 67–68.

44 **Firenk Suleyman Bey reached the island:** Vatin, *Sultan Djem*, 142.

45 **knew Cem personally from the truce negotiations in 1479:** Freely, *Jem Sultan*, 25.

45 **It took over a week:** Freely, *Jem Sultan*, 72.

46 **"most beautiful horse":** Quoted in Freely, *Jem Sultan*, 76.

47 **"an Armada," "a great many cannons":** Quoted in Freely, *Jem Sultan*, 30–32.

48 **comfortable on Rhodes . . . remained worried about his precarious position:** Vatin, *Sultan Djem*, 144, 146; Freely, *Jem Sultan*, 81.

48 **"observes those around him . . . everybody":** These quotes are from the English translation of Caoursin's account found in Freely, *Jem Sultan*, 81.

48 **Alméida, a slave woman:** Freely, *Jem Sultan*, 82. Alméida is not mentioned by name in Caoursin's text.

48 **Cem set sail:** *Encyclopaedia of Islam*, 2nd ed. (Leiden: Brill Online, 2012), s.v. "Djem" (Halil İnalcık).

48 **superb deal:** *Encyclopaedia of Islam*, s.v. "Djem" (İnalcık).

49 **Cem learned of this bargain:** Vatin, *Sultan Djem*, 19.

49 **the twenty-three-year-old prince:** On Cem's age, see Freely, *Jem Sultan*, 80.

49 **offered herself to the prince:** These French sources are referenced in Freely, *Jem Sultan*, 94.

49 **"charming well-made boys":** Quoted in Freely, *Jem Sultan*, 95. On Cem's sex life in Nice, see Freely, *Jem Sultan*, 93–95; Vatin, *Sultan Djem*, 156.

49 **"a man can stay there":** Quoted in Freely, *Jem Sultan*, 95.

50 **"the general good of Christendom":** Quoted in *Encyclopaedia of Islam*, s.v. "Djem" (İnalcık).

50 **arrived in Rome:** *Encyclopaedia of Islam*, s.v. "Djem" (İnalcık).

50 **"The humanists wrote":** James Hankins, "Renaissance Crusaders: Humanist Crusade Literature in the Age of Mehmed II," *Dumbarton Oaks Papers* 49 (1995): 112. I thank Francesca Trivellato for bringing this passage to my attention.

51 **married a Christian woman:** The suggestion is in Vatin, *Sultan Djem*, 156, n. 408.

51 **tall, rotund pope:** For an image of Pope Innocent, see "Pope Innocent VIII Died in a Rejuvenation Attempt in 1492," Alamy, https://www.researchgate .net/figure/Pope-Innocent-VIII-died-in-a-rejuvenation-attempt-in-1492 -Alamy_fig5_269710719 (accessed February 9, 2019).

51 **vowed never to help Rome:** *Encyclopaedia of Islam*, s.v. "Djem" (İnalcık).

51 **"even for the rule":** Quoted in Caroline Finkel, *Osman's Dream: The Story of the Ottoman Empire, 1300–1923* (New York: Basic Books, 2006), 87.

52 **"Stocky and robust":** Letter from Matteo Bosso, cited in Freely, *Jem Sultan*, 172.

52 **he forgave Bayezit:** *Encyclopaedia of Islam*, s.v. "Djem" (İnalcık).

54 **He handed over to Rome:** *Encyclopaedia of Islam*, s.v. "Djem" (İnalcık); Eamon Duffy, *Saints and Sinners: A History of the Popes*, 3rd ed. (New Haven: Yale University Press, 2006), 196; Freely, *Jem Sultan*, 162–63.

55 **Pope Innocent VIII . . . died:** Freely, *Jem Sultan*, 205–06.

57 **reached Naples in February 1495:** Vatin, *Sultan Djem*, 23.

57 **a wilting weariness:** Freely, *Jem Sultan*, 271–73.

58 **"Be in good spirits":** All quotes in this paragraph are from Freely, *Jem Sultan*, 272.

58 **dying in Naples:** On Cem's death, see Vatin, *Sultan Djem*, 65–69.

CHAPTER 4: LEARNING THE FAMILY BUSINESS

64 **Black Sea dolphin:** "Black Sea Dolphins," *Black Sea*, http://blacksea-education .ru/dolphins.shtml (accessed February 11, 2019).

64 **boasted ancient roots:** On the Ottomanization of these and other cities, see Ronald C. Jennings, "Urban Population in Anatolia in the Sixteenth Century: A Study of Kayseri, Karaman, Amasya, Trabzon, and Erzurum," *International Journal of Middle East Studies* 7 (1976): 21–57.

65 **subdue Trabzon:** Franz Babinger, *Mehmed the Conqueror and His Time*, trans. Ralph Manheim, ed. William C. Hickman (Princeton: Princeton University Press, 1978), 190–97.

65 **slow transition from a millennium of Christian rule:** Jennings, "Urban Population in Anatolia," 43–46.

65 **tenuous ties to Ottoman hegemony:** Heath W. Lowry, *The Islamization and Turkification of the City of Trabzon (Trebizond), 1461–1583* (Istanbul: Isis Press, 2009), 5–37.

65 **adhered to some form of Christianity:** Lowry, *Islamization and Turkification*, 36; Jennings, "Urban Population in Anatolia," 43.

67 **Venetian and Genoese merchants:** In this period, Venetians and Genoese made up around 4% of the city's population. Lowry, *Islamization and Turkification*, 36.

68 **When a Catholic Florentine merchant:** Halil İnalcık, "The Ottoman State: Economy and Society, 1300–1600," in *An Economic and Social History of the Ottoman Empire*, ed. Halil İnalcık with Donald Quataert, 2 vols. (Cambridge, UK: Cambridge University Press, 1994), 1:235–36.

69 **the middlemen of Eurasian trade:** İnalcık, "The Ottoman State," 1:222–23.

69 **Ottoman policy of "one mother, one son":** Leslie P. Peirce, *The Imperial Harem: Women and Sovereignty in the Ottoman Empire* (Oxford: Oxford University Press, 1993), 42–45.

69 **Circle of Justice:** Linda T. Darling, *A History of Social Justice and Political Power in the Middle East: The Circle of Justice from Mesopotamia to Globalization* (New York: Routledge, 2013), 2.

70 **cherries and hazelnuts:** On Trabzon's hazelnuts, see İnalcık, "The Ottoman State," 1:187.

71 **the world's most prolific producer:** *Wikipedia*, s.v. "Trabzon," https://en .wikipedia.org/wiki/Trabzon (accessed February 8, 2019).

71 **small farms were distributed as recompense for military service:** On the Ottoman landholding system, see Colin Imber, *The Ottoman Empire, 1300–1650: The Structure of Power*, 2nd ed. (New York: Palgrave Macmillan, 2009), 164–203, 239–42, 253–61.

71 **thoroughgoing program of Ottomanization:** Lowry, *Islamization and Turkification*.

72 **The Islamic institution of the pious foundation:** Ronald C. Jennings, "Pious Foundations in the Society and Economy of Ottoman Trabzon, 1565–1640: A Study Based on the Judicial Registers (Şerʿi Mahkeme Sicilleri) of Trabzon," *Journal of the Economic and Social History of the Orient* 33 (1990): 271–336.

72 **Gülbahar established the most opulent:** Jennings, "Pious Foundations," 289–90, n. 22; 330.

74 **Her mosque and Qur'anic school played a key role:** Jennings, "Pious Foundations," 289–90, n. 22; Lowry, *Islamization and Turkification*.

75   **Uncovering the full genealogical picture:** Peirce, *Imperial Harem*, 84–85.
75   **Suleyman the Magnificent:** Gábor Ágoston and Bruce Masters, eds., *Encyclopedia of the Ottoman Empire* (New York: Facts on File, 2009), s.v. "Süleyman I ('the Magnificent'; Kanuni, or 'the Lawgiver')" (Gábor Ágoston).
75   **plumpish, with long auburn hair and a prominent forehead:** *Wikipedia*, s.v. "Hafsa Sultan (wife of Selim I)," https://en.wikipedia.org/wiki/Hafsa_Sultan_(wife_of_Selim_I)#/media/File:BustOfAyseHafsaSultan_ManisaTurkey.jpg (accessed February 9, 2019).
75   **Sultanate of Women:** Peirce, *Imperial Harem*, 57–112.

CHAPTER 5: POWER AT THE EDGE

78   **"He was a sun":** Celia J. Kerslake, "A Critical Edition and Translation of the Introductory Sections and the First Thirteen Chapters of the 'Selīmnāme' of Celālzāde Muṣṭafā Çelebi" (D. Phil. thesis, University of Oxford, 1975), 39a.
78   **the provincial governorships:** On these appointments, see H. Erdem Çıpa, *The Making of Selim: Succession, Legitimacy, and Memory in the Early Modern Ottoman World* (Bloomington: Indiana University Press, 2017), 32–37.
79   **The regular rotation of governors:** On this practice in Trabzon, see Heath W. Lowry, *The Islamization and Turkification of the City of Trabzon (Trebizond), 1461–1583* (Istanbul: Isis Press, 2009), 28–29.
80   **cut deals with Kurdish chieftains:** Çıpa, *Making of Selim*, 7–8.
81   **alliances with the Karamanid tribal confederation:** Hakkı Erdem Çıpa, "The Centrality of the Periphery: The Rise to Power of Selīm I, 1487–1512" (Ph.D. diss., Harvard University, 2007), 226–31.
82   **One of Selim's payroll registers:** Çıpa, "Centrality of the Periphery," 220–31. See also Çıpa, *Making of Selim*, 78–106.
84   **Ak Koyunlu Confederacy:** *Encyclopaedia of Islam*, 2nd ed. (Leiden: Brill Online, 2012), s.v. "Aḳ Ḳoyunlu" (V. Minorsky).
85   **"The kingship . . . false person":** Kerslake, " 'Selīmnāme,' " 40a.
85   **"The carpets of justice":** Kerslake, " 'Selīmnāme,' " 39b.
85–86   **a teenager named Ismail:** Roger Savory, *Iran under the Safavids* (Cambridge, UK: Cambridge University Press, 1980), 20–26.

CHAPTER 6: COLUMBUS AND ISLAM

90   **At the age of nine:** Carol Delaney, *Columbus and the Quest for Jerusalem: How Religion Drove the Voyages that Led to America* (New York: Free Press, 2011), 25–26; Silvio A. Bedini, ed., *The Christopher Columbus Encyclopedia* (New York: Simon and Schuster, 1992), s.v. "Columbus, Christopher: Early Maritime Experience" (Helen Nader).
91   **"one of the maritime wonders," "coastal highway":** *Christopher Columbus Encyclopedia*, s.v. "Columbus, Christopher: Early Maritime Experience" (Nader).
94   **"Today many Mongols":** Quoted in Abbas Hamdani, "Columbus and the Recovery of Jerusalem," *Journal of the American Oriental Society* 99 (1979): 42.
94   **Several of these envoys:** Hamdani, "Columbus and the Recovery of Jerusalem," 42–43.
95   **Seven Cities of Cibola:** Peter Manseau, *One Nation, Under Gods: A New American History* (New York: Little, Brown, 2015), 32–33. Delaney expresses doubt

about Columbus's belief in the Seven Cities: Delaney, *Columbus and the Quest for Jerusalem*, 77–78.

95 **The 1325 map of Dalorto:** William H. Babcock, "The Island of the Seven Cities," *Geographical Review* 17 (1919): 98.

96 **became an apprentice sailor:** *Christopher Columbus Encyclopedia*, s.v. "Columbus, Christopher: Early Maritime Experience" (Nader).

96 **Columbus directly experienced the Muslim world:** Delaney, *Columbus and the Quest for Jerusalem*, 33.

97 **a letter he wrote from Hispaniola:** Charles Elton, *The Career of Columbus* (New York: Cassell, 1892), 55–56.

97 **sent him to Chios:** Delaney, *Columbus and the Quest for Jerusalem*, 33–34; Stuart B. Schwartz, *The Iberian Mediterranean and Atlantic Traditions in the Formation of Columbus as a Colonizer* (Minneapolis: University of Minnesota, the Associates of the James Ford Bell Library, 1986), 2.

97 **the Italian city-state's easternmost territory:** Schwartz, *Iberian Mediterranean and Atlantic Traditions*, 4.

100 **fire broke out on Columbus's vessel:** *Christopher Columbus Encyclopedia*, s.v. "Columbus, Christopher: Early Maritime Experience" (Nader).

100 **"garbled story":** *Christopher Columbus Encyclopedia*, s.v. "Columbus, Christopher: Early Maritime Experience" (Nader).

100 **London in these years:** This and the following paragraph are adapted from Roy Porter, *London: A Social History* (Cambridge, MA: Harvard University Press, 1994), 11–33.

102 **"Men of Cathay":** Quoted in David B. Quinn, "Columbus and the North: England, Iceland, and Ireland," *William and Mary Quarterly* 49 (1992): 284.

102 **Native Americans rode Atlantic currents eastward:** Jack D. Forbes, *Africans and Native Americans: The Language of Race and the Evolution of Red-Black Peoples*, 2nd ed. (Urbana: University of Illinois Press, 1993), 6–25.

CHAPTER 7: COLUMBUS'S CRUSADE

103 **indubitably one of Crusade:** Abbas Hamdani, "Ottoman Response to the Discovery of America and the New Route to India," *Journal of the American Oriental Society* 101 (1981): 323–24.

104 **Filipa Moniz:** Silvio A. Bedini, ed., *The Christopher Columbus Encyclopedia* (New York: Simon & Schuster, 1992), s.v. "Columbus, Christopher: Columbus in Portugal" (Rebecca Catz). No information about Filipa's appearance survives.

105 **navigational instruments and maps:** Kirstin Downey, *Isabella: The Warrior Queen* (New York: Nan A. Talese/Doubleday, 2014), 234–35.

105 **Prince Henry:** *Christopher Columbus Encyclopedia*, s.v. "Henry the Navigator" (Glenn J. Ames).

105 **Columbus took advantage of his new connections:** Carol Delaney, *Columbus and the Quest for Jerusalem: How Religion Drove the Voyages that Led to America* (New York: Free Press, 2011), 43–44.

105 **"was actuated by the zeal":** Quoted in Delaney, *Columbus and the Quest for Jerusalem*, 324.

106 **Mali Empire:** Michael A. Gomez, *African Dominion: A New History of Empire in Early and Medieval West Africa* (Princeton: Princeton University Press, 2018), 61–165.

108 **The papal conjoining of Muslim and non-Muslim:** Peter Manseau, *One Nation, Under Gods: A New American History* (New York: Little, Brown, 2015), 29–56.

109 **São Jorge da Mina:** Delaney, *Columbus and the Quest for Jerusalem*, 45–47; *Christopher Columbus Encyclopedia*, s.v. "Columbus, Christopher: Early Maritime Experience" (Helen Nader); *Wikipedia*, s.v. "Elmina Castle," https://en.wikipedia.org/wiki/Elmina_Castle (accessed February 9, 2019).

109 **João's fort immediately proved its worth:** *Wikipedia*, s.v. "Elmina," https://en.wikipedia.org/wiki/Elmina (accessed February 9, 2019).

111 **"fit and athletic . . . gay":** On Ferdinand's looks, see Downey, *Isabella*, 78. On Isabella's, 71. On their familial relations, 41.

111 **"Every day":** Quoted in Downey, *Isabella*, 178.

112 **Ottoman ships continued west:** *Wikipedia*, s.v. "List of Ottoman conquests, sieges and landings," https://en.wikipedia.org/wiki/List_of_Ottoman_conquests,_sieges_and_landings (accessed February 9, 2019).

114 **in the port of Bougie:** Andrew C. Hess, *The Forgotten Frontier: A History of the Sixteenth-Century Ibero-African Frontier* (Chicago: University of Chicago Press, 1978), 60.

114 **several successful raids against Spanish positions:** Hess, *Forgotten Frontier*, 60.

116 **Isabella had little time:** Delaney, *Columbus and the Quest for Jerusalem*, 56–58.

116 **Prince Henry the Navigator, was her great-uncle:** Downey, *Isabella*, 234.

116 **in some ways kindred spirits:** Downey, *Isabella*, 238–39.

117 **Columbus's appearance and personality:** *Christopher Columbus Encyclopedia*, s.v. "Iconography: Early European Portraits" (Carla Rahn Phillips); s.v. "Columbus, Christopher: Columbus in Portugal" (Catz).

117 **nose aquiline, and his light eyes "lively":** Robert Hume, *Christopher Columbus and the European Discovery of America* (Leominster, UK: Gracewing, 1992), 10–11.

117 **"was clearly a charismatic figure":** Delaney, *Columbus and the Quest for Jerusalem*, 59.

117 **"devoted to the Holy Christian Faith":** Quoted in Karine V. Walther, *Sacred Interests: The United States and the Islamic World, 1821–1921* (Chapel Hill: University of North Carolina Press, 2015), 10.

118 **joining the Spanish fight against the Moors:** Delaney, *Columbus and the Quest for Jerusalem*, 62–63.

118 **Vera, Vélez-Blanco, and Vélez-Rubio:** Downey, *Isabella*, 198.

118 **played a decisive role:** Washington Irving, *The Life and Voyages of Christopher Columbus* (New York: James B. Millar, 1884), 137–38.

118 **two Franciscan friars:** Irving, *Life and Voyages*, 69–70.

119 **elaborate regal encampment:** Delaney, *Columbus and the Quest for Jerusalem*, 65.

119 **stretched its resources:** Delaney, *Columbus and the Quest for Jerusalem*, 65.

119 **Granada:** Felipe Fernández-Armesto, *1492: The Year the World Began* (New York: HarperCollins, 2009), 29.

119 **Alhambra complex:** *Wikipedia*, s.v. "Alhambra," https://en.wikipedia.org/wiki/Alhambra (accessed February 9, 2019).

120 **"darker-complexioned . . . fair":** On Ferdinand, see Downey, *Isabella*, 78. On Isabella, 71.

120 **Boabdil left the palace:** Downey, *Isabella*, 201–02.

120 **"the extinction . . . all of Europe":** All quotes come from Downey, *Isabella*, 38.

120 **Celebratory bullfights . . . reenactments:** Downey, *Isabella*, 38.

121 **"was famed and celebrated":** Quoted in Downey, *Isabella*, 203–04.

121 **Not until the twentieth-century formation of Albania and Bosnia:** Fernández-Armesto, *1492*, 44.

122 **"project of discovering . . . bounds of desire":** Quoted in Irving, *Life and Voyages*, 77.

## CHAPTER 8: NEW WORLD ISLAM

123 **Sultan Bayezit marched his armies:** On Bayezit's moves that summer, see Colin Imber, *The Ottoman Empire, 1300–1650: The Structure of Power*, 2nd ed. (New York: Palgrave Macmillan, 2009), 35.

124 **"On 2 January . . . conversion":** Christopher Columbus, *The Four Voyages of Christopher Columbus: Being his own Log-Book, Letters, and Dispatches with Connecting Narrative drawn from the Life of the Admiral by his Son Hernando Colon and Other Contemporary Historians*, ed. and trans. J. M. Cohen (London: Penguin, 1969), 37.

124 **the three ships:** Jerald F. Dirks writes that the brothers Martín Alonso Pinzón and Vicente Yáñez Pinzón, who accompanied Columbus in 1492 as the captains of *La Pinta* and *La Niña* respectively, were from a Muslim family descended from the Marinid sultanate of Morocco. A third brother, Francisco Martín Pinzón, was the pilot of *La Pinta*. Jerald F. Dirks, *Muslims in American History: A Forgotten Legacy* (Beltsville, MD: Amana, 2006), 62–63.

125 **borrowing a technology from their Muslim rivals:** J. H. Parry, *The Establishment of the European Hegemony, 1415–1715: Trade and Exploration in the Age of the Renaissance*, 3rd ed. (New York: Harper and Row, 1966), 19–24; Abbas Hamdani, "Ottoman Response to the Discovery of America and the New Route to India," *Journal of the American Oriental Society* 101 (1981): 324–25, n. 8.

125 **"combined rig made possible":** Parry, *Establishment of European Hegemony*, 23.

125 **"the Arabs were their teachers":** Parry, *Establishment of European Hegemony*, 21.

125 **the *Pinta*'s rudder broke loose:** Silvio A. Bedini, ed., *The Christopher Columbus Encyclopedia* (New York: Simon & Schuster, 1992), s.v. "Voyages of Columbus" (William Lemos). This source also describes the behavior of the crew on the voyage.

126 **"many people of the island":** Columbus, *Four Voyages*, 53.

126 **the Taino people:** On Taino history and culture, see Sven Lovén, *Origins of the Tainan Culture, West Indies* (Tuscaloosa: University of Alabama Press, 2010); Antonio M. Stevens-Arroyo, *Cave of the Jagua: The Mythological World of the Taínos* (Albuquerque: University of New Mexico Press, 1988); Samuel M. Wilson, *Hispaniola: Caribbean Chiefdoms in the Age of Columbus* (Tuscaloosa: University of Alabama Press, 1990); Lesley-Gail Atkinson, ed., *The Earliest Inhabitants: The Dynamics of the Jamaican Taíno* (Kingston: University of the West Indies Press, 2006); Irving Rouse, *The Tainos: Rise and Decline of the People Who Greeted Columbus* (New Haven: Yale University Press, 1992).

126 **"the colour of Canary Islanders":** Columbus, *Four Voyages*, 55.

126 **As "naked":** Quoted in *Christopher Columbus Encyclopedia*, s.v. "Voyages of Columbus" (Lemos).

126 **"fine limbs":** Columbus, *Four Voyages*, 55.

126 **balls of cotton thread, and parrots:** Columbus, *Four Voyages*, 56.

126 **beads, baubles, and bits of colored glass:** *Christopher Columbus Encyclopedia*, s.v. "Voyages of Columbus" (Lemos).

126 **"would easily be made Christians":** Columbus, *Four Voyages*, 56.

126 **six evidently willing Tainos:** Rouse, *Tainos*, 142–43. Columbus also took these six Taino passenger-captives with him on his return voyage to Spain. There, they were baptized, with the king, queen, and their children serving as godparents. One of the six stayed in Spain, where he died two years later. The others returned to the Caribbean with Columbus on his second voyage, with one of them serving as his interpreter (145).

127 **"who wears much gold":** Quoted in *Christopher Columbus Encyclopedia*, s.v. "Voyages of Columbus" (Lemos).

127 **"another very large island":** Quoted in *Christopher Columbus Encyclopedia*, s.v. "Voyages of Columbus" (Lemos).

128 **"Not even a shoe string":** Quoted in *Christopher Columbus Encyclopedia*, s.v. "Voyages of Columbus" (Lemos).

128 **La Navidad:** *Christopher Columbus Encyclopedia*, s.v. "Settlements: La Navidad" (Kathleen Deagan).

130 **"[O]nce in the open sea":** Bernal Díaz, *The Conquest of New Spain*, trans. J. M. Cohen (London: Penguin, 1963), 17.

131 **the vocabulary of war with Islam:** Mercedes García-Arenal, "Moriscos e Indios: Para un Estudio Comparado de Métodos de Conquista y Evangelización," *Chronica Nova* 20 (1992): 153–75.

131 **"have no iron":** Columbus, *Four Voyages*, 55.

131 *almaizares*, **Moorish sashes:** Vanita Seth, *Europe's Indians: Producing Racial Difference, 1500–1900* (Durham, NC: Duke University Press, 2010), 48.

131 **"Moorish robes," "Moorish women":** Seth, *Europe's Indians*, 48.

131 **"like the Moors, the women":** Quoted in *Christopher Columbus Encyclopedia*, s.v. "Voyages of Columbus" (Lemos).

132 **"a familiar barbarian empire":** J. H. Elliott, "Cortés, Velázquez and Charles V," introductory essay in *Hernán Cortés: Letters from Mexico*, ed. and trans. Anthony Pagden (New Haven: Yale University Press, 1986), lxii.

132 **called Montezuma a sultan:** *Cortés: Letters from Mexico*, 112.

132 **styles of floor and roof tiles:** *Cortés: Letters from Mexico*, 110; Elliott, "Cortés," lxii.

132 **"Since the only political model":** Elliott, "Cortés," lxii.

132 *alarabs . . . mamelucos*: Serge Gruzinski, *What Time Is It There?: America and Islam at the Dawn of Modern Times*, trans. Jean Birrell (Cambridge, UK: Polity Press, 2010), 131–32. On the Chichimecs, see also Amber Brian, "Shifting Identities: Mestizo Historiography and the Representation of Chichimecs," in *To Be Indio in Colonial Spanish America*, ed. Mónica Díaz (Albuquerque: University of New Mexico Press, 2017), 143–66.

132 *genízaros*: Russell M. Magnaghi, "Plains Indians in New Mexico: The Genízaro Experience," *Great Plains Quarterly* 10 (1990), 92, n. 2; Ramón A. Gutiérrez, *When Jesus Came, the Corn Mothers Went Away: Marriage, Sexuality, and Power in New Mexico, 1500–1846* (Stanford, CA: Stanford University Press, 1991), 151.

132 **"the zambra of the Moors":** Peter Manseau, *One Nation, Under Gods: A New American History* (New York: Little, Brown, 2015), 43–44. See also David Sanchez Cano, "Dances for the Royal Festivities in Madrid in the Sixteenth and Seventeenth Centuries," *Dance Research* 23 (2008): 123–52. Generally on the *zam-*

*bra* and its perceived New World connections, see Karoline P. Cook, *Forbidden Passages: Muslims and Moriscos in Colonial Spanish America* (Philadelphia: University of Pennsylvania Press, 2016), 10–21.

133 **"ships that were said . . . than Spaniards":** All quotes from Karoline P. Cook, "Muslims and *Chichimeca* in New Spain: The Debates over Just War and Slavery," *Anuario de Estudios Americanos* 70 (2013): 16–18.

133 **"García [the Crown's agent]":** Quoted in Cook, "Muslims and *Chichimeca*," 18.

134 **"The conquest of the Indians began":** Quoted in Barbara Fuchs, *Mimesis and Empire: The New World, Islam, and European Identities* (Cambridge, UK: Cambridge University Press, 2001), 7.

134 **"began as a kind of proxy war":** Manseau, *One Nation, Under Gods*, 45.

134 **Santiago Matamoros, St. James the Moor-slayer:** Gruzinski, *What Time Is It There?*, 132–33.

134–135 *Mataindios . . . Mataespañois:* "The Transference of 'Reconquista' Iconography to the New World: From Santiago Matamoros to Santiago Mataindios," *Ballandalus*, https://ballandalus.wordpress.com/2014/02/11/the-transference-of-reconquista-iconography-to-the-new-world-from-santiago-matamoros-to-santiago-mataindios/ (accessed February 9, 2019).

## CHAPTER 9: CHRISTIAN JIHAD

137 **"No prince of Castile":** Quoted in Silvio A. Bedini, ed., *The Christopher Columbus Encyclopedia* (New York: Simon & Schuster, 1992), s.v. "Voyages of Columbus" (William Lemos).

137 **"tax payment," "like Christians":** Quoted in *Christopher Columbus Encyclopedia*, s.v. "Encomienda" (Paul E. Hoffman).

138 **sign statements that they believed Cuba to be mainland Asia:** *Christopher Columbus Encyclopedia*, s.v. "Voyages of Columbus" (Lemos).

138 **continued to bring interpreters:** Abbas Hamdani, "Columbus and the Recovery of Jerusalem," *Journal of the American Oriental Society* 99 (1979): 44.

139 **"[It] was brought out of malice":** Quoted in *Christopher Columbus Encyclopedia*, s.v. "Voyages of Columbus" (Lemos).

139 **Columbus died:** William D. Phillips, Jr., and Carla Rahn Phillips, *The Worlds of Christopher Columbus* (Cambridge, UK: Cambridge University Press, 1992), 238–40; *Christopher Columbus Encyclopedia*, s.v. "Columbus, Christopher: The Final Years, Illness, and Death" (Helen Nader).

139 **one of only two mentions:** *Christopher Columbus Encyclopedia*, s.v. "Columbus, Christopher: Columbus in Portugal" (Rebecca Catz).

139 **The Requirement:** I use the version of the text quoted in Patricia Seed, *Ceremonies of Possession in Europe's Conquest of the New World, 1492–1640* (Cambridge, UK: Cambridge University Press, 1995), 69.

141 **had to accept the superiority of Christianity:** Seed, *Ceremonies of Possession*, 71.

141 **"unique ritual demand for submission":** Seed, *Ceremonies of Possession*, 72.

142 **The first step of any *jihad*:** Seed, *Ceremonies of Possession*, 76.

142 **"refusal to acknowledge religious superiority":** Seed, *Ceremonies of Possession*, 78.

142 **"No other European state":** Seed, *Ceremonies of Possession*, 70.

142 **"Moors or Turks . . . Muhammad":** Quoted in Seed, *Ceremonies of Possession*, 92–93.

143 **challenge that authority's legitimacy:** Seed, *Ceremonies of Possession*, 94.

143 **"the veritable barbarian outcasts":** Quoted in Tzvetan Todorov, *The Conquest of America: The Question of the Other*, trans. Richard Howard (Norman: University of Oklahoma Press, 1999), 166.

144 **a mark of vassalage:** Seed, *Ceremonies of Possession*, 82.

144 **"indigenous peoples of the Americas":** Seed, *Ceremonies of Possession*, 87.

145 **"the Romans of the Muslim world":** Albert Hourani, "How Should We Write the History of the Middle East?," *International Journal of Middle East Studies* 23 (1991): 130.

145 **Spain asserted its Roman heritage:** On the Spanish uses of the legacy of the Roman Empire in their conquest of the Americas, see David A. Lupher, *Romans in a New World: Classical Models in Sixteenth-Century Spanish America* (Ann Arbor: University of Michigan Press, 2003).

145 **"As for your observation":** Bernal Díaz, *The Conquest of New Spain*, trans. J. M. Cohen (London: Penguin, 1963), 159. See also J. H. Elliott, "The Mental World of Hernán Cortés," *Transactions of the Royal Historical Society* 17 (1967): 45.

146 **"of good height":** On Montezuma's appearance, see Díaz, *Conquest of New Spain*, 224.

146 **"donated" his empire to Charles V:** Elliott, "Mental World of Cortés," 52–53; J. H. Elliott, "Cortés, Velázquez and Charles V," introductory essay in *Hernán Cortés: Letters from Mexico*, ed. and trans. Anthony Pagden (New Haven: Yale University Press, 1986), lxvii–lxviii.

146 **leaving—"donating"—Italy and the rest of western Europe to the pope:** Elliott, "Cortés," lxvii–lxviii.

146 **"monarch of the universe":** Quoted in Elliott, "Mental World of Cortés," 55.

CHAPTER 10: THE TAINO—MUSLIMS OF HISPANIOLA

150 **Livorno:** Ariel Salzmann, "Migrants in Chains: On the Enslavement of Muslims in Renaissance and Enlightenment Europe," *Religions* 4 (2013): 396.

150 **forcibly converted the Muslims and other non-Christians:** Sylviane A. Diouf, *Servants of Allah: African Muslims Enslaved in the Americas*, 2nd ed. (New York: New York University Press, 2013), 33–37.

151 **forays were organized mostly from . . . Santiago:** Jane Landers, "The Great Wolof Scare of 1521" (unpublished manuscript), 1. My sincerest thanks to Professor Landers for allowing me to read and cite her work.

151 **Valencians constituted about a third:** William D. Phillips, Jr., *Slavery in Medieval and Early Modern Iberia* (Philadelphia: University of Pennsylvania Press, 2013), 66–67.

151 **Black slaves who had lived in Christian or Muslim kingdoms:** For a very useful study of slavery and race in Morocco, see Chouki El Hamel, *Black Morocco: A History of Slavery, Race, and Islam* (Cambridge, UK: Cambridge University Press, 2013).

151 **the Wolof Empire split:** Michael A. Gomez, *Black Crescent: The Experience and Legacy of African Muslims in the Americas* (Cambridge, UK: Cambridge University Press, 2005), 9–12.

151 **"criminals, witches":** Martin A. Klein, "Slavery and the Early State in Africa," *Social Evolution and History* 8 (2009): 177.

152 **"In a new land":** Quoted in Diouf, *Servants of Allah*, 36.

153 **official sanction to individual direct transshipments:** Gomez, *Black Crescent*, 15.

153 **"bad customs":** Quoted in Landers, "Wolof Scare," 2, and Erin Woodruff Stone, "America's First Slave Revolt: Indians and African Slaves in Española, 1500–1534," *Ethnohistory* 60 (2013): 203.

153 **the history of sugar cultivation:** William D. Phillips, Jr., "Old World Precedents: Sugar and Slavery in the Mediterranean," in *The Caribbean: A History of the Region and Its Peoples*, ed. Stephan Palmié and Francisco A. Scarano (Chicago: University of Chicago Press, 2011), 70–71, 77–79.

154 **first Muslim slaves and sugar cane to the New World:** Genaro Rodríguez Morel, "The Sugar Economy of Española in the Sixteenth Century," in *Tropical Babylons: Sugar and the Making of the Atlantic World, 1450–1680*, ed. Stuart B. Schwartz (Chapel Hill: University of North Carolina Press, 2004), 86–87.

154 **boosting the development of the Caribbean economy:** William D. Phillips, Jr., "Sugar in Iberia," in *Tropical Babylons*, 34–35.

154 **"There are so many [blacks]":** Quoted in Landers, "Wolof Scare," 12.

155 **perhaps just a twentieth of the African population:** Ida Altman, "The Revolt of Enriquillo and the Historiography of Early Spanish America," *The Americas* 63 (2007): 611.

155 **"bellicose and perverse":** Quoted in Landers, "Wolof Scare," 1, 6. See also Stone, "America's First Slave Revolt," 195–217; Gomez, *Black Crescent*, 3–5.

155 **"wild and bloody expedition":** Quoted in Gomez, *Black Crescent*, 3.

157 **"planted with gallows":** Quoted in Landers, "Wolof Scare," 8–9.

157 **"The blacks were punished":** Quoted in Landers, "Wolof Scare," 9.

158 **"Among the few and poor goods":** Quoted in Altman, "The Revolt of Enriquillo," 595.

158 **"probably mostly men":** Altman, "The Revolt of Enriquillo," 598.

159 **natives from nearby islands:** On the interisland movement of Caribbean Indians, see Karen F. Anderson-Córdova, *Surviving Spanish Conquest: Indian Fight, Flight, and Cultural Transformation in Hispaniola and Puerto Rico* (Tuscaloosa: University of Alabama Press, 2017).

159 **rebels were able to sustain themselves:** Altman, "The Revolt of Enriquillo," 599.

160 **"know the land . . . needed":** Quoted in Altman, "The Revolt of Enriquillo," 599.

160 **"The island is large":** Quoted in Stone, "America's First Slave Revolt," 204–10.

160 **the Taino and the Muslims joined forces:** Stone, "America's First Slave Revolt."

160 **"rebel Indians and Negros":** Stone, "America's First Slave Revolt," 217, n. 70. The date October 1523 is given on 209.

160 **El Limona:** Stone, "America's First Slave Revolt," 204–10.

162 **"prideful . . . Africans from other lands":** Quoted in Landers, "Wolof Scare," 11.

162 **"It would be preferable":** Quoted in Altman, "The Revolt of Enriquillo," 611.

162 **the majority of the slaves taken to gold-rich Cartagena:** Diouf, *Servants of Allah*, 38.

162 **allowed Muslims to become a major force in the Americas:** Today's Muslim population in the Caribbean and throughout Latin America is mostly the

result of recent immigration from the Middle East and South Asia. See María del Mar Logroño Narbona, Paulo G. Pinto, and John Tofik Karam, eds., *Crescent over Another Horizon: Islam in Latin America, the Caribbean, and Latino USA* (Austin: University of Texas Press, 2015).

162 **"if counted as a whole"**: Diouf, *Servants of Allah*, 70.

162 **"the cursed sect of Mahomet"**: Quoted in Diouf, *Servants of Allah*, 38.

162-163 **accuse their Muslim slaves of proselytizing**: Diouf, *Servants of Allah*, 212–13; Gomez, *Black Crescent*, 18.

163 **greater reliance on galleys for transport in the Caribbean**: David Wheat, "Mediterranean Slavery, New World Transformations: Galley Slaves in the Spanish Caribbean, 1578–1635," *Slavery and Abolition* 31 (2010): 327–44.

163 **"Moors and Turks . . . prove to be the best"**: Quoted in Wheat, "Mediterranean Slavery," 330.

163 **Records from 1595**: Gomez, *Black Crescent*, 31–33.

163 **"The conquest of the earth"**: Joseph Conrad, *Heart of Darkness* (New York: Penguin, 2017), 7.

164 **Melchor de Castro . . . coat of arms**: Landers, "Wolof Scare," 8.


CHAPTER 11: FINDING OTTOMAN JERUSALEM

166 **"Your Highnesses ordained"**: Christopher Columbus, *The Four Voyages of Christopher Columbus: Being his own Log-Book, Letters, and Dispatches with Connecting Narrative drawn from the Life of the Admiral by his Son Hernando Colon and Other Contemporary Historians*, ed. and trans. J. M. Cohen (London: Penguin, 1969), 37–38.

167 **Jews had materially aided Granada's Muslims**: Silvio A. Bedini, ed., *The Christopher Columbus Encyclopedia* (New York: Simon & Schuster, 1992), s.v. "Jews: Expulsion from Spain" (Angel Alcalá).

167 **release funds that had been tied up by the war**: *Christopher Columbus Encyclopedia* s.v. "Jews: Expulsion from Spain" (Alcalá).

167–168 **"[I]t is evident . . . declaration"**: Quoted in Jane S. Gerber, *The Jews of Spain: A History of the Sephardic Experience* (New York: Free Press, 1992), 286–88.

169 **some 100,000 opted for conversion**: Gerber, *Jews of Spain*, 140.

170 **"If [our enemies] let us live"**: Quoted in Gerber, *Jews of Spain*, 138.

170 **"In the first week of July"**: Quoted in Gerber, *Jews of Spain*, 140.

170 **Portugal received . . . about 120,000**: Gerber, *Jews of Spain*, 139.

171 **"inhabited by lizards . . . abandonment"**: Quoted in Gerber, *Jews of Spain*, 141.

171 **"kindness of the King"**: Quoted in Gerber, *Jews of Spain*, 149. See also 139.

172 **Sicily . . . expelled its Jewish community**: *Wikipedia*, s.v. "History of the Jews in Sicily," https://en.wikipedia.org/wiki/History_of_the_Jews_in_Sicily (accessed February 10, 2019).

172 **a boatload of Jews escaping persecution in Pesaro**: Gerber, *Jews of Spain*, 150.

172 **"their weary feet could find rest"**: Quoted in Gerber, *Jews of Spain*, 150.

173 **"a paradise for the Jews"**: Franz Babinger, *Mehmed the Conqueror and His Time*, trans. Ralph Manheim, ed. William C. Hickman (Princeton: Princeton University Press, 1978), 106.

173 **Isaac Sarfati**: Babinger, *Mehmed the Conqueror*, 107.

174 **"our righteous Messiah":** Quoted in Gerber, *Jews of Spain*, 151.

174 **replace Italian Christian merchants with Ottoman Jewish traders:** The Ottomans made similar arguments in the sixteenth century in support of many of the empire's Armenian merchant families.

174 **Spanish Jews . . . in Trabzon:** Daniel Goffman, "Jews in Early Modern Ottoman Commerce," in *Jews, Turks, Ottomans: A Shared History, Fifteenth through the Twentieth Century*, ed. Avigdor Levy (Syracuse, NY: Syracuse University Press, 2002), 18–19.

174 **"You call Ferdinand":** Quoted in Gerber, *Jews of Spain*, 151.

175 **"Not long since banished":** Quoted in Gerber, *Jews of Spain*, 164–65.

175 **Joseph Hamon:** *Encyclopedia of Jews in the Islamic World* (Leiden: Brill Online, 2010), s.v. "Hamon Family" (Cengiz Sisman).

175 **Hebrew printing press:** Gerber, *Jews of Spain*, 158–60.

175 **The first Hebrew-language printed books:** Yaron Ben Na'eh, "Hebrew Printing Houses in the Ottoman Empire," in *Jewish Journalism and Printing Houses in the Ottoman Empire and Modern Turkey*, ed. Gad Nassi (Istanbul: Isis Press, 2001), 75.

176 **Numbers attest to the success of Jewish life:** Gerber, *Jews of Spain*, 153–58.

177 **"each congregation appears":** Quoted in Gerber, *Jews of Spain*, 154.

177 **two *conversos* married by Christian rite:** Gerber, *Jews of Spain*, 157.

178 **more lax kosher meat laws:** Gerber, *Jews of Spain*, 157.

179 **In Istanbul, the number of Jewish households:** Gerber, *Jews of Spain*, 153.

179 **twenty-one synagogues and eighteen Talmudic colleges:** Gerber, *Jews of Spain*, 172.

181 **Trabzon's population:** Ronald C. Jennings, "Urban Population in Anatolia in the Sixteenth Century: A Study of Kayseri, Karaman, Amasya, Trabzon, and Erzurum," *International Journal of Middle East Studies* 7 (1976): 42–47.

181 **Islam did not become the city's majority religion:** Jennings, "Urban Population in Anatolia," 42–47; Heath W. Lowry, *The Islamization and Turkification of the City of Trabzon (Trebizond), 1461–1583* (Istanbul: Isis Press, 2009).

181 **Jews remained a tiny minority in Trabzon:** For Trabzon's total population, see Jennings, "Urban Population in Anatolia," 43. For mentions of Trabzon's small Jewish population, see Rhoads Murphey, "Jewish Contributions to Ottoman Medicine, 1450–1800" in *Jews, Turks, Ottomans*, 61; Goffman, "Jews in Early Modern Ottoman Commerce," 19.

181 **"kill them [Jews] if they see them":** Quoted in Robert Dankoff, *An Ottoman Mentality: The World of Evliya Çelebi* (Leiden: Brill, 2004), 68–69. All quotes in this section, along with the story of the two young Muslim brothers, are from the writings of the prolific seventeenth-century scholar and traveler Evliya Çelebi.

## CHAPTER 12: HERESY FROM THE EAST

186 **Safavid Empire:** On the emergence and rise of the Safavids, see Roger Savory, *Iran under the Safavids* (Cambridge, UK: Cambridge University Press, 1980), 1–49; Andrew J. Newman, *Safavid Iran: Rebirth of a Persian Empire* (London: I. B. Tauris, 2009), 13–25; Stephen Frederic Dale, *The Muslim Empires of the Ottomans, Safavids, and Mughals* (Cambridge, UK: Cambridge University Press, 2010), 63–70; Abbas Amanat, *Iran: A Modern History* (New Haven: Yale University Press, 2017), 31–75.

188 **He spent hours in meditation:** Sholeh A. Quinn, "The Dreams of Shaykh Safi al-Din and Safavid Historical Writing," *Iranian Studies* 29 (1996): 127–47; N. Hanif, *Biographical Encyclopaedia of Sufis (Central Asia and Middle East)* (New Delhi: Sarup and Sons, 2002), s.v. "Safi Al-Din Ardabili (1252–1334)" (F. Babinger and R. M. Savory).

188 **interpreting Safi's visions:** Quinn, "Dreams of Safi."

188 **"Ṣafī, God has shown you":** Quoted in Savory, *Iran under the Safavids*, 8.

191 **A left-handed redhead:** *Encyclopaedia Iranica* (online edition, 2012), s.v. "Esmāʿīl I Ṣafawī: Biography" (Roger M. Savory); Wall text, "Şah İsmayıl—Commander and King," exhibition from April to December 2016, Azerbaijan National Academy of Sciences, Azerbaijan Historical Museum, Baku, Azerbaijan.

192 **Ismail supposedly directed that a ram be killed:** Wall text, "Şah İsmayıl," exhibition, Azerbaijan National Academy of Sciences.

192 **"I am the faith of the Shah":** Quoted in Dale, *Muslim Empires*, 68.

193 **"I am Very God":** Quoted in Savory, *Iran under the Safavids*, 23.

194 **"infidel dog":** Savory, *Iran under the Safavids*, 23. See also "Letters from Selîm and Ismāʿîl," in *The Islamic World*, ed. William H. McNeill and Marilyn Robinson Waldman (Chicago: University of Chicago Press, 1973), 338–44.

## CHAPTER 13: ENEMIES EVERYWHERE

198 **30 percent of the annual income of some Black Sea cities:** Halil İnalcık, "The Ottoman State: Economy and Society, 1300–1600," in *An Economic and Social History of the Ottoman Empire*, ed. Halil İnalcık with Donald Quataert, 2 vols. (Cambridge, UK: Cambridge University Press, 1994), 1:283.

198 **"I am making a raid":** Selim's call to arms, the account of the Georgian raid, and Selim's speech to the troops are from Celia J. Kerslake, "A Critical Edition and Translation of the Introductory Sections and the First Thirteen Chapters of the 'Selîmnâme' of Celālzāde Muṣṭafā Çelebi" (D. Phil. thesis, University of Oxford, 1975), 49a–52a.

199 **ten thousand Georgian women and children destined for slavery:** H. Erdem Çıpa, *The Making of Selim: Succession, Legitimacy, and Memory in the Early Modern Ottoman World* (Bloomington: Indiana University Press, 2017), 36.

203 **major crisis fanned the flames:** Çıpa, *Making of Selim*, 43–48; Caroline Finkel, *Osman's Dream: The Story of the Ottoman Empire, 1300–1923* (New York: Basic Books, 2006), 98–104.

204 **Şahkulu:** Finkel, *Osman's Dream*, 98.

204 **sent letters as far as Greece and Bulgaria:** Çıpa, *Making of Selim*, 44.

204 **"majestic and strong commander":** Quoted in Çıpa, *Making of Selim*, 35.

204 **April 9, 1511:** Finkel, *Osman's Dream*, 98.

205 **notching important victories against Ottoman forces:** Çıpa, *Making of Selim*, 45.

205 **some twenty thousand strong:** Finkel, *Osman's Dream*, 99.

205 **"destroyed everything":** Quoted in Finkel, *Osman's Dream*, 99.

205 **within two days:** Finkel, *Osman's Dream*, 99.

206 **beheaded him and burned the body:** Çıpa, *Making of Selim*, 45.

206 **Bayezit turned to his grand vizier:** Çıpa, *Making of Selim*, 45–46.

206 **confronted the rebels near . . . Sivas:** Çıpa, *Making of Selim*, 46.

207 **resettled most of them in the Peloponnese:** Finkel, *Osman's Dream*, 100.

207 **suggesting that he died either in the battle at Sivas or during the march to Iran:** Çıpa, *Making of Selim*, 46.

207 **benefited from Şahkulu's rebellion:** Çıpa, *Making of Selim*, 46–48.

208 **refused on the grounds that he was not personally leading them into war:** Çıpa, *Making of Selim*, 47–48.

208 **Murad . . . had defected to the Safavid side:** Çıpa, *Making of Selim*, 47.

208 **distinctive red helmet of the *Kızılbaş*:** Finkel, *Osman's Dream*, 103–04.

## CHAPTER 14: SUMMER IN CRIMEA

211 **"the straight-grown sapling":** Celia J. Kerslake, "A Critical Edition and Translation of the Introductory Sections and the First Thirteen Chapters of the 'Selīmnāme' of Celālzāde Muṣṭafā Çelebi" (D. Phil. thesis, University of Oxford, 1975), 53a.

211 **Selim had tried (and failed) to have him named governor:** H. Erdem Çıpa, *The Making of Selim: Succession, Legitimacy, and Memory in the Early Modern Ottoman World* (Bloomington: Indiana University Press, 2017), 34.

213 **"The protected city of Kaffa":** Kerslake, " 'Selīmnāme,' " 54a.

214 **ornate palace in western Crimea:** *Wikipedia*, s.v. "Bakhchisaray Palace," https://en.wikipedia.org/wiki/Bakhchisaray_Palace (accessed February 11, 2019).

214 **short, stocky:** For an image of Mengli and his son Mehemmed, see *Wikipedia*, s.v. "Mehmed I Giray," https://en.wikipedia.org/wiki/Mehmed_I_Giray#/media/File:Mengli_bayezid.jpg (accessed February 11, 2019).

215 **Between 1450 and 1586:** Orest Subtelny, *Ukraine: A History*, 3rd ed. (Toronto: University of Toronto Press, 2000), 106.

215 **10,000 gold ducats:** Leslie Peirce, *Empress of the East: How a European Slave Girl Became Queen of the Ottoman Empire* (New York: Basic Books, 2017), 21.

215 **Mengli who had gifted Hafsa:** Peirce, *Empress of the East*, 20.

215 **"firm and honest":** Kerslake, " 'Selīmnāme,' " 54b.

215 **"[Mengli] came to meet him":** The account of Selim's visit to Mengli's court comes from Kerslake, " 'Selīmnāme,' " 54b–59b.

217 **"even if Gabriel descended":** Quoted in Çıpa, *Making of Selim*, 38–39.

221 **Mengli Giray Khan ramped up his support:** Hakkı Erdem Çıpa, "The Centrality of the Periphery: The Rise to Power of Selīm I, 1487–1512" (Ph.D. diss., Harvard University, 2007), 42.

221 **"For such a long time":** Kerslake, " 'Selīmnāme,' " 58a.

222 **"My lord . . . have you come":** This exchange is from Kerslake, " 'Selīmnāme,' " 59a.

## CHAPTER 15: BOUND FOR ISTANBUL

224 **By the end of July, Selim had begun his march southward:** H. Erdem Çıpa, *The Making of Selim: Succession, Legitimacy, and Memory in the Early Modern Ottoman World* (Bloomington: Indiana University Press, 2017), 40–41.

225 **Hasan Pasha:** Çıpa, *Making of Selim*, 41.

225 **They negotiated a rapprochement:** Çıpa, *Making of Selim*, 41–42.

226 **He wrote an angry letter:** Çıpa, *Making of Selim*, 42.

226 **Selim procrastinated:** Çıpa, *Making of Selim*, 42.

226–227 **"[fierce as] lion-hunters"**: Celia J. Kerslake, "A Critical Edition and Translation of the Introductory Sections and the First Thirteen Chapters of the 'Selīmnāme' of Celālzāde Muṣṭafā Çelebi" (D. Phil. thesis, University of Oxford, 1975), 72a.
227 **Selim himself was almost killed**: Çıpa, *Making of Selim*, 50.
227 **Selim's soldiers sneaked him off the battlefield**: Kerslake, "'Selīmnāme,'" 73b.
227 **"such vessels . . . the right way"**: Kerslake, "'Selīmnāme,'" 73b.
227 **wary of becoming too beholden to them**: Çıpa, *Making of Selim*, 51.
228 **He sent word for Ahmed**: Kerslake, "'Selīmnāme,'" 74a–74b.
228 **"the hope of acceding"**: Kerslake, "'Selīmnāme,'" 74b.
229 **he mobilized quickly**: Çıpa, *Making of Selim*, 52–54.
229 **treasonous dogs**: Çıpa, *Making of Selim*, 52.
229 **"[This] vast company"**: Kerslake, "'Selīmnāme,'" 77a.
231 **seethed with rage**: Kerslake, "'Selīmnāme,'" 77b–78b.
231 **"His disposition"**: Kerslake, "'Selīmnāme,'" 78a.
231 **"become an independent sovereign"**: Kerslake, "'Selīmnāme,'" 78a.
231 **invasion and capture of the important city of Konya**: Çıpa, *Making of Selim*, 53.
232 **"his thought and discernment"**: Kerslake, "'Selīmnāme,'" 78a.
232 **Ahmed now aimed his torrent of violence against Korkud**: Kerslake, "'Selīmnāme,'" 79a–79b.
232 **"I came because I was afraid"**: Kerslake, "'Selīmnāme,'" 79b.
233 **commander-in-chief of the Janissaries**: Çıpa, *Making of Selim*, 54.
234 **"the dust of his happiness-promoting feet"**: Kerslake, "'Selīmnāme,'" 80b.

## CHAPTER 16: ONE AND ONLY SULTAN

235 **The decisive weapon**: Franz Babinger, *Mehmed the Conqueror and His Time*, trans. Ralph Manheim, ed. William C. Hickman (Princeton: Princeton University Press, 1978), 80–94.
236 **"in a tent whose height"**: Celia J. Kerslake, "A Critical Edition and Translation of the Introductory Sections and the First Thirteen Chapters of the 'Selīmnāme' of Celālzāde Muṣṭafā Çelebi" (D. Phil. thesis, University of Oxford, 1975), 82b.
236 **"with thousands of manifestations"**: Kerslake, "'Selīmnāme,'" 82b.
236 **"excellent kindness"**: The account of Selim's confrontations with Bayezit comes from Kerslake, "'Selīmnāme,'" 82b–83b.
237 **For about a week, they continued their meetings**: H. Erdem Çıpa, *The Making of Selim: Succession, Legitimacy, and Memory in the Early Modern Ottoman World* (Bloomington: Indiana University Press, 2017), 55.
238 **"everyone was flying . . . at the news"**: Kerslake, "'Selīmnāme,'" 84a.
238 **"The most brilliant sun"**: Kerslake, "'Selīmnāme,'" 84a.
239 **Selim's actions amounted to an unlawful coup**: Çıpa, *Making of Selim*, 56–58.
239 **what to do with his reviled father**: Kerslake, "'Selīmnāme,'" 84a–84b.
239 **Dimetoka—"a charming town"**: Kerslake, "'Selīmnāme,'" 84b.
239 **At dawn, in what must have seemed**: Kerslake, "'Selīmnāme,'" 84b; Fatih Akçe, *Sultan Selim I: The Conqueror of the East* (Clifton, NJ: Blue Dome Press, 2016), 36–37.
240 **"the provisions for the remainder"**: Kerslake, "'Selīmnāme,'" 85a.

240 **Bayezit's death seems suspicious:** Çıpa, *Making of Selim*, 56–58.
240 **"paradise-like in form":** Kerslake, "'Selīmnāme,'" 85b.
240 **exquisitely adorned mausoleum:** Kerslake, "'Selīmnāme,'" 86a.
242 **Korkud had made repeated requests:** Caroline Finkel, *Osman's Dream: The Story of the Ottoman Empire, 1300–1923* (New York: Basic Books, 2006), 103.
242 **They would strangle him:** Finkel, *Osman's Dream*, 103.
242 **He cut deals with local power brokers:** Çıpa, *Making of Selim*, 58.
242 **many of Ahmed's backers grew nervous:** Çıpa, *Making of Selim*, 58–59.
243 **Ahmed had sent his second son:** Çıpa, *Making of Selim*, 59; Finkel, *Osman's Dream*, 102.
243 **executing him along with the sons of some of his other half-brothers:** Çıpa, *Making of Selim*, 59.
244 **Selim devised a plan to trap Ahmed:** Finkel, *Osman's Dream*, 103.
244 **Ahmed was captured alive:** Finkel, *Osman's Dream*, 103.
245 **Selim had Ahmed strangled:** Finkel, *Osman's Dream*, 103; Çıpa, *Making of Selim*, 60.
245 **forces streamed into eastern Anatolia:** Çıpa, *Making of Selim*, 59–60; Finkel, *Osman's Dream*, 103.
246 **Machiavelli esteemed Selim:** Giuseppe Marcocci, "Machiavelli, the Iberian Explorations and the Islamic Empire: Tropical Readers from Brazil to India (Sixteenth and Seventeenth Centuries)," in *Machiavelli, Islam and the East: Reorienting the Foundations of Modern Political Thought*, ed. Lucio Biasiori and Giuseppe Marcocci (Cham, Switzerland: Palgrave Macmillan, 2018), 136.

CHAPTER 17: "THEIR ABODE IS HELL"

250 **Babur . . . had reached out:** Naimur Rahman Farooqi, "Mughal–Ottoman Relations: A Study of Political and Diplomatic Relations between Mughal India and the Ottoman Empire, 1556–1748" (Ph.D. diss., University of Wisconsin, Madison, 1986), 22–25.
250 **"fair, handsome, and very pleasing":** Quoted in *Encyclopaedia Iranica* (online edition, 2012), s.v. "Esmāʿīl I Ṣafawī: Biography" (Roger M. Savory).
250 **His mustache:** See for example "Şah İsmayıl—Commander and King," Exhibition from April to December 2016, Azerbaijan National Academy of Sciences, Azerbaijan Historical Museum, Baku, Azerbaijan, images 7 and 8.
250 **"as brave as a game cock":** Quoted in *Encyclopaedia Iranica*, s.v. "Esmāʿīl I Ṣafawī: Biography" (Savory).
251 **Ismail also enjoyed poetry, song, and dance:** *Encyclopaedia Iranica*, s.v. "Esmāʿīl I Ṣafawī: His Poetry" (Roger M. Savory and Ahmet T. Karamustafa).
251 **refused to observe the standard early sixteenth-century diplomatic protocol:** Adel Allouche, *The Origins and Development of the Ottoman–Ṣafavid Conflict (906–962 / 1500–1555)* (Berlin: Klaus Schwarz Verlag, 1983), 107.
251 **Isfahan:** *Encyclopaedia Iranica*, s.v. "Isfahan: Geography of the Oasis" (Xavier de Planhol).
251 **Shah Ismail mocked Selim's envoys:** Allouche, *Origins and Development*, 109–10.
252 **Selim's envoys departed Isfahan:** Allouche, *Origins and Development*, 106–10.
253 **Selim turned to the empire's religious establishment:** Allouche, *Origins and Development*, 110–12.

253 **Hamza Saru Görez stated unequivocally in his Ottoman Turkish** *fatwa*: Reproduced in M. C. Şehabeddin Tekindağ, "Yeni Kaynak ve Vesîkaların Işığı Altında: Yavuz Sultan Selim'in İran Seferi," *Tarih Dergisi* 17 (1967): 53–55.

253 **worse than Jews and Christians:** Tekindağ, "Yavuz Sultan Selim'in İran Seferi," 53–55; M. Sait Özervarlı, "Between Tension and Rapprochement: Sunni–Shi'ite Relations in the Pre-Modern Ottoman Period, with a Focus on the Eighteenth Century," *Historical Research* 90 (2017): 541.

253 **set out from Edirne on March 20, 1514:** Allouche, *Origins and Development*, 112.

254 **two hundred thousand soldiers:** Roger Savory, *Iran under the Safavids* (Cambridge, UK: Cambridge University Press, 1980), 40.

254 **Selim also moved to squeeze the Safavids economically:** Allouche, *Origins and Development*, 113.

254 **Selim reached Istanbul on March 29:** Allouche, *Origins and Development*, 116.

254 **drove the Safavid economy and supported nearly every facet of the state:** Rudolph P. Matthee, *The Politics of Trade in Safavid Iran: Silk for Silver, 1600–1730* (Cambridge, UK: Cambridge University Press, 2006), 15–32; Edmund M. Herzig, "The Volume of Iranian Raw Silk Exports in the Safavid Period," *Iranian Studies* 25 (1992): 61–79.

255 **Selim sent an envoy to Cairo:** Allouche, *Origins and Development*, 114. On the letters exchanged between Selim and al-Ghawri, see Celia J. Kerslake, "The Correspondence between Selīm I and Ḳānṣūh al-Ġawrī," *Prilozi za Orijentalnu Filologiju* 30 (1980): 219–34.

255 **Selim also dispatched one of his most trusted naval commanders:** Abbas Hamdani, "Ottoman Response to the Discovery of America and the New Route to India," *Journal of the American Oriental Society* 101 (1981): 326.

255 **letter to . . . 'Ubayd Allah Khan:** Allouche, *Origins and Development*, 115; *Encyclopaedia Iranica*, s.v. "Ottoman–Persian Relations: Under Sultan Selim I and Shah Esmā'il I" (Osman G. Özgüdenli).

256 **Selim marched out of Istanbul:** On Selim's troop levels, see *Encyclopaedia Iranica*, s.v. "Ottoman–Persian Relations" (Özgüdenli).

257–258 **"slayer of the wicked . . . face of the earth":** "Letters from Selîm and Ismâ'îl," in *The Islamic World*, ed. William H. McNeill and Marilyn Robinson Waldman (Chicago: University of Chicago Press, 1973), 338–42.

258 **"age seven to seventy":** Quoted in Tekindağ, "Yavuz Sultan Selim'in İran Seferi," 56. See also Caroline Finkel, *Osman's Dream: The Story of the Ottoman Empire, 1300–1923* (New York: Basic Books, 2006), 105.

259 **Selim and his troops arrived there on July 1:** Savory, *Iran under the Safavids*, 41.

259 **the army started toward Erzincan:** Allouche, *Origins and Development*, 118–19.

259–260 **Ismail began his message . . . "always falls":** "Letters from Selîm and Ismâ'îl," 342–44.

260 **the accoutrements of a Sufi:** Allouche, *Origins and Development*, 118.

260 **Ismail answered the challenge:** Elizabeth Fortunato Crider, "The Foreign Relations of the Ottoman Empire under Selim I, 1512–1520" (M.A. thesis, Ohio State University, 1969), 20.

260 **a Shiite uprising had broken out:** *Encyclopaedia Iranica*, s.v. "Ottoman–Persian Relations" (Özgüdenli).

260 **wear a** *chador* **(veil) instead of armor:** Allouche, *Origins and Development*, 118.

260 **sacked and burned everything before making their retreat:** Finkel, *Osman's Dream*, 105.

261 **His soldiers were weary:** *Encyclopaedia Iranica*, s.v. "Ottoman–Persian Relations" (Özgüdenli); Fatih Akçe, *Sultan Selim I: The Conqueror of the East* (Clifton, NJ: Blue Dome Press, 2016), 59.

261 **solar eclipse:** Akçe, *Sultan Selim*, 67; "Total Solar Eclipse of 1514 August 20," NASA Goddard Space Flight Center Eclipse Web Site: https://eclipse .gsfc.nasa.gov/SEsearch/SEsearchmap.php?Ecl=15140820 (accessed February 13, 2019).

262 **anticipated and even influenced later theories by the likes of Nicolaus Copernicus and Tycho Brahe:** George Saliba, *Islamic Science and the Making of the European Renaissance* (Cambridge, MA: MIT Press, 2007).

262 **reached the valley on August 22:** Allouche, *Origins and Development*, 119; Savory, *Iran under the Safavids*, 41.

262 **his forces far outnumbered those of the Safavids:** Allouche, *Origins and Development*, 119–20; Savory, *Iran under the Safavids*, 41–42.

262 **Ismail distributed wine to his soldiers:** Akçe, *Sultan Selim*, 76.

263 **Ottoman gunners . . . easily picking off their enemies:** Savory, *Iran under the Safavids*, 41–42; Abbas Amanat, *Iran: A Modern History* (New Haven: Yale University Press, 2017), 55–57. On the Ottomans' drummers, see Akçe, *Sultan Selim*, 76.

263 **Ismail himself hacked to death:** Wall text, "Şah İsmayıl," exhibition, Azerbaijan National Academy of Sciences.

263 **"The Persian horses":** Quoted in Savory, *Iran under the Safavids*, 43.

263 **Thousands of soldiers had died, along with:** Savory, *Iran under the Safavids*, 42; Amanat, *Iran*, 57.

263 **they solemnly buried their dead:** Akçe, *Sultan Selim*, 90.

264 **two small cannons and six arquebuses:** Finkel, *Osman's Dream*, 108.

264 **Preemptively they professed their loyalty:** Crider, "Foreign Relations," 22; *Encyclopaedia Iranica*, s.v. "Ottoman–Persian Relations" (Özgüdenli).

264 **entered the surrendered city on September 5:** Allouche, *Origins and Development*, 120.

264 **delivered in Selim's name:** Akçe, *Sultan Selim*, 93.

264 **Selim instructed his advisers to send letters:** Crider, "Foreign Relations," 22.

264 **Tabriz:** Wall text, "Şah İsmayıl," exhibition, Azerbaijan National Academy of Sciences.

265 **Selim dispatched some of the city's riches:** *Encyclopaedia of Islam*, 2nd ed. (Leiden: Brill Online, 2012), s.v. "Selim I" (Halil İnalcık).

266 **Ismail's favorite wife, Tajli Khanum:** Leslie P. Peirce, *The Imperial Harem: Women and Sovereignty in the Ottoman Empire* (Oxford: Oxford University Press, 1993), 37; Allouche, *Origins and Development*, 120–21. Some sources claim a different wife was captured. See Peirce, *Imperial Harem*, 297, n. 42.

266 **cutting off the noses of the four men:** Crider, "Foreign Relations," 23.

266 **they nearly mutinied:** Allouche, *Origins and Development*, 121; Savory, *Iran under the Safavids*, 42.

266 **one of the Ottomans' primary ideological and military foes:** On Ottoman–Safavid relations before and after 1514, see Allouche, *Origins and Development*; Jean-Louis Bacqué-Grammont, *Les Ottomans, les Safavides et leurs*

*voisins: contribution à l'histoire des relations internationales dans l'Orient islamique de 1514 à 1524* (Istanbul: Nederlands Historisch-Archaeologisch Instituut te Istanbul, 1987); İzzettin Çopur, *Yavuz Sultan Selim'in Çaldıran Meydan Muharebesi ve Mısır Seferi* (Ankara: Hipokrat Kitabevi, 2017).

266 **mangy Shiite dog:** Giovan Maria Angiolello, "A Short Narrative of the Life and Acts of the King Ussun Cassano," in *A Narrative of Italian Travels in Persia in the Fifteenth and Sixteenth Centuries*, ed. and trans. Charles Grey (London: Hakluyt Society, 1873), 122.

267 **rural areas between the cities of Bayburt, Erzincan, and Erzurum:** Allouche, *Origins and Development*, 121–23.

267 **an utterly devastating psychological blow:** Savory, *Iran under the Safavids*, 45–47.

267 **"most of his time was spent in hunting":** Quoted in Savory, *Iran under the Safavids*, 46.

267 **"always drunk":** Quoted in Rudi Matthee, *The Pursuit of Pleasure: Drugs and Stimulants in Iranian History, 1500–1900* (Princeton: Princeton University Press, 2005), 77.

268 **Portuguese captured the strategic island of Hormuz:** Allouche, *Origins and Development*, 122.

## CHAPTER 18: FRATERNAL EMPIRES

270 **religiously-tinged claims to universal sovereignty:** Tijana Krstić, *Contested Conversions to Islam: Narratives of Religious Change in the Early Modern Ottoman Empire* (Stanford: Stanford University Press, 2011).

271 **The increasingly bellicose Ottoman–Mamluk competition:** This and the next paragraph come from Elias I. Muhanna, "The Sultan's New Clothes: Ottoman–Mamluk Gift Exchange in the Fifteenth Century," *Muqarnas* 27 (2010): 199–200.

273 **"We have sent to you personally":** Quoted in Muhanna, "The Sultan's New Clothes," 200.

273 **essentially divided up the eastern Mediterranean:** On Ottoman–Mamluk relations, see Cihan Yüksel Muslu, *The Ottomans and the Mamluks: Imperial Diplomacy and Warfare in the Islamic World* (London: I. B. Tauris, 2014). See also Timothy Jude Fitzgerald, "Ottoman Methods of Conquest: Legal Imperialism and the City of Aleppo, 1480–1570" (Ph.D. diss., Harvard University, 2009), 172–76.

273 **two powers toggled back and forth between enmity and alliance:** Muslu, *Ottomans and Mamluks*.

274 **Barsbay . . . married an Ottoman princess:** Muslu, *Ottomans and Mamluks*, 100.

275 **a personal and political betrayal:** On Ahmed's son Suleyman in Egypt, see Hakkı Erdem Çipa, "The Centrality of the Periphery: The Rise to Power of Selim I, 1487–1512" (Ph.D. diss., Harvard University, 2007), 235.

275 **days of festivities in Mamluk Cairo:** Muslu, *Ottomans and Mamluks*, 110–17.

275 **buffer zone had begun to erode:** Muslu, *Ottomans and Mamluks*, 124–29.

276 **Qaitbay seized an old Byzantine hilltop castle . . . near the town of Kayseri:** Muslu, *Ottomans and Mamluks*, 128; "Zamantı Fortress, Turkiye Kayseri," *Heritage of the Great Seljuks*, http://www.selcuklumirasi.com/architecture-detail/zamanti-fortress?lng=en (accessed February 13, 2019).

276 **Bayezit struck back:** Muslu, *Ottomans and Mamluks*, 141–49.

276 **why he made Diyarbakir a focus of attention:** Elizabeth Fortunato Crider, "The Foreign Relations of the Ottoman Empire under Selim I, 1512–1520" (M.A. thesis, Ohio State University, 1969), 23.

277 **Khayr Bey:** Muslu, *Ottomans and Mamluks*, 160–62.

277 **Aleppo:** On early modern Aleppo, see Abraham Marcus, *The Middle East on the Eve of Modernity: Aleppo in the Eighteenth Century* (New York: Columbia University Press, 1989); Fitzgerald, "Ottoman Methods of Conquest."

278 **Khayr was tasked with journeying to the Ottoman capital:** Muslu, *Ottomans and Mamluks*, 258.

278 **Bayezit received two high-ranking military men:** Muslu, *Ottomans and Mamluks*, 160–61.

279 **began a secret correspondence with Bayezit's court:** Muslu, *Ottomans and Mamluks*, 161.

279 **Khain Bey instead of Khayr Bey:** Adel Allouche, *The Origins and Development of the Ottoman–Safavid Conflict (906–962 / 1500–1555)* (Berlin: Klaus Schwarz Verlag, 1983), 124, n. 83.

279 **"extraordinary talent":** Quoted in Leslie Peirce, *Empress of the East: How a European Slave Girl Became Queen of the Ottoman Empire* (New York: Basic Books, 2017), 82.

280 **the weakness of the Ottoman fleet:** Crider, "Foreign Relations," 20.

281 **seized the territories . . . capturing ʿAlaʾ al-Dawla:** Allouche, *Origins and Development*, 124–25; Muslu, *Ottomans and Mamluks*, 177–78.

281 **the possibility . . . of a Mamluk–Safavid alliance against the Ottomans:** Allouche, *Origins and Development*, 125–26.

281 **stalled his departure from Cairo:** George William Frederick Stripling, *The Ottoman Turks and the Arabs, 1511–1574* (Philadelphia: Porcupine Press, 1977), 40–51.

## CHAPTER 19: CONQUERING THE NAVEL

283 **fewer than six thousand souls:** Amnon Cohen and Bernard Lewis, *Population and Revenue in the Towns of Palestine in the Sixteenth Century* (Princeton: Princeton University Press, 1978), 94.

284 **he conquered Jerusalem:** Ibn Iyās, *An Account of the Ottoman Conquest of Egypt in the year A.H. 922 (A.D. 1516), Translated from the Third Volume of the Arabic Chronicle of Muḥammed ibn Aḥmed ibn Iyās, an Eye-Witness of the Scenes he Describes*, trans. W. H. Salmon (London: Royal Asiatic Society, 1921), 104. Ibn Iyās's original Arabic text is titled *Badāʾiʿ al-Zuhūr fī Waqāʾiʿ al-Duhūr*.

284 **al-Ghawri led his army out of Cairo on May 17, 1516:** George William Frederick Stripling, *The Ottoman Turks and the Arabs, 1511–1574* (Philadelphia: Porcupine Press, 1977), 41.

285 **His next stop was Damascus:** Stripling, *Ottoman Turks and Arabs*, 41; William Muir, *The Mameluke or Slave Dynasty of Egypt, 1260–1517 A. D.* (London: Smith, Elder, 1896), 197.

285 **its estimated ten thousand households:** Cohen and Lewis, *Population and Revenue*, 20.

285 **almost toppling the Mamluk sultan from his horse:** Stripling, *Ottoman Turks and Arabs*, 41.

285 **On July 10:** Stripling, *Ottoman Turks and Arabs*, 41.

285 **Mamluk soldiers ran amok:** Stripling, *Ottoman Turks and Arabs*, 45.

286 **Aleppo felt more like an occupied city:** Muir, *Mameluke Dynasty*, 198.

286 **Selim reached Elbistan:** Stripling, *Ottoman Turks and Arabs*, 43.

286 **The people of Aleppo cursed and jeered:** Stripling, *Ottoman Turks and Arabs*, 45.

286 **rumors began swirling among al-Ghawri's advisers:** Stripling, *Ottoman Turks and Arabs*, 44; Muir, *Mameluke Dynasty*, 198–99.

286 **a rousingly inspiring speech:** Stripling, *Ottoman Turks and Arabs*, 45–46.

288 **On the evening of August 23, 1516:** Stripling, *Ottoman Turks and Arabs*, 46.

288 **Although both sides brought approximately sixty thousand men:** On relative troop levels, see Stripling, *Ottoman Turks and Arabs*, 46; Fatih Akçe, *Sultan Selim I: The Conqueror of the East* (Clifton, NJ: Blue Dome Press, 2016), 145–46; Michael Winter, "The Ottoman Occupation," in *Islamic Egypt, 640–1517*, vol. 1 of *The Cambridge History of Egypt*, ed. Carl F. Petry (Cambridge, UK: Cambridge University Press, 1998), 498.

289 **spooked the Mamluks' horses:** Stripling, *Ottoman Turks and Arabs*, 47–48.

289 **treason best served Selim and his army:** Stripling, *Ottoman Turks and Arabs*, 47.

289 **"This is the moment":** Quoted in *Wikipedia*, s.v. "Battle of Marj Dabiq," https://en.wikipedia.org/wiki/Battle_of_Marj_Dabiq (accessed February 13, 2019).

289–290 **"was gripped by a sort of paralysis":** Quoted in *Wikipedia*, s.v. "Battle of Marj Dabiq." Hernia is mentioned in Stripling, *Ottoman Turks and Arabs*, 47. Most of what we know about the war comes from the chronicles of contemporary Mamluk historians writing from Cairo, such as Ibn Iyâs.

290 **closed the city's nine massive wooden gates:** Stripling, *Ottoman Turks and Arabs*, 48.

290 **gates were thrown open:** Stripling, *Ottoman Turks and Arabs*, 49.

290 **Selim received Khayr:** Stripling, *Ottoman Turks and Arabs*, 49; Muir, *Mameluke Dynasty*, 200.

290 **the citadel was the city's crown jewel:** On the Aleppo Citadel, see Julia Gonnella, *The Citadel of Aleppo: Description, History, Site Plan and Visitor Tour*, 2nd ed. (Geneva: Aga Khan Trust for Culture; Damascus: Syrian Directorate General of Antiquities and Museums, 2008).

291 **Governors, judges, tribal chieftains, and notables:** Stripling, *Ottoman Turks and Arabs*, 49.

291 **Selim also sent a military detachment to the Safavid border:** Stripling, *Ottoman Turks and Arabs*, 49.

292 **On September 16, Selim left Aleppo:** Stripling, *Ottoman Turks and Arabs*, 50.

292 **On October 9, Selim entered the city:** Stripling, *Ottoman Turks and Arabs*, 50.

293 **praying in iconic religious sites:** In this regard, see Leslie Peirce, *Morality Tales: Law and Gender in the Ottoman Court of Aintab* (Berkeley: University of California Press, 2003), 47–48.

294 **a severe case of constipation:** H. Erdem Çıpa, *The Making of Selim: Succession, Legitimacy, and Memory in the Early Modern Ottoman World* (Bloomington: Indiana University Press, 2017), 232.

294 **"When the sīn enters the shīn":** Ahmed Zildzic, "Friend and Foe: The Early

Ottoman Reception of Ibn 'Arabī" (Ph.D. diss., University of California, Berkeley, 2012), 92–93.

295 **Ibn 'Arabi visited him in a dream:** Akçe, *Sultan Selim*, 157–59.

295 **Osman . . . had studied under Ibn 'Arabi:** Akçe, *Sultan Selim*, 158.

296 **renewal of a peace treaty with Hungary:** Akçe, *Sultan Selim*, 171–72.

296 **snow began to fall:** Akçe, *Sultan Selim*, 164.

296 **met with representatives:** Başbakanlık Osmanlı Arşivi, Kâmil Kepeci Tasnifi, Evâmir-i Maliye Kalemine Tabi Piskopos Mukataası Kalemi, no. 2539, sh. 2 (1517). My thanks to Server Koray Er for this reference.

296 **increased the stipend . . . and reduced the visa fees:** Stripling, *Ottoman Turks and Arabs*, 51.

298 **Inside the mosque, Selim bowed his head:** Akçe, *Sultan Selim*, 178–79.

298 **fleet to meet him in Egypt with new arms and additional troops:** *Encyclopaedia of Islam*, 2nd ed. (Leiden: Brill Online, 2012), s.v. "Selīm I" (Halil İnalcık).

298 **enormous convoy of 106 ships:** Akçe, *Sultan Selim*, 172.

298 **secured the fertile coastal plains of Gaza:** Ibn Iyās, *Ottoman Conquest*, 106–07; *Encyclopaedia of Islam*, s.v. "Selīm I" (İnalcık).

299 **fifteen thousand camels carrying thirty thousand water bags:** *Encyclopaedia of Islam*, s.v. "Selīm I" (İnalcık).

299 **Aided by winter rains that firmed up the sandy terrain:** Akçe, *Sultan Selim*, 182.

299 **large, almond-shaped eyes:** For images of Tuman Bey, see "Tuman bay II," Getty Images, http://www.gettyimages.co.uk/detail/news-photo/tuman-bay-ii-last-mamluk-sultan-of-egypt-news-photo/526581572#tuman-bay-ii-last-mamluk-sultan-of-egypt-picture-id526581572 (accessed February 13, 2019); *Wikipedia*, s.v. "Tuman bay II," https://en.wikipedia.org/wiki/Tuman_bay_II#/media/File:Tumanbay_II_(cropped).jpg (accessed February 13, 2019).

300 **Tuman had devoted himself exclusively:** Stripling, *Ottoman Turks and Arabs*, 52–53.

300 **Tuman managed to assemble at Raidaniyya:** Ibn Iyās, *Ottoman Conquest*, 105.

300 **three Indian elephants:** Ibn Iyās, *Ottoman Conquest*, 105.

300 **a ditch embedded with vertical spears:** Stripling, *Ottoman Turks and Arabs*, 53.

300 **Tuman himself carried heavy stones:** Ibn Iyās, *Ottoman Conquest*, 107–08.

300 **transferring their goods to storehouses for safekeeping:** Ibn Iyās, *Ottoman Conquest*, 106.

301 **Tuman wanted to rush forward:** Ibn Iyās, *Ottoman Conquest*, 106, 108–09.

301 **each sultan tried to gauge:** Ibn Iyās, *Ottoman Conquest*, 109–10; *Encyclopaedia of Islam*, s.v. "Selīm I" (İnalcık).

## CHAPTER 20: CONQUERING THE WORLD

303 **The battle for Cairo:** *Encyclopaedia of Islam*, 2nd ed. (Leiden: Brill Online, 2012), s.v. "Selīm I" (Halil İnalcık); Ibn Iyās, *An Account of the Ottoman Conquest of Egypt in the year A.H. 922 (A.D. 1516), Translated from the Third Volume of the Arabic Chronicle of Muḥammed ibn Aḥmed ibn Iyās, an Eye-Witness of the Scenes he Describes*, trans. W. H. Salmon (London: Royal Asiatic Society, 1921), 111–12.

304 **the Ottoman guns outperformed:** George William Frederick Stripling, *The Ottoman Turks and the Arabs, 1511–1574* (Philadelphia: Porcupine Press, 1977), 53.

304 **more than twenty-five thousand Mamluk soldiers:** Stanford J. Shaw, *Empire of the Gazis: The Rise and Decline of the Ottoman Empire, 1280–1808*, vol. 1 of *History of the Ottoman Empire and Modern Turkey* (Cambridge, UK: Cambridge University Press, 1976), 84.

304 **The Mamluk capital now lay completely exposed:** Fatih Akçe, *Sultan Selim I: The Conqueror of the East* (Clifton, NJ: Blue Dome Press, 2016), 195.

304 **victory at Raidaniyya changed the world:** For studies of some of the consequences of this Ottoman victory, see Benjamin Lellouch and Nicolas Michel, eds., *Conquête ottomane de l'Égypte (1517): Arrière-plan, impact, échos* (Leiden: Brill, 2013).

305 **campaign of guerrilla warfare:** Shaw, *Empire of the Gazis*, 84; *Encyclopaedia of Islam*, s.v. "Selīm I" (İnalcık); Stripling, *Ottoman Turks and Arabs*, 55–56.

305 **allowed his soldiers to loot Cairo:** Ibn Iyās, *Ottoman Conquest*, 112–14.

305 **more pivotal for the empire than the conquest of Constantinople:** H. Erdem Çıpa, *The Making of Selim: Succession, Legitimacy, and Memory in the Early Modern Ottoman World* (Bloomington: Indiana University Press, 2017), 202–05.

305 **driving Tuman and his men into hiding:** William Muir, *The Mameluke or Slave Dynasty of Egypt, 1260–1517 A. D.* (London: Smith, Elder, 1896), 206–07.

306 **His body was strung up:** Stripling, *Ottoman Turks and Arabs*, 55–56; Muir, *Mameluke Dynasty*, 209.

306 **Selim entered Cairo:** Ibn Iyās, *Ottoman Conquest*, 114; *Encyclopaedia of Islam*, s.v. "Selīm I" (İnalcık).

306 **"Long live the victorious Sultan Selim!":** Ibn Iyās, *Ottoman Conquest*, 114.

307 **delivered their weekly sermons in Selim's name:** Ibn Iyās, *Ottoman Conquest*, 115.

308 **Selim recognized the sitting governors:** *Encyclopaedia of Islam*, s.v. "Selīm I" (İnalcık).

308 **The sharifs of Mecca:** Shaw, *Empire of the Gazis*, 84.

308 **Khayr Bey . . . was made governor of Egypt:** Michael Winter, "The Ottoman Occupation," in *Islamic Egypt, 640–1517*, vol. 1 of *The Cambridge History of Egypt*, ed. Carl F. Petry (Cambridge, UK: Cambridge University Press, 1998), 496–513.

308 **As the richest and most strategic of the provinces:** Stanford J. Shaw, *The Financial and Administrative Organization and Development of Ottoman Egypt, 1517–1798* (Princeton: Princeton University Press, 1962).

308 **a quarter of all the food consumed:** Alan Mikhail, *Nature and Empire in Ottoman Egypt: An Environmental History* (Cambridge, UK: Cambridge University Press, 2011), 82–123.

308 **Khayr, however, proved as cruel:** Winter, "Ottoman Occupation," 507.

309 **The ceremony to invest Selim with the caliphate:** Muir, *Mameluke Dynasty*, 205; Akçe, *Sultan Selim*, 223–25.

309 **"public service":** Muir, *Mameluke Dynasty*, 205.

309 **"servant of the two sacred cities":** Ibn Iyās, *Ottoman Conquest*, 115.

309 **caliph:** There is some dispute about Selim's adoption of the title caliph, with some historians claiming that he never used it during his lifetime and that his reputation as caliph was a later invention. See for example *Encyclopaedia of Islam*,

s.v. "Selīm I" (İnalcık); Caroline Finkel, *Osman's Dream: The Story of the Ottoman Empire, 1300–1923* (New York: Basic Books, 2006), 111; Stripling, *Ottoman Turks and Arabs*, 56. However, the evidence is clear: he used the title as early as 1518; see Giancarlo Casale, *The Ottoman Age of Exploration* (Oxford: Oxford University Press, 2010), 30–31. Moreover, other political leaders, even his enemies the Safavids, recognized him as caliph. In letters, the Safavids called Selim "Shāh on the Throne of the Caliphate" and "Caliph of God and of the Prophet Muḥammad"; quoted in Çıpa, *Making of Selim*, 236.

310 **One night in the spring of 1517:** Pınar Emiralioğlu, *Geographical Knowledge and Imperial Culture in the Early Modern Ottoman Empire* (Farnham, UK: Ashgate, 2014), 1–2; *Encyclopaedia of Islam*, s.v. "Pīrī Reʾīs" (S. Soucek).

310 **Piri Reis:** *Encyclopaedia of Islam*, s.v. "Pīrī Reʾīs" (Soucek).

310 **unfurled the drab gazelle-skin parchment:** Abbas Hamdani, "Ottoman Response to the Discovery of America and the New Route to India," *Journal of the American Oriental Society* 101 (1981): 327. For a detailed description of the map, see Gregory C. McIntosh, *The Piri Reis Map of 1513* (Athens, GA: University of Georgia Press, 2000).

310 **dozens of maps:** McIntosh, *Piri Reis Map*, 141–53.

311 **a raid off the coast of Valencia in 1501:** McIntosh, *Piri Reis Map*, 70, 72–73.

311 **several maps from those voyages:** Michel M. Mazzaoui, "Global Policies of Sultan Selim, 1512–1520," in *Essays on Islamic Civilization: Presented to Niyazi Berkes*, ed. Donald P. Little (Leiden: Brill, 1976), 240; McIntosh, *Piri Reis Map*, 72–73.

311 **feather headdress and an odd black stone:** McIntosh, *Piri Reis Map*, 72–73, 114.

311 **the first Ottoman vessel to enter the Atlantic:** *Wikipedia*, s.v. "Kemal Reis," https://en.wikipedia.org/wiki/Kemal_Reis (accessed February 15, 2019); Julia McClure, *The Franciscan Invention of the New World* (Cham, Switzerland: Palgrave Macmillan, 2017), 90.

311 **he may have even interviewed his uncle's Spanish captive:** Casale, *Ottoman Age of Exploration*, 25.

311 **Piri combined elements from more than a hundred maps:** A. Afetinan, *Life and Works of Pirî Reis: The Oldest Map of America*, trans. Leman Yolaç and Engin Uzmen (Ankara: Turkish Historical Association, 1975), 27, 30; Hamdani, "Ottoman Response," 328. For a list of all the maps Piri used, see McIntosh, *Piri Reis Map*, 141–53.

311 **"I have made maps":** Quoted in Casale, *Ottoman Age of Exploration*, 25.

311 **speaks of the Americas and their peoples:** For Piri's descriptions of the New World, see McIntosh, *Piri Reis Map*, 35–121; Afetinan, *Life and Works of Pirî Reis*, 26–42.

311 **"four kinds of parrots":** Quoted in Afetinan, *Life and Works of Pirî Reis*, 29.

311 **gold in the New World:** Afetinan, *Life and Works of Pirî Reis*, 31; McIntosh, *Piri Reis Map*, 70–71.

311 **Columbus's efforts to secure a patron:** Afetinan, *Life and Works of Pirî Reis*, 30.

311–312 **"the Portuguese infidels . . . one horn":** Quoted in Afetinan, *Life and Works of Pirî Reis*, 32, 34.

312 **Piri remained true to:** Hamdani, "Ottoman Response," 328.

312 **firsthand account of an Ottoman merchant:** Casale, *Ottoman Age of Explo-*

*ration*, 22; Pınar Emiralioğlu, "Relocating the Center of the Universe: China and the Ottoman Imperial Project in the Sixteenth Century," *Journal of Ottoman Studies* 39 (2012): 161–87.

312 **Vilayet Antilia:** Afetinan, *Life and Works of Pirî Reis*, 29; Hamdani, "Ottoman Response," 329. For references to Piri's labelling of the American mainland, see McIntosh, *Piri Reis Map*, 116. For a general discussion of the varied meanings of Antilia, see G. R. Crone, "The Origin of the Name Antillia," *Geographical Journal* 91 (1938): 260–62.

312 **ripped the map in half:** See the discussion in Casale, *Ottoman Age of Exploration*, 23–25; *Encyclopaedia of Islam*, s.v. "Pīrī Re'īs" (Soucek).

313 **Vasco da Gama:** On Vasco da Gama and the Order of Santiago, see Sanjay Subrahmanyam, *The Career and Legend of Vasco da Gama* (Cambridge, UK: Cambridge University Press, 1997), 60–61. Generally on Ottoman, Portuguese, and Mamluk rivalry in the Red Sea, see Jean-Louis Bacqué-Grammont and Anne Kroell, *Mamlouks, ottomans et portugais en Mer Rouge: l'affaire de Djedda en 1517* (Cairo: Institut français d'archéologie orientale, 1988).

314 **the Portuguese burned ten Mamluk ships:** Hamdani, "Ottoman Response," 326.

314 **the Portuguese blockaded the mouth of the Red Sea:** Hamdani, "Ottoman Response," 326.

315 **nineteen Portuguese ships from India:** Andreu Martínez d'Alòs-Moner, "Conquistadores, Mercenaries, and Missionaries: The Failed Portuguese Dominion of the Red Sea," *Northeast African Studies* 12 (2012): 8.

315 **Socotra:** *Wikipedia*, s.v. "Socotra," https://en.wikipedia.org/wiki/Socotra (accessed February 16, 2019).

315 **an even more threatening Portuguese naval battalion:** Martínez d'Alòs-Moner, "Conquistadores," 4–5, 8.

315 **Afonso de Albuquerque:** *Encyclopædia Britannica*, s.v. "Afonso de Albuquerque, Portuguese Conqueror" (Harold V. Livermore), https://www.britannica.com/biography/Afonso-de-Albuquerque (accessed February 24, 2019).

316 **In 1515, he sent one of his most experienced admirals:** Casale, *Ottoman Age of Exploration*, 39; Halil İnalcık, "The Ottoman State: Economy and Society, 1300–1600," in *An Economic and Social History of the Ottoman Empire*, ed. Halil İnalcık with Donald Quataert, 2 vols. (Cambridge, UK: Cambridge University Press, 1994), 1:321–25.

317 **"The Portuguese have not yet entered":** Quoted in Casale, *Ottoman Age of Exploration*, 42–43.

317 **"perfidious troublemakers":** Quoted in Casale, *Ottoman Age of Exploration*, 28.

317 **"in a state of incessant anarchy":** Quoted in Casale, *Ottoman Age of Exploration*, 43.

318 **Kamaran Island:** Casale, *Ottoman Age of Exploration*, 44.

318 **the first coffee drunk beyond the borders of the Ottoman Empire:** Elizabeth Horodowich, *A Brief History of Venice: A New History of the City and Its People* (London: Robinson, 2009), 164.

318 **the café:** The world's first coffeehouses opened in Syria in the 1530s and in Istanbul in the 1540s. Alan Mikhail, "The Heart's Desire: Gender, Urban Space and the Ottoman Coffee House," in *Ottoman Tulips, Ottoman Coffee: Leisure and Lifestyle in the Eighteenth Century*, ed. Dana Sajdi (London: I. B. Tauris, 2007), 137–38. A Lebanese Jew opened Europe's first café in Oxford in 1650. Coffee arrived in

Paris with the Ottoman ambassador in 1669. In 1700, two thousand cafés were thriving in London. In 1683, the same year the Ottoman army brought coffee to the gates of Vienna, Venice opened its first coffeehouse. And the first café in the Americas opened a few years later, in Boston in 1689. Mark Pendergrast, *Uncommon Grounds: The History of Coffee and How it Transformed Our World*, rev. ed. (New York: Basic Books, 2010), 8–14.

319 **coffee formed a common market from the Americas to the Malaccas:** For instructive ways of thinking about the early modern coffee market, see Steven Topik, "The Integration of the World Coffee Market," in *The Global Coffee Economy in Africa, Asia and Latin America, 1500–1989*, ed. William Gervase Clarence-Smith and Steven Topik (Cambridge, UK: Cambridge University Press, 2003), 21–49.

320 **twelve to fifteen thousand tons of coffee beans:** Michel Tuchscherer, "Coffee in the Red Sea Area from the Sixteenth to the Nineteenth Century," in *The Global Coffee Economy*, 55.

320 **coffee from Mocha represented about 90 percent:** Topik, "Integration of the World Coffee Market," 28.

320 **Java had replaced Yemen:** Topik, "Integration of the World Coffee Market," 28.

320 **2 or 3 percent of the world's production:** Topik, "Integration of the World Coffee Market," 29; Tuchscherer, "Coffee in the Red Sea Area," 55.

320 **cheaper to import coffee from Hispaniola to Cairo:** Topik, "Integration of the World Coffee Market," 29.

320 **"one of the most valuable":** Steven Topik and William Gervase Clarence-Smith, "Coffee and Global Development," in *The Global Coffee Economy*, 2.

CHAPTER 21: EMPIRE EVERYWHERE

324 **Selim's prized naval fleet finally arrived:** Stanford J. Shaw, *Empire of the Gazis: The Rise and Decline of the Ottoman Empire, 1280–1808*, vol. 1 of *History of the Ottoman Empire and Modern Turkey* (Cambridge, UK: Cambridge University Press, 1976), 84–85.

324 **beginning that march on September 13, 1517:** *Encyclopaedia of Islam*, 2nd ed. (Leiden: Brill Online, 2012), s.v. "Selīm I" (Halil İnalcık).

324 **the fleet set sail on its return trip:** Michael Winter, "The Ottoman Occupation," in *Islamic Egypt, 640–1517*, vol. 1 of *The Cambridge History of Egypt*, ed. Carl F. Petry (Cambridge, UK: Cambridge University Press, 1998), 504.

324 **a veritable intellectual army:** *Encyclopaedia of Islam*, s.v. "Selīm I" (İnalcık); Shaw, *Empire of the Gazis*, 85.

324 **lived out the rest of his days under house arrest in Istanbul:** William Muir, *The Mameluke or Slave Dynasty of Egypt, 1260–1517 A. D.* (London: Smith, Elder, 1896), 212; Caroline Finkel, *Osman's Dream: The Story of the Ottoman Empire, 1300–1923* (New York: Basic Books, 2006), 111.

324 **new center of the Muslim world and the seat of the global caliphate:** Fatih Akçe, *Sultan Selim I: The Conqueror of the East* (Clifton, NJ: Blue Dome Press, 2016), 225.

325 **On his way back to the capital:** *Encyclopaedia of Islam*, s.v. "Selīm I" (İnalcık).

325 **visited the recently completed shrine of Ibn 'Arabi:** Akçe, *Sultan Selim*, 229.

325 **Selim and his retinue fled plague-stricken Istanbul:** Marino Sanudo, *I Diarii di Marino Sanuto (MCCCCXCVI-MDXXXIII) Dall'autografo Marciano Ital.*

*Cl. VII Codd. CDXIX–CDLXXVII*, ed. Rinaldo Fulin, Federico Stefani, Nicolò Barozzi, Guglielmo Berchet, Marco Allegri, and la R. Deputazione Veneta di Storia Patria, 59 vols. (Venice: F.Visentini, 1879–1903), 26:134.

326 **Selim's primary delight in Edirne was hunting:** Sanudo, *Diarii*, 27:280, 305. On Ottoman hunting, see Alan Mikhail, *The Animal in Ottoman Egypt* (Oxford: Oxford University Press, 2014), 130–36.

326 **might have to wait in Edirne for days:** Sanudo, *Diarii*, 27:280.

326 **complained that he ignored important affairs of state and army:** Sanudo, *Diarii*, 27:305.

326 **two Italian hunting greyhounds:** Sanudo, *Diarii*, 28:232.

326 **prices of oats and vegetables skyrocketed in Syria:** Sanudo, *Diarii*, 26:188.

326 **the Janissaries . . . came to collect on their investment:** Sanudo, *Diarii*, 27:40, 79.

327 **Officials from as far afield as India and Hungary:** Sanudo, *Diarii*, 26:238, 247.

327 **He maintained the overland embargo:** Finkel, *Osman's Dream*, 111.

327 **"[The harbor of] Diu is waiting":** Quoted in Giancarlo Casale, *The Ottoman Age of Exploration* (Oxford: Oxford University Press, 2010), 28.

328 **"With the news of the Ottomans":** Quoted in Casale, *Ottoman Age of Exploration*, 28.

328 **received an ambassador from the ruler of Calicut:** Sanudo, *Diarii*, 26:163.

328 **Selim enthusiastically entered into this alliance:** Sanudo, *Diarii*, 27:141.

328 **instituted high tariffs on Portuguese merchants:** Sanudo, *Diarii*, 26:163; 27:513.

328 **They continued to complain about the Iranian silk embargo:** Sanudo, *Diarii*, 28:151.

328 **Venetian trade in Egyptian ports:** Sanudo, *Diarii*, 27:513.

328 **Venice and Hungary remained the strongest entities:** Finkel, *Osman's Dream*, 113.

328 **In 1517, he renewed the treaty:** Finkel, *Osman's Dream*, 113.

329 **Selim and King Vladislaus II of Hungary:** Finkel, *Osman's Dream*, 113.

329 **two sides frequently had to pump new life into their peace treaty:** Sanudo, *Diarii*, 26:238; 27:79, 305, 357, 474.

329 **renewed the empire's peace treaty with Poland:** Finkel, *Osman's Dream*, 113.

329 **Selim laughed when he heard this:** Sanudo, *Diarii*, 26:95.

330 **guarded their forests as a precious asset:** On Venetian forest management, see Karl Appuhn, *A Forest on the Sea: Environmental Expertise in Renaissance Venice* (Baltimore: Johns Hopkins University Press, 2009).

330 **planning an invasion of Rhodes:** Sanudo, *Diarii*, 26:22, 95.

330 **diplomats in Edirne attempted to insert into the document:** Sanudo, *Diarii*, 27:357.

330 **Selim grudgingly signed the treaty:** Sanudo, *Diarii*, 27:474.

331 **preparing for a war against the Safavid scourge:** Sanudo, *Diarii*, 26:15; 27:79, 141.

331 **deport several rich Shiite families:** Sanudo, *Diarii*, 26:344.

331 **Also worrisome was the sizable Shiite population of Tripoli:** Sanudo, *Diarii*, 26:344.

331 **Selim sent two hundred troops with sixteen cannons:** Sanudo, *Diarii*, 26:344.

331  purged two hundred families suspected of Shiite sympathies: Sanudo, *Diarii*, 26:188.

332  Shah Ismail moved a rebuilt force: Sanudo, *Diarii*, 26:344.

332  bitter cold and heavy snowfall: Sanudo, *Diarii*, 27:33.

332  Ismail had been able to capture several abandoned hilltop castles: Sanudo, *Diarii*, 26:359, 371.

332  Ottomans attempted to retake one of the captured castles: Sanudo, *Diarii*, 27:305.

332  Ottoman soldiers defecting to the Safavids: Sanudo, *Diarii*, 27:151.

332  steadily drew in European powers: Sanudo, *Diarii*, 27:379.

332  Selim's plan to travel to the front: Sanudo, *Diarii*, 27:601.

332  dispatched a thousand gunners and a thousand additional soldiers: Sanudo, *Diarii*, 27:600–01.

332  Safavids had sacked Mosul: Sanudo, *Diarii*, 27:619.

332  did the same in Baghdad: Sanudo, *Diarii*, 27:621.

333  between sixty and eighty thousand cavalry: Sanudo, *Diarii*, 27:619–20, 664.

333  many guns from the Portuguese: Sanudo, *Diarii*, 27:619.

333  1,500 Ottoman defectors: Sanudo, *Diarii*, 27:619, 664.

333  enlisted Georgians and Tatars: Sanudo, *Diarii*, 27:619.

333  dispatched an imposing fleet of a hundred ships: Sanudo, *Diarii*, 28:596.

333  He asked the empire's leading clerics: Finkel, *Osman's Dream*, 114.

333  mobilized a force of nearly fifteen thousand troops: Sanudo, *Diarii*, 27:620–21.

333  lack of food . . . angered the local population even more: Sanudo, *Diarii*, 27:664–65.

333  Selim's troops chased down internal enemies: Sanudo, *Diarii*, 28:661.

333  rebellion . . . erupted in . . . Amasya and Tokat: Sanudo, *Diarii*, 28:409.

334  "From Istambol's throne": Quoted in Finkel, *Osman's Dream*, 113–14.

## CHAPTER 22: FULCRUM OF THE ATLANTIC

335  the only way to secure . . . was to bring North Africa squarely under Spanish control: Andrew C. Hess, *The Forgotten Frontier: A History of the Sixteenth-Century Ibero-African Frontier* (Chicago: University of Chicago Press, 1978), 36–44.

336  a new Crusade against Islam in North Africa: Hess, *Forgotten Frontier*, 37.

336  captured the Moroccan coastal city of Melilla: Hess, *Forgotten Frontier*, 37; Henry Kamen, *Empire: How Spain Became a World Power, 1492–1763* (New York: HarperCollins, 2003), 30.

336  The hawks . . . carried the day: Hess, *Forgotten Frontier*, 37–38.

337  Rebellion of the Alpujarras: Hess, *Forgotten Frontier*, 37–38; L. P. Harvey, *Muslims in Spain, 1500–1614* (Chicago: University of Chicago Press, 2005), 35–37.

337  worked incessantly to eradicate any lingering remnants of Islam: Jane Landers, "The Great Wolof Scare of 1521" (unpublished manuscript), 10.

337  Isabella's health began to decline: Kirstin Downey, *Isabella: The Warrior Queen* (New York: Nan A. Talese/Doubleday, 2014), 403–11.

337  "In all the realms": Quoted in Downey, *Isabella*, 406.

337  deeply mourned the loss of his patron: Downey, *Isabella*, 427.

337 **"all these island territories"**: Bartolomé de Las Casas, *A Short Account of the Destruction of the Indies*, ed. and trans. Nigel Griffin (London: Penguin, 1992), 25.

338 **"permanent properties of the Crown"**: Downey, *Isabella*, 409.

338 **ordered that proceeds from the sale of her properties**: Downey, *Isabella*, 408.

338 **Isabella instructed that she be buried**: Downey, *Isabella*, 409–11.

338 **Isabella would continue to wage war against Islam**: Hess, *Forgotten Frontier*, 38.

338 **Pedro Navarro**: Hess, *Forgotten Frontier*, 38.

338 **expedition of four thousand men against the independent port of Bougie**: Hess, *Forgotten Frontier*, 39–42. On the size of this expedition, see Kamen, *Empire*, 32.

338 **Kemal Reis had temporarily captured Bougie**: Hess, *Forgotten Frontier*, 60.

338 **Tenes, Dellys, Mostaganem, and Peñon**: These Spanish gains in North Africa came alongside those of Portugal as well: "al-Qasr as-Saghīr in 1458, Anfia in 1469, Mussat in 1488, Tangiers and Arzila in 1471, Agadir in 1505, Safi in 1508, Azemour in 1513, Mazagan in 1514, and Marrakesh in 1515." Abbas Hamdani, "Ottoman Response to the Discovery of America and the New Route to India," *Journal of the American Oriental Society* 101 (1981): 329.

338 **farthest eastward extension of Spanish hegemony in North Africa**: Hamdani, "Ottoman Response," 329; Hess, *Forgotten Frontier*, 75–76; Kamen, *Empire*, 31–32.

339 **ongoing attempts to forcibly convert Muslims**: Harvey, *Muslims in Spain*; Brian A. Catlos, *Kingdoms of Faith: A New History of Islamic Spain* (New York: Basic Books, 2018), 393–97.

339 **Ottomans . . . chief suppliers of matériel, cash, and other resources**: Hess, *Forgotten Frontier*, 42; Hamdani, "Ottoman Response," 329.

340 **9,153 kilograms of American gold arrived in Seville**: Hess, *Forgotten Frontier*, 43.

340 **"frontier of opportunity"**: Hess, *Forgotten Frontier*, 43.

341 **Oruç and Hayreddin Barbarossa**: Hess, *Forgotten Frontier*, 61; Caroline Finkel, *Osman's Dream: The Story of the Ottoman Empire, 1300–1923* (New York: Basic Books, 2006), 125; *Encyclopaedia of Islam*, 2nd ed. (Leiden: Brill Online, 2012), s.v. "Khayr al-Dīn (Khiḍir) Pasha" (A. Galotta).

341 **Korkud had hired them**: Hess, *Forgotten Frontier*, 61; *Encyclopaedia of Islam*, s.v. "Khayr al-Dīn (Khiḍir) Pasha" (Galotta).

341 **working for the sultan of the Hafsid Empire**: Hess, *Forgotten Frontier*, 61; *Encyclopaedia of Islam*, s.v. "Khayr al-Dīn (Khiḍir) Pasha" (Galotta).

342 **the elders of Bougie appealed**: Hess, *Forgotten Frontier*, 61.

342 **as well as Pope Leo X, behind him**: On the blessing of Pope Leo X, see Marino Sanudo, *I Diarii di Marino Sanuto (MCCCCXCVI-MDXXXIII) Dall' autografo Marciano Ital. Cl. VII Codd. CDXIX-CDLXXVII*, ed. Rinaldo Fulin, Federico Stefani, Nicolò Barozzi, Guglielmo Berchet, Marco Allegri, and la R. Deputazione Veneta di Storia Patria, 59 vols. (Venice: F.Visentini, 1879–1903), 25:465.

342 **the brothers sent one of their men to Istanbul**: Hess, *Forgotten Frontier*, 62.

343 **sent ships to Granada to rescue Ibero-Muslims**: Hess, *Forgotten Frontier*, 62.

343 **"the Unbelievers took young women"**: Quoted in Hess, *Forgotten Frontier*, 228, n. 65.

344 **allowed them to recruit young boys from Anatolia:** Emrah Safa Gürkan, "The Centre and the Frontier: Ottoman Cooperation with the North African Corsairs in the Sixteenth Century," *Turkish Historical Review* 1 (2010): 143.

344 **attack the city of Bougie for a second time:** Hess, *Forgotten Frontier*, 63.

344 **the head of the Thaʿāliba tribe:** Hess, *Forgotten Frontier*, 63.

344 **dispute erupted over who should rule the city:** Hess, *Forgotten Frontier*, 63; *Encyclopaedia of Islam*, s.v. "Khayr al-Dīn (Khiḍir) Pasha" (Galotta).

345 **Selim's grand colonial ambitions were revealed:** Hess, *Forgotten Frontier*, 65–66.

345 **Ferdinand died:** Hess, *Forgotten Frontier*, 43–44.

345 **He had defied her final directive:** Downey, *Isabella*, 407–08.

345 **broke a deathbed promise . . . Germaine of Foix:** Downey, *Isabella*, 405, 431.

346 **appointed governor of Algeria . . . and also governor-general:** *Encyclopaedia of Islam*, s.v. "Khayr al-Dīn (Khiḍir) Pasha" (Galotta).

346 **Oruç would die in 1518:** *Encyclopaedia of Islam*, s.v. "Khayr al-Dīn (Khiḍir) Pasha" (Galotta).

347 **technique for attaching sails to wheeled cannons:** "Chapters of Turkish History: Barbarossa of Algiers," *Blackwood's Edinburgh Magazine* 52 (1842): 192.

347 **explained how Morocco differed . . . and why it would prove enormously difficult to conquer:** On Hayreddin's experiences in Morocco, see Hess, *Forgotten Frontier*, 65–66.

347 **a series of dynasties . . . had successfully resisted Spanish, Portuguese, and Mamluk penetration:** Hess, *Forgotten Frontier*, 50–58.

348 **boosted . . . Ahmad al-Aʿraj's confidence:** Hess, *Forgotten Frontier*, 51, 55. Al-Aʿraj means "the Lame," a moniker he received because of a problem with one of his legs.

348 **mocking them as a bunch of fishermen:** Hess, *Forgotten Frontier*, 55.

348 **he planned first to secure the interior:** On Selim's plan to invade Morocco, see Hess, *Forgotten Frontier*, 55–69.

349 **tocsins rang out across Spain:** Hess, *Forgotten Frontier*, 64–66.

349 **Hernán Cortés himself eventually returned from Mexico:** Hess, *Forgotten Frontier*, 74.

349 **fleet left Spain for its North African holdings:** Sanudo, *Diarii*, 26:54–55, 93.

350 **turned enemies into allies:** For references to some of the numerous requests from North Africa to Spain and France for military support against the Ottomans, see Sanudo, *Diarii*, 24:683; 26:371.

350 **Selim had ordered sixty thousand Ottoman troops:** Sanudo, *Diarii*, 26:419, 424.

350 **an impressive fleet in the Aegean:** Sanudo, *Diarii*, 27:177–78, 217.

350 **secured the island of Djerba:** Sanudo, *Diarii*, 27:453.

350 **collect troops on the volcanic island of Ischia:** Sanudo, *Diarii*, 28:171.

351 **asking the Venetian *bailo* in Istanbul:** Sanudo, *Diarii*, 28:310.

351 **settled on eighty thousand as the appropriate number of troops:** Sanudo, *Diarii*, 28:380–81.

351 **Ottoman and Spanish ambassadors traveled back and forth:** Sanudo, *Diarii*, 27:141, 186.

351 **guarantees of safe passage for Christian pilgrims to Jerusalem:** Sanudo, *Diarii*, 27:280.

352 **a new *mappamundi*:** Sanudo, *Diarii*, 28:630. The dragoman Ali Bey is also men-

tioned in E. Natalie Rothman, *Brokering Empire: Trans-Imperial Subjects between Venice and Istanbul* (Ithaca, NY: Cornell University Press, 2012), 168–69.

353 **"As the Ottomans were engaged":** Hamdani, "Ottoman Response," 329.

## CHAPTER 23: ETERNITY

356 **"like the prick of a thorn":** Fatih Akçe, *Sultan Selim I: The Conqueror of the East* (Clifton, NJ: Blue Dome Press, 2016), 241.

356 **a pimple with a whitened tip:** For suggestions about what Selim's ailment might have been, see H. Erdem Çıpa, *The Making of Selim: Succession, Legitimacy, and Memory in the Early Modern Ottoman World* (Bloomington: Indiana University Press, 2017), 257, n. 1.

356 **instructed a bath attendant to pop the pustule:** Akçe, *Sultan Selim*, 241.

356–357 **rumors started to swirl:** Marino Sanudo, *I Diarii di Marino Sanuto (MCCCCXCVI-MDXXXIII) Dall'autografo Marciano Ital. Cl. VII Codd. CDXIX-CDLXXVII*, ed. Rinaldo Fulin, Federico Stefani, Nicolò Barozzi, Guglielmo Berchet, Marco Allegri, and la R. Deputazione Veneta di Storia Patria, 59 vols. (Venice: F.Visentini, 1879–1903), 26:109, 231, 262–64; 27:149.

357 **his eyes began to yellow:** Sanudo, *Diarii*, 26:109.

357 **speculated that the boil was in fact a plague bubo:** For references to the presence of plague in Istanbul in these months, see Sanudo, *Diarii*, 26:134; 28:232; Nükhet Varlık, *Plague and Empire in the Early Modern Mediterranean World: The Ottoman Experience, 1347–1600* (Cambridge, UK: Cambridge University Press, 2015), 164–65.

357 **wheeled on a cart:** For Selim's final illness and death, see Akçe, *Sultan Selim*, 242–45.

358 **cause of death:** Akçe, *Sultan Selim*, 243; Varlık, *Plague and Empire*, 164–65; Çıpa, *Making of Selim*, 1; 257, n. 1.

358 **dispatched a single messenger to Manisa:** Akçe, *Sultan Selim*, 244–45.

359 **to cover his naked penis:** Akçe, *Sultan Selim*, 245.

359 **"tall and slender but tough":** Quoted in Alan Fisher, "The Life and Family of Süleymân I," in *Süleymân the Second and His Time*, ed. Halil İnalcık and Cemal Kafadar (Istanbul: Isis Press, 1993), 2.

359 **declaring their allegiance to Suleyman as their sovereign:** Leslie Peirce, *Empress of the East: How a European Slave Girl Became Queen of the Ottoman Empire* (New York: Basic Books, 2017), 67.

360 **rejoiced at the prospect that an inexperienced military strategist was now the Ottoman sultan:** Peirce, *Empress of the East*, 66.

360 **"a furious lion":** Quoted in Natalie Zemon Davis, *Trickster Travels: A Sixteenth-Century Muslim Between Worlds* (New York: Hill and Wang, 2006), 74.

361 **seizure of the Ottoman crown an illegitimate act:** Çıpa, *Making of Selim*, 1–2.

361 **threw themselves on the ground in sorrow:** Akçe, *Sultan Selim*, 245.

361 **"the army flowed":** Akçe, *Sultan Selim*, 245.

361 **assembled at the city's Edirne gate:** Akçe, *Sultan Selim*, 246; Peirce, *Empress of the East*, 67.

361 **helped to carry the bier:** Akçe, *Sultan Selim*, 246.

361 **commissioned a mosque complex for his father:** Peirce, *Empress of the East*,

67. For a description and images of the complex, see "Sultan Selim Külliyesi," Archnet, https://archnet.org/sites/2027 (accessed February 16, 2019).

362 **Hafsa died:** All quotes in this paragraph are from Peirce, *Empress of the East*, 113.

363 **one of the reasons historians have devoted so much attention to Suleyman:** Caroline Finkel, *Osman's Dream: The Story of the Ottoman Empire, 1300–1923* (New York: Basic Books, 2006), 115–16.

364 **"friendly . . . good judgement":** Quoted in Peirce, *Empress of the East*, 68.

364 **"He reflects constantly":** Quoted in Peirce, *Empress of the East*, 68.

364 **"shed more blood":** Quoted in Davis, *Trickster Travels*, 74.

365 **"Some Ottoman pundits":** Peirce, *Empress of the East*, 67.

## CHAPTER 24: SELIM'S REFORMATIONS

370 **used religion to advance their political and ideological legitimacy:** Tijana Krstić, *Contested Conversions to Islam: Narratives of Religious Change in the Early Modern Ottoman Empire* (Stanford: Stanford University Press, 2011).

370 **who had almost become a lawyer:** Carlos M. N. Eire, *Reformations: The Early Modern World, 1450–1650* (New Haven: Yale University Press, 2016), 133–34.

371 **the evils of the pope always exceeded the evils of the sultan:** Egil Grislis, "Luther and the Turks, Part II," *The Muslim World* 64 (1974): 285.

371 **wrote reams about the Ottomans:** C. Umhau Wolf, "Luther and Mohammedanism," *The Moslem World* 31 (1941): 161–62.

371 **contemplated sponsoring the first German translation of the Qur'an:** Wolf, "Luther and Mohammedanism," 167–68; David D. Grafton, "Martin Luther's Sources on the Turk and Islam in the Midst of the Fear of Ottoman Imperialism," *The Muslim World* 107 (2017): 680. He never carried out the translation.

371 **"the 'terrible Turk' ":** Grafton, "Martin Luther's Sources," 665.

371 **Leo X called for a new Crusade:** Chiara Palazzo, "The Venetian News Network in the Early Sixteenth Century: The Battle of Chaldiran," in *News Networks in Early Modern Europe*, ed. Joad Raymond and Noah Moxham (Leiden: Brill, 2016), 849–69.

371 **a small war in Belgrade in 1456:** Caroline Finkel, *Osman's Dream: The Story of the Ottoman Empire, 1300–1923* (New York: Basic Books, 2006), 59.

372 **"The humanists wrote":** James Hankins, "Renaissance Crusaders: Humanist Crusade Literature in the Age of Mehmed II," *Dumbarton Oaks Papers* 49 (1995): 112.

372 **Vatican spies reported:** Natalie Zemon Davis, *Trickster Travels: A Sixteenth-Century Muslim Between Worlds* (New York: Hill and Wang, 2006), 61.

372 **several reports claimed that twenty-seven Ottoman ships had arrived:** Kenneth M. Setton, "Pope Leo X and the Turkish Peril," *Proceedings of the American Philosophical Society* 113 (1969): 392.

372 **Leo interpreted lightning storms over Rome:** Davis, *Trickster Travels*, 60.

372 **another forty Ottoman ships (almost certainly misidentified):** Setton, "Pope Leo and the Turkish Peril," 397.

372 **In early 1518, Pope Leo . . . wrote again:** Finkel, *Osman's Dream*, 112–13.

373 **seeking a five-year truce:** Davis, *Trickster Travels*, 60.

373 **"While we waste time":** Quoted in Setton, "Pope Leo and the Turkish Peril," 410.

373 **"the diabolic Mohammedan rage":** Quoted in Davis, *Trickster Travels*, 60.

373 **"Instead of fearing the Turks":** Quoted in Grislis, "Luther and the Turks, Part II," 284.

375 **"an undistinguished Dominican":** Eire, *Reformations*, 146. On Tetzel, see 146–53.

375 **"as soon as the coin":** Quoted in Eire, *Reformations*, 149.

375 **The idea of indulgences arose in the twelfth century:** Ane L. Bysted, *The Crusade Indulgence: Spiritual Rewards and the Theology of the Crusades, c. 1095–1216* (Leiden: Brill, 2015).

376 **distributed widely across Germany:** Eire, *Reformations*, 150.

376 **never posted on the door of the church of Wittenberg:** Eire, *Reformations*, 149–50.

376 **focus on warfare betrayed an obsession with flesh:** Egil Grislis, "Luther and the Turks, Part I," *The Muslim World* 64 (1974): 186.

376 **The Church had often waged Crusades:** Martin Luther, "On War against the Turk," trans. Charles M. Jacobs, in *Luther: Selected Political Writings*, ed. J. M. Porter (Philadelphia: Fortress Press, 1974), 123.

377 **"The 'big wheels' of the church":** Quoted in Grislis, "Luther and the Turks, Part I," 181.

377 **"punished pious people by evil men":** Quoted in Grislis, "Luther and the Turks, Part I," 184.

377 **"best helpers":** Quoted in Grislis, "Luther and the Turks, Part I," 185.

377 **"Since the devil is a spirit":** Quoted in Grislis, "Luther and the Turks, Part I," 185.

378 **"In the East rules the Beast":** Quoted in Grislis, "Luther and the Turks, Part II," 275.

378 **"After the Turks":** Quoted in Wolf, "Luther and Mohammedanism," 163.

378 **"The Turk is the 'black devil' ":** Grislis, "Luther and the Turks, Part II," 275.

378 **"The pope kills the soul":** Quoted in Grislis, "Luther and the Turks, Part II," 276.

378 **"due to his lust":** Quoted in Grislis, "Luther and the Turks, Part II," 279.

378 **"The coarse and filthy Muḥammad":** Quoted in Grislis, "Luther and the Turks, Part II," 276.

379 **"as faithfully and diligently":** Quoted in Grislis, "Luther and the Turks, Part II," 278.

380 **"If the married women":** Quoted in Grislis, "Luther and the Turks, Part II," 278.

380 **Luther developed a much more nuanced view of Muslims:** Wolf, "Luther and Mohammedanism," 161–77.

380 **"They reject all images":** Quoted in Wolf, "Luther and Mohammedanism," 168.

380 **Luther saw a further formal similarity:** Wolf, "Luther and Mohammedanism," 163–64.

381 **Luther saw much to admire in Islam:** Grislis, "Luther and the Turks, Part II," 282–83.

383 **recent and older assertions:** Exemplary of this genre is Ayaan Hirsi Ali, *Heretic: Why Islam Needs a Reformation Now* (New York: HarperCollins, 2015).

CHAPTER 25: AMERICAN SELIM

386 **not a word about the Americas in his memoirs:** Vanita Seth, *Europe's Indians: Producing Racial Difference, 1500–1900* (Durham, NC: Duke University Press, 2010), 38.

387 **four times more works about the Muslim world:** Seth, *Europe's Indians*, 38.

387 *Mayflower,* **had begun its seafaring life trading with Muslims:** Nabil Matar, *Turks, Moors and Englishmen in the Age of Discovery* (New York: Columbia University Press, 1999), 98.

387 **John Smith:** Karen Ordahl Kupperman, *The Jamestown Project* (Cambridge, MA: Harvard University Press, 2007), 51–60.

387 **"the three Turkes heads," "Cape Tragabigzanda":** Quoted in Matar, *Turks, Moors and Englishmen,* 97. On Tragabigzanda, see also Kupperman, *Jamestown Project,* 57.

387 **"The lamentable noise":** Quoted in Karine V. Walther, *Sacred Interests: The United States and the Islamic World, 1821–1921* (Chapel Hill: University of North Carolina Press, 2015), 11.

387 **coat of arms proudly displayed in the bottom right corner:** Kupperman, *Jamestown Project,* 55–57.

387–388 **William Strachey . . . George Sandys:** Kupperman, *Jamestown Project,* 64–71; Jill Lepore, *These Truths: A History of the United States* (New York: W. W. Norton, 2018), 36.

388 **Native American dancing somehow had roots in Old World Muslim dances:** Matar, *Turks, Moors and Englishmen,* 101.

388 **"the fashion of the Turkes":** Quoted in Kupperman, *Jamestown Project,* 132.

388 **"If any great commander":** Quoted in Kupperman, *Jamestown Project,* 132.

388 **"If it should please God":** Quoted in Kupperman, *Jamestown Project,* 14. See also Matar, *Turks, Moors and Englishmen,* 93–94.

389 **when juxtaposed with their ongoing skirmishes:** Matar, *Turks, Moors and Englishmen,* 83–107.

389 **Barbary pirates:** On Barbary pirates and early America, see Paul Baepler, "The Barbary Captivity Narrative in Early America," *Early American Literature* 30 (1995): 95–120; Paul Baepler, "The Barbary Captivity Narrative in American Culture," *Early American Literature* 39 (2004): 217–46.

389 **North Africa remained the primary locale of England's overseas operations:** Matar, *Turks, Moors and Englishmen,* 43–82.

389 **more enslaved Englishmen in North Africa than free ones in North America:** Matar, *Turks, Moors and Englishmen,* 92, 96.

389 **"Conquerors in Virginia":** Matar, *Turks, Moors and Englishmen,* 15–16.

389 **"God hath given up":** Quoted in Walther, *Sacred Interests,* 14.

389 **no qualms about . . . the American and English enslavement of African Muslims and non-Muslims:** Walther, *Sacred Interests,* 12.

390 **Muslims might have constituted up to a tenth:** Michael A. Gomez, "Muslims in Early America," *Journal of Southern History* 60 (1994): 682.

390 **the question of whether or not a Muslim could be president of the United States:** Denise A. Spellberg, "Could a Muslim Be President? An Eighteenth-Century Constitutional Debate," *Eighteenth-Century Studies* 39 (2006): 485–506.

390 **"eternal enemy without":** Spellberg, "Could a Muslim Be President?," 485–86.

390 **a theoretical, though reluctant, yes:** Spellberg, "Could a Muslim Be President?," 487.

391 **Lincoln and his wife, Mary Todd, discussed a trip:** All quotes in this paragraph are from Hilton Obenzinger, *American Palestine: Melville, Twain, and the Holy Land Mania* (Princeton: Princeton University Press, 1999), 161.

391 **"dusky men . . . whole tribe":** Quoted in Obenzinger, *American Palestine*, 190.

391 **"These people about us":** Quoted in Obenzinger, *American Palestine*, 194.

392 **"Three Indian mounds":** Quoted in Obenzinger, *American Palestine*, 97.

392 **"Well do ye come":** Quoted in Obenzinger, *American Palestine*, 109.

392 **Washington Irving:** Zubeda Jalalzai, ed., *Washington Irving and Islam: Critical Essays* (Lanham, MD: Lexington, 2018).

392 **"Catholic Arabs?":** Quoted in Obenzinger, *American Palestine*, 109.

392 **"was a person . . . before":** Quoted in Obenzinger, *American Palestine*, 258.

393 **projected these stereotypes on screen:** Jack G. Shaheen, *Reel Bad Arabs: How Hollywood Vilifies a People* (Northampton, MA: Olive Branch Press, 2009).

393 **The Beatnik writers:** Brian T. Edwards, *Morocco Bound: Disorienting America's Maghreb, from Casablanca to the Marrakech Express* (Durham, NC: Duke University Press, 2005).

394 **white nationalists . . . have accounted for more terrorist attacks:** Janet Reitman, "U.S. Law Enforcement Failed to See the Threat of White Nationalism. Now They Don't Know How to Stop It," *New York Times Magazine*, November 3, 2018, https://www.nytimes.com/2018/11/03/magazine/FBI -charlottesville-white-nationalism-far-right.html (accessed February 17, 2019).

394 **regular targets of both discriminatory legislation and hate crime:** Tanvi Misra, "United States of Anti-Muslim Hate," *CityLab*, March 9, 2018, https:// www.citylab.com/equity/2018/03/anti-muslim-hate-crime-map/555134/ (accessed February 17, 2019).

394 **forty-three states introduced 201 bills:** Swathi Shanmugasundaram, "Anti-Sharia Law Bills in the United States," *Southern Poverty Law Center: Hatewatch*, February 5, 2018, https://www.splcenter.org/hatewatch/2018/02/05/anti-sharia -law-bills-united-states (accessed February 17, 2019); Michael Broyde, "Sharia in America," *Washington Post*, June 30, 2017, https://www.washingtonpost.com/news/ volokh-conspiracy/wp/2017/06/30/sharia-in-america/?noredirect=on&utm_ term=.e076f3b95241 (accessed February 17, 2019).

395 **"I would not advocate":** Quoted in Nick Gass, "Ben Carson: America's President Can't be Muslim," *Politico*, September 20, 2015, https://www.politico.com/ story/2015/09/ben-carson-muslim-president-213851 (accessed February 17, 2019).

395 **President Donald Trump tweeted an endorsement:** Aaron Rupar, "Trump's Unfounded Tweet Stoking Fears about Muslim 'Prayer Rugs,' Explained," *Vox*, January 18, 2019, https://www.vox.com/2019/1/18/18188476/trump-muslim -prayer-rugs-tweet-border (accessed February 17, 2019).

396 **not Jamestown, but a Spanish Catholic outpost in Florida:** Michael V. Gannon, *The Cross in the Sand: The Early Catholic Church in Florida, 1513–1870* (Gainesville: University of Florida Press, 1965).

396 **Islam is projected to supplant Christianity:** Pew Research Center, "The Future of World Religions: Population Growth Projections, 2010–2050," April 2, 2015, http://www.pewforum.org/2015/04/02/religious-projections-2010 -2050/ (accessed February 16, 2019).

CODA: SHADOWS OVER TURKEY

401 **claim that Muslims, not Christians, discovered America:** Associated Press in Istanbul, "Muslims Discovered America, says Turkish President," *Guardian*, November 16, 2014, https://www.theguardian.com/world/2014/nov/16/muslims-discovered-america-erdogan-christopher-columbus (accessed February 16, 2019).

402 **world's seventeenth largest:** Prableen Bajpai, "The World's Top 20 Economies," *Investopedia*, January 10, 2019, https://www.investopedia.com/insights/worlds-top-economies/ (accessed February 16, 2019).

403 **thieves stole a kaftan and crown:** Ömer Erbil, "Kaftan 12 Yıl Sonra Yeniden Türbede," *Hürriyet*, April 20, 2017, http://www.hurriyet.com.tr/gundem/kaftan-12-yil-sonra-yeniden-turbede-40432514 (accessed February 24, 2019); "Ardūghān Yuʿīd "Qafṭān al-Khilāfa" ilā Makānihi al-Aṣlī baʿda Muḥāwalat Tahrībihi min Qibali Tanẓīm Ghūlen al-Irhābī," *Daily Sabah*, April 18, 2017, https://www.dailysabah.com/arabic/history/2017/04/18/rdogan-returns-the-caftan-of-succession-to-his-original-place-after-an-attempt-to-smuggle-it-by-gulen-terrorist-organization (accessed February 24, 2019).

405 **"When man dies":** Quoted in Keely Lockhart, "Turkey Opens 'World's Widest' Suspension Bridge Linking Asia to Europe," *Telegraph*, August 27, 2016, https://www.telegraph.co.uk/news/2016/08/27/turkey-opens-worlds-widest-suspension-bridge-linking-asia-to-eur/ (accessed February 16, 2019).

# ILLUSTRATION

## CREDITS

. . .

Frontispiece      *Hünername*, Topkapi Palace Museum Library, H1523, f.217a

1    © A. Dagli Orti/De Agostini Picture Library/Bridgeman Images
6    *Hünername*, Topkapı Palace Museum Library, H. 1523, f. 049a
10    *Hünername*, Topkapı Palace Museum Library, H. 1523, f. 162b
13    Manuscript of the Zubdat al-Tarikh (Essence of History. . . . ) Turkey, first half of 17th century. . . . Manuscripts; codices; Ink, opaque watercolor, and gold on paper 10 7/16 x 6 3/8 x 1/4 in. (26.50 x 16.20 x 0.70 cm) The Edwin Binney, 3rd, Collection of Turkish Art at the Los Angeles County Museum of Art (M.85.237.38), www.lacma.org, Public Domain
15    ©Roland and Sabrina Michaud/akg-images
23    *Hünername*, Topkapı Palace Museum, Istanbul, Turkey/Sonia Halliday Photographs/Bridgeman Images
31    Lebrecht History/Bridgeman Images
35    *Selimname*, Topkapı Palace Museum Library, H. 1597-8, f. 052b
37    *Hünername*, Topkapı Palace Museum Library, H. 1523, f. 194b
43    Ghigo Roli/Bridgeman Images
47    De Agostini Picture Library/Bridgeman Images
56    Private Collection/Bridgeman Images
61    *Selimname*, Topkapı Palace Museum Library, H. 1597-8, f. 156a
63    ©De Agostini /Biblioteca Ambrosiana/akg-images
65    The Hebrew University of Jerusalem, Department of Geography - Historic Cities Research Project. Courtesy of Ozgur Tufekci.
73    Rolf Richardson/Alamy Stock Photo
77    ©Pictures From History/akg-images
87    ©WHA/World History Archive/akg-images
89    ©Roland and Sabrina Michaud/akg-images
91    ©UIG/Universal History Archive/akg-images
98    Werner Forman Archive/Bridgeman Images
103    ©Pictures From History/akg-images
110    Private Collection/Bridgeman Images
112    Photo ©CCI/Bridgeman Images
121    ©Gilles Mermet/akg-images
123    G. Dagli Orti/De Agostini Picture Library/Bridgeman Images

135 Classic Image/Alamy Stock Photo
136 Private Collection/Archives Charmet/Bridgeman Images
148 G. Dagli Orti/De Agostini Picture Library/Bridgeman Images
155 Chronicle/Alamy Stock Photo
156 Private Collection/The Stapleton Collection/Bridgeman Images
159 Hackenberg-Photo-Cologne/Alamy Stock Photo
165 ©Fototeca Gilardi/akg-images
178 Alan King engraving/Alamy Stock Photo
183 ©Roland and Sabrina Michaud/akg-images
185 ©Roland and Sabrina Michaud/akg-images
191 ©British Library Board. All Rights Reserved/Bridgeman Images
197 *Selimname*, Topkapı Palace Museum Library, H. 1597-8, f. 023b
210 *Selimname*, Topkapı Palace Museum Library, H. 1597-8, f. 032a
214 De Agostini Picture Library/M. Seemuller/Bridgeman Images
216 Chris Hellier/Alamy Stock Photo
224 *Selimname*, Topkapı Palace Museum Library, H. 1597-8, f. 044a
235 *Hünername*, Topkapı Palace Museum Library, H. 1523, f. 201a
241 *Selimname*, Topkapı Palace Museum Library, H. 1597-8, f. 062a
243 *Selimname*, Topkapı Palace Museum Library, H. 1597-8, f. 083b
247 *Selimname*, Topkapı Palace Museum Library, H. 1597-8, f. 176b
249 *Selimname*, Topkapı Palace Museum Library, H. 1597-8, f. 113a
265 ©Pictures From History/akg-images
270 ©akg-images
280 *Selimname*, Topkapı Palace Museum Library, H. 1597-8, f. 164b
283 *Selimname*, Topkapı Palace Museum Library, H. 1597-8, f. 216b
291 Dmitriy Moroz/Alamy Stock Photo
297 ©Roland and Sabrina Michaud/akg-images
303 *Selimname*, Topkapı Palace Museum Library, H. 1597-8, f. 235a
306 *Selimname*, Topkapı Palace Museum Library, H. 1597-8, f. 231b
316 World History Archive/Alamy Stock Photo
319 Gameover/Alamy Stock Photo
321 Leemage/Getty Images
323 Leemage/Getty Images
335 ©akg-images
339 Private Collection/Bridgeman Images
346 Science History Images/Alamy Stock Photo
354 *Selimname*, Topkapı Palace Museum Library, H. 1597-8, f. 267a
355 Age fotostock/Alamy Stock Photo
360 *Hünername*, Topkapi Palace Museum Library, H. 1524, H. 1524, f. 026a and 025b
362 By Alan Mikhail
364 The Picture Art Collection/Alamy Stock Photo
367 By Alan Mikhail
369 ©Roland and Sabrina Michaud/akg-images
376 Yale University Art Gallery, New Haven, CT, USA/Bridgeman Images
385 Virginia Museum of History & Culture/Alamy Stock Photo
393 Everett Collection, Inc./Alamy Stock Photo
399 Isik fidanci/Alamy Stock Photo
404 Anadolu Agency/Contributor/Getty Images

# COLOR INSERT

. . .

# INDEX

. . .

Page numbers in *italic* refer to illustrations and maps.

appoints Korkud governor of Teke, 204

approves Suleyman's governorship of Kefe, 212, 215, 217

armed forces of, 83

capitulation of, 231

Cem and, 31–59

challenge from Selim, 59

conversing with advisers, 35

defended against assassination attempt, 37

dies en route to Dimetoka, 240

Europe and, 58

funeral of, 241

imprisonment of, 239

Janissaries and, 34–36, 229

Khayr Bey and, 278–79

Knights Hospitaller of St. John and, 48–49

Machiavelli's assessment of, 246

Mamluk Empire and, 275

military philosophy of, 194–96, 200–203, 206–9, 251

moves to Istanbul, 22, 31–32, 35–36

proclaimed sultan, 35–36, 38

retirement to Dimetoka, 239

Selim and, 210–12, 224–28, 224, 233–34, 236–37

Shiite Muslims and, 182

succession from, 63–64, 79, 195–96, 200–203, 206, 208–13, 217–20, 222–23, 224–34, 251, 274–75

summons family from Amasya, 37

surrender of, 237

Şahkulu Rebellion and, 204–7, 331

welcomes Jews to his empire, 172–79

Baza, 118

Beijing, 93

Belgrade, 364, 365

Berbeci Muslims, 162

Berbers, 154

Bernáldez, Andrés, 170

Bethlehem, 392

Bin Laden, Osama, 396

Black Death, 170, 324

Black Sea, 210, 212, 212, 213, 220, 221, 224, 227, 278, 280, 352

Boabdil, 119–20, 121

Bolivia, 340

Bolu, 211, 258

Borgia clan, 56

Bosnia, 25, 121, 225

Bosphorus Bridge, 400

Bosphorus Strait, 36, 37, 230, 234, 400

Bosso, Matteo, 52

Bougie (Béjaïa), 114, 338, 342, 344, 350

Bowles, Jane, 393

Bowles, Paul, 393

Brazil, 132, 268

Bridge of Sighs, 120

Britain, 17, 29, 100–101, 222, 373

Americas and, 387–90

banishment of Jews from, 170

colonialism and, 387–90

Muslims and, 387–89

North Africa and, 389–90

British, Native Americans and, 387–90

Bulgaria, 174, 204, 217

Burma, 83

Burroughs, William, 393

Bursa, 6, 7, 21, 36, 68, 205, 243–44, 254, 331

Byzantine Empire, 6, 17, 29, 57, 64, 77, 84, 273

Ottoman capture of, 7, 180, 333

Plague of Justinian and, 324

Cairo, 7, 86, 130–31, 255, 276, 278, 284, 307, 317, 334, 372, 381

Cem in, 38–41, 50–51, 53

Citadel of, 307, 309

Jews in, 179

Selim's journey to, 281–82, 292, 296, 298–302, 303–20, 306

Calabria, 172

Calicut (Kozhikode), 314, 328

California, 391

caliphate, 271, 309–10, 324, 442–43n

Canada, 101, 268

Canary Islands, 96, 105, 125, 154

Caoursin, Guillaume, 48

Cape Ann, 387

Cape Bojadar, 106

Cape Catoche, 130–31

Cape Cod, 387

Cape of Good Hope, 349

Cape of Three Forks, 336

Cape Verde Islands, 96, 105, 150

ALAN MIKHAIL, professor of history and chair of the Department of History at Yale University, is widely recognized for his work in Middle Eastern and global history. He is the author of three previous books and over thirty scholarly articles that have received multiple awards in the fields of Middle Eastern and environmental history, including the Fuat Köprülü Book Prize from the Ottoman and Turkish Studies Association for *Under Osman's Tree: The Ottoman Empire, Egypt, and Environmental History* and the Roger Owen Book Award of the Middle East Studies Association for *Nature and Empire in Ottoman Egypt: An Environmental History*. In 2018, he received the Anneliese Maier Research Award of the Alexander von Humboldt Foundation for internationally distinguished humanities scholars and social scientists. His writing has appeared in the *New York Times* and the *Wall Street Journal*.